A Practitioner's Guide to the FCA Listing Regime 2018/2019

31st Edition

WITHDRAWN.

A Practitioner's Guide to the FCA Listing Regime 2018/2019

31st Edition

Introduced by

Nike Trost

Manager of the FCA's Primary Markets Policy Team

SWEET & MAXWELL

 THOMSON REUTERS

1st Edition   1998
31st Edition   2018

Published in 2018 by Thomson Reuters, trading as Sweet & Maxwell. Thomson Reuters is registered in England & Wales, Company No.1679046. Registered Office and address for service: 5 Canada Square, Canary Wharf, London, E14 5AQ.

For further information on our products and services, visit *www.sweetandmaxwell.co.uk*

Typeset by Letterpart Limited, Caterham on the Hill, Surrey, CR3 5XL.

Printed and bound by CPI Group (UK) Ltd, Croydon, CR0 4YY.

No natural forests were destroyed to make this product: only farmed timber was used and replanted.

A CIP catalogue record of this book is available from the British Library.

ISBN: 978-0-414-06915-2

Thomson Reuters, the Thomson Reuters Logo and Sweet & Maxwell ® are trademarks of Thomson Reuters.

Crown copyright material is reproduced with the permission of the Controller of HMSO and the Queen's Printer for Scotland.

Biographies

Nike Trost is the Manager of the FCA's Primary Markets Policy team, which has responsibility for the policy underpinning UK issuers raising equity and debt. Nike previously held a variety of roles in the UK Listing Authority with a focus on equity transactions.

Tom Soden is an Associate in the FCA's Primary Markets Policy team and has worked on various aspects of Listing Regime policy, including the FCA's Review of the Effectiveness of Primary Markets and the Shareholder Rights Directive. Joining the FCA in 2015, Tom previously worked at the European Securities and Markets Authority, on direct supervision of credit rating agencies, and before that at the UK Listing Authority, leading on enquiries relating to potential breaches of the Listing Regime.

Michael Bloch is a UK Counsel with extensive experience in a wide range of corporate finance and equity capital markets transactions, including IPOs, public and private acquisitions and disposals and auction processes, and private equity transactions, frequently on a cross-border basis.

Anne Kirkwood is a senior professional support lawyer in the Corporate Department at Allen & Overy. She specialises in the continuing obligations of listed companies and including advising on the law regulating prospectuses, MiFID II and the Market Abuse Regulation.

Linda Main is the head of KPMG's UK Capital Markets Group which provides services to companies of all sizes from all over the world which are considering an IPO in London. Linda's role is to advise clients on all stages of the IPO process from initial planning through to preparation for life as a public company. Her clients include companies of all sizes from the

UK and overseas seeking admission to the London markets. Linda is a member of the LSE's Aim Advisory Group. She is a regular speaker at conferences about the Listing Rules and the AIM Rules and contributes to various technical publications on the subject.

Chris Horton is a partner in the Corporate & Commercial group at Simmons & Simmons LLP and heads the equity capital markets team. Chris has a broad range of experience in cross-border and domestic equity capital markets transactions, advising sponsors, underwriters and issuers. Chris regularly advises clients on compliance with the Listing Rules. He has previously spent two years working in the ECM execution team at a leading investment bank.

Andrew Scott is a managing associate in the Corporate & Commercial group at Simmons & Simmons LLP with particular experience in equity capital markets transactions and Listing Rules compliance, advising sponsors, underwriters and issuers. Prior to joining Simmons & Simmons, Andrew worked at another major international law firm in London and Hong Kong where he specialised in ECM transactions.

Lucy Fergusson has been a Partner in the Corporate Department at Linklaters since 1996. She has extensive experience in corporate, securities and stock exchange law and regulation, mergers and acquisitions, and domestic and international capital raising. Lucy contributes to books and periodicals and speaks at conferences on topics related to equity capital markets and corporate governance.

Sarah Debney is a Senior Associate in the Corporate Department at Linklaters. She specialises in the continuing obligations of listed companies, including advising on the Market Abuse Regulation, and the law regulating prospectuses.

Simon Thomas is a Partner at Clifford Chance LLP. Simon joined Clifford Chance in 1996 and specialises in advising issuers and investment banks on equity capital markets transactions. Most recently, Simon advised on the London listings of Vivo Energy, TI Fluids, Bakkavor, Jackpotjoy, the Gym Group, John Laing, B&M European Value Retail, Nostrum Oil & Gas, Gulf Marine Services, Just Retirement and Crest Nicholson. He regularly acts for issuers and underwriters on UK and international listings, including those for Libstar, Coor Service Management, Eurocastle, Zenith Bank, Kcell, Jubilant Energy, Bilt Paper, Max Property Group, Commercial Bank of Qatar, DP World, Salamander Energy and Cineworld. He also advises issuers and underwriters on secondary offerings, including those for Provident Financial, Secure Income REIT, CRH, Cable & Wireless Communications, Just Retirement, Barclays, Redrow, Greencore, Swedbank, Enea, Travis Perkins, DTZ and FirstGroup. In addition, Simon advises on prospectus, circular and listing issues arising in connection with M&A transactions, including Evraz's disposal of the Nakhodka Trade Sea Port to Lanebrook, Greencore's acquisition of Peacock Foods, Just Retirement's successful offer for Partnership Assurance, Aviva's successful offer for Friends Life, Evraz's acquisition of the remaining interests in Raspadskaya, International Power's merger with GdF Suez's international energy division, Babcock's successful offer for VT Group and Kraft Foods' successful offer for Cadbury.

Joseph Newitt is a partner in the corporate and securities department at KWM Europe LLP and has worked for the King & Wood Mallesons network in both London and Australia. Joseph has particular expertise in domestic and cross-border M&A and equity capital markets. He has acted on a number of hybrid security issuances for predominantly Australian banks and financial institutions. Recent deal highlights include the £1.4 billion refinancing of the AA and South32's demerger from BHP and listing on the London Stock Exchange.

Greg Stonefield is a partner in the corporate and securities department at KWM Europe LLP. He has a broad corporate finance practice focusing on ECM related transactions (including IPOs (equity and GDRs), introductions, secondary offerings, block trades, private placements) and on domestic and international public and private M&A. He has significant experience in advising clients on the UKLA Listing Rules and

vii

Disclosure and Transparency Rules, the Prospectus Rules, the AIM Rules and general corporate law. He has a wealth of experience in representing both issuers and underwriters on equity transactions and in bringing overseas companies to the London Stock Exchange. He is a regular speaker at conferences covering London listings, capital markets trends and corporate governance.

Simon FT Cox is a consultant in the Corporate Department of Norton Rose Fulbright (formerly Norton Rose) LLP, having been a partner in the department from 1988 until May 2018. He has a wide-ranging corporate practice covering domestic and international securities and mergers and acquisitions work, with an emphasis on natural resources, transition and emerging markets and collective investment projects.

Contents

8   **Overseas Companies, Investment Entities, Debt and Specialist Securities and Mineral Companies and the High Growth Segment**

Simon FT Cox
Solicitor, Norton Rose Fulbright LLP

Chapter 1

The FCA Listing Regime

Nike Trost and Tom Soden
Financial Conduct Authority

1.1 Introduction

Listed companies are required to comply with a range of obligations which vary depending on the characteristics of the issuer and the security. The requirements stem broadly from the applicable framework of EU regulations and directives and are contained within:

- the Listing Rules (LRs), which set out the standards issuers must meet at the point of listing and on an ongoing basis;
- the Prospectus Rules (PRs), which set out the circumstances in which a company is required to prepare and publish a prospectus and the content of that prospectus;
- the Disclosure Guidance and Transparency Rules (DTRs), which require notifications and disclosures from listed issuers on an ongoing basis; and
- the Market Abuse Regulation (MAR), a directly applicable EU regulation targeted at ensuring market integrity and investor protection.[1]

This book refers to these requirements collectively as the Listing Regime. In this chapter, we outline how the regime has developed over the years and describe at a high level the role of the Financial Conduct Authority (FCA) within this framework. Setting the context for the following chapters, we then

---

[1] The LRs, PRs and DTRs are set out in the *FCA Handbook* available at: *https://www.handbook.fca.org.uk/* [Accessed 24 May 2018]; Regulation 596/2014 on market abuse (market abuse regulation) and repealing Directive 2003/6 and Directives 2003/124, 2003/125 and 2004/72 [2014] L173/1.

provide an introduction to the regime and each of the key component sourcebooks, directives and regulations. Finally, we describe recent policy initiatives and other regulatory developments of relevance to the regime.

1.2 Development of the Listing Regime

The FCA's Listing Regime came into force in May 2000 following the transfer of the UK Listing Authority and connected Listing Rules from the London Stock Exchange (LSE) to the FCA's predecessor, the Financial Services Authority.

The EU's Financial Services Action Plan led to the introduction of three directives targeted at developing a single EU wholesale market and open and secure retail markets in financial services: the Prospectus Directive (PD), the Transparency Directive (TD) and the Market Abuse Directive (MAD).[2] The FCA is the designated competent authority in the UK for the PD, TD and MAR, which began to apply across the EU from 3 July 2016, replacing the MAD.

As a result of the directives, including the subsequent amendments made to Pt VI of the Financial Services and Markets Act 2000 (FSMA), the Listing Rules were restructured into their present format to create a Listing Regime comprised of the LRs, PRs and DTRs. Further information on these sourcebooks is contained in ss.1.3–1.5 below.

The FCA has periodically revised and amended the rules to take account of new European legislation, such as the MAR,

---

[2] Directive 2003/71 on the prospectus to be published when securities are offered to the public or admitted to trading and amending Directive 2001/34 [2003] OJ L345/64; Directive 2013/50 amending Directive 2004/109 on the harmonisation of transparency requirements in relation to information about issuers whose securities are admitted to trading on a regulated market, Directive 2003/71 on the prospectus to be published when securities are offered to the public or admitted to trading and Directive 2007/14 laying down detailed rules for the implementation of certain provisions of Directive 2004/109 [2013] OJ L294/13; Directive 2014/57 on criminal sanctions for market abuse (market abuse directive) [2014] OJ L173/179.

and the UK's own domestic needs. The FCA does so with the overarching strategic objective of ensuring that markets function well and the following three operational objectives:

- to secure an appropriate degree of protection for consumers;
- to protect and enhance the integrity of the UK financial system; and
- to promote effective competition in the interests of consumers.

In setting the Listing Regime, the FCA aims to balance the interests of issuers and investors in order to enhance investor confidence and market attractiveness for issuers. This ultimately promotes greater access to capital and facilitates economic growth. Other entities also have significant roles in shaping the primary market landscape. For example, although there is a connection between the Listing Regime and indexation (premium listing is a current prerequisite for admission to Financial Times Stock Exchange (FTSE) indices), index providers decide whether to establish an index for a specific sector or group of issuers and to set the relevant entry requirements.

Similarly, whilst requirements for reporting on "comply or explain" provisions of corporate governance are addressed in the LRs and DTRs, the Financial Reporting Council (FRC) is responsible for the specification of relevant provisions in the Corporate Governance Code. Domestically, the Panel on Takeovers and Mergers is an independent body responsible for supervising and regulating takeovers to which the City Code applies, whilst the European Securities and Markets Authority (ESMA) has a key role in the development of European guidelines and technical standards which affect primary market regulation.

The following sections describe in more detail the concept of listing (including the eligibility criteria that issuers are required to meet) and introduce the key sourcebooks, regulations and directives that aim to ensure sufficient information is made available to investors at the point of admission and on an ongoing basis. For further information, the Knowledge Base section of the FCA's website[3] contains a library of published material and recent updates of relevance to the Listing Regime.

1.3 Listing and the Listing Rules

An issuer's decision to seek a listing is distinct from being "admitted to trading on a regulated market" (a key phrase in various EU directives), a decision taken by exchange operators such as the LSE. Unlike in some other EU countries, where exchanges are responsible for listing, the FCA is the UK's listing authority and is solely responsible for listing issuers' securities on the Official List, the definitive record of whether a company's securities are listed in the UK.

The Official List is divided into two listing segments: "standard" and "premium". The requirements for standard listing are derived from the applicable framework of EU directives and are consistent with regulatory frameworks for listed securities across the EU. Premium listing builds on those requirements by adding certain "super-equivalent" rules based on UK corporate governance traditions, which oblige issuers to satisfy additional conditions and, in the case of admission criteria, a greater degree of business maturity. These requirements include the need to demonstrate an independent business, a three-year revenue earning track record, sufficient working capital and unqualified financial statements.

Each security on the Official List is also allocated to a subsegment called a securities category. The securities category to which a security is allocated is determined by its characteristics and not what it might be convertible into. The set of obligations on an issuer imposed by the Listing Regime is determined by its listing segment and securities category. This

---

[3] Knowledge Base section of the FCA website available at: *https://www.fca.org.uk/markets/ukla/knowledge-base* [Accessed 24 May 2018].

structure facilitates choice by issuers, who are provided with a range of listing options dependent on their needs and investors.

Once issuers have been listed, the LRs set out the continuing conduct and governance obligations which seek to ensure that investors have the information they need to make properly informed and active investment and voting decisions. They also provide shareholders with the tools they need to hold the boards of issuers to account. In certain instances, a premium listed company is required to seek the advice of a sponsor – an advisory firm specially approved by the FCA to advise on the listing regime and make declarations to us in certain instances. These declarations and the FCA's oversight of sponsor firms aim to ensure appropriate due diligence is performed.

The relationship between the Listing Regime and the operation of effective corporate governance for listed issuers is an important aspect of the wider primary markets landscape. The super-equivalent elements of the LRs provide a clear set of criteria for high standards of corporate governance for premium listed issuers. For example, the LRs require premium listed issuers to state how they have applied the main principles of the Corporate Governance Code (as administered by the FRC) and whether they have complied with them and, if not, to provide an explanation for their non-compliance.

In the case of a statement of non-compliance, it is left to shareholders to decide whether they are content with the issuer's explanation and whether they want to use voting rights attached to their securities to influence the governance of the issuer. This flexible approach avoids a "one-size-fits-all" model and also leaves shareholders with the responsibility to assess the relative merits of issuers' compliance with the Code and to make consequent investment decisions, including whether to seek to influence the governance of the issuer.

In line with the FCA's objective to ensure the Listing Regime remains effective for issuers and investors, the FCA will keep the requirements under review to assess whether any amendments may be required in the event of future changes in the UK regulatory framework, including as a result of negotiations related to the UK's decision to leave the EU.

1.4   Disclosure when securities are issued

The rules governing disclosure when securities are issued are largely drawn from the PD. The PD applies to public offers of securities and to the admission of securities to trading on regulated markets. The Directive requires the prospectus to be approved by a competent authority (e.g. the FCA) before it can be published. The regime commenced in all EU Member States on 1 July 2005 and has been implemented in the UK through the FSMA and PRs. Its main provisions are to:

*   prescribe the contents and format of prospectuses;
*   set out procedures for the approval of prospectuses and how and where they must be published;
*   provide for the passporting of prospectuses on a pan-European basis; and
*   allow prospectuses drawn up under a third country's law to be treated as equivalent to the PD's requirements.

There have been two reviews of the PD by the European Commission (the Commission). The first started in 2009 and resulted in changes to:

*   require summaries to provide only the "key information" that investors need in order to be able to decide which offers and admissions of securities to consider further;
*   enable financial intermediaries selling securities to retail investors to use an issuer's prospectus provided a written agreement is in place and the prospectus is still valid;
*   create a proportionate disclosure regime for small and medium-sized enterprises and for rights issues;
*   provide clarity on the level of disclosure to be included in final terms for the issuance of debt securities; and

- raise the thresholds for some of the exemptions from publishing a prospectus.

The second review of the PD regime was launched in February 2015 with the publication of the Commission's proposal for a Level 1 regulation on prospectuses. It was an early and high priority in the Commission's Capital Markets Union Action Plan. The resulting Prospectus Regulation (the New Prospectus Regulation) came into force on 20 July 2017 and applies from 21 July 2019.[4] The New Prospectus Regulation will repeal the PD and the EU legislation made under the PD from that date. There were two early application measures:

- *admissions of less than 20%*: the PD previously provided that a prospectus does not need to be published for admissions of shares to regulated markets where the increase in any one year is less than a 10% increase in share capital. The new provision lifted the threshold to 20% and applied it to securities rather than just to shares. The FCA amended its PR 1.2 to take account of this change which came into effect immediately on 20 July 2017; and
- *offers below €8 million*: Member States will be able to set the threshold below which a prospectus does not need to be published for public offers at up to €8 million. This measure applies from 21 July 2018.

The other major changes relate to:

- *prospectus summary*: there will be a new, shorter summary;
- *universal registration document* (URD): URDs are designed to be published annually to alleviate the time it takes frequent issuers to publish a prospectus, whether for equity, debt or derivatives. Where an issuer has had two consecutive URDs approved by a Member State competent authority, it will not need to get subsequent URDs

---

4 Regulation 2017/1129 on the prospectus to be published when securities are offered to the public or admitted to trading on a regulated market, and repealing Directive 2003/71 [2017] OJ L168/12.

approved before they are published. Any resultant prospectus which includes the URD will, however, need to be
approved. The status of frequent issuer can be lost;

- *secondary issuances*: alleviation from disclosure requirements is provided for issuers making secondary issuances
of securities;
- *EU growth prospectus*: a new style of prospectus will be
available for use by small and medium-sized issuers,
mid-caps admitted to an "SME Growth Market" or small
issuances by non-listed issuers; and
- *wholesale debt markets*: the PD's alleviated disclosure
regime for issues of non-equity securities with a denomination of at least €100,000 is extended to securities with
lower denominations which are to be traded only on a
regulated market, or a specific segment of a regulated
market, to which only qualified investors have access.

1.5 Keeping the market updated

Key requirements for ongoing disclosure and notifications to
the market by issuers are set by the TD and MAR. These
disclosures are fundamental to providing investors with the
necessary information to determine whether to hold those
issuers' securities.

The TD is implemented in the UK through the DTRs, which
were updated in November 2015 following implementation of
the Transparency Directive Amending Directive.[5] The TD is
designed to enhance transparency in EU capital markets by
requiring issuers whose securities are admitted to trading on a
regulated market to produce periodic financial reports and
requiring shareholders in such companies to disclose major
holdings. The main provisions are:

---

[5] Directive 2013/50 amending Directive 2004/109 on the harmonisation of
transparency requirements in relation to information about issuers whose
securities are admitted to trading on a regulated market, Directive 2003/71 on the
prospectus to be published when securities are offered to the public or admitted
to trading and Directive 2007/14 laying down detailed rules for the implementation of certain provisions of Directive 2004/109 [2013] OJ L294/13.

- periodic financial reporting: there are requirements to provide annual and half-yearly reports;
- payments to governments: there is a requirement for issuers active in the extractive or logging of primary forest industries to prepare a report, on an annual basis, disclosing material payments to governments on both a country and project basis;
- notifiable interests and issuer scope: the TD requires notifications from vote holders when major holdings reach, exceed or fall below specific thresholds. The DTR thresholds and scope are similar to the Companies Act 1985 requirements but remain super-equivalent to the TD. Some entities, individuals or types of holdings are either fully or partially exempt from notification requirements. These include partial exemptions for market makers and trading book holdings. There are also exemptions for clearing and settlement houses, shares acquired for stabilisation purposes and custodians or nominees of holdings;
- dissemination of regulated information: Member States are required to ensure that an issuer discloses regulated information in a manner which ensures fast access to such information on a non-discriminatory and pan-European basis. In the UK, issuers are required to issue regulatory announcements via a Primary Information Provider. These are subsequently announced to the market through a Secondary Information Provider;
- storage of regulated information: under the TD, regulated information must be disseminated, filed and then stored in an Officially Appointed Mechanism (OAM). The TD requires that there is at least one OAM for the central storage of such information in each Member State. The FCA currently appoints a third-party provider to fulfil the role of OAM for the UK; and
- the DTRs also implement provisions of the Statutory Audit Directive and the Company Reporting Directive in relation to a number of corporate governance requirements.[6]

---

[6] Directive 2014/56 amending Directive 2006/43 on statutory audits of annual accounts and consolidated accounts [2014] OJ L158/196; Directive 2006/46 amending Directives 78/660 on the annual accounts of certain types of companies, 83/349 on consolidated accounts, 86/635 on the annual accounts and

The MAR began to apply across the EU from 3 July 2016, replacing the MAD. The objective of the MAR is to ensure market integrity and investor protection. It does this by updating the old regime to cover new markets, platforms and financial instruments as well as equipping regulators with new powers to prevent, detect and respond to market abuse. It also tackles market abuse across commodity and related derivative markets.

Central to the MAR is the control and public disclosure of inside information. Under the MAR, "inside information" is defined as being precise, non-public information that would be likely to have a significant effect on the price of financial instruments. Issuers are obliged to inform the public as soon as possible of any inside information which directly concerns that issuer. The MAR prohibits the unlawful disclosure of inside information as well as prohibiting insider dealing and market manipulation.

The MAR builds on the market abuse regime established under the MAD. Key changes between the two regimes include:

- an extension of the scope of the legislation to include financial instruments which are traded on multilateral trading facilities and organised trading facilities, spot commodities (when these are the underlying for commodities derivatives within the market abuse regime), benchmarks and emissions allowances;
- the introduction of new offences for *attempted* market abuse and manipulation of benchmarks (alongside the existing offences when market abuse and manipulation have taken place);
- an obligation to report suspicious orders and attempted market abuse alongside suspicious transactions;
- new circumstances under which an issuer may choose to delay the disclosure of inside information provided that certain conditions are met;

---

consolidated accounts of banks and other financial institutions and 91/674 on the annual accounts and consolidated accounts of insurance undertakings [2006] OJ L224/1.

- the introduction of a €5,000 annual threshold above which transactions by ersons discharging managerial responsibilities (PDMRs), and those of persons closely associated with them, must be disclosed; and restrictions on transactions PDMRs can carry out during a closed period;
- a new market soundings regime for the communication of information to investors prior to the announcement of a transaction; and
- changes to the presentation and dissemination of investment recommendations.

1.6 Other regulatory developments

In addition to the Listing Regime, listed issuers and their advisors may wish to be aware of regulatory developments and initiatives in other areas of capital markets regulation. Such initiatives and developments may have an impact on the obligations faced by issuers and their shareholders.

1.6.1 *Reforming the availability of information in the UK equity initial public offering process*

In October 2017, the FCA published Policy Statement (PS) 17/23 which finalises new Conduct of Business (COBS) rules intended to improve the range and quality of information available to investors during the initial public offering (IPO) process. This followed a consultation on the topic, launched in March 2017 (Consultation Paper (CP) 17/5).

Currently, the prospectus, which should be the primary source of information on companies seeking to raise finance through the IPO process, is made available very late in the process. Analysts within non-syndicate banks and independent research providers also generally lack access to the information they need to produce research on IPOs. As a result, "connected research" written by analysts within the book-running syndicate is the dominant source of information available to investors during a crucial stage of the process. This is of particular concern given the conflicts of interest that arise during the production of connected research.

The FCA has confirmed new rules to be included in COBS 11A which seek to ensure that a prospectus or registration document is published, and that providers of "unconnected research" have access to the issuer's management, before any connected research is released. The FCA also confirmed new guidance in COBS 12 intended to address conflicts of interest that arise when analysts within prospective syndicate banks interact with the issuer's management and its corporate finance advisers around the time that pitching efforts are taking place. These changes took effect from 1 July 2018.

1.6.2 Shareholder Rights Directive

In late 2016, agreement was reached on a package of revisions to the text of the Shareholder Rights Directive,[7] which is scheduled to be implemented over a 24-month period ending in mid-2019. The scope of the Directive has expanded considerably and includes new provisions in the following areas:

*   identification of shareholders, transmission of information and facilitation of exercise of shareholder rights;
*   transparency from institutional investors and asset managers regarding their investment strategies and engagement policies;
*   transparency from proxy advisors on a range of matters, including their voting policies, their approach to engagement with companies and conflicts of interest;
*   information to be provided in the remuneration report and the right of shareholders to vote on this and on the remuneration report; and
*   transparency and approval of related party transactions.

The original directive was implemented in the UK in all significant respects within companies legislation. However, the

---

[7] Directive 2007/36 on the exercise of certain rights of shareholders in listed companies [2007] OJ L184/17.

expanded scope of the revised directive will have direct impact for a wider range of parties within the "investment chain" that enables companies to identify and communicate with their shareholders and for shareholders to exercise their rights.

1.6.3 Benchmarks

Benchmarks are fundamental elements of financial markets' infrastructure. Trustworthy benchmarks help individual savers and institutional investors to measure prices and assess investments. Markets need to be able to trust that benchmarks are fair and accurately reflect the underlying markets. Ensuring benchmarks are anchored in observable transactions, rather than judgements, makes them more robust against manipulation.

The FCA identified in its 2018/19 Business Plan that it is potentially unsustainable, and undesirable, for market participants to rely indefinitely on reference rates that do not have active underlying markets to support them. Given this, the FCA will not require banks to continue to submit to London Inter-bank Offered Rate (LIBOR) after the end of 2021. Issuers who currently use the rate will need to plan actively during the next three years for the possibility that the LIBOR will not be produced after this date. The FCA is working closely with the Bank of England and other market participants under the risk-free rate working group to develop Sterling Overnight Index Average (SONIA) as an alternative sterling risk-free rate.

Chapter 2

The Statutory Framework for Listing

Lucy Fergusson and Sarah Debney
Partner and Senior Associate, Linklaters LLP

2.1 Introduction

The Listing Regime is a voluntary regime, in the sense that companies can choose whether or not to have their securities listed. A listing of securities, particularly shares, on an exchange such as the London Stock Exchange enables companies to access capital and shareholders to trade their shares. In return for these advantages, listed companies face a wide range of obligations, including eligibility requirements, initial and ongoing disclosure requirements and behavioural restrictions that apply both to the companies themselves and to directors and others working for them. The focus of this chapter is on the rules that apply to issuers as a consequence of a listing on the main market of the London Stock Exchange. This collection of rules, primarily overseen by the Financial Conduct Authority (FCA) in its role as the UK Listing Authority (UKLA), is referred to as the Listing Regime. This chapter summarises the key concepts underlying the UK Listing Regime and seeks to cast light on the sometimes complex interaction between the EU legislative framework, the relevant UK law and the rules of the FCA.

2.2 Overview of the statutory framework

The UK Listing Regime is largely based on EU legislation supplemented and enforced by the FCA under powers conferred on it by the Financial Services and Markets Act 2000 (FSMA). Under the draft Withdrawal Agreement currently being negotiated between the UK and the EU (in connection with Brexit), EU law will generally continue to apply to and in the UK after the exit date (expected to be 29 March 2019) until the end of the transition period (31 December 2020) and UK law will remain broadly unchanged. The UK will also have to continue to implement EU legislation that comes into effect during the transition period. The European Union (Withdrawal) Bill, which is expected to receive royal assent in summer 2018, will convert EU law into UK law and give the UK Government powers to make changes to "correct deficiencies" in retained EU law through secondary legislation to ensure the UK legal system continues to function correctly outside the EU. These changes are expected to take effect at the end of the transition period.

In some areas, the relevant EU legislation lays down detailed mandatory requirements while, in other areas, such as liability and enforcement, it is left to Member States to make their own provisions. In addition, the FCA's rules impose certain "super-equivalent" obligations on issuers or other persons, which are not derived from EU legislation. An explanation of the Listing Regime should start with the EU legislation that governs the capital markets.

2.2.1 The EU foundations of the Listing Regime

The majority of the rules that make up the UK Listing Regime derive, directly or indirectly, from EU legislation designed to facilitate capital raising and enhance public confidence in capital markets by: (1) ensuring clear, fair and transparent markets throughout the EU; and (2) the harmonisation of rules, to ensure a level playing field, reduce compliance costs and enhance comparability between different investments.

EU financial markets legislation is made under the so-called "Lamfalussy" legislative process, which is a four-level approach that aims to speed up the legislative process by passing relatively high level framework directives or regulations (Level 1) which delegate the making of the rules containing more technical details (Level 2) to the European Commission, supported by advice from other bodies (Level 3). Level 4 consists of the process of monitoring and enforcing the implementation of the directives across the EU Member States.

In relation to the capital markets, the European Securities and Markets Authority (ESMA) is the body that provides advice on regulatory matters to the European Commission. ESMA was established with the ultimate goal of developing a "single rulebook" for the capital markets in the EU. Its overall objectives are to ensure the integrity, transparency, efficiency and orderly functioning of securities markets as well as enhancing investor protection. ESMA's powers include:

(1)   the ability to draft legally binding "technical standards";
(2)   the ability to ensure consistent application of EU law through "a fast track procedure"; and
(3)   powers to resolve disagreements between national authorities.

The key EU measures underlying the Listing Regime are:

(1)   the Prospectus Directive (2003/71),[1] which governs the contents, approval and publication of prospectuses in connection with applications for admission to a regulated market and offers of securities to the public. Except where the context requires otherwise, references in this chapter to the "Prospectus Directive" include this directive and the Level 2 Prospectus Regulation (809/2004) (PD Regulation),[2] each as amended. The PD Regulation sets out, amongst other things, the detailed contents requirements

---

[1]   Directive 2003/71 on the prospectus to be published when securities are offered to the public or admitted to trading and amending Directive 2001/34 [2003] OJ L345/64.
[2]   Regulation 809/2004 implementing Directive 2003/71 as regards information

of prospectuses. A new EU Prospectus Regulation (2017/1129) (New Prospectus Regulation) came into force in July 2017,[3] the bulk of whose provisions apply from 21 July 2019. The regulation will replace the Prospectus Directive and implementing legislation;

(2) the Transparency Obligations Directive (2004/109)[4] dealing with financial reporting and other ongoing disclosure obligations of, and relating to, issuers. Except where the context requires otherwise, references in this chapter to the "Transparency Directive" include this directive, as amended, and the Level 2 Directive (2007/14)[5] made under it;

(3) the Market Abuse Regulation (596/2014)[6] governing insider dealing, market manipulation and the disclosure of inside information. Except where the context requires otherwise, references in this chapter to the "Market Abuse Regulation" include this regulation and the Level 2 measures made under it. The Market Abuse Regulation came into effect on 3 July 2016 and replaced the Market Abuse Directive (2003/6)[7];

(4) the Consolidated Admissions and Reporting Directive (2001/34) (CARD),[8] which consolidated earlier directives dealing with requirements for admission to listing and

---

contained in prospectuses as well as the format, incorporation by reference and publication of such prospectuses and dissemination of advertisements [2004] OJ L149/1.

[3] Regulation 2017/1129 on the prospectus to be published when securities are offered to the public or admitted to trading on a regulated market, and repealing Directive 2003/71 [2017] OJ L168/12.

[4] Directive 2004/109 on the harmonisation of transparency requirements in relation to information about issuers whose securities are admitted to trading on a regulated market and amending Directive 2001/34 [2004] OJ L390/38.

[5] Directive 2007/14 laying down detailed rules for the implementation of certain provisions of Directive 2004/109 on the harmonisation of transparency requirements in relation to information about issuers whose securities are admitted to trading on a regulated market [2007] OJ L69/27.

[6] Regulation 596/2014 on market abuse (market abuse regulation) and repealing Directive 2003/6 and Directives 2003/124, 2003/125 and 2004/72 [2014] OJ L173/1.

[7] Directive 2003/6 on insider dealing and market manipulation (market abuse) [2003] OJ L96/16.

[8] Directive 2001/34 on the admission of securities to official stock exchange listing and on information to be published on those securities [2001] OJ L184/1.

continuing obligations. The CARD remains in force only so far as conditions of eligibility for listing are concerned; and

(5) the IAS Regulation (1606/2002),[9] which requires the adoption of international accounting standards (as approved by the EU Commission) in consolidated accounts by companies with securities admitted to trading on a regulated market.

The directives referred to above are primarily implemented in the UK through the FSMA and rules made by the FCA, as described below. Regulations have direct effect in the EU and so do not require separate legislation to implement them in each Member State, although, in the context of the Listing Regime, the FSMA contains powers for the FCA to enforce regulations, such as the Market Abuse Regulation.

2.2.2 Listing and admission to trading on a regulated market

When a company first comes to the public market by way of an initial public offering (IPO), it will need to decide which market is appropriate for it. Levels of regulation will be an important factor in making this choice. Different markets have been established in the UK to offer a choice of levels of regulation. The key variables include whether "official listing" is involved, the choice of "listing segment" (see s.2.4 below) and whether or not the market that the securities are admitted to trading on is a "regulated market".

In the context of the FCA's Listing Regime, companies are regulated both as entities admitted to the "Official List" and under the rules that apply to the market on which they are traded, as described in this section and in s.2.2.7 below.

The FCA is required to maintain the Official List under s.74 of the FSMA and s.103 of the FSMA defines the term "Official List" simply as "the list maintained by the FCA". In practice, it

---

[9] Regulation 1606/2002 on the application of international accounting standards [2002] OJ L243/1.

is the list of securities that have satisfied the requirements of the Listing Rules (defined below) for admission to listing.

The Prospectus and Transparency Directives apply where securities are admitted to trading on an European Economic Area (EEA) "regulated market". A "regulated market" for these purposes is a market for securities which meets the requirements set out in the definition of "regulated markets" in the Markets in the Financial Instruments Directive (2004/39).[10] The European Commission is required to publish annually in the *Official Journal of the European Union* a list of regulated markets, notified to it by the Member States.

The Market Abuse Regulation applies more broadly to securities:

(1) admitted to trading on a regulated market or multilateral trading facility or for which a request for admission to trading has been made;
(2) traded on an organised trading facility; or
(3) not admitted to trading on any of these venues but where the price or value of those securities depends on or has an effect on the price or value of securities admitted to trading on these venues (for example, credit default swaps and contracts for difference).

In the UK, the FCA is responsible for maintaining the list of regulated markets for which the UK is the home Member State.

Regulated markets include:

(1) the London Stock Exchange's Main Market, which is the main regulated market for listed securities. This is split into premium and standard listing segments;
(2) the London Stock Exchange's High Growth Segment, which is part of the Main Market, and thus a regulated market, but is for equity securities which are not listed.

---

[10] Directive 2004/39 on markets in financial instruments amending Directives 85/611 and 93/6 and Directive 2000/12 and repealing Directive 93/22 [2004] OJ L145/1.

Launched in 2013, the High Growth Segment is designed for trading companies with growing revenues that are not yet in a position to meet the eligibility requirements for listing but that aspire to do so in the longer term;

(3) the London Stock Exchange's Specialist Fund Market, a regulated market for certain closed-ended funds which are not listed; and

(4) the ICAP Securities and Derivatives Exchange (ISDX) Main Board, a small and mid-cap stock exchange, again for companies which are not listed.

On the other hand, the London Stock Exchange also operates the Professional Securities Market (PSM), which is not a regulated market but is a market for listed debt securities and depositary receipts aimed at professional investors. The PSM is an exception to the general requirement of the Listing Rules that securities admitted to listing must be admitted to trading on a regulated market.

The London Stock Exchange's Alternative Investment Market (AIM) is not a "regulated market" for these purposes and securities traded on it are not admitted to listing. However, the AIM is a multilateral trading facility for the purpose of the Market Abuse Regulation.

2.2.3 Part VI of the FSMA

The UK law implementing the directives relating to listing, admission to trading on a regulated market and offers of securities to the public is largely contained in Pt VI of the FSMA. Part VI of the FSMA has been modified several times to reflect, in particular, new and amended EU directives, the Market Abuse Regulation and as part of wider reforms made by the Financial Services Act 2012.

Part VI of the FSMA gives the FCA the power to make and enforce rules (collectively known as "Pt 6 Rules") for purposes connected with official listing, public offers and securities traded on regulated markets. The Pt 6 Rules comprise rules on:

(1) admission to the Official List, including rules on applications for listing, suspension of listing, sponsors and continuing obligations, under ss.75, 77, 79, 88 and 96 of the FSMA (Listing Rules or LRs);

(2) prospectuses and related requirements in respect of transferable securities (Prospectus Rules or PRs). The Prospectus Rules implement parts of the Prospectus Directive and their scope is laid down by s.84 of the FSMA (as set out in s.2.2 above, this is likely to change from July 2019 when the New Prospectus Regulation comes fully into effect);

(3) the disclosure of periodic financial and other information by issuers; and the notification of major shareholdings in issuers. These rules (Transparency Rules) are made under s.89A–N of the FSMA;

(4) various aspects of corporate governance required by EU company law and applicable to companies with securities admitted to trading on a regulated market, which have been made under s.89O of the FSMA (Corporate Governance Rules); and

(5) primary information providers (PIPs) which provide regulatory information services for the purposes of the Pt 6 Rules. These rules are made under s.89P–V of the FSMA.

The Pt 6 Rules also contain the Disclosure Guidance which provides guidance on parts of the Market Abuse Regulation, which replaced the more substantive Disclosure Rules in place previously (see s.2.5.2.1 below).

The Transparency and Corporate Governance Rules, as well as the Disclosure Guidance and the rules of PIPs, are combined in a single part of the *FCA Handbook*, the *Disclosure Guidance and Transparency Rules Sourcebook* (DTR): Chs 1, 2 and 3 contain the Disclosure Guidance; Chs 1A, 4, 5 and 6 contain the Transparency Rules; and Chs 1B, 7 and 8 contain the Corporate Governance Rules and rules on PIPs.

Part VI of the FSMA also contains key substantive provisions regarding prospectuses and (for certain securities which are outside the scope of the Prospectus Directive) listing particulars including: (1) when a prospectus or listing particulars are required; (2) the general obligations of disclosure; (3) liability provisions; and (4) the FCA's ancillary powers.

2.2.4 The FCA's objectives

The FCA's strategic objective is to make sure that the financial markets and markets for regulated financial services function well. The operational objectives of the FCA, set out in s.1B(3) of the FSMA, are:

(1) consumer protection: the FCA must secure an appropriate degree of protection for consumers. This includes having regard to the amount of risk involved in different types of investment, the varying levels of experience and expertise that different consumers may have and consumers' potential expectations for different types of investments;

(2) market integrity: this objective means the FCA must act to protect and enhance the integrity of the UK financial system; and

(3) competition: this objective obliges the FCA to promote effective competition in the interest of consumers in the markets for regulated financial services or services provided by recognised investment exchanges in carrying on certain regulated activities. Note that this is not a focus on the competitive position of the UK markets as an end in itself but a focus on competition for the benefit of consumers.

2.2.5 The FCA Handbook

The *FCA Handbook* is comprised of a large number of different sets of rules and guidance, including the Listing Rules, Transparency Rules, Disclosure Guidance and Prospectus Rules. In addition, parts of the FCA's *Supervision Manual* (SUP), *Decision Procedure and Penalties Manual* (DEPP) and the *Enforcement Guide* (EG) are also relevant as these deal with the

FCA's supervision and enforcement policies and procedures as they apply to the Pt 6 Rules, the Market Abuse Regulation and persons subject to these rules.

The *Handbook*'s "General Provisions" (GEN) state that a purposive approach should be taken to the construction of the *Handbook*, meaning that the spirit as well as the letter of the rules should be followed.

2.2.6   Guidance

2.2.6.1   FCA guidance

A feature of the *FCA Handbook* is that guidance is incorporated alongside the rules to which it relates. Rule numbers are suffixed with the letter "R" while paragraphs containing guidance are suffixed with the letter "G".

The FCA may give guidance outside the *Handbook* under procedures laid down by s.139A–B of the FSMA. These require general guidance to be the subject of formal consultation. The FCA has issued a number of Procedural Notes and Technical Notes under these provisions to give guidance on the UKLA's practices and specific aspects of the Listing Rules, Transparency Rules and Prospectus Rules. These notes are published by the UKLA in the Knowledge Base on its website. Many of the notes in the Knowledge Base are based on previously published Technical Notes (which themselves replaced information in the UKLA's *List!* newsletters published over a period of a number of years), which did not constitute formal guidance. The FCA seeks to keep the UKLA Knowledge Base up to date by consulting and publishing new notes or revising existing guidance notes when necessary. Each separate technical and procedural note has a version number to make clear when a note has been amended.

The FCA may also give individual guidance on a case-by-case basis and this provides a means for issuers to understand or obtain a decision from the FCA on the application of specific rules to their particular circumstances.

If a person acts in accordance with general guidance in the circumstances contemplated by that guidance, the FCA will treat the person as having complied with the relevant aspects of the rule to which it relates.

2.2.6.2 ESMA guidance

As described in s.2.2.1 above, ESMA publishes Level 3 guidance in the form of recommendations on the application of specific provisions of the directives to assist in their uniform implementation across Member States. While the competent authorities in each Member State are not bound to act in accordance with such guidance, it is expected that most will do so in most cases.

The most significant set of Level 3 recommendations in the listing context are those relating to the content of prospectuses (the ESMA recommendations for the consistent implementation of the PD Regulation implementing the Prospectus Directive, dated 20 March 2013—ESMA Prospectus Recommendations). The ESMA Prospectus Recommendations cover topics such as the format of disclosure of historical financial information but also in effect lay down additional disclosure provisions, either by adding additional levels of detail to items of information prescribed by the PD Regulation or by adding information requirements for specific types of issuer, such as mining, property, start-up and research-based companies. ESMA also publishes questions and answers on the Prospectus Directive (ESMA Q&As). These are answers given to questions posed by market participants and competent authorities in relation to the practical application of the legislation and cover a broad range of topics, such as the information that must be filed with a competent authority and when a supplementary prospectus may be required. The FCA states in the Prospectus Rules (PR 1.1.8G) that it will take into account whether the ESMA Prospectus Recommendations and ESMA Q&As have been complied with in determining whether Pt VI of the FSMA, the Prospectus Rules and the PD Regulation have been complied with.

ESMA also provides key guidance on the Market Abuse Regulation. It has published guidelines on delaying the disclosure of inside information and guidelines for recipients of market soundings. It also maintains a Q&A document in which it publishes questions posed by the public and competent authorities, and the answers given by ESMA, in relation to the practical application of the Market Abuse Regulation. The goal of this document is to promote common supervisory approaches.

2.2.7 Stock exchange rules and markets

Under the Listing Rules, in order to be listed, securities must be admitted to trading on a regulated market, such as the London Stock Exchange's Main Market or, in the case of securities outside the scope of the Prospectus Directive and other specialist securities (i.e. securities normally bought and traded by a limited number of knowledgeable investors), on a recognised investment exchange's market for listed securities.

Under Pt XVIII of the FSMA, recognised investment exchanges are required to make rules not only to ensure that business is conducted in an orderly manner but also to require issuers to make disclosure of proper information to enable investors to assess the value of their securities. In the case of the London Stock Exchange, the former requirement is met by the "Rules of the London Stock Exchange" while the disclosure requirement is met, in the case of the London Stock Exchange's Main Market, by its "Admission and Disclosure Standards" which set out the rules on procedures to be followed by issuers applying for admission of securities to trading on each of its markets, other than the AIM (for which there are separate rules). The Admission and Disclosure Standards are relatively brief, having been designed to minimise any overlap with the FCA's Listing Rules; however, they do include additional rules and guidance for the High Growth Segment (see s.2.2.2 above) in Sch.5. The London Stock Exchange does, however, retain a discretion, albeit unlikely to be exercised in practice, to refuse to admit securities to trading on its markets, even if they have been admitted to the Official List.

The Market Abuse Regulation applies to securities admitted to trading on regulated markets, multilateral trading facilities and organised trading facilities. By contrast, markets which are not regulated markets (e.g. the AIM and PSM) are outside the scope of the Prospectus Directive and the Transparency Directive so the provisions of the Transparency Rules and Prospectus Rules generally do not apply to them. An exception is the major shareholding disclosure provisions under the Transparency Rules (DTR 5). These provisions do apply to AIM issuers, other than those which are not incorporated under the Companies Act 2006 or otherwise incorporated and which do not have a principal place of business in the UK (see the definition of "issuer" in the *FCA Handbook* Glossary).

2.2.8 Fees

The FCA levies fees from issuers under the Listing Rules and Prospectus Rules. Listing Rule fees comprise annual fees and, if applicable, transaction vetting fees in relation to specific transactions in relation to which documentation is submitted to the FCA, including an initial fee for consideration of the eligibility for listing of a new applicant. Fees are charged under the Prospectus Rules for the approval or vetting of prospectuses and other documents. An administration fee must be paid by an issuer which is late in publishing its annual or half-yearly report under the Transparency Rules. Fees are also payable by sponsors and PIPs in connection with approval by the FCA.

2.2.9 Other rules

Apart from the Pt 6 Rules, listed issuers must comply with a number of other regulations, including the Market Abuse Regulation and the financial promotion regime under s.21 of the FSMA. These are discussed briefly below.

It should also be noted that UK companies, by being listed or traded on a regulated market, become subject to a number of provisions under the Companies Act 2006 that only apply to publicly traded companies. Some of these derive from EU company law, such as provisions relating to shareholder meetings, whilst others are UK specific, such as additional requirements relating to executive remuneration and information to be included in the annual report. These company law provisions are not discussed further in this chapter.

2.2.10 Focus of this chapter

The remainder of this chapter seeks to provide an overview of the different sources of the rules that make up the Listing Regime. It focuses, in particular, on the following:

(1) the initial disclosure document: prospectuses and listing particulars;
(2) applying for listing: the listing segments and eligibility;
(3) life after listing: continuing obligations;
(4) financial promotions and advertisements;
(5) insider dealing and market manipulation; and
(6) the FCA's enforcement powers.

2.3 Initial disclosure: Prospectuses and listing particulars

Where a new class of securities is being admitted to listing, a disclosure document will be required. For shares and most other securities, this will be a prospectus but for certain securities it will be listing particulars. Part VI of the FSMA contains separate but parallel regimes for prospectuses and for listing particulars. The provisions in relation to prospectuses (ss.84–87R) derive from the Prospectus Directive.

Listing particulars are required in cases where an application for listing is being made and the prospectus regime is not applicable. This may either be because of the nature of the securities being admitted to listing, or because they are being admitted to listing, but are not being admitted to trading on a regulated market and are only being offered through an offering which is exempt from the prospectus requirements (this is the case with securities being admitted to the PSM). The provisions on listing particulars (ss.79–82) were originally based on the CARD (see s.2.2.1 above), whose provisions regarding listing particulars were repealed by the Prospectus Directive.

2.3.1 *The prospectus regime*

The FCA's Prospectus Rules, together with ss.84–87R of the FSMA, are devoted to the implementation of the Prospectus Directive. The aim of this directive is stated to be "to ensure investor protection and market efficiency, in accordance with high regulatory standards" (Recital 10 to the Prospectus Directive). The focus of the Directive is to achieve this by laying down requirements as to when a prospectus is required, what it should contain and how it should be published. There are also rules on advertisements and other communications in the context of an offer or the admission to trading of securities.

The Prospectus Directive is a "maximum harmonisation" measure. In other words, the standards it lays down cannot generally be supplemented by additional requirements imposed by individual Member States. In particular, the PD Regulation stipulates the items of information to be included in prospectuses and has direct effect in Member States. The UK, or any other Member State, cannot impose requirements regarding the contents of prospectuses beyond those required by the PD Regulation.

Part VI of the FSMA provides the framework for the UK implementation of the Prospectus Directive by empowering the FCA to make rules for that purpose and specifically in relation to:

(1) prospectuses;
(2) related documents, such as final pricing statements; and
(3) other communications.

Part VI of the FSMA also contains substantive provisions which need to be read alongside the rules made by the FCA, including:

(1) definitions of key terms, such as the meaning of an "offer of securities to the public";
(2) determining the general level of disclosure required in prospectuses and the nature of liability of prospectuses; and
(3) designating when a supplemental prospectus is required and conferring a statutory right of withdrawal in certain circumstances once a prospectus has been published.

As set out in s.2.2 below, the New Prospectus Regulation on the requirements for prospectuses came into force in July 2017. The bulk of the provisions will not come into effect until July 2019, at which point it will replace the Prospectus Directive. In general, the scope and content requirements for a prospectus remain the same, although certain changes are made, for example, in relation to the exemptions to the requirement for a prospectus (see s.2.3.2 below).

2.3.2 *Requirement for a prospectus*

A prospectus is required in the circumstances laid down by the Prospectus Directive as implemented by ss.85 and 86 of the FSMA. Under these provisions, subject to certain exemptions, a prospectus is required when transferable securities:

(1) are offered to the public in the UK; or
(2) are admitted to trading on a regulated market in the UK.

A prospectus can be required for a public offer of existing shares or other securities, even if they are already admitted to trading on a regulated market.

The definition of "transferable securities" refers to Directive 2014/65 on markets in financial instruments and amending Directive 2002/92 and Directive 2011/61 [2014] OJ L173/349 (commonly known as MiFID II). Essentially, "transferable securities" means securities that are negotiable on capital markets, other than money market instruments with a maturity of less than 12 months.

To determine whether a prospectus is required in connection with any issue or offering of shares, it is necessary to consider:

(1) whether the securities are of a kind to which the Prospectus Rules apply (see s.2.3.2.1 below);
(2) whether the securities are being offered only in circumstances falling within the private placement exemption described in s.2.3.2.3 below and, if not, whether an exemption as described in s.2.3.2.4 below applies; and
(3) whether an application for admission to trading is being made. If so, a prospectus will be required unless an exemption as described in s.2.3.2.4 below applies.

Where securities are being admitted to trading on a regulated market, as well as being offered in the UK, an exemption may be available under one limb of the prospectus requirement but not the other. For example, a prospectus may be required in connection with admission to trading of securities, even though the offering of them falls within an exemption.

Failure to publish an approved prospectus when this is required is a criminal offence under s.85(3) of the FSMA and can also give rise to civil liability for breach of statutory duty to anyone who has suffered loss as a result of such failure (s.85(4) of the FSMA).

2.3.2.1   Exempt securities

Schedule 11A of the FSMA sets out securities to which the Prospectus Directive, and therefore the prospectus requirement, does not apply. These include units in open-ended collective investment schemes, and securities issued by EEA governments and local authorities. Offers with a total value of less than €5 million are also exempt. Other exemptions are left by the FSMA to be specified by the Prospectus Rules. However, the FCA has no discretion under the Prospectus Directive in this area and the exemptions laid down in the Prospectus Rules (described in s.2.3.2.4 below) are a direct lift from the directive.

2.3.2.2   *Meaning of "offer of securities to the public"*

The term "offer of transferable securities to the public" has a wide definition in the Prospectus Directive. It means a communication, in any form and by any means, to any person, which presents sufficient information on the securities to be offered and on the terms on which they are offered to enable an investor to decide to buy or subscribe for the securities in question. Included in this definition is a placing of securities by a financial intermediary.

This definition is reflected in s.102B of the FSMA but with an important carve-out from the potentially very broad scope of the definition. Section 102B(5) of the FSMA makes clear that the definition does not catch a communication in connection with trading on:

(1)   a regulated market;
(2)   a multilateral trading facility; or
(3)   a prescribed market under s.130A(3) of the FSMA.

This makes clear that, for example, the display of prices in a secondary market trading context will not be an offer to the public.

2.3.2.3   *Private placement exemption*

Article 3(2) of the Prospectus Directive, as transposed by s.86(1) of the FSMA, permits an offer of securities to the public without a prospectus being required provided it is only made to "qualified investors" (broadly, professional investors and substantial corporations) and to fewer than 150 other persons, other than qualified investors, per Member State.

This private placement exemption (though that term is not used in the FSMA) facilitates cross-border offerings of both listed and unlisted securities. However, there is scope for variations in the precise manner of implementation across the EU. For example, s.86(1) of the FSMA, unlike the Prospectus

Directive, clarifies that an offer "directed at" qualified investors or fewer than 150 other persons, as well as one only "made to" such persons, will be exempt. In addition, s.86(2) of the FSMA ensures that offers to discretionary investment managers will not be "looked through" to the managers' underlying clients so that an offer can still be treated as being made only to qualified investors even where brokers allocate securities to retail investors, provided such brokers can do so without reference to the client.

There are also exemptions for offers of securities with a denomination of at least €100,000 and where each investor must invest at least €100,000.

2.3.2.4   Other exemptions

Other exemptions from the requirement for a prospectus are based on the circumstances in which the offer or application to listing is made.

They are set out in PRs 1.2.2R (in relation to public offers) and 1.2.3R (in relation to admission to trading). The exemptions set out in PR 1.2.2R broadly correspond with those in PR 1.2.3R(2)–(6) and cover in particular:

(1)   shares issued in substitution for other shares of the same class;
(2)   employee share plans;
(3)   scrip dividend issues; and
(4)   takeovers and mergers, provided an equivalent document is produced (see s.2.3.2.5 below).

However, as in art.4 of the Prospectus Directive, from which the exemptions are taken, the wording of the exemptions in PRs 1.2.2R and 1.2.3R is not identical and they need to be read with care.

In the case of the prospectus requirement in the context of admissions to trading, two provisions of the New Prospectus

Regulation which came into effect in July 2017 provide exemptions from the prospectus requirement where:

(1) a new issue of shares represents 20% of a class already admitted to trading. Note that this exemption only applies to admissions to trading. A prospectus will still be required if the securities are to be offered to the public (and an applicable exemption does not apply). The 20% figure is calculated on a rolling 12-month basis so that issues made over a period of 12 months are aggregated. This rule replaced the similar exemption under the Prospectus Directive and formerly implemented in PR 1.2.3. However, this related to shares representing less than 10% of a class already admitted to trading, rather than 20%; and

(2) the shares, of a class already admitted to trading, are the result of a conversion or exchange of other securities. This exemption will not apply if the resulting shares equal 20% or more of the number of shares, of the same class, already admitted to trading on the same regulated market, over a period of 12 months (save in the case of securities of financial institutions in certain circumstances). This represents a stricter approach than under the Prospectus Directive which gave an exemption for shares resulting from the conversion or exchange of a transferable security without the 20% limit.

Two further exemptions under the New Prospectus Regulation will come into effect in July 2018. These provide that the New Prospectus Regulation shall not apply to offers of securities to the public with a total consideration in the EU of:

(1) less than €1 million, calculated over a period of 12 months; and

(2) an amount, less than €8 million and calculated over a period of 12 months, to be determined by each Member State. This is an optional exemption which Member States can implement, if they wish. The FCA has not yet indicated whether the UK plans to implement this exemption.

These exemptions are a change from the existing rules. In art.1(2)(h) of the Prospectus Directive (implemented by Sch.11A to the FSMA), a prospectus is not required for an offer where the total consideration in the EU, calculated over 12 months, is less than €5 million. Another de minimis exemption also exists in art.3(2)(e) of the Prospect Directive (implemented by s.86(1)(e) of the FSMA). This provides that a prospectus is not required for an offer with a total consideration in the EU, calculated over 12 months, of less than €100,000. Given the higher threshold in Sch.11A to the FSMA, this second de minimis exemption has not had much significance in the UK. Both exemptions will be replaced by the provisions of the New Prospectus Regulation.

2.3.2.5   Equivalent documents for takeovers and mergers

The exemptions in PRs 1.2.2R and 1.2.3R for securities offered in connection with takeovers and mergers are subject to the publication of a document considered by the FCA to be equivalent to a prospectus. This will need to be approved by the FCA and contain substantially the same contents as a prospectus but does not carry the statutory baggage that the prospectus has under the FSMA, in terms of the liability regime (see s.2.3.7 below), the updating requirement of supplemental prospectuses (see s.2.3.6.4 below) and so on. In particular, the withdrawal rights provisions of s.87Q(4) of the FSMA do not apply to equivalent documents. On the other hand, equivalent documents do not benefit from the ability to be "passported" (see s.2.3.5 below). Since it is possible to opt to publish a prospectus instead of an equivalent document, bidders in securities exchange offers need to make a judgement as to the advantages and disadvantages of choosing to use an equivalent document over a prospectus according to the circumstances of the particular offer.

2.3.3   Requirement for listing particulars

Listing particulars are required in connection with an application for admission to the Official List in circumstances where a prospectus is not required. This includes certain issues of securities within Sch.11A to the FSMA, most importantly open-ended collective investment schemes and non-equity securities issued by the government of an EEA Member State, a local or regional authority of an EEA Member State or public international bodies of which an EEA Member State is a member. It also applies in the case of applications for admission of securities to be listed on the Official List and traded on the PSM.

It is nevertheless possible under s.87 of the FSMA for certain issuers who would otherwise be exempt from the requirement for a prospectus to opt in to the prospectus regime (and thereby benefit from the passport arrangements). This opt-in right applies, in particular, to non-equity securities issued by the government of an EEA Member State, a local or regional authority of an EEA Member State or public international bodies of which an EEA Member State is a member.

2.3.4 Home state and approval of prospectus

Where a prospectus is required, it must be approved by the competent authority of the "home state" in relation to the issuer of the securities, before publication. In the UK, under Pt VI of the FSMA, the FCA has responsibility for determining eligibility for listing, reviewing and approving the prospectuses of issuers whose home state is the UK.

2.3.4.1 Home state

Even where securities are to be admitted to the Official List in the UK and nowhere else, it will not necessarily be the case that the UK is the home state. The home state principle is an important element of the Prospectus Directive regime and essentially limits the choice that issuers have in determining who they will be regulated by, at least in the context of equity securities and low-denomination non-equity securities.

In summary, the home state for issuers incorporated in the EEA will be:

(1) in the case of equity securities or non-equity securities with a denomination of less than €1,000 (or its equivalent in another currency), the state in which the issuer is incorporated (even if it is not making an offer to the public or seeking admission of the securities to a regulated market in that Member State); and

(2) in the case of other securities, the state which the issuer chooses as its home state.

For the purposes of the Prospectus Directive and home state determination, "equity securities" are shares and other instruments linked to equity, such as warrants over an issuer's own shares or bonds convertible into the issuer's shares or shares of another group entity (but not bonds exchangeable into shares of an entity outside the issuer's group).

An issuer whose home state is the UK (either automatically or through choice) is required by DTR 6.4 to disclose this to the competent authority of:

(1) the EEA state where it has its registered office (where applicable);

(2) the home state; and

(3) each host state.

If this is not done within a period of three months from the date the issuer's securities are admitted to trading, a default home state will apply.

The home state rules for non-EEA issuers are complex and are discussed in Ch.8 below.

2.3.4.2 *Approval of prospectus*

The FCA may not approve a prospectus unless satisfied that:

(1) the UK is the relevant home state;

(2) the prospectus contains the necessary information (see s.2.3.6.2 below); and

(3) all other applicable requirements imposed by the FSMA, the Prospectus Directive or the PD Regulation have been complied with (s.87A of the FSMA).

Under s.87J of the FSMA, the FCA can, in particular cases, require the inclusion in a prospectus of additional information if it considers this necessary for investor protection. It can also require information or documents to be provided to it not only by the issuer or other person applying for approval of the prospectus but also by:

(1) a person controlling, or controlled by, the applicant;
(2) an auditor or manager of the applicant; and
(3) a financial intermediary involved in the offer to the public or admission to trading on a regulated market.

Section 87C and D of the FSMA lay down timing and procedural requirements in connection with the FCA's approval of prospectuses.

Article 13.5 of the Prospectus Directive, implemented by s.87F of the FSMA, permits a home competent authority to transfer the task of approving a prospectus to another authority, if the latter agrees. PR 3.1.13G states that the FCA will consider doing this at the request of the person seeking approval of the prospectus or where it considers it would be more appropriate for the other authority to perform the function. Section 87E of the FSMA deals with transfers of applications for approval to another competent authority by the FCA and s.87F of the FSMA deals with transfers by another competent authority to the FCA. When an application is transferred to the FCA, it will be treated as though the UK were the home state.

2.3.5   *The passport for prospectuses*

The passporting of prospectuses is an important aspect of the regime created by the Prospectus Directive. Once a prospectus has been approved by the relevant competent authority as compliant with the PD Regulation and with the other general form and content requirements under the Prospectus Directive, no further disclosure or approval process can be insisted upon by any other competent authority.

A prospectus approved in the relevant home state can, therefore, be used for admission to trading or a public offer in any other EEA Member State (the host state), subject only to the following conditions:

(1)   notification by the competent authority which approved the prospectus to the competent authority in each host state; and
(2)   translation of the prospectus summary, if required under the rules of the host state (art.17(1) of the Prospectus Directive).

Section 87I of the FSMA, which implements art.18 of the Prospectus Directive, sets out the obligations of the FCA in relation to issuing certificates of approval for these purposes and additional requirements are set out in PR 5.3.2R.

The limited translation obligation is particularly important because translation of a full prospectus would generally be time-consuming and costly. The simplicity and ease of pass-porting means that it is common, particularly in the context of offerings to existing shareholders on a pre-emptive basis and cross-border mergers and takeovers.

2.3.6   Form, contents and publication of prospectuses and listing particulars

The Prospectus Directive and PD Regulation prescribe in detail the required form and contents of prospectuses. The level of prescription is intended to have the effect of ensuring better and more uniform disclosure by issuers so as to increase investor confidence in the markets, facilitate comparisons between issuers in different jurisdictions and hence encourage cross-border investment. The detailed substantive require-ments of the regime in relation to the form, contents and publication requirements for prospectuses and listing particulars are outside the scope of this chapter. However, the sources of the relevant requirements are worth noting.

2.3.6.1 *Form of prospectus*

Article 5 of the Prospectus Directive, implemented by PR 2.2, permits a prospectus to take one of a variety of forms:

(1) a single document, including a summary. The summary is required to follow a prescribed format in order to facilitate comparability of different securities and must contain the "key information" required to enable investors to understand the nature and risks of the issuer and the securities and to aid them when considering whether to invest in the securities;

(2) a tripartite document, comprising a registration document (containing information relating to the issuer), a securities note (containing information relating to the securities) and the summary; or

(3) in the case of non-equity securities, a base prospectus plus a document containing the final terms of the issue.

The PD Regulation stipulates that a single document prospectus must begin with a detailed table of contents followed by the summary and risk factors (in that order) before the other contents requirements are fulfilled. However, as reflected in s.87A(5) of the FSMA and PR 2.1.3R, a summary is not required for a prospectus relating to non-equity securities that have a denomination of at least €100,000 or an equivalent amount, unless the prospectus relates to an offer of the securities to the public.

2.3.6.2 *Contents of prospectus*

The overriding obligation laid down by the Prospectus Directive, as implemented by s.87A(1) and (2) of the FSMA, is for a prospectus to contain "the information necessary to enable investors to make an informed assessment of:

1.   the assets and liabilities, financial position, profits and losses, and prospects of the issuer of the transferable securities and any guarantor; and
2.   the rights attaching to the transferable securities".

The FCA may not approve a prospectus unless it is satisfied that the prospectus contains this information (defined in s.87A as the "necessary information") and that all other information and procedural requirements under Pt 6 of the Prospectus Directive have been complied with. The necessary information must be presented in a form which is comprehensible and easy to analyse, and must be prepared having regard to the particular nature of the transferable securities and their issuer.

The specific contents requirements of prospectuses are set out in the PD Regulation, which lays down a "building block approach", under which different annexes set out different requirements for different types of securities (equities, debt, global depositary receipts, derivatives etc). Where securities fit within more than one annex, generally speaking, the requirements of all relevant annexes must be satisfied. The annexes to the PD Regulation are set out as Appendix 3 to the Prospectus Rules.

A particular feature of the disclosure requirements is the distinction drawn between securities with a denomination of €100,000 (or the equivalent in another currency) ("wholesale securities") and those with a lower denomination ("retail securities"). As might be expected, a more onerous disclosure regime applies to retail securities.

The ESMA Prospectus Recommendations provide detailed guidance on how to comply with a number of the specific items of disclosure laid down by the prospectus regime. They also provide some recommendations for additional disclosure in respect of property, mining, start-up, research-based and shipping companies.

Section 87B of the FSMA, in accordance with art.8.2 of the Prospectus Directive, sets out the cases in which the FCA has the power to grant derogations from this general duty of disclosure or from the specific contents requirements under the PD Regulation, namely:

(1) where disclosure would be contrary to the public interest;
(2) where disclosure would be seriously detrimental to the issuer, provided non-disclosure would not be likely to mislead a person considering the acquisition of the securities as to any facts, knowledge of which is essential for an informed assessment; and
(3) where the information is of minor importance only and not such as to influence the assessment of the issuer.

2.3.6.3 Publication of prospectus

The requirements for publication of a prospectus are set out in PR 3.2 and derive from art.14 of the Prospectus Directive and from the PD Regulation.

2.3.6.4 Supplementary prospectuses

Under art.16 of the Prospectus Directive, implemented by s.87G of the FSMA, a supplementary prospectus must be published if there arises or is noted a significant new factor, material mistake or inaccuracy relating to the information included in a prospectus approved by the FCA. "Significant" means significant in terms of the "necessary information" required to make an informed assessment under s.87A(2) of the FSMA. A supplementary prospectus must give sufficient information to correct any mistake or inaccuracy which gave rise to the need for it.

The requirement for a supplementary prospectus is triggered by any change or inaccuracy that comes to light during the "relevant period". This begins at the time when the prospectus is approved and ends with the closure of the offer to which the prospectus relates or the time when trading in those securities on a regulated market begins, as applicable. However, if the prospectus is prepared for the purposes of admission to a regulated market and for an accompanying offer, then the "relevant period" ends on the later of admission or the closing of the offer.

It is the duty, under s.87G(5) of the FSMA, of any person who is responsible for a prospectus to give notice to the issuer and any other person who requested approval of the prospectus, if he or she becomes aware of any new factor, mistake or inaccuracy which may give rise to the need' for a supplementary prospectus.

The ESMA has now also produced regulatory technical standards in relation to when an issuer must publish a supplementary prospectus and these are reflected in PR 3.4.4R. The list is not exhaustive but is phrased as the minimum situations in which a supplement may be required and includes the situations where:

(1) new annual audited financial statements are published by the relevant issuer;
(2) an amendment to a profit forecast or a profit estimate already included in the prospectus is published by the relevant issuer;
(3) there is a change in control in respect of the relevant issuer; and
(4) there is any new public takeover bid by third parties and the outcome of any public takeover bid in respect of the equity of the relevant issuer.

2.3.6.5   Withdrawal rights

Under art.16 of the Prospectus Directive, as implemented in s.87Q of the FSMA, the publication of a supplementary prospectus triggers a right for any investor who has already agreed to buy or subscribe for the securities to withdraw their acceptance for a period of two working days after the date on which the supplementary prospectus was published. These rights do not apply if the securities had already been delivered to the investor before the event to which the supplementary prospectus related occurred.

In addition, if a prospectus does not disclose the offer price or number of shares being offered, or at least give maximum figures, or the criteria for determining the price or offer size, withdrawal rights apply on publication of the price and number of shares in a final pricing statement (art.8 of the Prospectus Directive, implemented in s.87Q of the FSMA).

2.3.6.6 *Form, contents and publication of listing particulars*

Listing Rule 4 sets out requirements relating to listing particulars for:

(1) units in open-ended collective investment schemes and other securities under Sch.11A to the FSMA (being securities to which the Prospectus Directive does not apply) excluding (principally) non-equity securities issued or guaranteed by EEA governments or local authorities and EEA public international bodies or central banks, and securities issued where the total amount of the offer or issue is less than €5,000,000; and

(2) other specialist securities which are to be admitted to the PSM. "Specialist securities" are defined as securities which, because of their nature, are normally bought and traded by a limited number of investors who are particularly knowledgeable in investment matters.

The regime for listing particulars is no longer based on any EU provisions since provisions previously in the CARD on listing particulars were repealed by the Prospectus Directive. The FSMA and the FSMA 2000 (Official Listing of Securities) Regulations 2001 (SI 2001/2956) (Official Listing Regulations) contain requirements for listing particulars which are essentially unchanged from the previous rules.

The general duty of disclosure in listing particulars submitted to the FCA for approval, under s.80 of the FSMA, is similar to the general disclosure obligation for prospectuses under s.87A. However, s.80 makes some qualifications which are not present in the s.87A disclosure regime for prospectuses:

(1) the information to be included is that which investors and their professional advisers would reasonably require and reasonably expect to find in the listing particulars. The nature of the persons likely to consider acquiring the securities may be taken into account in determining what information they might reasonably require and might reasonably expect to find;

(2) the information required is that which is within the knowledge of the persons responsible for the document or which it would be reasonable for them to obtain by making enquiries; and

(3) in deciding what information is material, one may take into account matters which investors and their advisers might already have within their knowledge or information which may be available to them either as a result of the continuing obligations or other statutory requirements (e.g. a previous listing document or annual accounts) or as a result of any disclosure requirements imposed by a recognised investment exchange.

Like s.87B of the FSMA for prospectuses, s.82 of the FSMA permits derogations from disclosure in listing particulars in cases where disclosure would be contrary to the public interest or seriously detrimental to the issuer. In addition, in the case of such securities as the FCA specifies under s.82(1)(c), information that is unnecessary for persons of the kind who may be expected normally to buy or deal in securities of that kind may be omitted. LR 4.2.11R specifies specialist securities for these purposes. In addition, no summary is required for listing particulars in relation to specialist securities.

Section 81 of the FSMA contains an obligation to prepare supplementary listing particulars, which is broadly similar to the supplementary prospectus obligation in s.87G of the FSMA.

In relation to specific form and contents requirements, LR 4 follows the requirements laid down by the PD Regulation, save that securities with a denomination of less than €100,000 can use the annexes for wholesale securities rather than retail securities (LR 4.2.4R).

Similarly, the approval and publication requirements in LR 4 broadly treat listing particulars as though they were prospectuses and subject to the requirements of the Prospectus Rules.

2.3.7 Liability for prospectuses and listing particulars

The Prospectus Directive obliges Member States to ensure that at least civil liability attaches to persons responsible for the prospectus, except that no civil liability may attach to any person solely on the basis of a summary, including any translation of a summary, unless it is misleading, inaccurate or inconsistent when read together with the prospectus or does not contain the required key information (art.6, implemented in s.90 of the FSMA). It is left open to Member States to determine the precise nature of the liability.

Section 90 of the FSMA provides for the payment of statutory compensation where loss is suffered by persons as a result of misleading statements or omissions in either prospectuses or listing particulars approved by the FCA. This right is available to any person who has:

(1) acquired any of the securities in question; and
(2) suffered loss in respect of them as a result of any untrue or misleading statement, or the omission of any matter required to be included in the prospectus or listing particulars or a supplementary document, or as a result of failure to publish a supplementary document.

A claimant does not need to show express reliance on a misstatement in acquiring the securities in question. All that is necessary is for the loss to have resulted from the misstatement. The right to compensation is available for those who subscribe or purchase the securities pursuant to the offer or invitation contained in a prospectus or listing particulars. The right may also be available to subsequent purchasers of the securities in the market who can demonstrate that their loss resulted from the statement or omission. However, the currency of a prospectus or listing particulars will lapse with time, thanks to the defences provided in paras 1 and 2 of Sch.10 to the FSMA (see ss.2.3.9.3–2.3.9.4 below).

Prospectus Rules 3.1.2AR and 3.1.2BR provide that an applicant for the approval of a prospectus or supplementary prospectus must take all reasonable care to ensure that its prospectus or supplementary prospectus contains:

(1) all the necessary information required by s.87A of the FSMA;
(2) the relevant information required by the annexes of the PD Regulation; and
(3) no omission likely to affect its import.

An applicant who breaches these rules will be liable to sanction by the FCA (see s.2.8 below).

2.3.8   Who is liable? Persons responsible for prospectuses and listing particulars under section 90 of the FSMA

Prospectus Rule 5.5 defines the persons responsible for a prospectus or supplementary prospectus in relation to which the UK is the home state. Part 3 of the Official Listing Regulations defines the persons responsible for listing particulars and supplementary listing particulars.

The PD Regulation requires the persons responsible for prospectuses to be identified in the document and to make a declaration (a "responsibility statement") stating that, having taken reasonable care to ensure that such is the case, the information contained in the document is, to the best of their knowledge, in accordance with the facts and contains no omission likely to affect its import.

2.3.8.1 *Persons always responsible*

The responsible persons will always include:

(1) the issuer of the securities;
(2) any person who accepts, and is stated in the particulars as accepting, responsibility for the document or any part of it; and
(3) any other person who has authorised the contents of the document; this will include experts, such as accountants, whose reports or statements are included in a prospectus since, under the PD Regulation, such experts must authorise the contents of that part of the document (see, for example, Annex 1, para.23, set out in PR Appendix 3). It has sometimes been argued that sponsors should be regarded as having authorised the contents of a prospectus where they are sponsoring the issue. Whether this is the case may depend upon their actual role but it is more likely that they should be considered as advisers (see s.2.3.9.9 below).

Those who accept responsibility for, or authorise, parts of a prospectus are only responsible for that part.

2.3.8.2 *Persons requesting admission to trading*

Under the Prospectus Directive regime, it is possible for someone other than the issuer to request admission to trading on a regulated market and, accordingly, responsibility can also apply to a person who has requested admission of the securities to trading. If the issuer has not authorised the request for admission to trading neither it nor its directors will be responsible.

2.3.8.3 *Offerors*

In the case of an offer of securities to the public, if the prospectus relates to an offer by a person other than the issuer, such as a selling shareholder, the selling shareholder or other offeror will be responsible for the prospectus except where he is making the offer in association with the issuer and the prospectus is drawn up primarily by the issuer or persons acting on the issuer's behalf.

2.3.8.4   *Directors and future directors*

The position of directors will depend upon the nature of the securities. Prospectus Rule 5.5 applies different rules to:

(1)   equity shares, warrants or options to subscribe for equity shares which are issued by the issuer of the shares and other securities having similar characteristics to such shares, warrants or options; and
(2)   any other securities, including debt and convertible securities.

In the case of equity securities within (1) above, the following persons will be responsible for the prospectus (in addition to those mentioned in ss.2.3.8.1–2.3.8.3 above):

(a)   the directors of the issuer: where the issuer is a body corporate, this includes all persons who were directors at the date of the document;
(b)   each person who has authorised himself to be named, and is named, as having agreed to become a director of the issuer either immediately or in the future: it is common in recommended takeover offers, for example, to state that certain directors of the target company will join the board of the offeror upon the offer becoming unconditional. Those directors will thereby become responsible for the information concerning the offeror as well as the information concerning their own company;
(c)   the directors of the offeror: if the offeror is a body corporate and is responsible as mentioned in s.2.3.8.3 above, its directors at the date of the prospectus will also be responsible; and
(d)   the directors of the person requesting admission: if this person is a body corporate who is not the issuer, its directors at the date of the prospectus will be responsible.

Under PR 5.5.4R, responsibility for prospectuses in relation to securities within (2) above does not apply to persons within (a)–(d) above.

Under the Official Listing Regulations, directors and future directors (as in (b) above) will be responsible for listing particulars, except in the case of specialist securities. Listing Rule 4.2.13R provides that, in relation to listing particulars for specialist securities, directors may, but need not, give a responsibility statement.

2.3.8.5   Guarantor

In the case of securities which are not equity securities within (1) in s.2.3.8.4 above, if there is a guarantor for the issue, the guarantor will also be a person responsible for the prospectus.

2.3.9   Exemptions from, and defences to, statutory liability

There are a number of important exclusions from, or defences to, liability provided by the Prospectus Rules (in relation to prospectuses) by the Official Listing Regulations (in relation to listing particulars) and by Sch.10 to the FSMA (in relation to both).

2.3.9.1   Publication without knowledge (Prospectus Rule 5.5.6R and regulation 6(2))

A director is not a "person responsible" and therefore is not liable if the document was published without his knowledge or consent and on becoming aware of publication he gives reasonable public notice of that fact.

2.3.9.2   Part not included in agreed form and context (Prospectus Rule 5.5.8R and regulation 6(3))

A person who accepts responsibility for, or authorises the contents of, the document only in relation to certain specified parts or only in certain specified respects is only liable to the extent specified and only if the material in question is included in (or substantially in) the form and context to which he has agreed.

2.3.9.3 *Reasonable belief as to statement (Schedule 10 paragraph 1 of the FSMA)*

A person is not liable if he shows that, at the time when the document was submitted to the FCA, he:

> "reasonably believed, having made all such enquiries (if any) as were reasonable, that the statement was true and not misleading or that the matter whose omission caused the loss was properly omitted".

However, he must, in addition, show that one of four further conditions has been fulfilled, namely that:

(1) he continued in that belief until the securities were acquired;
(2) the securities were acquired before it was reasonably practicable to bring a correction to the attention of those persons likely to acquire them;
(3) before the securities were acquired, he had taken all reasonable steps to secure that a correction was brought to the attention of those persons likely to acquire them; or
(4) he continued in that belief until after commencement of dealings in the securities following their admission to the Official List or regulated market and the securities were acquired after such a lapse of time that he ought reasonably to be excused.

2.3.9.4 *Statements by experts (Schedule 10 paragraph 2 of the FSMA)*

A responsible person will not be liable for losses caused by an expert's statement where, at the time the document was submitted to the FCA, he believed on reasonable grounds that the expert was competent to make or authorise the statement and had consented to its inclusion in the form and context in which it was included. Again, four additional conditions have to be fulfilled, equivalent to those relevant for the defence described in s.2.3.9.3 above.

2.3.9.5 Correction issued (Schedule 10 paragraphs 3 and 4 of the FSMA)

Even if reasonable belief in the accuracy of the document cannot be proved, there is still a defence if the person responsible can show that:

(1) before the securities were acquired a correction was suitably published; or
(2) he took all reasonable steps to secure such publication and reasonably believed that it had taken place before the securities were acquired.

2.3.9.6 Statement by an official or in an official document (Schedule 10 paragraph 5 of the FSMA)

It is a defence to show that the statement concerned is an accurate and fair reproduction of a statement made by an official person or contained in a public official document.

2.3.9.7 Plaintiff's knowledge of misstatement/omission (Schedule 10 paragraph 6 of the FSMA)

It is a defence to show that the person suffering the loss acquired the securities with knowledge that the statement was false or misleading or of the omitted matter. Where a supplementary prospectus or listing particulars should have been published, it is a defence to show that the person suffering loss acquired the securities with knowledge of the change or new matter which required such publication.

2.3.9.8   Reasonable belief that supplements not required (Schedule 10 paragraph 7 of the FSMA)

A person is not liable for failing to produce a supplementary document if he reasonably believed that the change or new matter was not such as to make it necessary to produce one.

2.3.9.9   Professional advisers (Prospectus Rule 5.5.9R and regulation 6(4))

Responsibility does not attach to professional advisers who provide advice as to the contents of the listing document in a professional capacity, by reason only of their giving advice. There is obviously a thin line here between giving advice and "authorising the contents". Happily for the legal profession, lawyers are generally thought to fall on the right side of the line so far as this provision is concerned.

2.3.10   Other sources of liability on prospectuses

2.3.10.1   Negligent misstatement and misrepresentation

In addition to the statutory obligation to compensate investors, there may be common law liability on a prospectus or listing particulars, including for negligent misstatement or misrepresentation (s.90(6) of the FSMA).

The scope of the duty of care arising under the law of negligence was narrowed in the line of cases of which *Caparo Industries Plc v Dickman*[11] is the most prominent. In *Al Nakib Investments (Jersey) Ltd v Longcroft*,[12] the plaintiffs brought an action against the directors of the company as well as the company itself, alleging that, inter alia, they had purchased shares in the company in the market in reliance on a rights issue prospectus and that this prospectus contained untrue and misleading statements. Following the old case of *Peek v*

---

[11] *Caparo Industries Plc v Dickman* [1990] 2 A.C. 605; [1990] 2 W.L.R. 358; [1955–95] P.N.L.R. 523 HL.

[12] *Al Nakib Investments (Jersey) Ltd v Longcroft* [1990] 1 W.L.R. 1390; [1990] B.C.C. 517; [1991] B.C.L.C. 7 Ch D.

Gurney,[13] the court held that, whilst directors owed a duty of care to those who subscribed for shares under the rights issue in reliance on the prospectus, they did not owe a duty of care to a shareholder or anyone else who relied on the prospectus for the purpose of deciding whether to purchase shares through the stock market, and the relationship between the directors and those investors was not sufficiently proximate for a duty of care to arise.

However, in *Possfund Custodian Trustee Ltd v Diamond*,[14] in a preliminary hearing of the defendants' attempt to strike out the plaintiffs' claim that a duty of care was owed to the plaintiffs in respect of purchases of shares in the after-market following the issue of a prospectus, the court held that it was at least arguable that a duty of care was owed to investors in such circumstances and that the plaintiffs' claim deserved full consideration at trial. Lightman J, in the concluding remarks of his judgment, gave support to the view, expressed in a leading textbook, that the decision in *Peek* was "outmoded" and that the decision in *Al Nakib* "[should] be reviewed by a higher court".[15]

A claim at common law for fraudulent misrepresentation would require the claimant to establish that the defendant knew or was reckless as to whether a statement was untrue. A claim under s.2(1) of the Misrepresentation Act 1967 only requires a showing of negligence but this remedy only applies to statements made by a party to the subsequent contract. Accordingly, the company but not the directors (unless, perhaps, they are selling shareholders) could be liable and there may be no liability where the prospectus relates to shares being sold by third parties.

---

[13] *Peek v Gurney* (1873) L.R. 6 H.L. 377; [1861–1873] All E.R. Rep. 116 HL.
[14] *Possfund Custodian Trustee Ltd v Diamond* [1996] 1 W.L.R. 1351; [1996] 2 B.C.L.C. 665; *Times*, 18 April 1996 Ch D.
[15] *Possfund* [1996] 1 W.L.R. 1351 at 1366.

2.3.10.2   Criminal liability and market abuse

The general offences in ss.89 and 90 of the Financial Services Act 2012 relating to misstatements made dishonestly or recklessly so as to induce others to deal in securities will potentially apply to false statements made in a prospectus or listing particulars, as will the market abuse regime under the Market Abuse Regulation. The FCA has the power to bring charges under the criminal provisions of ss.89 and 90 of the Financial Services Act 2012.

2.3.10.3   Penalties under the FSMA

Issuers, directors and sponsors may also be liable to sanctions under s.91 of the FSMA for breach of the Prospectus Rules or Listing Rules, Pt VI of the FSMA or the PD Regulation. The FCA also has powers to stop a public offer or prohibit admission to trading (see s.2.8.4 below).

2.4   Applying for listing

For those companies seeking admission of their securities to the Official List, the Listing Rules set out the application process, and eligibility requirements, as well as obligations that apply on a continuing basis to listed issuers.

Before considering the application process, it is appropriate to consider the structure of the regime for official listing more broadly.

2.4.1   Introduction to the Listing Rules

The Listing Rules contain eligibility requirements and continuing obligations, which differ according to the type of security and issuer. Under the Listing Rules, the Official List is divided into two segments: premium and standard. Equity shares can be listed on either the premium or the standard segment but all other securities must be listed on the standard segment. The premium and standard segments are subdivided into listing categories according to the type of security and the type of entity issuing them. A particular issuer may, of course, fall within both segments, having equity shares which are premium listed and other classes of securities which have standard listings.

Certain eligibility criteria for companies seeking admission to listing are imposed by the CARD. The most significant of these in practice is the minimum "free float" requirement for companies listing shares. The remainder of the Listing Rules are not based on EU legislation.

The FCA is currently reviewing some parts of the UK Listing Regime, including the operation of the standard listing segment. At the time of writing, the outcome of the review in respect of the standard listing segment has not been published.

2.4.1.1 *Premium listing*

The premium listing segment is open to equity shares only and imposes super-equivalent eligibility requirements alongside the minimum standards on eligibility required by the CARD. Additional continuing obligations are also included, supplementing those that apply under the DTR, notably the obligation to disclose compliance with the UK Corporate Governance Code, rules on shareholder approval of significant and related party transactions, and rules governing relationships with controlling shareholders.

The premium segment is divided into four categories: commercial companies; closed-ended investment funds; open-ended investment companies; and sovereign-controlled companies (established in July 2018). The additional eligibility requirements and continuing obligations which apply to commercial companies are set out in LRs 6–12. In addition to many of the requirements in those chapters, specific requirements for closed and open-ended investment entities are set out in LR 15 and LR 16 respectively.

It is important to note that the FCA is free to apply, and derogate from, its own super-equivalent rules in such a manner as it thinks fit. By contrast, it generally has, at most, limited flexibility to derogate from the obligations based on EU legislation.

2.4.1.2 *Standard listing*

The standard listing segment meets the EU minimum standards, with only a few additional requirements, and is available to both UK and non-UK issuers. Standard listing is open to shares and other securities that are not eligible for premium listing. It is divided into five categories: shares; global depositary receipts (GDRs); debt and debt-like securities; securitised derivatives; and miscellaneous securities (including options and warrants). Which chapter of the Listing Rules these will fall into will in some cases depend on whether they are treated as specialist securities under LR 17. Standard listing is not available for the equity shares of closed or open-ended investment entities, unless they also have at least one class of equity shares with a premium listing.

The breadth of the standard listing category is in line with the power of the FCA to list "such securities and other things as it may consider appropriate" under s.75 of the FSMA. Her Majesty's (HM) Treasury has a broad authority to issue orders excluding certain categories or descriptions of things from eligibility for admission to the Official List. Currently, the only category of securities excluded is certain securities of non-public UK companies (reg.3 of the Official Listing Regulations).

2.4.2 *Conditions for listing*

Before applying for listing, an issuer will need to establish that it satisfies the relevant conditions for listing. Those applicable to all securities are set out in LR 2, with additional requirements set out in individual chapters for each category of security.

2.4.3 *Sponsors*

The sponsor regime is one of the key features of the UK premium listing regime since the role of a sponsor is both to guide issuers on understanding their responsibilities under the Listing Rules and DTRs, and also to confirm to the FCA that the company's responsibilities under the rules have been met. Section 88 of the FSMA allows for the Listing Rules to require issuers to have a sponsor and sets up the framework for the FCA to approve sponsors. Listing Rule 8 lays down the circumstances in which a sponsor will be required, defines the duties of the sponsors both to the FCA and to issuers whom they advise and sets out the criteria for approval as a sponsor.

Section 88A of the FSMA empowers the FCA to sanction sponsors, including the power to publicly censure sponsors for breach of any of their obligations under the Listing Rules, impose financial penalties and suspend the approval of the sponsor (for a period not exceeding 12 months). In August 2016, the FCA imposed a fine of £530,502 on Cenkos, an authorised firm and sponsor, for, among other things, not having appropriate systems and controls in place and failing to act with the level of diligence and professional care that the FCA expects of a sponsor.

The FCA may also suspend the approval of a sponsor to advance its operational objectives (as described in s.2.2.4 above), in which case there is no set time limit on the length of the suspension (s.88E of the FSMA). The FCA has stated that it envisages this power would be used when the FCA had already made its concerns clear to the sponsor and needed to act urgently to prevent a sponsor acting, in order to protect consumers or the integrity of the UK financial system.

An investor does not have a right of action under the FSMA against a sponsor who breaches the Listing Rules. Section 138D of the FSMA provides that private persons who can show that they have suffered loss as a result of a breach of any FCA rule by an authorised person may, unless the relevant rule expressly excludes that right, bring an action for damages against that authorised person for breach of statutory duty. However, the Pt 6 Rules are excluded from this provision (under s.138D(5) of the FSMA).

2.5 Continuing obligations

Once listed, a company will be subject to a range of continuing obligations under the Listing Rules as well as under the Transparency Rules and the Market Abuse Regulation.

While the continuing obligations are discussed in detail elsewhere, it is worth pausing to consider, because they are somewhat different in nature from the other rules, the Listing Principles, which apply to premium listed issuers.

2.5.1 The Listing Principles

The Listing Principles, which are set out in LR 7, were originally adopted in 2005, following a general review of the Listing Rules.

At that time, the Listing Principles applied only to premium listed companies. From May 2014, however, the Listing Rules were amended to apply two Listing Principles to all companies, including standard listed companies, with additional Premium Listing Principles applying only to those with a premium listing. The new Premium Listing Principles include two Principles on the voting rights attached to classes of shares.

The Listing Principles applicable to all issuers require them to:

(1) take reasonable steps to establish and maintain adequate procedures, systems and controls to enable them to comply with their obligations; and
(2) deal with the FCA in an open and co-operative manner.

The additional Premium Listing Principles are as follows:

(1) the company must take reasonable steps to enable its directors to understand their responsibilities and obligations as directors;

(2) the company must act with integrity towards the holders and potential holders of its premium listed shares;

(3) all shares in a class that has been admitted to premium listing must carry an equal number of votes on any shareholder vote;

(4) where the company has more than one class of shares admitted to premium listing, the aggregate voting rights of the shares in each class should be broadly proportionate to the relative economic interests of those classes;

(5) the company must ensure that it treats all holders of the same class of its listed shares that are in the same position equally in respect of the rights attaching to those listed shares; and

(6) the company must communicate information to holders and potential holders of its listed shares in such a way as to avoid the creation of a false market in those listed shares.

The FCA sets out its policy on disciplinary breaches of the Listing Principles in the *Decision Procedure and Penalties Manual* (DEPP 6.2.16G–6.2.18G). Examples of where enforcement action on the basis of a breach of a Listing Principle would be taken are where there is no specific other rule breach but there is behaviour which "clearly contravenes" a Listing Principle. In addition, the FCA may find it appropriate to take action where there have been a number of breaches of detailed rules which individually do not merit disciplinary action but which cumulatively suggest a breach of a Listing Principle.

A significant instance of a company being fined for a breach of Listing Principles without any other rule breach was the case of Prudential Plc, which was fined for failing to deal with the UKLA in an open and co-operative manner in March 2013. This was in the context of a transaction on which the UKLA took the view it should have been consulted at an earlier stage and illustrates the breadth of scope of the Listing Principles. In addition, a number of companies have been fined on the basis that they have breached both DTR 2.2.1 (on disclosure of information) and the Listing Principles on communication so as to avoid a false market, or having adequate procedures, systems and controls.

2.5.2   *The Disclosure Guidance and Transparency Rules*

2.5.2.1   *The Disclosure Guidance*

The Disclosure Guidance is made up of DTRs 1, 2 and 3. These provisions give some guidance in relation to the issues covered by arts 17 (disclosure of inside information), 18 (insider lists) and 19 (managers' transactions) of the Market Abuse Regulation, including:

(1) the application of the *FCA Handbook* (see s.2.2.5 above) and consultation with the FCA in relation to persons covered by arts 17, 18 and 19 of the Market Abuse Regulation (DTR 1);
(2) penalties that may be imposed by the FCA in relation to a breach of arts 17, 18 and 19 of the Market Abuse Regulation (DTR 1);
(3) the disclosure of inside information (DTR 2); and
(4) disclosure of dealings in an issuer's shares or debt by persons discharging managerial responsibilities (DTR 3).

Prior to the Market Abuse Regulation, these issues were covered by the Disclosure Rules, which formed part of the *FCA Handbook*. Disclosure Rules 1, 2 and 3 implemented parts of the Market Abuse Directive (disclosure of inside information, insider lists and disclosure of dealings by persons discharging managerial responsibilities).

When the Market Abuse Directive was replaced by the Market Abuse Regulation in July 2016, much of the content of the Disclosure Rules was deleted but certain parts were retained as guidance, hence the term "Disclosure Guidance".

2.5.2.2   The Transparency Rules

The Transparency Rules (in DTRs 4 and 6) implement the provisions of the Transparency Directive regarding the reporting obligations of issuers whose transferable securities are admitted to trading on a regulated market and whose home state is the UK.

Under DTR 4, all issuers must produce annual reports (subject to exemptions for wholesale debt issuers, state authorities and certain other public bodies) and issuers of shares and debt securities must produce half-yearly reports.

Disclosure Guidance and Transparency Rule 6 deals with issuers' continuing obligations and access to information, namely the way companies communicate with shareholders and the market. Under DTR 6, issuers are required to release "regulated information" to a Regulatory Information Service (RIS) so that the information is disseminated to the market. "Regulated information" for these purposes means information which the issuer is required to disclose under the Transparency Directive, arts 17–19 of the Market Abuse Regulation, the Listing Rules or the DTRs.

Disclosure Guidance and Transparency Rule 5 implements the provisions of the Transparency Directive on major shareholding disclosures and requires shareholders (or those with rights to acquire shares or to exercise control of voting rights held directly or indirectly as a shareholder or through a direct or indirect holding of financial instruments) of an issuer to inform the issuer of changes to major holdings in that issuer's shares. The disclosable percentage interests in relation to UK issuers are 3% and every whole percentage figure above 3%. In relation to non-UK issuers whose home state is the UK, the interests in shares and related financial instruments are disclosable at 5%, 10%, 15%, 20%, 25%, 30%, 50% and 75%.

Notification must be effected as soon as possible and in any event no later than two trading days (in respect of a UK issuer) or four trading days (in respect of a non-UK issuer) after the time when the investor knew, or should have known, of the change. Under DTR 5, issuers also have to publish regular statements of their total issued share capital.

While the FCA generally adopted a "copy out" approach in transposing the provisions of the Transparency Directive on major shareholding disclosure into DTR 5, it took advantage of the flexibility under the directive to impose more stringent provisions by requiring the lower disclosure thresholds and a shorter notification timetable that apply to holdings in UK-incorporated issuers. The rules in DTR 5 were also extended in 2009 to capture interests in UK issuers in the form of contracts for differences and other financial instruments with a similar economic effect to an interest in shares. However, amendments to the Transparency Directive under Directive 2013/50[16] followed the FCA's approach by requiring all member states to require disclosure of holdings in financial instruments with a similar economic effect to an interest in shares. The FCA amended DTR 5 to bring it into line with these new provisions on 26 November 2015.

2.5.3 *Liability for ongoing disclosure*

2.5.3.1 *Section 90A of the FSMA*

The statutory liability regime relating to prospectuses is discussed above (see ss.2.3.7–2.3.9). Liability for information published by issuers under their ongoing obligations is prescribed by Sch.10A to the FSMA which applies to all information published via a RIS, including information whose availability is announced by a RIS, such as annual reports. This therefore covers information published under the Listing Rules, Transparency Rules and the Market Abuse Regulation.

---

[16] Directive 2013/50 amending Directive 2004/109 on the harmonisation of transparency requirements in relation to information about issuers whose securities are admitted to trading on a regulated market, Directive 2003/71 on the prospectus to be published when securities are offered to the public or admitted to trading and Directive 2007/14 laying down detailed rules for the implementation of certain provisions of Directive 2004/109 [2013] OJ L294/13.

The regime in Sch.10A to the FSMA was introduced by the Companies Act 2006 and amended in 2010 with the intention of providing certainty as to the extent of the liability of issuers for their publications and, importantly, to limit the scope of such liability, creating a safe harbour that would protect companies and their directors from speculative litigation while encouraging directors to be open and transparent in their reporting of ongoing developments. The regime was initially introduced as a response to the Transparency Directive, without a great deal of prior consultation. Accordingly, the Government commissioned Professor Paul Davies to review the regime, and adopted the recommendations he made in his *Final Report* of June 2007, in extending and clarifying the regime and its application.

Under the regime, any issuer publishing false or misleading statements will be liable to compensate an investor who suffered loss as a consequence of the false or misleading information, but only if a director of the issuer knew or was reckless as to whether information was misleading or untrue, or knew that an omission constituted dishonest concealment of a material fact. Other liabilities are excluded, subject to certain exceptions (see below). The exclusion of liability applies both to the issuer, in respect of any loss arising as a result of misleading statements or omissions in publications to which Sch.10A to the FSMA applies, and to persons (other than the issuer) for all liabilities other than to the issuer itself.

As well as clarifying the basis of liability, the regime provides a safe harbour by excluding other liabilities in relation to the information to which it applies, while specifically preserving liability: under s.90 of the FSMA; under rules made by the Takeover Panel under s.954 of the Companies Act 2006; for breach of contract; under the Misrepresentation Act 1967; or where express responsibility has been assumed to a particular person for a particular purpose.

2.5.3.2   Negligent misstatement

Schedule 10A to the FSMA excludes negligence misstatement in respect of market announcements. However, in respect of information published prior to October 2010, investors may be able to bring a common law negligent misstatement claim against a company if it can be shown they have suffered loss as a result of misleading announcements made to the market. While the *Caparo* case established that a company has no duty of care to potential purchasers of securities in the case of annual accounts, it is not clear that this was the case in respect of market announcements. Hence, it has been held, in *Hall v Cable and Wireless Plc*, that allegations of negligence against an issuer which had failed to disclose information which, when subsequently announced, caused a fall in its share price, were at least arguable.[17] There may still, however, be complex questions of reliance and causation of loss to be established before a claim could succeed. In the same case, the judge dismissed claims based on breach of statutory duty, market abuse and negligent misrepresentation pursuant to the Misrepresentation Act 1967, confirming that:

(1)   an issuer cannot be sued for breach of statutory duty in relation to breaches of Pt 6 Rules, given the clear scheme and modes of enforcement provided by the FSMA;
(2)   there is no direct cause of action for market abuse by a person who has suffered a loss as a result of it; and
(3)   as the loss that was alleged to have been caused by misleading statements of the company arose as a result of market purchases of shares from a third party, the requirement under s.2(1) of the Misrepresentation Act 1967 that the misleading statement be made by a contracting party was not satisfied.

2.5.3.3   Dishonest delay

Schedule 10A to the FSMA also imposes liability on issuers for dishonest delay in disclosing information on the market. This

---

[17]   *Hall v Cable and Wireless Plc* [2009] EWHC 1793 (Comm); [2011] B.C.C. 543; [2010] 1 B.C.L.C. 95.

arose from a recommendation from Professor Davies in his *Final Report* to introduce a new liability for dishonest delay in making RIS announcements. The creation of a new liability to investors for delays in publishing information was a particular concern to issuers when it was proposed, on the basis that it could encourage litigation and put undue pressure on issuers to make announcements in circumstances where delay is legitimate. However, under the provisions in Sch.10A to the FSMA, for the issuer to be liable, there has to have been dishonesty on the part of a director. For these purposes, there is a special definition of dishonesty. A person's conduct will be dishonest if regarded as such by persons who regularly trade on the market in question and the person was aware (or must be taken to have been aware) that it was so regarded.

2.5.4 *Corporate governance rules*

The provisions of DTR 7 implement provisions of EU company law dealing with audit committees and corporate governance statements in annual reports. For premium listed issuers, there is some overlap between these requirements and the requirement to make a statement of compliance regarding the UK Corporate Governance Code under the super-equivalent provisions in LR 9.

2.6 Market abuse

The Market Abuse Regulation came into force on 3 July 2016 and covers the following areas that used to be contained in the DTRs (see s.2.5.2.1 above):

(1) disclosure of inside information (art.17);
(2) insider lists (art.18); and
(3) dealings by persons discharging managerial responsibilities (art.19).

The FCA also has the authority to impose unlimited fines for breaches of these rules (see s.2.8 below).

The Market Abuse Regulation also contains the rules on:

(1) insider dealing (art.8);
(2) market manipulation (art.12), which includes:
    (a) entering a transaction, placing an order to trade or any other behaviour which gives false or misleading signals, or secures the price of investments at an abnormal or artificial level;
    (b) entering into a transaction, placing an order to trade or any other activity or behaviour that uses fictitious devices, deceptions or contrivances;
    (c) disseminating information which gives false or misleading signals;
    (d) transmitting false or misleading information or providing false or misleading inputs in relation to benchmarks; and
(3) unlawful disclosure of inside information (art.10).

The regulation also sets out two safe harbours, subject to compliance with detailed conditions, to cover stabilisation activities and share buybacks (art.5). However, non-compliance with the safe harbour does not necessarily mean that market abuse is being committed.

The regulation, in art.11, also sets out a procedure to be followed when conducting market soundings. This procedure will prevent certain market soundings being an unlawful disclosure of inside information (art.10). Among other things, the procedure requires the party conducting the market sounding to obtain the consent of the recipient to receiving inside information and inform them of the restrictions that would then apply to them. There are detailed requirements in relation to exactly what information may be disclosed, timing of disclosures, obtaining the recipient's consent and record-keeping.

Section 123 of the FSMA gives the FCA the power to impose unlimited fines upon any person who has engaged in market abuse under the Market Abuse Regulation.

2.7 Financial promotions and advertisements

2.7.1 *The financial promotion regime*

The financial promotion regime under the FSMA is of concern to listed companies since, for example, many communications made to the market, or to shareholders or to employees in connection with an employees' share scheme, are capable of falling within the regime. Fortunately, an exemption will often be available, enabling companies to avoid the need to have their communications approved by an authorised person.

The financial promotion regime is established under s.21 of the FSMA. This prohibits the communication of an invitation or inducement to engage in a regulated activity (a "financial promotion") unless it is approved or communicated by an authorised person. A number of exemptions apply under the Financial Services and Markets Act 2000 (Financial Promotion) Order 2005 (SI 2005/1529) (as amended) (Financial Promotion Order). In particular, art.70 of the Financial Promotion Order exempts prospectuses (including prospectuses passported from other EEA states), listing particulars, supplementary prospectuses and listing particulars, and any other document required or expressly permitted to be published under the Prospectus Rules or Listing Rules. However, advertisements under the Prospectus Rules are excluded from this exemption (see s.2.7.2 below).

Other exemptions that are of particular relevance to listed companies include promotions that are required or permitted by market rules (art.67), certain promotions of securities already admitted to markets in the EEA (art.69), promotions to members or creditors of the company (art.43) and communications of or including the company's annual accounts and/or directors' report (art.59).

Listed companies seeking to take advantage of these exemptions need, where relevant, to ensure that they satisfy the detailed terms of any exemption they are seeking to rely on. For example, an announcement of a placing of shares could be a financial promotion which is exempt under art.69 of the Financial Promotion Order but, if historic pricing information is included, the announcement must also include a warning that past performance cannot be relied on as a guide to future performance. Issuers should also be aware of potential problems caused by different media of communication. For example, whilst a circular posted to shareholders may fall within art.43 of the Financial Promotion Order, publication of the same circular on the company's website may not be within that exemption since the communication is no longer only made to shareholders, given the public nature of the internet.

A further analysis of the financial promotion regime is outside the scope of this chapter. Guidance on the regime is published by the FCA within Ch.8 of its *Perimeter Guidance Manual* (PERG) (the guidance is of general application and not only relevant to authorised persons).

2.7.2 *Advertisements and other communications under the Prospectus Rules*

The Prospectus Directive governs the content of ancillary marketing activities in the context of an offer to the public or admission of securities to trading on a regulated market as well as the prospectus itself. The rules set out in PR 3.3 derive from art.15 of the Prospectus Directive and relate to advertisements and other communications where a prospectus is required.

A wide range of "advertisements" is covered. The PD Regulation describes an advertisement as an announcement relating to a specific offer to the public or admission to trading that aims specifically to promote the potential subscription or acquisition of securities. The regime applies to any advertisement disseminated to the public:

(1) whether by the issuer, the offeror, financial intermediaries or underwriters; and
(2) by almost any media, including seminars and presentations, standard form letters, press advertising, telephone or text messages, fax, email, internet advertising, TV,

radio, videotext, brochures, posters and other printed materials (art.34 of the PD Regulation).

An advertisement must not be issued unless:

(1) it states that a prospectus has been or will be published and indicates where investors are, or will be, able to obtain it;

(2) it is clearly recognisable as an advertisement, containing a bold and prominent statement to the effect that it is not a prospectus but an advertisement and that investors should only subscribe or purchase on the basis of the prospectus;

(3) the information in the advertisement is not inaccurate or misleading; and

(4) information in the advertisement is consistent with the information in the prospectus (if it is already published) or required to be in the prospectus (if it is published afterwards) (PR 3.3.2R).

Where it appears that advertisements do not comply with these provisions, the FCA has the power to prevent or suspend their publication.

In addition to the specific requirements set out above for "advertisements", there is also a broader obligation in PR 3.3.4R to ensure that all information concerning an offer of securities to the public or admission of securities to trading on a regulated market, in respect of which a prospectus is required, is consistent with that contained in the prospectus. This applies to information communicated in oral or written form, even if not for advertising purposes.

Finally, even for offers of securities where no prospectus is required because relevant exemptions apply (e.g. an AIM offering or secondary block trade, in each case to qualified investors only), art.15 of the Prospectus Directive, implemented in PR 5.6.1R, lays down a requirement for equality of information to potential investors.

2.8   The FCA's enforcement powers

2.8.1   *General*

The FCA has a powerful enforcement armoury, including powers to investigate, to publish information, to censure, to suspend the marketing of securities and, above all, to impose unlimited fines on both companies and individuals. These powers, under s.91 of the FSMA, relate to actual or suspected breaches of provisions of Pt VI of the FSMA, of Pt 6 Rules or of a provision otherwise made in accordance with the Prospectus Directive (such as the PD Regulation) (Pt VI provisions). The FCA has a similar range of powers, of enforcement against sponsors, including power to suspend authorisation (see s.2.4.3 above) and PIPs. Section 123 of the FSMA gives the FCA power to impose unlimited fines and censure for breaches of the Market Abuse Regulation and the DEPP and the EG also give the FCA investigative and punitive powers to enforce the regulation. In addition, the FCA is the prosecuting authority (except in Scotland) for misleading statements or conduct under ss.89 and 90 of the Financial Services Act 2012 and insider dealing under the Criminal Justice Act 1993.

Under s.91 of the FSMA, the FCA may not bring an action for breach of rules made under Pt VI of the FSMA after the end of three years, beginning on the first day the FCA knows (or has information from which it can reasonably be inferred) that the entity has contravened the requirement or restriction.

The FCA's policy on enforcement is described in its EG. In general terms, it will seek to use its enforcement powers to pursue its statutory objectives and in such a way as both to change the behaviour of the person subject to the enforcement action and to deter future non-compliance by others—the policy known as "credible deterrence".

2.8.2 Gathering and publication of information

The FCA has information-gathering powers under LR 1.3 under which issuers must promptly provide to the FCA any information necessary to protect investors and ensure the smooth operation of the market, to verify compliance with the Listing Rules or to enable the FCA to decide upon an application for listing. There are similar powers to gather information under s.122A–C of the FSMA in relation to market abuse.

The Listing Rules allow the FCA to require an issuer to publish information in such form as the FCA considers appropriate to protect investors or to ensure the smooth operation of the market. If an issuer fails to comply with such a requirement, the FCA may publish the information itself. Similar powers exist under s.122G and H in the FSMA in relation to market abuse.

2.8.3 Investigations

Under s.97 of the FSMA, the FCA may appoint one or more persons, who will usually be members of the FCA staff, to question or demand information or documents where circumstances suggest that there may have been a breach of Pt VI provisions.

An investigator appointed under s.97 of the FSMA is treated as an investigator under s.167(1) of the FSMA, which sets out the FCA's general investigative powers, including powers to investigate market abuse under the Market Abuse Regulation. The FCA describes its policy with regard to such investigations in EG 3.

The FCA's investigative powers extend to any persons connected with the target of the investigation, including members of the same corporate group, any shareholders holding more than 10% of the company, or any partnership of which the company is a member, present or former brokers, auditors, lawyers, or employees of the company, or any member of its corporate group. The powers include the power to apply to a magistrate for a warrant to search or seize documents for information. Section 177 of the FSMA makes it a criminal offence to falsify, conceal or destroy documents relevant to an investigation, to provide false or misleading information or to intentionally obstruct rights conferred by a warrant.

In many cases, where the company or individuals concerned are willing and able to co-operate with an inquiry, the FCA will conduct investigations into breaches of Pt VI provisions without using its formal investigative powers. These powers may be used where, for example, obligations of confidentiality would otherwise inhibit individuals from providing information to the FCA.

2.8.4   Suspension and cancellation of offers, admission to trading or listing

2.8.4.1   Stopping offers and admissions to trading

Section 87K–L of the FSMA gives the FCA powers to suspend an offer to the public being made in the UK or a request for admission to trading for a period of up to 10 business days. This includes requiring a person to cease any advertising activity relating to the offer or request for a period of up to 10 business days.

These powers are exercisable if the FCA has reasonable grounds for suspecting that a relevant Pt VI provision has been infringed.

If the FCA has reasonable grounds for suspecting that a Pt VI provision will be infringed, or finds that such a provision has been infringed, it can require the offeror to withdraw a public offer.

2.8.4.2   Suspending and prohibiting trading

In the case of securities that have been admitted to trading, if the FCA suspects that a Pt VI provision has been infringed, it may require the market operator to suspend trading for up to 10 business days (s.87L of the FSMA). If the FCA finds that a relevant Pt VI provision has been infringed, it can also require the market operator to prohibit trading in the securities on the regulated market in question.

Section 122I of the FSMA allows the FCA to suspend trading in the UK in any financial instrument covered by the Market Abuse Regulation where it considers it necessary for the exercise of its functions under the regulation. Disclosure Guidance and Transparency Rule 1.4 sets out examples of where the FCA may require the suspension of a financial instrument. These include where an issuer fails to make an announcement required by the Market Abuse Regulation.

2.8.4.3 *Suspending and cancelling listing*

Sections 77 and 78 of the FSMA give the FCA powers to suspend or cancel the listing of securities in accordance with provisions set out in the Listing Rules. Listing Rule 5 sets out the FCA's requirements and procedures in relation to the suspension, cancellation and restoration of listing. In order to cancel the listing of securities, the FCA must be satisfied that there are special circumstances which preclude normal regular dealings in them.

In accordance with art.18(1) of the CARD, the FCA can suspend the listing of securities if the smooth operation of the market is, or may be, temporarily jeopardised, or if it is necessary to protect investors. The FCA may also suspend listing at the request of an issuer if it thinks that the circumstances justify suspension.

Examples of where the FCA may cancel listing include where the securities are no longer admitted to trading, where a suspension of listing of the security has lasted for more than six months or where the FCA believes that insufficient shares are held by the public (subject to a reasonable time being allowed to restore the percentage of shares in public hands).

2.8.5 Public censures and private warnings

Under s.87M of the FSMA, the FCA may publicly censure an issuer which it finds has failed to comply with its obligations under Pt VI provisions by publishing a statement to that effect. It may also publicly censure the issuer and any other person on whom it would be entitled to impose a financial penalty under s.91 of the FSMA (see s.2.8.6 below). Section 123 of the FSMA empowers the FCA to censure a person who has contravened any provision of the Market Abuse Regulation, any of ss.122A, B, C, G, H, I, 123A or B of the FSMA, or any requirement relating to the Market Abuse Regulation under Pt 11 of the FSMA.

As with financial penalties, the FCA will consider a range of factors before issuing a public censure, including:

(1)   whether there was systematic compliance failure;
(2)   the extent of co-operation with the FCA;
(3)   the extent to which FCA guidance was followed; and
(4)   the past record of the person to be disciplined.

Private warnings may be issued by the FCA in response to breaches that are minor in nature or degree or have been fully remedied. Such warnings are intended to serve as an indication by the FCA that it was close to imposing a formal disciplinary sanction. Private warnings will be kept on record by the FCA as part of the issuer's or director's compliance history.

2.8.6 Financial penalties

The FCA may impose unlimited financial penalties on:

(1)   issuers, offerors and applicants for admission to trading for breaches of Pt VI provisions;
(2)   directors or former directors of such persons who were knowingly involved in such a breach;
(3)   persons who have contravened any provision of the Market Abuse Regulation, any of ss.122A, B, C, G, H, I,

123A or B of the FSMA or any requirement relating to the Market Abuse Regulation under Pt 11 of the FSMA;

(4) persons holding shares or voting rights who infringe provisions of the Transparency Rules;

(5) sponsor firms for breaches of the Listing Rules relating to sponsors or for breaching the terms of their authorisation as sponsor; and

(6) PIPs, in respect of any breach of requirements or restrictions imposed on them by the rules in DTR 8.

The FCA is required under s.93 of the FSMA (and under ss.88C and 89S for sponsors and PIPs) to publish a statement of policy, listing the factors it may take into account when deciding the level of financial penalties for breaches of Pt VI provisions. This statement of policy is set out in the FCA's *Decision Procedure and Penalties Manual* at DEPP 6.

Factors prescribed under the FSMA that the FCA must have regard to under its penalties policy are the seriousness of the misconduct, the extent to which the breach was deliberate or reckless and whether the person upon whom the fine is to be imposed is an individual. As described in DEPP 6, the FCA has a five-step model for determining the level of penalties:

(1) Step 1: disgorgement—the FCA will seek to deprive a person of the financial benefit derived directly from the breach (which may include the profit made or loss avoided) where it is practicable to quantify this. The FCA will ordinarily also charge interest on the benefit;

(2) Step 2: seriousness of the breach—the FCA will determine a figure that reflects the seriousness of the breach;

(3) Step 3: mitigating and aggravating factors—the FCA may increase or decrease the amount of the financial penalty arrived at after Step 2 to take into account factors which aggravate or mitigate the breach. Mitigating factors include the degree of co-operation shown once the breach was discovered and remedial steps taken to ensure that breaches will not occur in the future;

(4) Step 4: adjustment for deterrence—if the FCA considers the figure arrived at after Step 3 is insufficient to deter the

person who committed the breach, or others, from committing further or similar breaches then the FCA may increase the penalty; and

(5) Step 5: settlement discount—the amount of the financial penalty which might otherwise have been payable may be reduced to reflect the stage at which the FCA and the person concerned reached a settlement agreement.

In a Final Notice published in March 2013 announcing the imposition of fines on Lamprell Plc for Listing Principle and Disclosure Rule breaches, the FCA set out in more detail how it will apply the five-step process, in particular Step 2, in cases involving listed issuers. This approach uses a formula based on the listed company's market capitalisation and is expected by the FCA "to lead to significantly higher penalties than in the past". The formula applies a percentage of up to 0.5% of the issuer's market capitalisation, depending on the seriousness of the breach.

2.8.7 *Procedure and appeals*

When exercising its decision-making powers in relation to the imposition of formal disciplinary measures—as well as applications for, or the cancellation or suspension of, listing, or the approval of a sponsor—the FCA must follow certain statutory notice procedures under ss.387–395 of the FSMA. Decisions on whether or not to issue a particular notice, or concerning the statutory notice once given, will be taken by either the Regulatory Decisions Committee or the FCA staff under executive procedures. The Regulatory Decisions Committee is a committee of the FCA board, which exercises regulatory powers on behalf of the FCA. Its members, apart from the chairman, are not FCA employees but are external members appointed for fixed periods.

Details of the individual procedures to be followed are published by the FCA in the *Decision Procedure and Penalties Manual*. In summary, in the case of disciplinary actions, the FCA must give a warning notice to the person to be sanctioned, setting out details of the enforcement action it proposes to take and of the person's right to make representations. Under new powers conferred in 2013, the FCA can make public the fact that it has issued a warning notice, together with a brief summary of the facts leading to the warning notice. Following representations, or if none are received, the next stage in the FCA's procedure is to publish a decision notice, setting out its decision on the matter, or a notice of discontinuance if proceedings are not being taken or are being discontinued. The recipient may appeal a decision by referring it to the Upper Tribunal, which is established under s.3 of the Tribunals, Courts and Enforcement Act 2007. If no reference to the Upper Tribunal is made, or following such a reference if the FCA's decision is confirmed, it will issue a Final Notice, setting out the reasoning behind its decision including summaries of any arguments against the decision made by the person sanctioned and a statement of the factors determining the nature and amount of any penalty imposed.

Supervisory notices are used by the FCA to give notice of decisions relating to suspension or discontinuation of listing.

2.8.8   Restitution orders

Where persons have suffered a loss as a result of a breach of the Market Abuse Regulation or the FCA's rules or profits have accrued to a person who has contravened such a provision or been knowingly involved in a contravention, the FCA may, under ss.382 and 384 of the FSMA, apply to the court for an order for payment of such amount as the court considers just. The FCA is obliged to distribute amounts paid to it under this provision to those who have been adversely affected by the breach.

In March 2017, the FCA required Tesco Stores Ltd and Tesco Plc (together, Tesco) to pay restitution to shareholders who suffered a loss as a result of a false market in certain Tesco securities, created by the publication of incorrect trading information. This was the first time the FCA had ordered the payment of restitution by a listed company in a market abuse case.

Chapter 3

Application Procedure and Publication of Prospectuses

Simon Thomas
Partner, Clifford Chance LLP

3.1 Introduction

3.1.1 Background

This chapter considers the regime governing sponsors, requirements for listing shares on the Official List of the Financial Conduct Authority (FCA), the types of transactions in which shares may be brought to listing, and the procedures for listing applications and publication of prospectuses. The treatment of debt and specialist securities or depositary receipts is not addressed in this chapter.

The regime is contained in the Prospectus Rules (PRs), the Listing Rules (LRs), and the Disclosure Guidance and Transparency Rules, each of which form part of the *FCA Handbook*. Formal guidance appears alongside the various rules in the *FCA Handbook*, whilst informal guidance (of a non-binding nature) is set out in technical and procedural notes arranged under key themes and topics (Technical Notes and Procedural Notes). These notes are available on the FCA's website. In addition, further informal guidance is published from time to time by the European Securities and Markets Authority (ESMA). The ESMA's guidance, which takes the form of recommendations and does not constitute EU legislation, is intended to facilitate the consistent implementation of the EU's

Financial Services Action Plan throughout the Member States of the EU. In practice, the ESMA's guidance is followed by the FCA.

3.1.2   *Structure of the UK's Listing Regime*

The Listing Rules are constantly evolving. Since April 2007, the Financial Services Authority (the FSA, the predecessor to the FCA) and the FCA have held numerous discussions with market participants to solicit their views as to the need to introduce further changes to the Listing Rules, primarily as part of an ongoing commitment to review the appropriateness of the regime.

The current structure of the Listing Regime has been in place since April 2010 and consists of two listing segments, "premium" and "standard". Both segments constitute a listing on the Official List.

A premium listing is the UK's "super-equivalent" Listing Regime, i.e. a company is subject to more stringent eligibility criteria (such as having to demonstrate a three-year revenue earning track record and appoint a sponsor) and continuing obligations (for example, requiring prior shareholder approval in the event of substantial or related party transactions) than those prescribed by the various EU directives. Prior to 1 July 2018, only voting equity shares in a commercial company, a closed-ended investment company or an open-ended investment company were eligible for a premium listing.

On 1 July 2018, changes to the Listing Rules took effect creating a new premium listing category for commercial companies controlled by a shareholder that is a sovereign country. When assessing eligibility for this category, a company must demonstrate that substantive control (that is, 30% or more of the voting rights of the company) is being exercised by the state in question. The new category also extends to companies listing interests in their equity in the form of global depositary receipts (GDRs), facilitating state-controlled GDRs issuers to step up to a premium listing and access a broader range of investors.

A standard listing is the UK's "directive minimum" listing regime. In other words, in general terms, a company need only comply with the minimum eligibility requirements and continuing obligations of the various EU directives. Voting equity shares in a commercial company are eligible for either a standard listing or a premium listing. Further classes of voting equity shares in an investment company may only be admitted with a standard listing if the investment company already has (and only for so long as it maintains) a premium listing of another class of voting equity shares. Other types of securities, such as depositary receipts (although note the comments above about rule changes that enable state-controlled GDR issuers to be eligible for a premium listing), debt and specialist securities and securitised derivatives, are only eligible for a standard listing.

Both UK incorporated companies and overseas incorporated companies are eligible for a premium listing. Overseas companies with a premium listing are required to offer their shareholders pre-emption rights on secondary issues to provide uniformity with the regime for UK companies. Overseas companies are also required to "comply or explain" against the corporate governance recommendations set out in the UK Corporate Governance Code.

Similarly, both UK incorporated companies and overseas incorporated companies are eligible for a standard listing.

A company that wishes to move from a premium listing to a standard listing must obtain the prior approval of 75% of shareholders at a general meeting. If a company wishes to move from a standard listing to a premium listing, it must demonstrate to the FCA that it has satisfied all of the eligibility requirements which apply for a premium listing (including appointing a sponsor). A company is not required, however, to publish a prospectus at the time of moving from a standard listing to a premium listing (assuming that no further shares are offered to the public and no application is made to admit further shares to trading on a regulated market at the time of migration).

In February 2017, the FCA published discussion paper DP17/2, intending to prompt a broad discussion about the effectiveness of the UK primary markets in providing access to capital for issuers and investment opportunities for investors. Key areas of focus include: (1) whether the standard listing regime is fit for purpose; (2) whether a new listing category should be introduced to facilitate dual-listings for international companies with an existing listing; (3) whether exchange-traded funds should be required to list on the premium segment; and (4) what structural changes could be made to better support the growth of science and technology companies in their "step-up" and pre-revenue phases. Feedback on DP17/2 was mixed. There was broad support for the premium listed segment, whilst feedback on standard listings was more varied, with some respondents highlighting the flexibility it offers, whilst others noted concerns that the "standard" label can be seen as unhelpful. The majority of respondents did not favour the introduction of different requirements for international and UK companies. In its "Feedback Statement", FS17/3, published in October 2017, the FCA identified three areas that it believes merit further consideration: (1) the positioning of the standard v premium listing; (2) the provision of patient capital to companies requiring long-term investment (particularly in the context of supporting the growth of science and technology companies); and (3) retail access to debt markets. The FCA intends to engage further with stakeholders on these issues.

3.1.3 Scope of this chapter

For the purposes of this chapter (so as to describe the most demanding standard), we describe the regime as it would apply to a premium listing of a commercial company (as opposed to a sovereign-controlled company or an investment entity).

The Prospectus Rules and Listing Rules cover not only applications for listing but also the making of offers to the public. They also contemplate that an applicant for listing may be a person other than a company issuing new securities. In this chapter, however, we seek to answer the following questions in relation to a company proposing to seek an initial listing of its shares on the Official List of the FCA:

(1) is the company required to appoint a sponsor in connection with its application for admission to listing? If it does require a sponsor, what responsibilities will the sponsor have?
(2) what requirements will the company have to fulfil in order to obtain a listing?
(3) in what ways may the company bring its shares to listing?
(4) what application procedures will the company need to follow in order to obtain a listing? and
(5) what does the company need to do to publicise its application for listing?

Each of these questions is considered in turn in ss.3.2–3.6 below.

3.1.4   Current legislative framework

Before dealing with the detailed content of this chapter, it is worth recalling that the listing of securities within the EU is governed by a framework of European directives. Part VI of the Financial Services and Markets Act 2000 (FSMA) deals with listing and delegates decisions on the admission of securities to official listing to the "competent authority". The FCA is the "competent authority" in the UK.

Securities are "admitted to listing" by the FCA (in its capacity as the competent authority in the UK). In addition, securities must also be "admitted to trading" by the London Stock Exchange (the Exchange) (or any other recognised investment exchange—RIE). In the usual case where securities are to be listed, there will therefore be a two-stage process of applying to the FCA for the securities to be admitted to listing and applying to the Exchange (or other RIE) for the securities to be admitted to trading. In practice, these processes run in parallel and the two events are announced and occur simultaneously. Continuing obligations under the Listing Rules, the disclosure requirements set out in arts 17, 18 and 19 of the EU Market Abuse Regulation (MAR disclosure requirements)[1] and the requirements of the Transparency Rules are policed by the FCA, whilst compliance is also required by the Exchange with its Admission and Disclosure Standards.

3.1.5 *Terminology*

References in this chapter to "chapters" or "appendices" are to chapters or appendices of the Prospectus Rules or Listing Rules published by the FCA. References to relevant paragraphs of the Prospectus Rules or Listing Rules setting out the detailed rules are, for example, described in the format "PR 1.2.3R" (the "R" signifying that the particular paragraph is a formal rule) or "LR 2.2.12G" (the "G" signifying that the particular paragraph is formal FCA guidance). This is the format used in the relevant rulebooks themselves.

3.2 Sponsors

Starting with the first question; a company wants to obtain the benefits of having its shares publicly traded. It is a condition of an application for admission to trading on the Exchange that the shares are listed or proposed to be listed by the FCA.

Is the company required to appoint a sponsor in connection with its application for admission to listing? If it does require a sponsor, what responsibilities will the sponsor have?

Chapter 8 of the Listing Rules sets out the requirements relating to sponsors, who will normally be corporate brokers or investment banks but may also be other professional advisers,

---

[1] Regulation 596/2014 on market abuse (market abuse regulation) and repealing Directive 2003/6 and Directives 2003/124, 2003/125 and 2004/72 [2014] OJ L173/1.

such as lawyers and accountants in appropriate circumstances (although this is rarely the case).

It is worth noting that the sponsor regime is a UK specific concept and the contents of Ch.8 of the Listing Rules are not prescribed by EU legislation. The impact of the UK's exit from the EU in 2019 should not mean that significant changes are required to the sponsor regime itself.

3.2.1 *When must the company appoint a sponsor?*

The Listing Rules (LR 8.2.1R) set out the circumstances in which a company must appoint, or have in place, a sponsor. Every new applicant for listing of shares must appoint a sponsor. Applications for listing by existing listed companies which do not require a prospectus may be made by the listed company without appointing a sponsor, for example, where the capital of the listed company is being increased by less than 20% over a 12-month period (exemptions from the requirement to produce a prospectus are set out in PRs 1.2.2.R and 1.2.3R).

A company with or seeking a premium listing of its shares must appoint a sponsor when it:

(1) makes an application for listing which requires it to submit a prospectus, a supplementary prospectus or an equivalent document (LR 8.2.1R(1)) to the FCA for approval. An "equivalent document" refers to those documents that are equivalent to a prospectus and are prepared in the context of a takeover or a merger. Listing Rule 8.2.1R(1) also requires a sponsor to be appointed when a company with a premium listing submits a supplementary prospectus to the FCA for approval;

(2) is required to submit to the FCA a Class 1 circular (LR 8.2.1R(2)) or other circular in connection with a major reconstruction or refinancing which is required by LR 9.5.12R to include a working capital statement (LR 8.2.1R(3));

(3) is required to submit to the FCA a circular for the proposed purchase of its own shares which is required by

LR 13.7.1R(2) to include a working capital statement as exercise in full of the authority sought would result in the purchase of 25% or more of the company's issued share capital (LR 8.2.1R(4));

(4) is required to obtain confirmation from a sponsor that the terms of a proposed smaller related party transaction are fair and reasonable (LR 8.2.1R(6));

(5) is required to submit to the FCA a related party circular which includes a statement by the board of the company that the transaction or arrangement is fair and reasonable (LR 8.2.1R(7));

(6) is required to submit to the FCA an eligibility letter from a sponsor in connection with a new applicant's application for admission to listing (LR 8.2.1R(8));

(7) is required to make an announcement or request a suspension in connection with a reverse takeover (LR 8.2.1R(9)); confirms to the FCA in connection with a reverse takeover that the disclosure requirements in relation to financial information and inside information to which the target is subject by virtue of having its securities admitted to an investment exchange or trading platform are not materially different from the MAR disclosure requirements (LR 8.2.1R(10)); makes a disclosure announcement in connection with a reverse takeover where the target is not subject to a public disclosure regime confirming that the announcement contains sufficient information about the target to provide a properly informed basis for assessing its financial position and that it has made the necessary arrangements to enable it to keep the market informed without delay of any developments concerning the target which would be required to be released if the target were part of the company (LR 8.2.1R(11)); or submits to the FCA a letter in relation to its eligibility as enlarged following completion of a reverse takeover (LR 8.2.1R(12));

(8) provides confirmation to the FCA of its severe financial difficulty, leaving it with no alternative but to dispose of a substantial part of its business within a short time frame to meet its ongoing working capital requirements or reduce

its liabilities, meaning that it is not able to prepare a circular to obtain prior shareholder approval (LR 8.2.1R(13));

(9) is required to assess the appropriateness of an investment exchange or multilateral trading facility on which a publicly traded target is admitted pursuant to LR 13.5.27BR (LR 8.2.1R (14));

(10) is required to provide a written opinion to the FCA in respect of the terms of any joint venture arrangements with a related party (LR 8.2.15); and

(11) makes an application to transfer its listing from a standard listing to a premium listing or from one category of premium listing to another (LR 8.2.1AR).

In addition, where it appears to the FCA that a listed company with a premium listing has, or may have, breached the Listing Rules, the MAR disclosure requirements or the Transparency Rules, the FCA may notify the company that the appointment of a sponsor is required (LR 8.2.1R(5)). Broadly, this is to ensure that proper advice is given on the application of the Listing Rules.

Companies with a premium listing must also seek the guidance of a sponsor where they are proposing to enter into a transaction which could be a Class 1 transaction or reverse takeover, or which could be a transaction with a related party (LRs 8.2.2R and 8.2.3R).

In addition to the specific situations listed above, the FCA encourages the appointment of a sponsor on an ongoing basis to advise on the application and continuing requirements of the Listing Rules and the MAR disclosure requirements. There is, however, no formal requirement to appoint a sponsor on an ongoing basis.

A company must notify the FCA in writing (copied to the sponsor) of the resignation or dismissal of any sponsor appointed by it and include in such notification, if a sponsor is dismissed, the reasons for the dismissal (LR 8.5.2R).

The Listing Rules place companies seeking a, or with an existing, premium listing under a positive obligation to co-operate with its sponsor by providing the sponsor with all information reasonably requested by the sponsor for the purpose of carrying out its sponsor services (LR 8.5.6R).

3.2.2 Can a company have more than one sponsor?

The Listing Rules recognise that a company may appoint more than one sponsor (LR 8.5.3R).

In January 2014, the FCA published Consultation Paper (CP) 14/2, in which it sought market participants' views on the merits and disadvantages of the joint sponsor regime. Whilst recognising the benefits that the appointment of joint sponsors can bring to a deal, the FCA identified a number of potential concerns about the practice, including: (1) a reluctance of the part of the largest, most active sponsors to act as joint sponsor other than in the primary contact role, creating a perception of a two-tier system, whereby one sponsor is the "lead" and the other the "junior"; (2) the apparent lack of arrangements or understanding between sponsors as to how the joint role will work leading to the potential that one sponsor may rely on the work of the other while retaining full responsibility for it under Ch.8 of the Listing Rules; and (3) a failure of communication between the joint sponsors leading to a disparity of information between them. The consultation responses received by the FCA were overwhelmingly in favour of retaining the joint sponsor regime. Following this, in September 2014, the FCA published a formal consultation on joint sponsors in which it proposed amending LR 8.5.3R so that the requirement for a listed company to advise the FCA of the sponsor that will take responsibility for contact with the FCA in connection with the sponsor service applies in respect of administrative matters only, thereby removing the perception of there being a "lead" sponsor. The FCA also sought to clarify that, in respect of non-administrative matters, all sponsors should be equally involved. In addition, the FCA proposed the introduction of new guidance setting out its expectation that, where joint sponsors are appointed, they should co-operate with each other, including establishing arrangements for the sharing of information as appropriate to the service being carried out. These rule changes took effect on 1 February 2015.

Accordingly, the company must ensure that one sponsor takes primary responsibility for contact with the FCA in respect of administrative matters and must inform the FCA in writing of the relevant sponsor's contact details. In respect of each transaction, the sponsor must appoint a key contact who has sufficient knowledge about the company and the proposed transaction to be able to answer queries from the FCA about it (LR 8.6.19R). Key contacts must possess technical knowledge of the rules, guidance and the ESMA publications relevant to sponsor services and understand the responsibilities and obligations of a sponsor under Ch.8 of the Listing Rules and must also be authorised to make representations to the FCA for, and on behalf of, the sponsor. Sponsors are required to have a minimum of at least two key contacts (LR 8.6.7D(G)) and, for the most active sponsors, they are likely to have considerably more.

The FCA considers all sponsors to be jointly responsible for compliance with responsibilities set out in the Listing Rules and the sponsor declarations given pursuant thereto (LR 8.3.14). As a result, multiple sponsors are responsible for ensuring that nothing falls between them and that they do not fail to deal with any relevant issues.

3.2.3 *Qualifications of a sponsor*

The sponsor's relationship with the FCA is governed by the FSMA. Section 88 of the FSMA designates the FCA as the competent authority with statutory responsibility for the approval and regulation of sponsors. Pursuant to s.88(3) of the FSMA, the FCA has the power to specify in listing rules the circumstances in which a person is qualified for being approved as a sponsor. These circumstances are set out in LR 8.6.

Under LR 8.6.5R, a sponsor must satisfy the following conditions in order to be approved and placed on the list of sponsors maintained by the FCA. It must satisfy the FCA that it:

(1) is an authorised person under the FSMA (usually corporate brokers or investment banks) or a member of a designated professional body under the FSMA (presently lawyers, accountants and actuaries);

(2) is competent to perform sponsor services (defined as a service relating to a matter referred to in LR 8.2 that a sponsor provides or is requested or appointed to provide and that is for the purpose of the sponsor complying with the responsibilities of a sponsor (as set out in LR 8.3 or LR 8.4)); and

(3) has appropriate systems and controls in place to ensure that it can carry out its role as sponsor in accordance with Ch.8 of the Listing Rules.

Guidance in relation to the requirement described in (2) above (LR 8.6.5R(2)) enables the FCA to take into account the quality of the advice or guidance given by sponsors, outside of situations in LR 8.2, where such advice is relevant to a sponsor's competence. With regard to the requirement described in (3) above (LR 8.6.5R(3)), the guidance on what constitutes appropriate systems and controls focuses on sponsors having, among other things, clear and appropriate reporting lines, together with effective systems and controls for the supervision of employees engaged in providing sponsor services that ensure the performance of sponsor services with due care and skill and compliance with the Listing Rules, as well as effective systems and controls to identify and manage conflicts (LR 8.6.12G).

A sponsor is not required to carry out a regular review to ensure that it meets the approval criteria set out in LR 8.6.5R on the basis that any such requirement duplicates the need for a sponsor to meet the approval criteria at all times (as required by LR 8.6.6R). It is implicit that sponsors are unable to comply with LR 8.6.6R unless they monitor their eligibility appropriately and on an ongoing basis. The obligations of sponsors relating to record management also make clear that sponsors must ensure they keep records sufficient to demonstrate the basis upon which they comply with their ongoing eligibility obligations under LR 8.6.6R. In addition, a sponsor must notify the FCA should it become aware of any matter which, in its reasonable opinion, would be relevant to the FCA in considering whether the sponsor continues to comply with LR 8.6.6R (LR 8.7.8R(1)). A sponsor must also notify the FCA where it identifies or otherwise becomes aware of material deficiencies in its sponsor systems and controls (LR 8.7.8R(9)).

Listing Rule 8.7.7R requires a sponsor firm to submit an annual confirmation to the FCA stating that it continues to meet the approval criteria (LR 8.6.5R) and the annual confirmation must detail the basis upon which the sponsor firm considers itself to meet the approval criteria (LR 8.7.7(1A)R). Sponsors should complete an annual notification form (available on the FCA's website) which should be submitted in January of every year.

Sponsors must also pay an annual fee in order to remain on the FCA's list of sponsors.

The FCA's rules on sponsor competence requirements are set out in LR 8.6.7R and are supplemented with more detailed guidance. The rules include a requirement that a sponsor must have recent "on-the-job" experience of providing sponsor services; and, in particular, that it would need to demonstrate that it has been providing sponsor services during the preceding three-year period. In addition, LR 8.6.7R(2) requires a sponsor to ensure that it has a sufficient number of employees with the skills, knowledge and expertise necessary in order for it to provide sponsor services. The FCA has published two Technical Notes (UKLA/TN/714.2, last updated March 2017 and UKLA/TN/715.1, last updated February 2015) which set out, respectively, guidance on the competence requirements set out in LR 8.6.7R(2)(b) and guidance on the practical implications of the competence requirements for sponsors and applicants. In particular, a sponsor must assess the skills of its employees to ensure that they meet the prescribed competency requirements, which include knowledge of: (1) the rules, guidance and the ESMA publications directly relevant to the provision of sponsor services; (2) the procedural requirements and processes of the FCA; (3) the due diligence processes required in order to provide sponsor services; (4) the responsibilities and obligations of a sponsor as set out in Ch.8 of the Listing Rules; and (5) if relevant, specialist industry sectors.

Acknowledging that sponsors usually have more than one interest in a transaction, the independence criteria contained in the Listing Rules allow sponsors to identify and manage potential conflicts of interests, not by a list of prescriptive factors which are determinative of independence but by reference to high-level guidance on identifying and managing conflicts so as to ensure that conflicts of interest do not adversely affect the ability of a sponsor to perform its functions properly or affect the market's confidence in sponsors (LR 8.3.7AG). In identifying conflicts of interests, a sponsor is required to take into account circumstances that could compromise its ability to fulfil its obligations to the FCA in relation to the provision of a sponsor service (LR 8.3.8G(2)) in addition to those that could create a perception in the market that a sponsor may not be able to perform its functions properly (LR 8.3.8G(1)).

Under LR 8.3.9R, a sponsor must take all reasonable steps to put in place and maintain effective organisational and administrative arrangements to ensure that conflicts do not adversely affect its ability to perform its functions, whilst LR 8.3.10G provides that disclosure alone of a conflict of interest will not usually be considered to be an effective organisational or administrative arrangement.

Listing Rule 8.3.11R acknowledges that, notwithstanding any conflict management arrangements that a sponsor may implement, there may be circumstances where a sponsor should decline to act.

The FCA published a Technical Note on Sponsors: Conflicts of interest (UKLA/TN/701) which sets out examples of transactions that may affect market confidence in sponsors and advises that firms contact the Sponsor Supervision Team at an early stage of a transaction if they have concerns about their ability to act.

In March 2017, the FCA published a Consultation Paper, CP 17/5, in which it sought views on an updated version of this Technical Note (UKLA/TN/701.3) as a result of a call for views (CFV) on sponsor conflicts that it undertook in September 2014 (the outcome of the CFV was delayed due to a market study that the FCA undertook in relation to investment and corporate banking in 2015, the outcome of which was published in October 2016).[2] Feedback on the FCA's CFV on sponsor conflicts was mixed,[3] with the sponsor community of the view that the current rules and guidance on sponsor management of conflicts of interest were operating well, whilst some members of the investor stakeholder community supported greater disclosure of the relationships between advisers and issuers, as well as disclosure of fees for sponsor and non-sponsor services. As a result, the FCA concluded that the current rules around sponsor conflicts were, broadly speaking, operating effectively and remain fit for purpose and so it did not propose to take forward plans for greater fee or relationship disclosure in the context of sponsor conflicts.

However, the FCA decided to consult on an updated draft of Technical Note UKLA/TN/701 in order to provide greater clarity and guidance on specific aspects of the existing rules, including the operation of the "perception" test in LR 8.3.8G.[4] The Technical Note, which, following consultation, was published in final form in August 2017, encourages sponsors to assess a perceived conflict from the point of view of a

---

[2] FCA, "Investment and corporate banking market study", MS 15/1 (2015); FCA, *Investment and corporate banking market study: Final report*, MS 15/1.3 (October 2016).

[3] Consultation Paper on "Feedback and Policy Statement on CP 14/02, consultation on joint sponsors and call for views on sponsor conflicts", CP 14/21 (September 2014).

[4] FCA, *Primary Market Bulletin* No.17 (March 2017).

theoretical "reasonable market user", a person likely to have general knowledge of the type of transaction in question, the primary markets and the operation of integrated investment banks. They would be aware that banks have in place systems and procedures to manage conflicts but would not necessarily conclude that conflicts can be managed in all circumstances. The assessment would inevitably have to flex, depending on the circumstances of the transaction. Having carried out such an assessment, the sponsor may decide not to act or to seek guidance from the Sponsor Supervision Team.

The updated Technical Note also offers greater guidance to sponsors on the factors to take into account when a sponsor is acting as a lender in connection with a transaction, including indicating a threshold exposure which, if exceeded, should require the sponsor to contact the FCA to discuss the potential conflict before it can accept the mandate.

3.2.4 Services to be provided by a sponsor

The services to be provided by a sponsor are set out in LRs 8.3 and 8.4. A key requirement is that a sponsor must guide the company in understanding and meeting its responsibilities under the Listing Rules, the MAR disclosure requirements and the Transparency Rules and, when required, provide assurance to the FCA that those responsibilities have been met. Any service, assurance, guidance or advice that is provided in relation to the application or interpretation of the Listing Rules, the MAR disclosure requirements and the Transparency Rules must be provided with due care and skill (LR 8.3.3R). The standard of care and skill set out in LR 8.3.3R only applies when a sponsor is required by LR 8.2R. Sponsors must, however, deal with the FCA in an open, co-operative and prompt manner at all times.

With regard to the standard of care which the FCA expects of a sponsor in relation to communications with the regulator and information provided by third parties, a sponsor must take such reasonable steps as are sufficient to ensure that any communication or information which it provides to the FCA in carrying out a sponsor service is, to the best of its knowledge and belief, accurate and complete in all material respects. In addition, as soon as is possible, a sponsor must provide to the FCA any information of which it becomes aware that materially affects the accuracy or completeness of information it has previously provided (LR 8.3.1AR). The FCA has also sought to reinforce the responsibility for communication with the FCA which is based on information received from a third party, such as the company or another adviser. In assessing whether the sponsor has discharged its obligations, the FCA will take into account, amongst other things, whether the sponsor has appropriately used its own knowledge, judgement and expertise to review and challenge information provided by third parties (LR 8.3.1BG). In its 2012 consultation,[5] the FSA elaborated further, indicating that it would be reasonable for the sponsor to discuss with the third party and, at the very least, have knowledge of and understand the basis of any opinion or advice provided by the third party. These obligations extend to any written or oral communication between the sponsor and the FCA. In addition, sponsors are required to provide the FCA with any explanation or confirmation as the FCA reasonably requires for the purposes of ensuring that the Listing Rules are being complied with by a company with, or applying for, a premium listing (LR 8.3.1R(1A)).

Listing Rule 8.7.8R states that a sponsor is obliged to notify the FCA in writing as soon as possible on the occurrence of a range of specified events, including where the sponsor ceases to satisfy the criteria to act as a sponsor (e.g. due to deficiencies highlighted as a result of the annual review referred to in s.3.2.3 above, it is no longer an authorised person or it no longer has appropriate systems and controls to perform its role as sponsor in accordance with its obligations) where the sponsor, or any employee who provides sponsor services, is convicted of any offence of fraud, theft or dishonesty or is subject to any bankruptcy or similar proceedings or is disqualified by a court from acting as a director of, or in a management capacity in, or conducting the affairs of, any

---

[5] FSA, Consultation Paper on "Enhancing the effectiveness of the Listing Regime and feedback on CP 12/2", CP 12/25 (October 2012).

company. Notification must also be made if the sponsor, or an employee who provides sponsor services, is subject to public criticism, regulatory intervention or disciplinary action, or on a change of the sponsor's name. Notifications may be made initially by telephone and followed up in writing to the Sponsor Supervision Team at the FCA (rather than through any other FCA personnel).

Sponsors are also required to notify the FCA (LR 8.7.8(10)R) in the event of a change of control of the sponsor or if the sponsor's group carries out any restructuring which results in a reorganisation of those involved in providing sponsor services.

The FCA has noted in its Technical Note on Sponsor notifications (UKLA/TN/711.1, last updated July 2013) that there needs to be a high degree of self-monitoring by a sponsor. As sponsors are only required to confirm compliance with the approval criteria to be a sponsor on an annual basis, sponsors need to be mindful that events, such as personnel changes or ad hoc changes to departmental procedures, may trigger a notification requirement under LR 8.7.8R.

Specific services to be provided by sponsors are considered in the following paragraphs.

3.2.4.1 Application for admission to listing

Where an applicant is applying to have its shares admitted to a premium listing on the Official List of the FCA for the first time, under LR 8.4.2R, the sponsor must only submit the application if it has come to a reasonable opinion, after having made due and careful enquiry, that:

(1) the company has satisfied all requirements of the Listing Rules relevant to an application for listing;
(2) the company has satisfied all applicable requirements of the Prospectus Rules (unless the prospectus is being passported from another Member State);

(3) the directors of the company have established procedures for ongoing compliance with the Listing Rules, the MAR disclosure requirements and the Transparency Rules;

(4) the directors of the company have established procedures which provide a reasonable basis for them to make proper judgements on an ongoing basis as to the financial position and prospectus of the company and its group; and

(5) the directors of the company have a reasonable basis to conclude that the company and its group have sufficient working capital for at least the next 12 months.

The Listing Rules contain no guidance as to the steps a sponsor would normally be expected to take in coming to its opinion, even though the requirements place greater demands on sponsors than existed previously. However, the FCA has provided commentary on both technical and non-technical matters on a variety of issues, including on the role and responsibility of sponsors, through the UK Listing Authority (UKLA) Technical Notes. For example, the UKLA's Technical Note on The sponsor's role on working capital confirmations (UKLA/TN/704.3, last updated March 2017) makes it clear that a sponsor is expected to apply its judgement, experience, knowledge and expertise on the Listing Rules, the MAR disclosure requirements and the Transparency Rules when deciding whether a company has a reasonable basis on which to make the working capital statement. To do this, the sponsor must have regard to the company's circumstances and the context of the transaction. The Technical Note also makes it clear that a sponsor cannot rely solely on the part played by the directors of the company or by the reporting accountants appointed by the company in the working capital exercise, meaning that the work of these third parties would, on its own, not be sufficient evidence that a sponsor had discharged its obligations to make due and careful enquiry.

In the absence of formal guidance, sponsors have tended to follow established market practices to discharge their obligations. In particular, in relation to the confirmation required to be given in LR 8.4.2R(3) (described in (3) above), sponsors generally require companies coming to the market for the first time to adopt a specifically developed compliance manual to act as a guide to ongoing compliance with the Listing Rules, the MAR disclosure requirements and the Transparency Rules.

In practice, companies can assume that sponsors will require appropriate "comfort letters" from companies and their other advisers as part of sponsors' diligence in connection with their confirmations.

In addition, where an applicant is applying to have its shares admitted to premium listing for the first time, the sponsor is required to:

(1) complete a Declaration on an Application for Listing, the form of which can be found on the FCA's website. This is a confirmation given by the sponsor that, among other things, it has acted with due care and skill in relation to the provision of sponsor services; it has taken reasonable steps to satisfy itself that the directors of the company understand their responsibilities and obligations under the Listing Rules, the MAR disclosure requirements and the Transparency Rules; and it has come to a reasonable opinion, after having made due and careful enquiry, as to the matters addressed in LR 8.4.2R (described above). It also includes a confirmation that the sponsor has maintained accessible records which are sufficiently capable of demonstrating that the sponsor has provided sponsor services and otherwise complied with its obligations under the Listing Rules, including the basis for each confirmation set out above;

(2) complete a Shareholder Statement, the form of which is available on the FCA's website (listed companies complete a Pricing Statement);

(3) ensure that all matters known to it which, in its reasonable opinion, should be taken into account by the FCA in considering the application for admission to listing and whether the admission of the shares would be detrimental to investors' interests, have been disclosed with sufficient prominence in the prospectus or otherwise in writing to

the FCA (this is also required to be confirmed in the Declaration on Application for Listing). The FCA's Technical Note on Sponsor Services: Principles for Sponsors (UKLA/TN/710.1), published in July 2013, makes clear that sponsors need to ensure that companies and their advisers are under an obligation to inform the sponsor immediately of any such information up to the date of admission to listing; and

(4) submit a letter stating how the company satisfies the requirements for listing set out in LRs 2 and 6 (see s.3.3 above). Historically, the FCA has reviewed a company's eligibility first before reviewing drafts of the prospectus, requiring that the eligibility letter be submitted and all substantive eligibility issues be resolved before the first submission of the draft prospectus could be made. In July 2013, the FCA changed its practice such that the eligibility review process now happens at the same time as the review of the prospectus (see UKLA/PN/901.3, last updated March 2017). As a result, the eligibility letter is now submitted by the sponsor at the same time as the draft prospectus is submitted for review rather than in advance of the first submission of the prospectus.

3.2.4.2   *Directors*

When providing sponsor services, any guidance or advice given by the sponsor on the application or interpretation of the Listing Rules, the MAR disclosure requirements and the Transparency Rules, a sponsor must take reasonable steps to satisfy itself that the directors of the company understand their responsibilities and obligations under the Listing Rules, the MAR disclosure requirements and the Transparency Rules (LR 8.3.4R). Depending on the circumstances, sponsors often provide the company's management team with a presentation explaining the company's key continuing obligations and require that the company's own legal advisers provide the directors with a memorandum setting out such responsibilities and obligations and deliver a "teach-in" session at a meeting of the board of directors. This forum is used to explain these responsibilities and obligations and the directors are given an opportunity to clarify any uncertainty they may have.

3.2.5 What disciplinary action can the FCA take against a sponsor?

The FCA has broad powers to sanction sponsors. In particular, in the event of a breach of the Listing Rules by a sponsor, the FCA has the ability to impose a financial penalty and suspend the approval of a sponsor for a period not exceeding 12 months. The FCA may also suspend the approval of a sponsor to advance its operational objectives and, in these circumstances, there is no time limit on the length of suspension. In a Consultation Paper, CP 12/37, the FSA indicated that it envisaged this power would be used when it had already made its concerns clear to the sponsor and needed to act urgently to prevent a sponsor acting, in order to protect consumers or the integrity of the UK financial system.

The FCA also has the power to impose restrictions or limitations on the sponsor work that may be carried out by existing sponsors or an entity seeking approval to become a sponsor. The FCA may do this where it concludes that an existing sponsor's, or an entity seeking to become a sponsor's, experience and expertise or systems and controls are appropriate for only certain types of sponsor services (rather than the full range of sponsor services).

This power may be invoked in relation to an existing sponsor to advance the FCA's operational objectives. As with the FCA's power to suspend a sponsor further to its operational objectives, it is envisaged that restrictions or limitation would only be imposed on sponsors where urgent action is required.

3.2.6 Appointment of an agent by a sponsor

Listing Rule 8.7.16 provides that a sponsor may not delegate any of its functions or permit another person to perform those functions.

3.2.7   *Direct access*

Although the FCA expects to discuss all issues relating to a transaction or any draft or final document with the company's sponsor, the FCA will, in appropriate circumstances, communicate directly with the company (LR 8.3.2G). The Listing Rules provide guidance reinforcing that a sponsor remains responsible for communications with the regulator even in circumstances where it is relying on representations made by a listed company or an applicant for listing or a third party, such as an adviser (LR 8.3.2AG). If a sponsor does provide information to the FCA which is based on information it has received from a third party, in assessing whether the sponsor has discharged its duty to take such reasonable steps as are necessary to ensure that the information is, to the best of the sponsor's knowledge and belief, accurate and complete in all material respects, the FCA has indicated that the sponsor would be required to ensure that the relevant third party had been provided with information that was, to the best of its knowledge and belief, accurate and complete in all material respects and for the sponsor to discuss with the third party and, at the very least, to have knowledge of and understand the basis of any opinion or advice provided by the third party. The FCA will have regard, amongst other things, to whether the sponsor has appropriately used its own knowledge, judgement and expertise to review and challenge information provided by a third party (LR 8.3.1BG).

3.3   Requirements for listing

Having decided that companies seeking a premium listing need a sponsor and examined what the responsibilities of the sponsor are, the second question to answer is: what conditions will such companies have to satisfy in order to obtain a premium listing?

The eligibility requirements for a premium listing are set out primarily in Chs 2 and 6 of the Listing Rules, dealing with, respectively, the requirements for all securities and those specifically for equity securities. These are dealt with in ss.3.3.1 and 3.3.2 below. The FCA has clarified that, in circumstances where a company with an existing premium listing introduces a new holding company, the eligibility requirements in Ch.6 will not be applied provided that the existing company is not entering into a transaction that would be classified as a reverse takeover (LR 6.1.1(2)R).

The FCA may make the admission of securities to listing subject to any special conditions which it considers appropriate to ensure investor protection and of which it has explicitly informed the applicant (LR 2.1.4R). These could include, for example, undertakings from the principal shareholders not to dispose of their shareholding for a specified period following admission.

The requirements for listing of closed-ended investment funds, open-ended investment companies, debt/specialist securities, GDRs, securitised derivatives and sovereign-controlled commercial companies are dealt with in Chs 15, 16, 17, 18, 19 and 21 of the Listing Rules, respectively, and are outside the scope of this chapter.

3.3.1   Listing requirements: All securities

3.3.1.1   Incorporation

An applicant must be duly incorporated or otherwise validly established according to the relevant laws of its place of incorporation or establishment, and must be operating in conformity with its memorandum and articles of association or equivalent constitutional documents (LR 2.2.1R). Although no longer explicit in the Listing Rules, a company incorporated in the UK must be registered or re-registered as a public limited company before its shares can be listed.

3.3.1.2   Validity

To be listed, the shares must be in conformity with the laws of the applicant's place of incorporation, be duly authorised according to the requirements of the applicant's constitution and have any necessary statutory or other consents (LR 2.2.2R).

3.3.1.3 Admission to trading

The shares must be admitted to trading on a regulated market for listed securities operated by a RIE (shares admitted to trading on the Exchange meet this requirement) (LR 2.2.3R). In practice, the sponsor will apply to the Exchange (or another RIE) for admission of the company's shares to trading at the same time as it applies to the FCA for admission of the shares to listing. The FCA may suspend or cancel the listing of the shares if they cease to be admitted to trading (LRs 5.1 and 5.2).

3.3.1.4 Transferability

Under LR 2.2.4R, the shares must be freely transferable, fully paid and free from all liens and from any restriction on the right of transfer (except any restriction imposed for failure to comply with a notice under s.793 of the Companies Act 2006).

The FCA may allow partly paid shares to be listed if it is satisfied that their transferability is not restricted and that investors have been provided with all appropriate information to enable dealings in such shares to take place on an open and proper basis (LR 2.2.5G).

In exceptional circumstances approved by the FCA, an applicant may retain the power not to approve a transfer of shares provided that the exercise of such a power would not disturb the market in those shares (LR 2.2.6G). In practice, the FCA regards very few restrictions on transferability as being permissible under LR 2.2.4R. In particular, the FCA has noted in its Technical Note on Restrictions on transfer (UKLA/TN/101.2, last updated March 2015) that it has permitted the use of restrictions on transfer if they are necessary to avoid falling within onerous legislative requirements, for example, in articles of association (primarily of investment companies) to prevent breach of onerous overseas legislative requirements. The FCA, however, will not permit a broad power being granted to refuse to register a transfer if a certain shareholder may cause the company in question to suffer, for example, "a pecuniary tax, financial or other material disadvantage". The only other notable restrictions which the FCA has allowed relate to protecting the wider public interest, for example, where a government requires the right to prevent transfers as a pre-requisite to selling off strategic industries to prevent such businesses becoming controlled by foreign entities. Any such restrictions need to be considered in light of the principle of equality of treatment of all shareholders (LR 7.2.1AR), although a power initiating a compulsory sell down by shareholders where shareholders are selected according to fully disclosed pre-set formulae is not likely to offend this principle, whereas a broad power allowing management to choose shareholders on a case-by-case basis would.

Whilst, as mentioned above, it is a listing requirement that the shares to be listed are freely transferable, shareholders are free to enter into agreements between themselves which restrict their freedom to transfer the shares held by them.

3.3.1.5   *Market capitalisation*

Except where shares of the same class are already listed, the expected aggregate market value of all shares to be listed (ignoring shares held by the company in treasury, where relevant) must be at least £700,000 for shares (LR 2.2.7R).

The FCA may admit shares of lower value if it is satisfied that there will be an adequate market for the shares (LR 2.2.8G). It is, however, unlikely that a listing would be sought for shares with a lower expected market value as the costs involved in achieving such a listing are likely to prove prohibitive.

3.3.1.6   *Whole class to be listed*

An application for listing of shares of any class must:

• if no shares of that class are already listed, relate to all shares of that class, issued or proposed to be issued; or

- if shares of that class are already listed, relate to all further shares of that class, issued or proposed to be issued.

This requirement is set out in LR 2.2.9R.

3.3.2   Listing requirements: Equity securities

3.3.2.1   *Historical financial information and revenue earning track record*

A new applicant for a premium listing must have published or filed historical financial information which:

(1)   covers at least three years;
(2)   represents at least 75% of the applicant's business for the three-year period;
(3)   has a latest balance sheet date that is not more than six months before the date of the prospectus and not more than nine months before the date the shares are admitted to listing (although this requirement does not apply in the context of a reverse takeover where a company is seeking to apply for re-admission on the enlarged group); and
(4)   includes the consolidated accounts in respect of the company and all its subsidiary undertakings.

In determining what amounts to 75% of the applicant's business, the FCA will consider the size, in aggregate, of all the acquisitions that the applicant has entered into during the three-year period and up to the date of the prospectus, relating to the size of the applicant as enlarged by the acquisition. In ascertaining the size of the acquisitions relative to the applicant, the FCA will take into account factors such as the assets, profitability and market capitalisation of the businesses. In practice, this means the FCA will apply the "class tests" set out in the Annex to LR 10 to assess the size of any acquisitions relative to the applicant.

The historical financial information must have been audited or reported on in accordance with the International Financial Reporting Standards (IFRS) as adopted by the EU (EU IFRS) or, for EU applicants, in accordance with their national accounting standards. For non-EU applicants, the financial information must be prepared in accordance with EU IFRS or to an accounting standard which is considered to be equivalent to EU IFRS (LR 6.2.4R). The generally accepted accounting principles of Japan, the US, China, Canada and the Republic of China have all been deemed equivalent. Non-EU applicants may also present historical financial information in accordance with IFRS provided that the notes to the audited financial statements that form part of the historical financial information contain an explicit and unreserved statement that the financial statements comply with IFRS in accordance with International Accounting Standard (IAS) 1 Presentation of Financial Statements.

The historical financial information must not be subject to a modified report, unless the presence of an emphasis of matter paragraph arises in respect of one of the earlier years and the opinion on the final period is unmodified or the opinion on the historical financial information for the final period includes an emphasis of matter paragraph (with regard to going concern, but the applicant can satisfy the requirement to have sufficient working capital for the next 12 months at the date of the prospectus (LR 6.2.5)).

The applicant must take all reasonable steps to ensure that the person providing the opinion on the historical financial information is independent of it and it must obtain a written confirmation from the person providing the opinion that it complies with guidelines on independence issued or approved by its national accountancy or auditing bodies (LR 6.2.6R).

The company's three-year historical financial information must demonstrate that the company has a revenue-earning track record and put prospective investors in a position to make an informed assessment of the business.

The FCA may, however, take the view that, even where the company's business has been in existence for the requisite three-year period, if a significant part or all of the company's business has one or more of the following characteristics, it may fail to satisfy this eligibility condition:

(1) a business strategy places significant emphasis on the development or marketing of products or services which have not formed a significant part of the company's historic financial information;
(2) the value of the business on admission will be determined, to a significant degree, by reference to future developments rather than past performance;
(3) the relationship between the value of the business and its revenue or profit-earning record is significantly different from those of similar companies in the same sector;
(4) there is no record of consistent revenue, cash flow or profit growth throughout the historic revenue earning period;
(5) where the business has undergone a significant change in its scale of operations during the period of the historic financial information or is due to do so before or after admission; or
(6) there are significant levels of research and development expenditure or significant levels of capital expenditure.

The FCA has published a Technical Note (UKLA/TN/102.1, January 2018) which provides guidance on the historical financial information and track-record requirements.

Mineral and scientific research based companies have traditionally been exempt from some or all of the listing requirements relating to historical financial information described above.

Following its 2017 Consultation Paper, CP 17/4, the FCA has revised and extended the concessions available to companies in certain specialist areas.

A mineral company that has been operating for a period of less than three years may still apply for admission to listing, provided that it has published or filed historical financial information since the inception of its business. However, the applicant must still ensure that any historical financial information will put prospective investors in a position to make an informed assessment of the business for which a listing is sought. The requirement to demonstrate a revenue-earning track record does not apply to a mineral company seeking a premium listing of its shares. If a mineral company does not hold controlling interests in a majority (by value) of the properties, fields, mines or other assets in which it has invested, it must demonstrate that it has a reasonable spread of direct interests in mineral resources and has rights to actively participate in their extraction.

The exemption for scientific research-based companies that do not have a three-year track record of historical financial information requires that, in such circumstances, the company must:

(1) demonstrate its ability to attract funds from sophisticated investors;
(2) intend to raise at least £10 million at the time of listing;
(3) have a capitalisation before listing of at least £20 million (based on a proposed issue price and excluding the value of any shares which have been valued in the six months before listing);
(4) have as its primary reason for listing the raising of finance to bring identified products to a stage where it can generate significant revenues; and
(5) demonstrate that it has a three-year track record of operations in laboratory research and development including:
     (a) details of patents granted or progress as to their application;
     (b) the successful completion or progress of testing the effectiveness of an applicant's products.

As of 1 January 2018, the FCA introduced an additional exemption from compliance with the rules regarding the revenue earning track record for property companies (LR 6.12). A property company is a company which is primarily engaged in property activities, including: (1) the holding of properties (directly or indirectly) for letting and retention as investments; (2) the development of properties for letting and retention as investments; (3) the purchase and development of properties for subsequent sale; or (4) the purchase of land for development properties for retention as investments.

If a property company does not have a revenue-earning track record: (1) it will be required to demonstrate that it has three years of development of its real estate assets represented by increases of the gross asset value of its real estate assets, evidenced by the required historical financial information required and supported by a published property valuation report; or (2) it must demonstrate that 75% of the gross asset value of its real estate assets, as supported by a published property valuation report, are revenue generating at the time the application for premium listing is made. The property valuation report will need to be made available in the applicant's prospectus.

Where an applicant is relying on the modified Listing Rules referred to above but cannot comply with the requirement to have published or filed historical financial information that covers at least three years because it has been operating for a shorter period, the company must have published or filed historical financial information since the inception of its business.

The Statutory Audit Directive (2006/43) (as amended)[6] affects the ability of non-EU applicants to list their shares, or GDRs, on the regulated market of the Exchange (or other RIEs) and to maintain such listing. Where a company's shares or GDRs are admitted (or to be admitted) to trading on a regulated market in any EU Member State and its auditors are regulated in a non-EU country, the directive requires that its auditor must either be registered in that Member State and be subject to that Member State's system of oversight, quality assurance, investigation and penalties or seek a derogation from the requirement

---

[6] Directive 2006/43 on statutory audits of annual accounts and consolidated accounts, amending Directives 78/660 and 83/349 and repealing Directive 84/253 [2006] OJ L157/87.

to be registered on the basis of reciprocity. Registration on the basis of reciprocity is only available where the relevant non-EU country's auditors or audit entities are subject to equivalent systems of oversight, quality assurance, investigations and penalties to those in the EU. It is the European Commission's responsibility to determine whether there is equivalence. To ensure compliance, the directive provides that audit reports issued by auditors from non-EU countries which are neither registered nor able to rely on a derogation shall have no legal effect. As such, the directive needs to be considered by non-EU applicants in the context of the requirements of LR 6.2 and the continuing obligations to publish audited financial statements, once listed, under the Transparency Rules.

To date, the European Commission has determined that the following non-EU countries have equivalent oversight systems and therefore may be exempted from the auditors' registration obligations under the directive: Abu Dhabi, Australia, Brazil, Canada, China, Croatia, Dubai International Financial Centre, Guernsey, Indonesia, the Isle of Man, Japan, Jersey, Malaysia, Mauritius, New Zealand, Singapore, South Africa, South Korea, Switzerland, Taiwan, Thailand, Turkey and the US.

An auditor registered in a non-EU country which is not considered to be subject to equivalent oversight systems is required to register in an EU Member State and supply to the competent authority in the UK certain information about itself, the auditing standards and independence requirements applied to the audit concerned, a description of its internal quality control systems and certain information about the last quality assurance review of the auditor. When seeking a listing to the regulated market of the Exchange, non-EU applicants will therefore need to check whether their auditors are duly registered with the competent authority in the UK.

3.3.2.2 Independent business

An applicant must also be able to demonstrate that it will be carrying on an independent business as its main activity (the "independence test") (LR 6.4).

Factors that may indicate that the applicant does not satisfy the independence test include situations where:

(1) the majority of revenue generated by the applicant is attributable to business conducted directly or indirectly with one person or group;
(2) where the applicant does not have strategic control over the commercialisation of its products and/or its ability to earn revenue and/or freedom to implement its business strategy; or
(3) where the applicant cannot demonstrate that it has access to financing other than from one person or group (LR 6.4.3G).

An applicant for admission of shares to a premium listing that has a "controlling shareholder" (broadly, any party who exercises or controls on their own or with any persons with whom they are acting in concert 30% or more of the shares in the company) is required to enter into a binding agreement with that shareholder in order to demonstrate that it is able to carry on an independent business as its main activity (LR 6.51R).

The agreement must contain legally binding undertakings that:

(1) transactions and arrangements between the controlling shareholder (and/or any of its associates) and the applicant will be conducted at arm's length and on normal commercial terms;
(2) neither the controlling shareholder nor any of its associates will take any action that would have the effect of preventing the applicant from complying with its obligations under the Listing Rules; and
(3) neither the controlling shareholder nor any of its associates will propose or procure the proposal of a shareholder resolution which is intended (or appears to be intended) to circumvent the proper application of the Listing Rules.

Separate rules apply if the controlling shareholder is a sovereign state.

The FCA has issued a new Technical Note (UKLA/TN/102.1, January 2018) with further guidance on how to interpret the independence test.

The independence test discussed above along with the requirement to put in place a binding agreement with any controlling shareholder apply to mineral companies, scientific research based companies and property companies.

A company with a premium listing with a controlling shareholder must ensure that the election and re-election of an independent director be approved by both the shareholders of the company and the independent shareholders (i.e. excluding the controlling shareholder) of the company. Where either resolution is defeated, the company may not propose a further resolution to elect or re-elect the proposed director until 90 days have passed since the original vote. Any further resolution may be passed by a single vote of the shareholders of the company (i.e. including the controlling shareholder). An applicant for a premium listing will need to demonstrate to the FCA that its constitution will allow it to comply with this requirement. For an applicant incorporated in England and Wales, it may be that no changes need be made to its articles of association to allow it to comply with this requirement.

3.3.2.3 Working capital

In connection with any application for a premium listing, the company must ensure that it and its subsidiary undertakings have sufficient working capital for the group's requirements for at least the next 12 months from the date of publication of the prospectus (LR 6.1.7R). If a prospectus is being prepared, a statement to this effect is required to be included pursuant to the Prospectus Rules.

In the case of an application for listing of shares by a company which already has a premium listing, the FCA may grant admission where the company does not have sufficient working capital if the prospectus contains satisfactory proposals for the provision of additional working capital (LR 6.1.17G).

A company whose business is entirely or substantially that of banking, insurance or the provision of similar financial services may not be required to comply with the working capital requirements if the FCA is satisfied that the company's solvency and capital adequacy are regulated by the FCA or by another regulatory body and the company is meeting its solvency and capital adequacy requirements and is expected to do so for the next 12 months without having to raise new capital (LR 6.1.18G).

As of 1 January 2018, the FCA deleted guidance from the Listing Rules which referred to the FCA's ability to dispense with the requirement for an applicant and its subsidiary undertakings to be able to demonstrate they have sufficient working capital to meet the group's requirements for at least the next 12 months on the basis that this requirement has not been waived since the listing function was conducted by the FCA (or its predecessor, the FSA) and it is unlikely to do so in the future.

In light of the number of secondary issues by listed companies in 2009 with prospectuses which contained "qualified" working capital statements, it is worth highlighting some issues regarding such "qualified" statements. Recommendations[7] published by the Committee of European Securities Regulators (CESR—an organisation now superseded by ESMA) provide that a working capital statement in a prospectus must be either "clean" or "qualified" and the decision is "binary".

A "qualified" working capital statement is one which opens with a negative qualified statement, for example, one which indicates that the company "does not have" sufficient working capital for at least 12 months from the date of the document. Whilst a listed company (unlike a new applicant) is permitted to make a "qualified" working capital statement by virtue of LR 6.1.7R, in such circumstances, the FCA has indicated that it expects the prospectus to include satisfactory proposals for

---

[7] Now contained in ESMA, *ESMA update of the CESR recommendations: The consistent implementation of Regulation 809/2004 implementing the Prospectus Directive*, ESMA/2013/319 (20 March 2013).

providing the additional working capital that the company thinks is necessary. These proposals should contain:

(1) specific proposed actions, for example, a refinancing or renegotiation of new credit terms and/or facilities, a decrease in discretionary capital expenditure, a revised strategy or acquisition programme or asset sales;

(2) the relative timing of such actions, for example, indicating when action is required and whether, for example, such action is required immediately or at a specified time later in the 12-month period; and

(3) the implications of such actions not being taken, for example, whether the company will enter into administration or receivership and, if so, when.

In order for the working capital statement to be considered to be "clean", it must state that the company has "sufficient working capital" for at least 12 months from the date of the prospectus. It is not permissible to include any reference in the working capital statement to:

(1) a future tense, i.e. that the company "will have" sufficient working capital as this could point to an unidentified future time or debt facilities yet to be agreed within the 12 months in question;

(2) assumptions, sensitivities, risk factors or caveats. This is because adding such disclosures detracts from the value of the statement and, in effect, seeks to transfer risk to investors; or

(3) trade creditors, debtors or uncommitted new facilities. Only references to cash, bank and other committed facilities which are currently available to the company and its group, made on the basis that the transaction proceeds, and taking into account underwritten, guaranteed or firm placed proceeds only, are permitted. The FCA's position that underwritten, guaranteed or firm placed proceeds may be taken into account by a company in determining whether its working capital position is not a position which is widely held by other European securities

regulators and is the subject of debate between the various regulators at the ESMA level.

With regard to (2) above, in its Technical Note on Working capital statements and risk factors (UKLA/TN/321.1, last updated December 2012), the FCA reminded market participants that it will challenge risk factors included in draft prospectuses in circumstances where the proposed disclosure conflicts with or undermines other Listing Rule or Prospectus Rule requirements (for example, by qualifying the working capital statement with references to the requirement for further additional funding in the near future) and gave market participants specific guidance on the interplay between risk factors and working capital statements.

In relation to (3) above, in circumstances where the working capital statement would be qualified if the proposals fail, for example, where the working capital statement is made taking into account the proceeds of the proposals, additional disclosure is required to be included regarding the importance of any vote required in connection with the proposals. For example, if the company takes into account the proceeds of a rights issue when making its working capital statement, and the rights issue is conditional upon, amongst other things, shareholder approval, a description of the implications of the vote not being passed is required to be disclosed. This disclosure must appear in a section before any description of the directors' recommendation regarding the vote.

As a result of the challenging market conditions in 2008 and 2009, the FSA reminded sponsors in *List!* (Issue No.20, January 2009) of the heightened risks that they face in connection with working capital statements. In particular, the FSA noted that in transactions with a "rescue" element, particular attention should be paid to an issuer's working capital position. Whilst the company and its directors bear overall responsibility for the working capital statement, the sponsor must confirm that it has come to a reasonable opinion, after having made due and careful enquiry that the directors of the company have a reasonable basis on which to make their working capital

115

statement. The FSA specifically highlighted that the sponsor's role is "in addition" to the part played directly by the directors of the company or by a reporting accountant appointed by the company in the working capital exercise. In particular, the sponsor cannot simply take the directors' working capital statement and the exercise conducted by the reporting accountants at face value, the sponsor is expected to "review" and "challenge" the work done by the company and reporting accountant and, through its own knowledge and experience of the company and its operating environment, ensure that the conclusion reached on the company's working capital position is the right one under the circumstances. The FSA also highlighted that it is important for sponsors to carry out sufficient due diligence when performing their role in connection with a working capital statement and be aware of, amongst other things: the inherent difficulties in making accurate forecasts and projections; the need to have an appropriate basis for each of the assumptions used in the working capital model; whether sensitivities run consider all probable outcomes and give the necessary comfort that the issuer has sufficient headroom; and whether financing facilities are in place and will remain so throughout the working capital period. In addition, where the sponsor or a member of the sponsor's group has an interest in the company (for example, through an existing loan facility) and the company is in financial distress and the transaction has a "rescue element", the sponsor must ensure that any relevant conflict is identified and properly managed. Where a conflict cannot be managed, the sponsor must decline to act. See s.3.2.3 above for more information on sponsor conflicts.

The FSA also asked sponsor firms to consider whether they need to revisit their systems and controls over working capital and make appropriate enhancements to reflect the current environment, including: introducing enhanced review procedures; providing additional training to staff on undertaking due diligence in times of financial distress; and ensuring communication between the sponsor, the issuer and the reporting accountant is clear and effective.

Whilst not all of these provisions have been replicated in the FCA's two Technical Notes on Working capital statements— Basis of preparation (UKLA/TN/320.1) and on Working capital statements and risk factors (UKLA/TN/321.1), the description of the sponsor's role and its obligations in these historic editions of *List!* remain a useful guide to the steps a sponsor should take in discharging its extended obligations under the Listing Rules.

3.3.2.4 Shares in public hands

Where an application for a premium listing has been made for a class of shares, at least 25% of that class (ignoring shares held by the company in treasury, where relevant) must be in the hands of the public in one or more European Economic Area (EEA) countries no later than the time for admission (LR 6.1.14R). Account may also be taken of holders in a non-EEA country if the shares are also listed in that state.

A percentage lower than 25% may be acceptable to the FCA if it considers that the market will operate properly with a lower percentage in public hands having regard to the number of shares of the relevant class in issue and the extent of their distribution to the public (LR 6.14.5G).

The FCA has clarified that the minimum free-float requirement is intended to ensure that there is sufficient liquidity in the shares rather than ensuring shareholders have sufficient power to counterbalance a dominant shareholder (CP 12/25). This clarification stemmed from investor concerns about a number of companies which had obtained derogations from complying with LR 6.1.19R (now LR 6.1.14R) under the discretion in LR 6.1.20AG (now LR 6.14.5G) on the grounds that, despite falling short of the 25% threshold, such companies placed a large number of shares in public hands at the time of listing and thus there would be liquidity in the shares by virtue of the size of such companies' market capitalisation. There is guidance in LR 6.1.14.5G on the circumstances in which the FCA will permit a modification of the minimum 25% free-float requirements. In particular, the FCA may take into account the following factors:

(1) whether shares of the same class are held (even though they are not listed) in non-EEA states; (2) the number and nature of the public shareholders; and (3) in relation to a premium listing, whether the expected market value of the shares in public hands at admission exceeds £100 million.

The "public" for the purposes of the shares in public hands test does not include a director of the applicant or any of its subsidiary undertakings. In addition, connected persons of such directors, the trustees of any employees' share scheme or pension fund, and any person who by virtue of any agreement has a right to nominate a person to the board of directors of the applicant, will not be regarded as being part of the "public". Furthermore, any shareholder whose interest is 5% or more of the shares of the relevant class will be excluded from the "public" for these purposes (LR 6.14.3R(1)(e)), as will any persons acting in concert with such a shareholder. Shares subject to a lock-up period of longer than 180 calendar days are excluded from the free-float calculation (LR 6.14.3R(2)). When assessing the number of shares held in public hands, the FCA may also disregard shareholdings held by different investment managers within a corporate group where the investment decisions are made independently by the individual in control of the relevant fund and those decisions are unfettered by the organisation to which the investment manager belongs (LR 6.14.4G).

As mentioned above, the FCA's view is that the purpose of LR 6.14.3R(1)(e) is to ensure sufficient liquidity within the secondary market of shares rather than to encourage wide public participation in an initial public offering (IPO). As such, it has confirmed that LR 6.14.3R(1)(e) seeks to ensure that persons or concert parties do not control significant holdings of shares that are not available for trading on the secondary market. Listing Rule 6.14.3R(1)(e) is less interested in who may be the ultimate beneficiary of the shares but rather who controls the investment decision in relation to those shares.

Where the percentage of shares in the hands of the public falls below the threshold stipulated by the FCA, the listing may be suspended or cancelled. The FCA will, however, normally allow a reasonable period of time for the relevant level of public ownership to be restored before a listing is suspended (LR 5.2.2G).

3.3.2.5 Settlement

In October 2015, the FCA deleted the provisions in the Listing Rules requiring that an applicant's articles of association or other constitutional documents and the terms of the shares which are the subject of an application for listing be compatible for electronic settlement, which includes settlement by a "relevant system" such as CREST. These provisions have been superseded by the requirements of the EU Central Securities Depositories Regulation[8] which requires securities that are the subject of transactions on a trading venue to be capable of being settled in a dematerialised form. It remains the case, therefore, that there must be nothing inherent in the applicant's constitutional documents which prevents electronic settlement.

The FCA recognises that the securities of many overseas companies cannot be settled in CREST without the use of Depository Interests, which allows intermediaries and investors to trade in the company's securities whilst settlement is effected electronically in CREST, and there may be external factors which affect the eligibility of shares for electronic settlement.

3.3.2.6 Pre-emption rights

English company law requires companies incorporated under the laws of England and Wales to offer pre-emption rights to their shareholders. The Listing Rules extend this obligation to overseas issuers of premium listed equity shares who, in general terms, are required to offer pre-emption rights to their shareholders.

---

[8] Regulation 909/2014 on improving securities settlement in the European Union and on central securities depositories and amending Directives 98/26 and 2014/65 and Regulation 236/2012 [2014] OJ L257/1.

3.3.2.7 Externally managed companies

Over the last ten years or so, a number of special purpose acquisition companies (SPACs), that is to say, cash shell companies incorporated with the intention of acquiring, running and transforming target businesses, have listed in London. Many of such SPACs have outsourced significant management functions to an offshore advisory firm, with the board of the listed company comprising entirely of non-executive directors. The advisory firm is typically formed by the founders of the SPAC and it signs a contract with the listed company to provide advice to the listed company on the identification of potential target businesses, their acquisition and, post-acquisition, their integration. When a SPAC first lists, it is not eligible for premium listing as it does not have an independent business with a three-year track record of historical financial information, so it obtains a standard listing. At the time the SPAC acquires a business, it will generally reconsider its options and often it will apply for a premium listing. The advisory firm is, in substance, providing the executive management function of the listed company and such an arrangement places the de facto management of the company beyond a number of key controls within the Listing Rules and reduces the ability of shareholders to hold the de facto management of the company to account. Having looked at such structures, in 2012, the FSA reached the conclusion that externally managed companies were at odds with the legitimate expectations of stakeholders in the listing regime and contrary to the high standards of UK corporate practice. As a result, in October 2012, a new rule and guidance was added to the Listing Rules making companies with external management ineligible for premium listing. In particular, a company seeking a premium listing must satisfy the FCA that the discretion of its board to make strategic decisions on behalf of the company has not been limited or transferred to a person outside of the group and that the board has the capability to act on key strategic matters in the absence of a recommendation from a person outside of the group (LR 6.13.1R). In considering whether a company has satisfied this requirement, the FCA will consider, among other things, whether the board of the company consists solely of non-executive directors and whether significant elements of the decision-making of, or planning for, the company take place outside the group (LR 6.13.2G).

In practice, the implications of this rule are that an externally managed SPAC will need to collapse its external management structure upon or following its acquisition of a business if it wishes to transfer its listing from a standard listing to a premium listing.

3.4 The methods in which shares may be brought to listing

Once a company has appointed its sponsor and identified the applicable requirements for a premium listing, the next question that arises is what are the different methods by which the company can list its shares?

Listing Rule 9.5 sets out certain transactions by which shares may be brought to listing; some are available only to new applicants (see s.3.4.1–3.4.3 below) and others are available also to companies which are already listed (see s.3.4.4 and 3.4.5 below).

The Listing Rules focus on the special features of certain transactions in which shares may be brought to listing without purporting to deal exhaustively with all such transactions. New applicants should therefore expect to discuss with the FCA transactions which are not specifically addressed (such as introductions and intermediaries' offers).

In all cases, the shares in issue must be sufficiently widely held that their marketability when listed can be assumed. In cases of doubt, the FCA should be consulted at an early stage.

3.4.1 *Offer for sale or subscription*

An offer for sale is an invitation to the public by, or on behalf of, a third party to purchase shares of the company already in issue or allotted, and may be in the form of an invitation to tender at or above a stated minimum price (LR Appendix 1). An offer for subscription is an invitation to the public by, or on behalf of, a company to subscribe for shares of the company not yet in issue or allotted, and again may be in the form of an invitation to tender at or above a stated minimum price (LR Appendix 1).

These types of offers were commonly used in the context of the large UK privatisations but have been rarely used since that time (although there were public offers in the Super-Group IPO in March 2010, the Ocado IPO in July 2010 and the Saga IPO in May 2014). More recently, the privatisation of Royal Mail in 2015, the first major privatisation by way of IPO in the UK for many years, was structured to allow the general public to participate in a direct offer for subscription.

In an offer for sale or subscription, the company must ensure that letters of allotment or acceptance are all issued simultaneously and numbered serially and, where appropriate, split and certified by the company's registrars. Where the shares may be held through CREST, as opposed to in paper form, the company must ensure that shareholders holding on either basis receive equal treatment. Letters of regret must be posted at the same time or no later than three business days thereafter.

If a letter of regret is not posted simultaneously with the letters of allotment or acceptance, the company must insert a notice to this effect in a national newspaper to appear on the morning following posting of the letters of allotment or acceptance (LR 9.5.11R).

3.4.2 Placing

A placing is a marketing of shares which are already in issue but which have not yet been listed, or of shares which have yet to be issued, to specified persons which does not involve an offer to the public or to existing holders of the company's shares generally (LR Appendix 1). An institutional placing is the most common route for achieving a listing, although it is sometimes combined with an intermediaries offer (see s.3.4.3 below).

In the case of a placing of new shares where the company's shares are already listed, the placing price cannot be at a discount of more than 10% to the middle market price of the shares at the time of the placing agreement between the issuer and the underwriter or placing agent or, in the case of an offer, at the time of announcing the terms (LR 9.5.10R(1)). The FCA has published guidance to clarify that, where a placing is agreed during the course of a trading day, the source of any on-screen intra-day price should be discussed in advance with the FCA and the FCA will consider whether there is sufficient liquidity and the source is one that is widely accepted by the market (LR 9.5.10AG). Note however that, in practice, the discount at which placing shares are normally offered is limited to not more than 5% to the middle market price of the shares in order to comply with the Pre-Emption Group Statement of Principles, which are guidelines for issuers that set out the views of the UK institutional investor community in relation to non-pre-emptive issues of shares for cash.

3.4.3 Intermediaries offer

Although not addressed in any detail in the Listing Rules, it is worth noting the availability of this type of transaction. An intermediaries offer is a means of accessing retail investors without conducting an offer for sale or subscription. Under an intermediaries offer, existing shares, or shares which have yet to be issued, are offered by, or on behalf of, the company to intermediaries (such as stockbrokers and share shops) who in turn allocate the shares to their own clients (LR Appendix 1).

This is the most commonly used method for accessing the retail investors in the UK, although retail offers have not in recent years been popular (except where there has been thought to be a robust commercial rationale to include retail investors). Examples of intermediaries offers in significant IPOs in recent times include those conducted by Direct Line Insurance Group Plc in 2012, esure Group Plc, Merlin Entertainments Plc and Royal Mail Plc in 2013, Pets at Home and TSB Banking Group in 2014, HSS Hire Group and John Laing Group in 2015, Countryside Properties Plc in February 2016 and Global Ports Holding Plc in May 2017.

3.4.4 Rights issues

A rights issue is an offer made to existing shareholders to subscribe or purchase further shares in proportion to their existing shareholdings. The offer is made through the issue of a renounceable letter (or other negotiable instrument) which may be traded (as "nil paid" rights) for a period before payment for the shares is due (LR Appendix 1).

In a placing of rights arising from the rights issue before the official start of dealings, the company must ensure that:

(1)   the placing relates to at least 25% of the maximum number of shares offered or such lesser amount as may be agreed by the FCA if it is satisfied that a requirement of at least 25% would be detrimental to the success of the issue (LR 9.5.2G);

(2)   the placees are committed to take up whatever is placed with them;

(3)   the price paid by the placees does not exceed the price at which the shares that are the subject of the rights issue are offered by more than one half of the calculated premium over the offer price (the premium being the difference between the offer price and the theoretical ex-rights price); and

(4)   the shares which are the subject of the rights issue are of the same class as shares already listed.

These provisions are contained in LR 9.5.1R.

In a rights issue, the FCA may list the shares at the same time as the shares are admitted to trading in "nil paid" form. Upon the shares being paid up and the allotment becoming unconditional in all respects, the listing will continue without the need for a further application for listing of fully paid up shares (LR 9.5.3G).

If existing shareholders do not take up their rights to subscribe in a rights issue (LR 9.5.4R):

(1) the company must ensure that the shares to which the offer relates are offered for subscription on terms that any premium obtained over the subscription price (net of expenses) is to be for the account of such holders save that, if the proceeds for an existing holder do not exceed £5, the proceeds may be retained for the company's benefit; and
(2) the shares may be allotted to the underwriters if, on the expiry of the subscription period, no premium (net of expenses) has been obtained.

The following details must also be notified to a regulated information service (RIS) without delay (LR 9.5.5R):

(1) the issue price and principal terms of the issue; and
(2) the results of the issue and, if any rights not taken up are sold, details of the sale, including the date and price per share.

The current EU Prospectus Directive[9] regime contains a reduced disclosure regime for rights issue prospectuses in respect of companies with shares admitted to trading on a regulated market. The regime provides that a full prospectus is not required for rights issues provided that statutory pre-emption rights have not been disapplied. Instead, a "proportionate disclosure regime" applies. Whilst this regime provides

---

[9] Directive 2003/71 on the prospectus to be published when securities are offered to the public or admitted to trading and amending Directive 2001/34 [2003] OJ L345/64.

companies with the flexibility of preparing a prospectus with reduced disclosure requirements, as many issuers and under-writers want to preserve the flexibility to place any "rump" with investors in certain non-EEA jurisdictions, for example, the US, market practice and/or local securities laws still dictate that a more comprehensive disclosure document is prepared, thereby limiting the benefits of the new proportionate disclo-sure regime for these types of offer.

The European prospectus regime has been under review for some time. A New Prospectus Regulation came into force in July 2017, with the bulk of its provisions coming into effect on 21 July 2019.[10] The New Prospectus Regulation repeals and replaces the existing Prospectus Directive and has direct effect across EU Member States. Recognising that the current proportionate disclosure regime has not been a success, the New Prospectus Regulation contains provisions for a new simplified disclosure regime for certain secondary issuances. The regime will apply in the case of an offer of securities to the public or of an admission to trading of securities on a regulated market by an issuer whose securities have been admitted to trading on a regulated market or a small and medium-sized enterprise (SME) growth market for at least 18 months and who issues more securities of the same class. This regime will only require the inclusion of minimal financial information covering the last financial year (such information may be included by reference). The European Commission is currently consulting on the delegated acts that will specify the nature of the other information that would need to be included. The new regime is intended to reflect the fact that such issuers are already subject to ongoing disclosure requirements and, therefore, that the prospectus should not need to include the same amount of information that would be required for the protection of investors in the case of a new applicant. Given the concerns referred to above in circumstances where an issuer wants to access non-EEA jurisdictions, it is unclear whether this reduced disclosure regime will be used by issuers any

---

[10] Regulation 2017/1129 on the prospectus to be published when securities are offered to the public or admitted to trading on a regulated market, and repealing Directive 2003/71 [2017] OJ L168/12.

more than the existing proportionate disclosure regime. It is also currently unclear what position the UK will take in relation to reflecting amendments to the EU prospectus regime into UK national law where such amendments will take effect after the UK's exit from the EU on 29 March 2019.

3.4.5   Open offers

An open offer is an invitation to existing shareholders to subscribe or purchase shares in proportion to their holdings which is not made on a renounceable letter (or another negotiable document) (LR Appendix 1).

The timetable for an open offer must be approved by the RIE on which the company's shares are traded (LR 9.5.7R).

A listed company must ensure that the open offer remains open for acceptance for at least 10 business days. For the purposes of calculating the period of 10 business days, the first business day is the date on which the offer is first open for acceptance (LR 9.5.7AR).

The following requirements relate to communication of information on an open offer (LR 9.5.8R):

(1)   if the offer is subject to the approval of shareholders in general meeting, the announcement must state that this is the case; and

(2)   the circular dealing with the offer must not contain any statement which might be taken to imply that the offer gives the same entitlements as a rights issue unless it is an offer with a compensatory element.

If existing shareholders do not take up their rights to subscribe in an open offer with a compensatory element (LR 9.5.8AR):

(1)   the listed company must ensure that the shares to which the offer relates are offered for subscription or purchase on terms that any premium obtained over the subscription or purchase price (net of expenses) is to be for the account of

the holders, except that, if the proceeds for an existing holder do not exceed £5, the proceeds may be retained for the company's benefit; and

(2)   the shares may be allotted or sold to underwriters, if on the expiry of the subscription period no premium (net of expenses) has been obtained.

In 2009, Lloyds Banking Group Plc and Songbird Estates Plc were the first issuers to undertake secondary offerings using an open offer with a compensatory element and LR 9.5.8AR was added to the Listing Rules in June 2011 to formalise this variation to open offers in order to cover this method of listing shares.

3.5   Listing application procedures

Having considered whether a company need appoint a sponsor, the applicable requirements for a premium listing and the types of transaction by which a company may obtain a listing, the next question to consider is what are the application procedures to obtain a premium listing?

The procedures which an applicant for listing must follow are set out in the Prospectus Rules and Ch.3 of the Listing Rules.

Historically, for issues of equity securities, a single prospectus has been approved. However, as a result of the FCA consultation in relation to reforming the availability of information in the UK IPO process (see CP 17/5 and Policy Statement (PS) 17/23) and the consequent rule changes that took effect on 1 July 2018, it is expected that companies seeking an IPO of their equity shares will initially prepare a registration document before preparing either a single prospectus or a securities note and a summary document (which together with the registration document will comprise a tri-partite prospectus). For secondary issues of equity, such as a rights issue or open offer, a single prospectus may still be prepared. For the purpose of this s.3.5, it is assumed that a prospectus is being approved and published as a single document. If it is prepared in separate parts, namely a registration document, a securities note and a summary (such as, for example, on the demutualisation and IPO of Standard Life in June 2006), each separate part must be approved individually and the procedures described in this s.3.5 apply to each separate part individually (see PR 3.1.11R).

3.5.1 General

The formal application procedure requires the following:

(1) submission of certain information 10 working days before the intended approval and publication of the prospectus (the "10-day documents") or, in the case of a new applicant for listing (that has not previously made an offer to the public), 20 working days (PRs 3.1.1R and 3.1.3R) (see s.3.5.4 below);
(2) submission of further documents (some of which are updates of the 10-day documents), no later than two business days before the hearing of the application for admission (the "48-hour documents") (see s.3.5.5 below);
(3) submission of certain items or documents on the day of the hearing (the "on-the-day documents") (see s.3.5.7 below); and
(4) a listing hearing to consider the application on a date agreed with the FCA in advance of submitting documents (LR 3.2.3G), the outcome of which is that admission is granted. The FCA has clarified that admission to listing will not be granted on a conditional basis.

Admission becomes effective (when the decision is announced by the FCA) and subsequent documents are lodged.

The Prospectus Rules impose timing requirements by reference to "working days" whilst the Listing Rules refer to "business days". To all intents and purposes, at least in a UK context, these are the same.

Draft prospectuses are normally filed well in advance of other documentation to ensure that there is sufficient time available for the FCA to review and comment on the draft prospectus in the hope of avoiding any last-minute delays. The FCA does, however, require all draft documents which are submitted (including draft prospectuses) to be substantially complete and requires a cross-reference list to be submitted with the draft prospectus which identifies where the relevant items required by the Prospectus Rules can be found in the draft prospectus (PR 3.1.1AR). The FCA has indicated in its Procedural Note on Review and Approval of Documents (UKLA/PN/903.3, last updated March 2017) that a document would not normally be considered to be substantially complete if any of the following information was omitted: (1) the summary; (2) financial information or expert's report required under the Listing Rules or the Prospectus Rules; (3) working capital disclosure; (4) the terms and conditions of the transaction; and (5) disclosure required by the litigation, material contracts and significant charge statements. Failure to comply with these requirements may result in extended review periods when subsequent drafts are submitted or the FCA rejecting the draft submitted.

The FCA is also entitled to carry out enquiries and request further information which it considers appropriate, to request the company to answer questions and to require verification, in any manner which it specifies, of any information provided by the company (LR 3.2.6G).

3.5.2 *Admission to trading*

As previously mentioned, the application procedure for obtaining admission to trading runs largely in parallel with the application procedure for admission to listing. The application to trading procedure principally involves an initial dialogue with the Exchange (or other RIE) to agree the process, followed by the completion and submission of the appropriate forms and payment of the relevant fee. The procedure to be followed is set out in the Admission and Disclosure Standards issued by the Exchange.

3.5.3   Admission becoming effective

Although admission to listing is granted at the listing hearing, admission of the shares which are the subject of the application only becomes effective when the decision of the FCA to admit the shares to listing has been announced (LR 3.2.7G). This is achieved by the decision being either:

(1)   disseminated by a RIS; or
(2)   posted on a designated notice board at the FCA, if the decision is made at a time when, in the opinion of the FCA, those electronic systems are not available for any reason. In this case, the FCA will cause the decision to be disseminated forthwith upon the electronic systems next becoming available.

As admission to listing is conditional upon the shares being admitted to trading and vice versa, in practice, both the Exchange and the FCA make simultaneous announcements confirming admission to trading on the Exchange and the admission to listing on the Official List of the FSA.

3.5.4   10-day documents

Prospectus Rule 3.1.3R sets out the various information and documents which must be submitted at least 10 working days (20 working days in the case of a new applicant) before the intended date of approval and publication of the document to which they relate.

Without listing all of the relevant information or documents (full details of which are set out in PR 3.1.3R), it is worth noting that the "10-day documents" include drafts of the following documents:

(1)   a completed Form A (an application form for approval of the prospectus by the FCA in the form issued by the FCA as available on the FCA's website);
(2)   the prospectus;

(3) a completed checklist identifying where in the prospectus each item required to be disclosed in the Prospectus Rules can be found (unless the order of the prospectus follows the order of the disclosure requirements in the relevant Annex to the Prospectus Directive Regulation)[11]; and

(4) contact details of individuals available to answer questions from the FCA.

3.5.5   48-hour documents

Again, without listing all of the relevant documents, the following documents (full details of which are set out in LR 3.3.2R) must be lodged in final form with the FCA before midday at least two business days prior to the consideration of the application for admission to listing:

(1) an application form for admission of the shares to the Official List (in the form issued by the FCA as available on its website), signed by a duly authorised officer of the company (namely, a director or the company secretary);

(2) either the prospectus as approved by the FCA or, if the prospectus has been approved by the competent authority in another EEA country and is being "passported" into the UK, a copy of the prospectus together with a certificate of approval and, if applicable, a translation of the summary into English;

(3) if there is no prospectus, the application form for admission referred to in (1) above must state that no prospectus is required and the reasons why (LR 3.3.2A(R));

(4) written confirmation of the number of shares to be allotted pursuant to a board resolution allotting the shares; and

(5) if a prospectus has not been produced, a copy of the RIS announcement detailing the number and type of shares that are the subject of the application and the circumstances of their issue.

---

[11] Regulation 809/2004 implementing Directive 2003/71 as regards information contained in prospectuses as well as the format, incorporation by reference and publication of such prospectuses and dissemination of advertisements [2004] OJ L149/1.

The FCA has said that it will not, except in exceptional circumstances, admit shares to listing until all of the 48-hour documents and the items to be lodged on the day have been received.

The onus is therefore on the company and its advisers to ensure that the Listing Rules and Prospectus Rules relating to an application are complied with in a timely manner to avoid the risk of delaying the consideration of the application and the commencement of dealings. There is, however, an exception to this requirement where a copy of the relevant resolution relating to either the issue or allotment of the relevant shares is not available for lodging as a 48-hour document.

3.5.6 Delays in obtaining allotment resolution

If written confirmation of the number of shares to be allotted pursuant to a board resolution cannot be lodged at least two business days prior to the consideration of the application for admission to listing, such resolution or resolutions—or failing which confirmation in writing from the company or its sponsor that the shares in question have been allotted—will be required to be delivered to the FCA no later than one hour ahead of the intended time of admission to listing becoming effective.

3.5.7 Items to be lodged on the day

The applicant must lodge with the FCA no later than 09.00 on the day of the consideration of the application for admission to listing (LR 3.3.3R) a duly completed Shareholder Statement (in the case of a new applicant) or Pricing Statement (in the case of a company whose shares are already listed).

3.5.8 Documents to be lodged later

A written confirmation of the number of shares that were allotted must be submitted to the FCA as soon as practicable after admission, if the number is lower than the number that was announced as being admitted to listing (LR 3.3.5R).

3.5.9 Additional documents

While the number of documents to be lodged with the FCA as part of the application procedure has been progressively reduced over the years, the company is still required to retain certain documents for not less than six years so that, if necessary, they can be provided to the FCA at its request (LRs 3.3.6R and 3.3.7R). These include:

(1) any agreement to acquire any assets, business or shares in consideration for, or in relation to which, the company's shares are being issued;

(2) any letter, report, valuation, contract or other documents referred to in the prospectus, listing particulars, other circular or document issued in connection with those shares;

(3) the applicant's constitution as at the date of admission;

(4) the annual report and accounts of the applicant for each of the periods which form part of the applicant's financial record contained in the prospectus;

(5) any interim accounts made up since the date to which the last annual report and accounts were made up and prior to the date of admission;

(6) in the case of an application in respect of shares issued pursuant to an employee share scheme, the scheme documents;

(7) where listing particulars or another document are published in connection with any scheme requiring court approval, any court order and the certificate of registration issued by the Registrar of Companies; and

(8) copies of board resolutions of the applicant allotting or issuing the shares.

3.5.10 Formal applications and block listings

Where a company issues shares on a regular basis (e.g. pursuant to an employee share scheme) in circumstances where there is no requirement to produce a prospectus, it may either:

(1) adopt a simplified application procedure for each issue (a "formal application"); or

(2) make an application in respect of a specified number of shares in any particular case (a "block listing").

Listing Rules 3.5.1R–3.5.6R deal with block listings mechanisms as well as the application procedures for such listings. The FCA has published a Procedural Note on Block Listings (UKLA/PN/907.2, last updated March 2015) in which it indicates that an issuer that is contemplating only infrequent allotments, is seeking flexibility "just in case", for reasons of convenience, or is merely trying to limit fees would not be in a position to justify a block listing. Whilst the FCA indicates that it does not intend to be prescriptive about when a block listing may be appropriate, a block listing would only be granted where there was a justifiable and demonstrable need.

3.6 Publication and availability of prospectuses

The final question to address in this chapter is what does the company need to do to publicise its application for listing under the Listing Rules and the Prospectus Rules?

Chapter 4 of the Listing Rules and Ch.3 of the Prospectus Rules set out the provisions relating to the requirement for companies to publish and make available prospectuses, reflecting the provisions of the Prospectus Directive.

3.6.1 Prior approval

A prospectus must not be published until it has been formally approved by the FCA (PR 3.1.10R). The FCA will only approve the relevant document on the day on which it is to be published (see s.3.6.2 below) and, therefore, the relevant logistics need to be carefully co-ordinated.

It has been customary, in the context of an IPO undertaken by way of an institutional placing, to produce a draft unapproved prospectus, clearly marked as such (commonly called a "pathfinder", a "red" or a "prelim"), for the purpose of marketing to institutional investors. A draft unapproved prospectus may only be circulated to investment professionals or other categories of persons who fall within an exemption from the financial promotion regime contained in s.21 of the FSMA. This approach is permitted under the advertisement regime in PR 3.3, provided that the draft unapproved prospectus is clearly marked as an advertisement, makes reference to the fact that a prospectus is to be published in due course and gives details of where copies of the prospectus may be obtained. It has also been possible for marketing to be conducted using a prospectus which has been approved by the FCA and does not specify the final offer price but rather includes an indicative price range.

The ability to market the offer to institutional investors using a draft unapproved prospectus may change as a result of rule changes which took effect on 1 July 2018 from the FCA's desire to increase the availability and quality of information in the UK IPO process.

As a result of its March 2017 consultation (CP 17/5), the FCA amended its *Conduct of Business Sourcebook* in order to ensure that an approved prospectus or registration document is published much earlier in the IPO process. The FCA's stated intention is to restore the primacy of an approved prospectus document as the document on which investors make their investment decision, improve the range and quality of information available to investors and facilitate the availability of such information early enough in the process to support more balanced investor education and price discovery.

The effect of the new rules is that a company will likely publish an approved registration document during the private phase of the IPO process, up to seven days prior to making a public "intention to float" announcement. It is not currently expected at the time of writing that the management roadshow will be undertaken with a tri-partite prospectus. It is more likely that the management roadshow will then be undertaken with an approved price-range prospectus (or perhaps with an unapproved "pathfinder" prospectus depending on whether the offer is being marketed only to institutional investors and then the FCA's views on whether this is compatible with the intentions behind the reforms to the UK IPO process).

After the roadshow, where an approved price-range prospectus is used, the final offer price will be set and announced to the market via the publication of a short pricing statement or, if a significant new matter has arisen since the date of publication of the prospectus, by way of a supplemental prospectus (which must also be approved by the FCA). Where the offer is priced outside of the indicative price range set out in the approved price-range prospectus, this may also trigger the need for a supplemental prospectus.

These reforms amount to a significant change to the timing of availability of information during the UK IPO process. If investors have agreed to subscribe or purchase shares on the basis of an approved price-range prospectus, investors are entitled to withdraw their applications within two working days of the final offer price or the actual number of shares being offered being notified to the FCA, unless the criteria for determining the final offer price or the offer size is disclosed or the maximum price is included (s.87Q of the FSMA). Where a prospectus relates to an offer of securities to the public (as opposed to an institutional-only placing of securities which is exempt), and a supplemental prospectus is required to be published, investors who have already agreed to subscribe for, or purchase the securities, have the right to withdraw their application.

3.6.2 Publication

Once approved by the FCA, a prospectus must formally be filed with the FCA and made available to the public (PR 3.2.1R).

The most common route for publication is by making copies available, in printed form, free of charge to the public at the registered office of the company and at the offices of the financial intermediaries distributing the shares.

Alternative methods of making a prospectus available to the public include publishing it:

(1) by making copies available, in printed form, free of charge to the public at the offices of the Exchange (or other RIE where admission to trading is sought);

(2) in one or more newspapers with wide circulation in the EEA states in which the offer is made or admission to trading is sought;

(3) in electronic form on the company's website and, if applicable, on the websites of the financial intermediaries distributing the shares; or

(4) in electronic form on the website of the Exchange (or other RIE where admission to trading is sought).

These provisions are set out in PR 3.2.4R. If a prospectus is published either in a newspaper or on the website of the Exchange (or other RIE where admission to trading is sought), the prospectus must also be made available in electronic form on the company's website (PR 3.2.4AR).

As prospectuses are increasingly being published in electronic form on the company's website, this brings into sharp focus the need to police compliance with local securities laws around the world. A company considering using this method of publication will want to ensure that appropriate safeguards, such as firewalls, are utilised.

3.6.3 *Period of time available*

The prospectus must be filed and made available to the public as soon as practicable. In any event, it must be available at a reasonable time in advance of admission to trading and certainly no later than the commencement of dealings (PR 3.2.2R).

In an IPO, the prospectus must be available to the public at least six working days before the end of the offer. This period does not, however, begin until the prospectus is approved and published. The rule changes that took effect on 1 July 2018 mean that the approved prospectus is likely to be published before commencement of the management roadshow and well in advance of admission to trading.

Chapter 4

Contents of Prospectuses

Michael Bloch and Anne Kirkwood
Allen & Overy

4.1 Introduction

A European Economic Area (EEA) prospectus must meet an onerous overarching disclosure standard and contain prescribed information about the securities, their issuer and the offer.[1]

The Prospectus Directive (2003/71)[2] provides the EEA framework for the drawing up, form and content of prospectuses that are published when securities are offered to the public or admitted to trading on a regulated market, amongst other topics. The Prospectus Directive harmonises requirements for preparing prospectuses across the EU. In itself, it provides only a framework of principles. Detailed provisions concerning prospectus format and content, the use of incorporation by reference and the advertisements regime are set out in Regulation 809/2004 (existing PD Regulation).[3]

The Prospectus Directive was amended on 31 December 2010 by Directive 2010/73 (PD Amending Directive),[4] which carried

---

[1] This chapter has been updated as at 21 July 2018.
[2] Directive 2003/71 on the prospectus to be published when securities are offered to the public or admitted to trading and amending Directive 2001/34 [2003] OJ L345/64.
[3] Regulation 809/2004 implementing Directive 2003/71 as regards information contained in prospectuses as well as the format, incorporation by reference and publication of such prospectuses and dissemination of advertisements [2004] OJ L149/3.
[4] Directive 2010/73 amending Directives 2003/71 on the prospectus to be published when securities are offered to the public or admitted to trading and

forward the framework's original objectives of ensuring investor protection and market efficiency.

It was further amended, on 23 May 2014, by Directive 2014/51 (Omnibus II).[5] In March 2016, the Financial Conduct Authority (FCA) issued the Prospectus Rules Sourcebook (Omnibus 2 Directive Regulatory Technical Standards) Instrument 2016 (FCA 2016/27) which effected changes in relation to the information that may be incorporated by reference in a prospectus and the issue of advertisements in connection with a securities offer.

The test for whether a prospectus is required, as opposed to listing particulars, turns on the nature of the securities being offered. Listing particulars (and not a prospectus) are required for only specified securities (such as non-equity securities issued by a Member State or by Member State central banks and continuous or repeated issues of certain vanilla non-equity securities by credit institutions) (Listing Rule (LR) 4.1.1). In view of this, this chapter does not comment further on the contents requirements for listing particulars. In most cases, it will be the rules governing prospectuses that will be relevant.

The contents of prospectuses published in the UK are primarily governed by Pt VI of the Financial Services and Markets Act 2000 (FSMA), the existing PD Regulation, the FCA's Prospectus Rules (PRs), the guidance of the European Securities and Markets Authority (ESMA) on the content of prospectuses and ESMA's prospectus FAQs (Version 28, March 2018). The FCA is responsible for the rules relating to prospectuses within the UK. When the FCA acts in this capacity it is referred to as the UK Listing Authority (UKLA). The PRs primarily govern the contents of prospectuses and are complemented by the LRs,

---

2004/109 on the harmonisation of transparency requirements in relation to information about issuers whose securities are admitted to trading on a regulated market [2010] OJ L327/1.

[5]   Directive 2014/51 amending Directives 2003/71 and 2009/138 and Regulations 1060/2009, 1094/2010 and 1095/2010 in respect of the powers of the European Supervisory Authority (European Insurance and Occupational Pensions Authority) and the European Supervisory Authority (European Securities and Markets Authority) [2014] OJ L153/1.

the Disclosure Guidance and Transparency Rules and the market soundings regime under the Market Abuse Regulation 596/2014 (MAR).[6]

The Prospectus Directive provides for "maximum harmonisation" of rules, which means that Member States cannot impose additional restrictions. The UKLA is, however, able to impose listing requirements and, subject to the EU Transparency Directive[7] and the MAR, continuing obligations on listed companies as the directive does not prevent the imposition of requirements that do not relate to the drawing up, content or dissemination of a prospectus.

This chapter focuses on the contents for prospectuses for equity. The requirements for debt and specialist securities are considered in Ch.8 below.

4.1.1   Forthcoming changes under the New Prospectus Regulation 2017/1129

The text of the New Prospectus Regulation 2017/1129,[8] which entered into force on 20 July 2017 (being the 20th day following its publication in the *Official Journal of the European Union*), will affect prospectus content. The New Prospectus Regulation will be directly applicable, without any implementing legislation, in all EU Member States, subject to Brexit, from the following dates:

- in the case of the majority of the provisions of the New Prospectus Regulation, from 21 July 2019;
- in the case of offers of securities to the public with a total consideration in the EU of: (1) less than €1 million,

---

[6]   Regulation 595/2014 on market abuse (market abuse regulation) and repealing Directive 2003/6 and Directives 2003/124, 2003/125 and 2004/72 [2014] OJ L173/1.

[7]   Directive 2004/109 on the harmonisation of transparency requirements in relation to information about issuers whose securities are admitted to trading on a regulated market and amending Directive 2001/34 [2004] OJ L390/38.

[8]   Regulation 2017/1129 on the prospectus to be published when securities are offered to the public or admitted to trading on a regulated market, and repealing Directive 2003/71 [2017] OJ L168/12.

calculated over a period of 12 months; and (2) an amount of up to €8 million, calculated over a period of 12 months, to be determined by each Member State. This is an optional exemption which Member States can implement, if they wish, under art.3(2)(b) of the New Prospectus Regulation. On 21 July 2018, the UK implemented this exemption at a threshold of up to €8 million; and

- in the case of two exemptions, described below in ss.4.1.1.1.4 and 4.1.1.1.5, from 20 July 2017.

4.1.1.1 Key provisions regarding prospectus content in the New Prospectus Regulation (Level 1) text

4.1.1.1.1 Risk factors

Issuers will be required to assess the materiality of risk factors based on the probability of occurrence and expected magnitude of their negative impact and may (but not must) disclose this assessment using a scale of low, medium or high. Risk factors will need to be presented in a limited number of categories depending on their nature, with the most material risk factors being mentioned first in each category.

On 13 July 2018, ESMA published its Consultation Paper on "Guidelines on risk factors under the New Prospectus Regulation", for consultation until 5 October 2018. A final report containing a final version of the Guidelines is expected to be published in Q1 2019.

ESMA has been mandated to develop these Guidelines under art.16(4) of the New Prospectus Regulation, in order to "assist competent authorities in their review of the specificity and materiality of risk factors and of the presentation of risk factors across categories depending on their nature" (p.8 of the Consultation Paper). As the draft Guidelines expand on concepts provided for under art.16, it is to be expected that the final Guidelines will come into application in July 2019, subject to Brexit. Market participants will be expected to take the

Guidelines into account when drawing up a prospectus as competent authorities will be applying them in their review process.

The consultation makes some proposals which may, depending on the outcome under the final Guidelines, impact on risk factor disclosure practice, depending on whether the relevant competent authority showed flexibility as to their application or not. For example, providing quantitative information and having to justify where this is not available and also having to justify the use of mitigating language, which is considered to compromise the materiality of risk factor disclosure, might be a challenging area to comply with.

4.1.1.1.2   Summaries

The summary shall be read as an introduction to the prospectus with a focus on the information investors need to decide which securities they want to study further. The new page limit will be seven sides of A4, subject to extension in certain circumstances, e.g. one additional side per any guarantor. The maximum number of risk factors to be included in the summary will be 15.

4.1.1.1.3   Disclosure test

There is an acknowledgement in the general duty of disclosure that the "necessary information which is material to an investor" in a prospectus may differ depending on the nature of the issuer, the type of securities, the circumstances of the issuer and the targeted investors.

4.1.1.1.4   Lighter touch regime for certain "listed" issuers

An exemption from the prospectus requirement for admission to trading of a fungible issue representing over 12 months less than 20% of securities already listed has applied since 20 July 2017. From an equity securities perspective, this extends the allowance under the previous regime from up to 10% to up to 20%. Issuers with a premium listing of shares may find this extension of limited utility as the Pre-Emption Group has stated there will be no corresponding change to the *Pre-Emption Guidelines*.[9] In addition, commercial considerations may still dictate a need to publish a prospectus even in the absence of a legal requirement to do so.

In addition, a reduced disclosure regime will apply (from July 2019, subject to Brexit) for "secondary issuances", e.g. an issue of equity or debt securities by an issuer which has had equity listed on an EEA regulated market for 18 months.

4.1.1.1.5   Convertible bonds

A new 20% limit over 12 months on shares which can be admitted to trading on an EEA regulated market without a prospectus following a conversion has applied since 20 July 2017. There was no such cap in the previous prospectus regime. There are some carve-outs from this limit relating to regulatory and solvency capital instruments.

4.1.1.1.6   Implementation

As noted above, the New Prospectus Regulation requirements will apply from July 2019 with a limited number of provisions applying sooner. It is not yet clear how much time there will be between the finalisation of the European Commission's (the Commission's) delegated acts at Level 2, which will set out much of the detail relating to the new requirements in the regulation (see below) and the application date for the bulk of the new requirements.

4.1.1.1.7   Areas covered by Commission mandates to ESMA on Level 2 delegated acts

Under mandates from the Commission to ESMA to advise on the development of delegated acts, ESMA has consulted on delegated acts covering, amongst other things:

---

[9]   Financial Reporting Council, "Pre-Emption Group Statement", PN 35/17 (27 July 2017)—no intention to change the pre-emption thresholds following the New Prospectus Regulation coming into force.

- the format of the prospectus and the schedules defining the specific information items;
- the information to be included in a simplified prospectus for a "secondary issuance";
- the criteria for scrutiny and procedures for approval of prospectuses;
- the general equivalence criteria for third-country prospectuses;
- advertisements; and
- prospectus supplements.

ESMA has published:

- on 28 March 2018, its *Final Report: Technical advice under the Prospectus Regulation* (ESMA31-62-800). This report is concerned with the format of the prospectus, the base prospectus and the final terms, the content of the share registration document, the content of the securities note, the content of the registration document for securities issued by third countries and their regional and local authorities, the content of the building block for pro forma financial information, the list of specialist issuers, the content of the secondary issuance regime; and
- on 17 July 2018, its *Final Report: Draft regulatory technical standards under the Prospectus Regulation* (ESMA31-62-1002). This report is concerned with the key financial information for inclusion in the prospectus summary, data and machine readability, advertisements, supplements and publication.

In each case, the measures remain subject to the endorsement by the European Commission, at the date of publication.

4.2 The "informed assessment" test

The overarching disclosure standard is that a prospectus must contain the necessary information to enable investors to make an informed assessment of the assets and liabilities, financial position, profits and losses, and prospects of the issuer of the securities and of any guarantor and the rights attaching to those securities (Prospectus Directive art.5(1) and PR 2.1.1). The UKLA may only approve a prospectus if this requirement is met (s.87A of the FSMA). These provisions explain that the "necessary information" must be prepared having regard to the particular nature of the securities and their issuer, and must be presented in a form which is "comprehensible and easy to analyse".

Whatever specific prospectus content requirements apply in a particular case, it is always important to consider whether the fundamental "informed assessment" test has been satisfied. It does not necessarily follow that a prospectus is complete merely because all of the detailed information required by the Prospectus Rules has been included (PR 3.1.2A).

The "informed assessment" test under s.87A of the FSMA is cast in wider terms than the previous "informed assessment" test, which still applies, by virtue of s.80 of the FSMA, in relation to listing particulars. The test under s.80 refers to such information as investors and their professional advisers would reasonably require and reasonably expect to find in the document; whereas the test under s.87A refers to the information "necessary" to assess the various factors listed. In practice, this distinction is unlikely to have a significant effect on the high standards of care that are required in preparing a prospectus.

The importance of the positive duty of disclosure is reinforced by the requirement for a prospectus to contain a responsibility statement, which is a declaration by those responsible to the effect that the information given is to the best of their knowledge in accordance with the facts and contains no omission likely to affect its import. There is also a duty on the applicant, mirroring the responsibility statement, to take reasonable care that the prospectus is, to the best of its knowledge, in accordance with the facts and contains no omission likely to affect its import.

Under Ch.8 of the FCA's Listing Rules, a sponsor of new applicants or new issuances also has to think beyond the specific disclosure requirements of the Prospectus Rules. A sponsor must:

(1) give a Sponsor's Declaration to the UKLA, pursuant to LR 8.4.3, confirming that all matters known to it which, in its reasonable opinion, should be taken into account by the UKLA in considering the application for admission to listing have been disclosed with sufficient prominence in the prospectus or otherwise in writing to the UKLA;

(2) confirm that it has come to a reasonable opinion, based on professional experience and after having made due and careful enquiry, that the applicant has satisfied the applicable requirements of the Prospectus Rules;

(3) confirm in their declaration that, to the best of their knowledge and belief, they have provided all the necessary services in LRs 8.2, 8.3 and 8.4 with due care and skill. These responsibilities include an obligation to guide the issuer in understanding and meeting its ongoing responsibilities under the Listing Rules and Disclosure Guidance and Transparency Rules (LR 8.3.1(2)); and

(4) submit a letter to the FCA setting out how the applicant satisfies the criteria for listing in the Listing Rules.

4.3 Structure and content requirements

4.3.1 General

The statutory basis for the specific contents of prospectuses (as opposed to the general disclosure provision already considered) is to be found in s.84 of the FSMA, which makes provision for prospectus rules to prescribe matters such as the required form and contents of a prospectus (including a summary) and various procedural matters.

The specific contents of prospectuses are determined by the existing PD Regulation and the PD Amending Directive. Chapter 2 of the Prospectus Rules sets out specific and detailed requirements relating to both the content and the format of a prospectus. It should be noted that ESMA's recommendations for the consistent implementation of the Prospectus Directive should be borne in mind in relation to compliance with prospectus content requirements.[10] The ESMA Q&As should also be considered, where necessary.

A "building block" approach is applied by the existing PD Regulation and is copied out, by virtue of s.84 of the FSMA, into the Prospectus Rules at PR Appendix 3. The "building block" approach uses a number of separate schedules that each contain the minimum information requirements for different types of securities or issuers. A prospectus for a given security uses the combination of schedules and building blocks specified for that security by Annex XVIII to the existing PD Regulation. The "schedules" are arranged so that Annexes I, IV, VII, IX, XI, XV, XVI and XVII set out the minimum require-ments relating to an issuer and Annexes III, V, XII and XIII set out the minimum disclosure requirements relative to the securities.

The Prospectus Directive regime does not allow a competent authority to relax the contents requirements for particular types of issue. In terms of the structure, a prospectus is required to comprise four parts:

(1)   a table of contents;
(2)   the summary (where required);
(3)   risk factors; and
(4)   other information as required by the schedules and building blocks.

The issuer or other person required to prepare the prospectus must include the required information in that particular order.

---

[10] ESMA, *ESMA update of the CESR recommendations: the consistent implementation of Regulation 809/2004 implementing the Prospectus Directive*, ESMA/2013/319 (20 March 2013).

4.3.2 Separate documents

A prospectus must consist of three principal components, which can either be standalone documents which together comprise a tripartite prospectus or which are combined in a single document:

(1) a summary;
(2) a registration document containing information relating to the issuer; and
(3) a securities note providing details of the securities to be offered.

4.3.2.1 Summary

A summary must be written concisely, in non-technical language and must provide the key information relevant to understanding the securities which are the subject of the prospectus and, when read with the rest of the prospectus, must be an aid to investors considering whether to invest in the securities. The length of the summary should take into account the complexity of the issuer and of the securities offered but should not exceed 7% of the length of the prospectus or 15 pages, whichever is the longer. The summary is intended to be a standalone document and must not contain cross-references to other parts of the prospectus. A summary, however, is not required in the listing of non-equity securities with a denomination of at least €100,000 (or an equivalent amount unless a host Member State has exercised the option in art.19.4 of the Prospectus Directive to require a summary to be drawn up in official language).

A summary should be constructed on a modular basis so as to contain the key information items set out in Annex XXII of the existing PD Regulation. This information is organised in five mandatory tables with the following headings: "Introduction and Warnings"; "Issuer and Any Guarantor"; "Securities"; "Risks"; and "Offer". The order of the sections and of the items within each section are mandatory. Where an item is not applicable to a prospectus, it should be included with a "not applicable" reference.

Within the "Introduction and Warnings" table, there is a warning note that the summary should be read as an introduction to the prospectus and that any decision to invest in the securities should be based on a consideration of the prospectus as a whole. The scope of civil liability for the summary under s.90 of the FSMA is consistent with this approach. A person responsible for the contents of the prospectus is liable to pay compensation under s.90 in respect of the summary, including any translation of it, only to the extent that, when read together with the other parts of the prospectus, the summary is misleading, inaccurate or inconsistent or does not provide key information (s.90(12) of the FSMA). "Key information" is the information which is essential to enable investors to understand the relevant securities to which the prospectus relates and to decide whether to consider the offer further (s.87A(9) of the FSMA). This includes: the essential characteristics and risks associated with the issuer and any guarantor, including their assets, liabilities and financial positions, and the investment in the relevant security, including any rights attaching to them; the general terms, including an estimate of the expenses charged to an investor by the issuer; the details of the admission to trading; and the reasons for the offer and proposed use of proceeds (s.87A(10) of the FSMA).

There is a higher threshold for the inclusion of risks in the prospectus summary than for the risk section in the main body. The summary should only contain the "key risks" whereas the risk section should contain all "material risks" (see further s.4.4.3 below). In its Technical Note on Risk factors (UKLA/TN/621.3, last updated March 2015), the UKLA has emphasised that the difference in threshold is intentional and that it will challenge the disclosure of non-key risks in the summary. The UKLA has prescribed pro forma wording that can be used by issuers to remind investors to consider all the risk factors and not just those in the summary.

4.3.2.2 *Registration documents*

The registration document contains company-specific information about the issuer. Registration documents that have been approved and filed with the UKLA will be valid for 12 months (subject to the requirement to update with supplements, if necessary, and, for new applicants, the requirement set out in PR 6.1.3R(1)(b) that the latest balance sheet should not be dated more than nine months before the date the shares are admitted to listing). The approved registration document can be combined with a summary and an offer-specific securities note for making further offerings or applications for admission to trading within that 12-month period. The summary and securities note will, however, require separate UKLA approval.

This "tripartite" document system replaced the former shelf registration system, of which only a limited number of issuers took advantage. Article 9 of the New Prospectus Regulation introduces the new concept of a "universal registration document", which is intended for use by frequent issuers of securities which have their registered offices in a Member State and which is based on an existing French concept. The Commission is of the view that this new form of disclosure document, which would set out disclosure on an issuer and form one of the constituent parts of a prospectus alongside a securities note and a summary, will bring a number of benefits for frequent issuers. These benefits would include fast track approval of a prospectus, which includes a universal registration document as one of its components, the ability to satisfy the Transparency Directive's ongoing financial disclosure requirements through inclusion of such disclosure in the universal registration document and the ability to use such a document without its prior approval by a competent authority after three years of approval in the normal manner. Market participants are waiting for the finalisation of delegated acts setting out the minimum content requirements for these documents.

In the case of an offer programme of non-equity securities (including warrants in any form) or of non-equity securities issued in a continuous or repeated manner by credit institutions, the issuer may issue a "base prospectus" and supplement it as necessary. The contents of a base prospectus are essentially the same as that of an ordinary prospectus except that it is permissible to omit items which are not known at the time of approval and can only be known at the time of the individual issue. Where neither the base prospectus nor any supplementary prospectus contains the final terms, the document which is issued to set these out is known as "final terms". An indication of what the final terms will contain and how they will be published must be given in the base prospectus. It is worth noting that, although the base prospectus for an offering programme is only valid for up to 12 months, the base prospectus for non-equity securities issued by a credit institution is valid until no more securities are being issued in a continuous or repeated manner. Issuers should bear in mind that under these circumstances the updating requirements in the Prospectus Directive apply during the whole period in which the prospectus is valid. The use of a base prospectus and final terms, for non-equity securities, is not considered further.

4.3.2.3 Securities note

The securities note provides information on the securities and the offer. It must include information on the securities offered or on the securities for which admission to trading is sought, as well as any information which should normally be provided in the registration document if there has been a material change or recent development liable to affect investors' decision since the last approved registration document or approval of the last supplement. Specific content requirements for the securities note are set out in further detail in this chapter, particularly at s.4.4.12 below.

4.3.3 Building blocks

For the registration document, the level of disclosure is determined by the type of security concerned. There are individual arrangements for: shares; debt and derivatives in denominations per unit of less than €100,000; debt and derivatives in denominations per unit of €100,000 or more; asset-backed securities; bank debt and derivatives; closed-end collective investment undertakings; states; regional/local authorities; and public international bodies. Annex XVIII is the Table of Combinations, or Road Map, the purpose of which is to help guide the issuer through disclosure requirements. Recital 6 to the existing PD Regulation states:

> "In most cases, given the variety of issuers, the type of securities, the involvement or not of a third party as a guarantor, whether or not there is a listing etc., one single schedule will not give the appropriate information for an investor to make his investment decision. Therefore the combination of various schedules should be possible."

For transactions with a major effect on the issuer's business, defined as a more than 25% variation in one or more indicators of size, there is an additional building block concerning the provision of financial information on the acquired entity. This does not apply where merger accounting is required.

For the securities note, one or more of four schedules will apply for: shares; debt in denominations per unit of less than €100,000; debt in denominations per unit of €100,000 or more; and derivative securities. There are additional building blocks in respect of guarantees, asset-backed securities and the underlying share for convertible or otherwise exchangeable securities.

Together, these are intended to cover most scenarios. Complex or unusual securities should be handled by combining the building blocks. However, for securities with features that are completely different from the types listed, the UKLA may derogate from the restriction on seeking information over and above that specified.

4.3.4   ESMA and UKLA guidance

4.3.4.1   Further guidance on the contents of the prospectus may be found in the recommendations issued by the ESMA

ESMA published, and regularly updates, a "Q&As" guide which is intended to provide market participants with common positions agreed by ESMA members. The guidance can be helpful in determining the scope of the obligations under the Prospectus Directive regime. The Q&As include responses to questions relating to passporting, risk factors, supplementary prospectuses and disclosure of pro forma financial information. The latest edition is Version 28, dated March 2018.

The UKLA has published a series of technical and procedural notes (Technical Notes), which bring together the still valid and, in some cases, updated articles from *List!* (including updated rule references where relevant), key guidance themes and topics. Where relevant, these are referred to throughout this chapter.

The Technical Notes consider a number of topics, including eligibility for listing, governance, working capital, profit forecasts, regulatory announcements, prospectus content and sponsors. While the Technical Notes are not formal FCA guidance, these publications offer useful pointers to the UKLA's approach to the prospectus regime. The Technical Notes have thrown light on troublesome areas such as the disclosure requirements in limited access situations. The UKLA has also published a series of articles entitled "Factsheet" which, although again they do not contain formal UKLA guidance, do provide very useful question and answer format pointers on UKLA processes and procedures.

4.3.5   Incorporation by reference

The Prospectus Directive (art.11) and the Prospectus Rules permit the incorporation of certain information into the prospectus (except the summary) by reference to previously or simultaneously published documents that have been approved by the UKLA or filed with it. (ESMA confirmed that this may be the case even for information from prospectuses which are no longer valid.) Some competent authorities (for example, the UKLA) permit the incorporation by reference of documents that have been approved by, or filed with, another competent authority where this was the competent authority in the issuer's home Member State at the time of approval or filing.

There are detailed rules in art.28 of the existing PD Regulation and PR 2.4 regarding the types of documents that might be incorporated by reference, for example, the issuer's annual and interim financial information. Any information being so incorporated must be the latest available to the issuer and a hard copy of it must be submitted with the prospectus to the UKLA for vetting and approval.

Article 28.2 of the existing PD Regulation provides (as confirmed in the ESMA Q&As) that an issuer can incorporate by reference a document drawn up in a different language than that of the prospectus, provided that the language of the incorporated document is one of the languages accepted in the home/host Member State, as relevant. (This means that, if, for example, an issuer wanted to make a non-exempt public offer in the UK, a passported prospectus would not be acceptable if it incorporated by reference French language financial statements.)

4.4 Specific contents requirements

4.4.1 *General*

The Prospectus Directive is a "maximum harmonisation" directive, which also means that the UKLA cannot impose a higher disclosure standard than is set out in the existing PD Regulation. However, there are specific regimes in relation to property companies, mineral companies, investment companies, scientific research-based companies, companies with less than three years' existence and shipping companies.

This chapter will consider the contents requirements by reference to the most onerous schedule, namely that applying to a prospectus relating to shares or transferable securities equivalent to shares. For other types of security for which a prospectus is required, the regime is in general more relaxed, particularly in the case of wholesale debt securities.

Please see Ch.8 below for the disclosure requirements applicable to debt securities.

4.4.2   *Persons responsible and auditors*

The most important item in s.1 ("Persons Responsible") of Annex I to the existing PD Regulation is the declaration of responsibility for the information given in the prospectus. The schedule requires a list of "persons responsible" being:

> "all persons responsible for the information given in the Registration Document and, as the case may be, for certain parts of it, with, in the latter case, an indication of such parts".

The Prospectus Directive requires responsibility to attach at least to the issuer or its administrative, management or supervisory bodies, the offeror, the person asking for admission to listing or the guarantor. Otherwise, it leaves the choice of who is to be regarded as responsible for the prospectus to the Member States.

Prospectus Rules 5.5.3 and 5.5.4 set out the persons responsible for prospectuses relating to equity and non-equity securities, respectively. Equity securities are shares and other transferable securities comprised in a company's share capital, as well as any other type of transferable securities issued by that company or any entity in the same group as that company, giving the right to acquire securities as a consequence of them being converted or the rights conferred by them being exercised.

For equity securities, the persons responsible are the issuer, its existing and named future directors, each person who is a senior executive of any external management company of the issuer, those who expressly accept responsibility in the prospectus, the offeror and its directors, the applicant for listing and its directors and, finally, anyone who authorises the contents of the prospectus. For non-equity securities, including convertible securities, directors do not have to accept responsibility. The persons responsible are the issuer, those who expressly accept responsibility, the offeror or applicant, any guarantor in relation to information about the guarantee and anyone who authorises the contents of the prospectus. It is worth noting that the Prospectus Directive requires someone to be responsible for the whole of the prospectus (including information sourced from third parties) so that "split" responsibility statements are not possible. Statements of responsibility for parts of a prospectus remain possible but only for those who accept responsibility for or who "authorise the contents" of the prospectus (PR 5.5.8). Note that ESMA confirmed the position that one person must take responsibility for the whole prospectus, notwithstanding that there might be different persons responsible for particular parts, and provided guidance on the issue of responsibility of a guarantor. Issuers should also be mindful of not including other disclosures in the prospectus which could be seen to qualify the responsibility statement.

The meaning of the expression "authorise the contents" is not clear. It may mean that it imposes liability on senior management below board level to whom the board has delegated the responsibility for finalising the document, or on whom the board is relying in relation to the provision of information for inclusion in it. Alternatively, it could mean that it imposes liability on a residual category of persons who have had some measure of control over the document. The market consensus view is that professional advisers, such as lawyers and accountants who may in practice also have influence on the drafting, will not be responsible for the prospectus provided all that they have done is to give advice as to its contents in a professional capacity (PR 5.5.9).

Note that the defences available in Sch.10 and 10A to the FSMA against liability under s.90 of the FSMA apply to prospectuses (s.90(11) of the FSMA) and take account of the information available to different categories of persons. A person responsible for any false or misleading statement in the prospectus will not incur liability to compensate persons suffering any resultant loss if, among other exceptions, he/she satisfies the court that at the time when the document was submitted to the UKLA, he/she reasonably believed, having made such enquiries (if any) as were reasonable, that the statement was true and not misleading or that the matter, the omission of which caused the loss, was properly omitted.

4.4.3 *Selected financial information and risk factors*

Sections 3 ("Selected Financial Information") and 4 ("Risk Factors") of Annex 1 to the existing PD Regulation require the inclusion of selected financial information and prominent disclosure of risk factors specific to the issuer or its industry. Risk factors should be grouped together in a coherent manner and risk factors considered to be of the greatest or most immediate significance should be given due prominence at the beginning of the risk factors section or the relevant group within the risk factors section.

Risks that require disclosure could include circumstances having an adverse impact on supply, on the prices at which supplies can be secured, on the selling price of goods or on the issuer's competitive position in various markets.

In its Technical Note on Risk factors (UKLA/TN/621.3), the UKLA said that it was of the view that there had been an increasing tendency for the risk factors section to include more generic, standardised risk factors which do not appear to be directly relevant for the particular issuer. The UKLA therefore reminded issuers that only risks specific to them or their industries should be included in the prospectus. Simple statements of fact that contain no explanation of the risks in the context of the issuer's business would not be sufficient.

The UKLA has discussed the interaction between risk factors and working capital statements in its Technical Note on Working capital statements and risk factors (UKLA/TN/321.1, last updated December 2012). See s.4.4.12 below for discussion on this important topic.

The selected financial information must provide the key figures that summarise the financial condition of the issuer in respect of the three financial years preceding the issue of the prospectus (or such shorter period that the issuer has been in operation). If selected information for interim periods is provided, comparative data for the same period in the previous financial year must also be provided. ESMA offered guidance in its Q&As covering situations in which the issuer changes an accounting policy in its financial statements between reporting periods.

4.4.4   *Information about the issuer and business overview*

A number of different sections require the inclusion of information concerning the issuer's business and group structure. Section 5 ("Information about the Issuer") of Annex 1 to the existing PD Regulation requires certain formal information regarding the issuer, together with a description of the important events in the development of its business. Disclosure is also required under s.5 of the main investments made in the last three years and in the current financial year and the principal investments currently being made (including their geographical location and method of financing), together with information about all future investments in respect of which firm commitments have been made. Any information given as to future investment programmes should be factored into the projections underlying the working capital statement required by s.3.1 of Annex III to the Prospectus Rules, or any other projections on the basis of which statements in the prospectus are being made.

The disclosure requirements in relation to the issuer's core business are contained in s.6 ("Business Overview") of Annex 1 to the existing PD Regulation. If it has more than one main business or geographical market, it will be necessary to break down the activities or markets into categories to enable investors to assess the relative importance of each activity. The main categories of products sold and/or services performed and any significant new products sold and/or activities undertaken must be stated. Total revenues during the past three financial years must be broken down by category of activity and into geographical markets. Where any of this information has been influenced by exceptional factors, that fact should be explained. In addition, the document must explain the basis for any statement made by the issuer regarding its competitive position.

Another potentially important area of disclosure in this context is the requirement in s.6.4 of Annex 1 to the existing PD Regulation to provide summary information regarding the extent to which the issuer is dependent on patents, licences, industrial, commercial or financial contracts, or new manufacturing processes if these are material to the issuer's business or its profitability. Depending on the particular circumstances, if the issuer is concerned about protecting commercial confidentiality in respect of important business arrangements, it may be possible to persuade the UKLA that the extent of the disclosure can be tempered in order to avoid the risk of serious detriment to the issuer (providing that the omission is not likely to mislead investors with regard to facts and circumstances that are essential for the assessment of the securities in question).

Section 7 ("Organisational Structure") of Annex 1 to the existing PD Regulation requires a brief description of the issuer's group (if relevant) and the issuer's position in the group. This section also requires a list of significant subsidiaries, which must include specified details such as the name and country of incorporation or residence.

Section 8 ("Property, Plants and Equipment") of Annex 1 to the existing PD Regulation requires the disclosure of information about existing or planned material tangible fixed assets (including real estate) owned or leased, together with information about environmental issues that may affect their use.

Section 9 ("Operating and Financial Review") of Annex 1 to the existing PD Regulation is a key section from the perspective of investors as it requires a description of the issuer's financial condition and changes in its financial condition, as well as results of operations for each year and the interim period for which financial information is required, to the extent not covered elsewhere in the document. This should include an explanation of the causes of material changes from year to year in the financial information to the extent necessary to understand the issuer's business as a whole. When discussing a company's development and performance for a given year of the track record, the UKLA recommends that issuers consider drawing a comparison with the preceding year. Under s.9, if there have been any significant factors materially affecting the issuer's income from operations, then these must be disclosed. Strikes or the elimination of an important supply source are examples of factors which might call for disclosure in this area. It may also be necessary to consider circumstances arising more than 12 months ago, if the effect of those circumstances upon the financial position of the group has only materialised in the last 12 months. Where the financial statements disclose material changes in net sales or revenues, there needs to be a narrative description of the reasons for the changes. In addition, information must be included regarding any governmental, economic, fiscal, monetary or political policies, or factors that have materially affected, or could materially affect, the issuer's operations, whether directly or indirectly. There is clearly considerable scope for the commentary on these matters to overlap with the risk factors section of the document. It will be important to ensure that a consistent message is given throughout the prospectus about the environment in which the issuer operates and the risks that it faces.

Information must be given under s.11 ("Research and Development, Patents and Licences") of Annex 1 to the existing PD Regulation concerning the issuer's policy as to research and development where this has been material over each of the past three financial years. In addition, s.17 ("Employees") of Annex 1 to the existing PD Regulation requires the disclosure of details of the average number of employees or their

163

numbers at the end of the financial year and of any material changes which have occurred in the last three financial years (together, if possible and material, with a breakdown of persons employed by main categories of activity and geographical location).

Finally, s.12 ("Trend Information") of Annex 1 to the existing PD Regulation requires the prospectus to include information on the most significant recent trends in production, sales and inventory, costs and selling prices since the end of the last financial period. To this is added information on known trends, uncertainties, demands, commitments or events that are "reasonably likely" to have a material effect on the issuer's prospects for at least the current financial year. Section 12 therefore has a forward-looking limb and a backward-looking limb. According to the UKLA, initial submissions commonly lack one of the two. In relation to the forward-looking limb, issuers should also be careful that their disclosure is not an unintentional profit forecast as this will be subject to s.13 ("Profit Forecasts or Estimates") of Annex 1 to the existing PD Regulation. As already noted above, it is important to consider whether the "informed assessment" test is met; it is particularly important for an issuer to consider whether the current trading and prospects information included in the prospectus gives a fair and balanced picture when measured against that wider test and when considered in the light of the other information in the prospectus.

4.4.5   The management

Through disclosure, the issuer should explain how a new applicant's directors and senior management collectively have appropriate experience to manage the group's business. Section 14 ("Administrative, Management, and Supervisory Bodies and Senior Management") of Annex 1 to the existing PD Regulation supports that approach by providing for the inclusion of information about the management expertise and experience of members of the issuer's administrative, management or supervisory bodies, its partners, founders and any senior managers. This includes names, business addresses and functions within the issuer, together with an indication of the principal activities performed by the relevant directors or managers outside the issuer where these are significant with respect to the issuer. Other details to be included are items such as the names of all companies and partnerships in which the relevant director or member of management has been a member of the administrative, management or supervisory bodies or a partner in the previous five years and details of bankruptcies, receiverships and liquidations with which the individual has been associated as a member of an administrative, management or supervisory body, a partner, a founder or a senior manager. Also disclosable are convictions in relation to fraudulent offences in at least the last five years and details of public criticisms. An appropriate negative statement is required where there is no relevant information to disclose.

Section 15 ("Remuneration and Benefits") of Annex 1 to the existing PD Regulation requires the prospectus to disclose the amount of remuneration paid on an individual rather than aggregate basis, including deferred or contingent compensation, and benefits in kind granted to the individuals listed above by the issuer or any member of the group during the last completed financial year under any description whatsoever. Amounts set aside by the issuer or its subsidiaries to pay pensions or retirement benefits to the individuals listed above must also be disclosed. Details of the terms of office and any benefits to be provided on termination of employment should be given.

Any potential conflicts of interest must be clearly stated or a negative statement made. Any arrangement or understanding with major shareholders, customers, suppliers or others which allows them to appoint a member of the issuer's senior management or administrative, management or supervisory bodies must also be disclosed.

Section 16 ("Board Practices") of Annex 1 to the existing PD Regulation requires the prospectus to include information on the terms of office and service contracts of the management and other key persons including benefits payable on termination. Information about the audit and remuneration committees and details regarding compliance with domestic corporate governance requirements must also be given.

The prospectus must also disclose the interests of the directors in the issuer's capital, including stock options, and any restrictions on their disposal. Details of any schemes involving employees in the capital of the issuer must be given. Finally, the prospectus must summarise the provisions of the memorandum and articles of association of the issuer with respect to the members of the administrative, management and supervisory bodies.

4.4.6 *Financial information*

Section 20 ("Financial Information Concerning the Issuer's Assets and Liabilities, Financial Position and Profits and Losses") of Annex 1 to the existing PD Regulation, supplemented by ss.9, 10 and 13, contains most of the requirements in relation to financial information about the issuer. Three years of audited financial information must be presented and prepared in accordance with the International Financial Reporting Standards (IFRS) or "equivalent" accounting standards.

The European Commission has acknowledged the equivalence of the US and Japanese Generally Accepted Accounting Principles (GAAPs) and the GAAPs of Canada, China and South Korea.[11] The European Commission has provided for extensions of the transitional equivalence status of India until 31 March 2016 because of delays in India's implementation of the IFRS; there has been no further update since.

Where a country's standards are not equivalent to the IFRS, the accounts must be restated. The UKLA has stated in the past that it encourages issuers and their advisers to contact them at

---

[11] Regulation 311/2012 amending Regulation 809/2004 implementing Directive 2003/71 as regards elements related to prospectuses and advertisements [2012] OJ L103/13.

an early stage if they are intending to present financial information under an equivalent standard.

An accountants' report on the financial and other information contained in the prospectus has not been routinely required for some time but, in practice, in relation to new issues, sponsors continue to instruct reporting accountants to produce a long-form report. An independent accountants' or auditors' report will be required where the building block for pro forma financial information is applicable. This applies in any case where there is a variation of more than 25% relative to one or more indicators of the size of the issuer's business as a result of a particular transaction, except where merger accounting is required.

Dividend policy and restrictions thereon and dividends per share for the last three years must be shown, as adjusted, where the number of shares has changed, to make it comparable.

Section 20.8 of Annex I to the existing PD Regulation, copied out into the FCA's Prospectus Rules at PR Appendix 3, states that, if quarterly or half yearly financial information has been published by an issuer since the date of the last audited financial statements, such information must be included in the prospectus. If the quarterly or half-yearly financial information was audited or reviewed, the audit or review report must also be included in the prospectus. If not, a negative statement to that effect must be included.

Where more than nine months have elapsed since the end of the financial year to which the last published annual accounts relate, the prospectus must contain interim financial informa-tion covering at least the first six months of the current financial year together with an indication that the statement is unaudited (if that is the case) (s.20.6 ("Interim and Other Financial Information") of Annex 1 to the existing PD Regulation). Whether or not nine months have elapsed since the last published annual accounts, the latest published quarterly or half-yearly financial information must be included in the prospectus. The interim financial information must include comparative statements for the same period in the prior financial period except that the requirement for comparative balance sheet information may be satisfied by presenting the year's end balance sheet.

Section 25 ("Information on Holdings") of Annex 1 to the existing PD Regulation requires information to be given on undertakings in which the issuer holds a proportion of capital likely to have a significant effect on the assessment of its own assets and liabilities, financial position or profits and losses. Section 10 ("Capital Resources") of Annex 1 to the existing PD Regulation requires information on the issuer's short and long-term capital resources, including cash flow, borrowing and material restrictions on the use of capital resources. ESMA advised that this description should include information on ratios such as interest cover and gearing. Detailed information on indebtedness is a part of the securities note, not the registration document. Issuers of equity securities are no longer asked to consider whether there has been a change in the indebtedness of the group which would require disclosure as a significant change in its financial position, although this type of information may require disclosure as a risk under s.4, a change under s.9 or 20, or a trend under s.12. In any event, the issuer must disclose its borrowing requirements and funding structure.

The Prospectus Rules address the situation where issuers have complex financial histories, where financial information covering the principal business of the issuer is not included in the financial statements drawn up by the issuer but is contained in financial statements drawn up by other parties. It may be necessary to include standalone information for any acquired entity if an issuer has made material acquisitions or disposals in the three-year track period or was about to do so and has made a "significant commitment" or was about to do so (art.4 of the existing PD Regulation). The intention is to require the inclusion of all historical financial information necessary for investors to make informed assessments of the financial condition and prospects of issuers with complex financial histories.

4.4.7 *Profit forecasts*

Care is needed to ensure that the description of the issuer's trading position and prospects do not inadvertently constitute a profit forecast that would need to be reported on in the prospectus by the inclusion of a report prepared by independent accountants or auditors. The 28th edition of ESMA's Q&As published on 28 March 2018 specifically states that a "substance over form" approach should be taken when determining whether a statement is a profit forecast and gives more detail on what kind of information may fall within the definition of a "profit forecast". This makes it even more likely that forward-looking statements previously published by a listed issuer will be considered to constitute forecasts. If the issuer chooses to give a profit forecast or estimate, it must comply with the various requirements in s.13 ("Profit Forecasts or Estimates") of Annex 1 to the existing PD Regulation as to disclosure of the assumptions on which the forecast is based and the inclusion of reports from reporting accountants. There has to be a clear distinction drawn between assumptions about factors which the directors and management can influence and factors which are exclusively outside their influence. Assumptions must be readily understandable by investors, be specific and precise, and not relate to the general accuracy of the estimates underlying the forecast.

In its Q&A No.84, ESMA helpfully confirms that cumulative figures for a full financial year as disclosed in Q4 reports should be considered interims and not a profit forecast.

4.4.8 *Legal and arbitration proceedings*

Information has to be given under s.20.8 of Annex 1 to the existing PD Regulation on any governmental, legal or arbitration proceedings (including any such proceedings that are pending or threatened of which the issuer is aware) which may have, or have had in the recent past (covering at least the previous 12 months), a significant effect on the group's financial position. Sometimes the issuer is conscious of circumstances that could give rise to proceedings but is reluctant to disclose their existence in case the resultant publicity, particularly in the context of a disclosure about litigation, increases the likelihood of proceedings being instituted. However, this is unlikely to be acceptable given that an appropriate negative statement is required where there is none.

Ultimately, it is likely that any conflict in this area can only be satisfactorily resolved in favour of fair disclosure of the relevant circumstances and of what the directors reasonably believe, in light of the legal advice which they have received, to be the strength of the company's position.

The existence of circumstances that could give rise to proceedings, but which are neither threatened nor pending, would not seem to call for disclosure under this section. In deciding whether or not it is necessary to disclose the existence of circumstances that could give rise to proceedings, careful attention must, however, be given not only to the precise wording of the litigation disclosure statement itself but also to the general "informed assessment" requirement.

This disclosure obligation also extends to proceedings which have been concluded but which have had a significant effect on the group's position in the recent past.

4.4.9   *Material contracts*

An important area covered by s.22 ("Material Contracts") of Annex 1 to the existing PD Regulation concerns the disclosure of material contracts. The Prospectus Rules require the inclusion of details of contracts entered into in the two years before publication of the document and of any other contract entered into at any time which contains an obligation or entitlement which is material to the group as at the date of the document. There is no hard and fast rule by which to identify a material contract but such a contract is normally recognisable—in short, it is something which is "significant" to the company. This is a matter of judgement, much depends on the particular company in question. Regard should also be had to the general "informed assessment" test under s.87A of the FSMA, considered above.

There is an exception from the disclosure requirement for contracts entered into in the ordinary course of business. The word "ordinary" should be stressed since it is quite possible that a particular contract of considerable importance to the company's business is entered into in the course of that business but not in the ordinary course. Moreover, it is always important to remember that a particularly significant contract, for example, with a supplier on whom the issuer is materially dependent, may have been entered into in the ordinary course of business but will still require disclosure, either under the general "informed assessment" test or under the specific disclosure requirements in relation to business activities, considered above. However, such a contract may not constitute a "material contract" which is required to be summarised. The test of what is material has to be determined at the date of the prospectus—if any active provisions under a contract that was material a year ago cease to be, such contract may no longer be material and may not call for disclosure.

4.4.10 *Major shareholders and related parties*

The protection of minority shareholder interests from controlling shareholders is covered by the criteria for admission to a premium listing, as set out in the Listing Rules.

Listing Rule 6.5.1 requires new applicants for a premium listing to demonstrate that, despite having a controlling shareholder, they are able to carry on an independent business as their main activity. The Listing Rules provide guidance on the circumstances that may suggest an applicant is not carrying on an independent business, which focus on the influence of any controlling shareholder(s) over the applicant's business (LR 6.5.3). A "controlling shareholder" includes any person who exercises or controls, on their own, or together with any

171

person with whom they are acting in concert, 30% or more of the votes able to be cast on all or substantially all matters at a general meeting of the applicant (see the Glossary to the *FCA Handbook*). It is worth noting that applicants that have controlling shareholders are required to put in place certain protections to preserve the independence of the applicant's business, including a relationship agreement between the applicant and its controlling shareholder(s) (LR 6.5.4) and provisions within its constitution governing the election of independent directors (LR 9.2.2E–F). Furthermore, sponsors are required to confirm that the company can comply with the "Listing Principles" (set out in s.7.2 below), one of which is equality of treatment for members.

In addition, information must be included in the prospectus regarding the holders of notifiable interests in the issuer's capital (in the UK, those interested in 3% or more of the issuer's total voting rights and capital), so far as known to the issuer. Under s.18 ("Major Shareholders") of Annex 1 to the existing PD Regulation, the issuer must also state whether it is directly or indirectly owned or controlled and by whom. The statement must describe the nature of the control and the measures in place to ensure that control is not abused.

The s.18 ("Major Shareholders") rules also require disclosure of any arrangements known to the issuer, the operation of which may result in a change of control over it. Section 19 ("Related Party Transactions") of Annex 1 to the existing PD Regulation requires disclosure of certain related party transactions during the last three financial years.

4.4.11   Other matters

Where a statement or report attributed to a person as an expert is included in the prospectus, the prospectus must state the expert's name, business address, qualifications and material interests (if any) in the issuer. If the report has been produced at the issuer's request, a statement must be added to confirm that it is included, in the form and context in which it is included, with the consent of the person who has authorised the contents of that part of the registration document. There has been some debate as to whether extracts from, or references to, market research reports are to be treated as having been prepared by experts. The answer will generally depend on whether the relevant report has been published and is in the public domain or whether it has been commissioned by the issuer for the purposes of the transaction.

Fine detail is required by s.21 ("Additional Information") of Annex 1 to the existing PD Regulation about the company's issued share capital. The amounts of authorised and issued share capital have to be stated. Details of recent share issues and those holding options over the share capital of the company also have to be disclosed.

Section 24 ("Documents on Display") of Annex 1 to the existing PD Regulation requires the prospectus to contain a statement that, for the life of the registration document, copies of the following documents, where applicable, may be inspected:

(1) the memorandum and articles of association of the issuer;
(2) all reports, letters or other documents, historical financial information and valuations and statements prepared by any expert at the issuer's request, any part of which is included or referred to in the listing particulars; and
(3) the historical financial information of the issuer or, in the case of a group, the historical financial information for the issuer and its subsidiary undertakings for each of the two financial years preceding the publication of the registration document.

ESMA has clarified that it is not necessary to display material contracts and only a summary of their details is required to be disclosed in the prospectus. The UKLA has separately confirmed this point and further clarified that it does not follow from the ESMA clarification that non-material contracts should be put on display.

4.4.12 The share securities note

The securities note may be published separately from the registration document and requires a similar declaration of responsibility. The securities statement must also contain prominent disclosure of risk factors material to the given securities (in contrast to the risk factors material to the issuer or its industry that are required to be disclosed in the registration document).

Section 3.1 of Annex III to the Prospectus Rules deals with a very important matter—the statement as to the adequacy of the issuer's working capital. The requirement is to include a statement by the issuer that, in its opinion, it has sufficient working capital for its present requirements or, if not, how it proposes to provide the additional working capital needed. ESMA's update of the CESR's[12] recommendations on the subject of working capital include[13]:

(1) working capital should be sufficient for at least the next 12 months;

(2) financing facilities that are taken into account should exist at the date of the prospectus and issuers are expected to have undertaken appropriate procedures to support the statement made (including sensitivity analysis); and

(3) there should be no disclosure of detailed assumptions underlying the working capital statement, unless it is qualified. The basis for this is that detailed disclosure of assumptions to a clean working capital statement will put the onus on the investors to reach their own conclusion as to the adequacy of working capital and hence detract from the value of the working capital statement. Note that, while it is not normally acceptable to have detailed assumptions alongside a clean working capital statement, the UKLA has taken the view that this does not prevent the continuation of the practice of disclosing the basis on

---

[12] CESR—the former Committee of European Securities Regulators.

[13] ESMA, *ESMA update of the CESR recommendations: the consistent implementation of Regulation 809/2004 implementing the Prospectus Directive*, ESMA/2013/319 (20 March 2013).

which the working capital statement is made (for instance, "taking into account existing bank facilities").[14]

ESMA's recommendations also state that issuers should ensure that there is very little risk that the basis of a working capital statement is later called into question. In practice, the margins of available cash and facilities as against cash requirements may be considerable and the extent of verification necessary to support the working capital statement will be tailored accordingly. Nevertheless, the financial projections which are normally produced to support the working capital statement can be an invaluable cross-check against much of what is of real substance in the prospectus, such as the current trading position and the future prospects and investment intentions of the issuer. The UKLA emphasises that:

> "[t]he document as a whole … is consistent with the risk factor disclosure".[15]

In its Technical Note on Working capital statements and risk factors (UKLA/TN/321.1), the UKLA reminded market participants that there is the potential for a significant degree of overlap between the risk factors section of a prospectus and the issuer's working capital statement. Issuers might, instead of providing a qualified statement, have a desire to draft the risk factors broadly and generically or to include in the risk factors section potential caveats (such as a disclaimer that states the risk factors are not intended to qualify the issuer's working capital statement) to a clean statement. However, the UKLA is of the view that certain risk factor disclosures are fundamentally inconsistent and can never be reconciled with a clean working capital statement. In such circumstances, the UKLA will be prepared to challenge an issuer's prospectus and/or working capital statement.

---

[14] Technical Note on Working capital statements—Basis of preparation (UKLA/TN/320.1, last updated December 2012).
[15] Technical Note on Working capital statements and risk factors (UKLA/TN/321.1), p.2.

The UKLA has stressed that it will not be appropriate for an issuer to simply remove or redraft the risk factors if the effect would lead to deficient disclosure which prevents investors from making informed assessments of the financial condition and prospects of the issuer. Instead, the UKLA will either require the issuer to address the facts underlying the risk factors or provide the working capital statement on a qualified basis. As has been emphasised by the UKLA, a prospectus should present a clear picture of the issuer's position that is consistent as a whole. The UKLA encourages issuers to maintain a meaningful dialogue with it if there are concerns that certain risk disclosures might not be consistent with a clean working capital statement. It should be noted, however, that, as the UKLA has clarified, not all risk factors dealing with matters of funding or finance are necessarily inconsistent with a clean working capital statement. Similarly, disclosure of the risks, which, if they were to materialise, would cause severe impact, may be found to be consistent with a clean working capital if the probability of such risks materialising is sufficiently low.

The UKLA has also pointed out that some issuers might try to express risk factors in a way which suggests the risk will only operate "in the longer term" or after the period covered by the 12-month working capital statement. The UKLA has made it clear that they will test the genuineness of such disclosure and seek to ensure that the disclosure is appropriate and accurate and not simply used as a way of taking the risk factor outside the strict 12-month period of the working capital statement.

Where the prospectus is being published in connection with the issue of shares in consideration for an acquisition, it can also be of importance to ensure that the combined working capital requirements of the issuer's group and of the business or businesses being acquired are capable of being adequately met. The Prospectus Rules are silent on this, although it is a condition of listing that an applicant and its subsidiary undertakings have sufficient working capital available for the group's requirements for at least the next 12 months (LR 6.7.1).

In respect of certain circulars, LR 13.4.3 confirms that, where the issuer is itself already listed, the working capital statement must take account of the working capital needs of the enlarged group on the basis that the acquisition has taken place, if the offer is recommended by the board of the offeree at the time of the publication of the offer document. If the offer has not been recommended, the UKLA will allow the working capital statement on the combined basis to be given later in a circular which must be published within 28 days after the offer has become or been declared unconditional. Where the offer is agreed or recommended, this requirement should present no particular problems, save that the requirement to treat competing offerors equally in relation to the provision of information should be remembered.

In any event, in order to make the working capital statement in the prospectus, it will be of vital importance for the directors of the offeror and offeree companies, and their advisers, to take into account all potential cash outflows consequent upon the offer, to review all relevant financial projections and to satisfy themselves as to the reasonableness of the assumptions on which those projections are based. In a recommended or agreed offer, it is normal for the directors of the offeror company, if they alone are making the working capital statement in relation to the enlarged group, to require appropriate assurances from the directors of the offeree company as to the adequacy of the working capital available to the offeree company and its subsidiaries. The directors of the offeree company may have to qualify any such assurances if they will cease to have control of the activities of the offeree company and its subsidiaries once the offer has become unconditional.

The securities note also requires a detailed statement of capitalisation and indebtedness (including contingent and indirect indebtedness) as at a date no earlier than 90 days prior to the date of the document. ESMA has published clarification on the meaning of the terms "indirect" and "contingent indebtedness" and stated that, where an event which could be described as a significant change occurs between the 90-day period and the date of the prospectus, the issuer must reflect this change in its capitalisation and indebtedness statement.[16]

The purpose of the offer and a fairly detailed breakdown of how the proceeds will be used and prioritised must also be set out.

4.5 Omission of information

There are essentially three grounds on which omission of information may be sought, which remain unchanged from the previous regime. The first ground for omission is that the information is of minor importance. The second ground for omission is that the omission of the information would not be likely to mislead investors but, if it were to be disclosed, it would be seriously detrimental to the issuer. The third ground is that the disclosure would be contrary to the public interest, in which case it is not relevant that the non-disclosure would be likely to mislead investors.

4.6 Approval

A prospectus cannot be published until approved by the UKLA. So far as new applicants—who do not have securities admitted to trading on a regulated market and have not previously made an offer of securities to the public—are concerned, the draft should be submitted to the UKLA at least 20 clear business days prior to the intended publication date (in other cases, the usual period is 10 clear business days). Any request for omission of information from the prospectus must be submitted to the UKLA with this draft.

---

[16] ESMA, *ESMA update of the CESR recommendations: the consistent implementation of Regulation 809/2004 implementing the Prospectus Directive*, ESMA/2013/319 (20 March 2013), para.3.2.

Under art.2 of Regulation 2016/301,[17] reproduced in PR 3.1.-1EU, draft documentation must be submitted in a searchable electronic format.

A prospectus can be submitted for approval even though the final offer price and amount of securities to be offered are not yet determined. The UKLA can approve a prospectus without those details, provided that the prospectus discloses the criteria and/or the conditions in accordance with which those items will be determined, or the maximum price, and final details must then be filed with the UKLA and published (PR 2.3.2). In practice, in part because of the manner in which the UKLA applies the publication rules, the approach of preparing a pathfinder (which has the status of an "advertisement", under PR 3.3.2) is still being followed in institutional placings. The UKLA has indicated that, where a pathfinder is sent to institutional placees only, it will be regarded as an advertisement relating to a public offer even though the institutional placing itself does not trigger a prospectus.

4.7 Supplementary prospectuses (shares)

A supplement is required if a "significant new factor, material mistake or inaccuracy relating to the information included in the prospectus which is capable of affecting the assessment of the securities" occurs between the time that the prospectus has been approved and the final closing of the offer of securities under the prospectus or admission of those securities to trading (art.16 of the Prospectus Directive). The PD Amending Directive amended art.16 of the Prospectus Directive to clarify that the obligation to produce a supplement will end at the *later of* the final closing of the offer period or the time when trading of such securities on a regulated market begins.

---

[17] Regulation 2016/301 supplementing Directive 2003/71 with regard to regulatory technical standards for approval and publication of the prospectus and dissemination of advertisements and amending Regulation 809/2004 [2016] OJ L58/13.

The production of a supplement triggers a cooling-off period of at least two working days for investors who have agreed to purchase or subscribe for securities before the supplement is published (art.16.2 of the Prospectus Directive).

The provision in art.16(2) as amended by the PD Amending Directive says that the withdrawal right is exercisable "within two working days after the publication of the supplement". Note, however, that an issuer or offeror will be able to extend this period. While the drafting is unclear, the amendments may be interpreted as providing that the walk-away right is only triggered if the prospectus has been produced in the context of a non-exempt offer to the public, i.e. not where a supplement has been produced in the context of a prospectus prepared for admission to trading on a regulated market only. The position of supplements in the context of a base prospectus and final terms is beyond the scope of this chapter and is not considered (please see Ch.8 below). It is also unclear what the intention is behind the inclusion in this section of the reference to the arising of the new factor, mistake or inaccuracy before the final closing of the offer and the delivery of the securities.

4.8 Proportionate disclosure regime for rights issues

The PD Amending Directive creates a proportionate disclosure regime for offers of shares by companies whose shares of the same class are admitted to trading on a regulated market or a multilateral trading facility, which are subject to appropriate ongoing disclosure requirements and rules on market abuse, provided that the issuer has not disapplied the statutory pre-emption rights (art.7.2(g) of the PD Amending Directive).

It is the practice in several Member States for rights issues to be made by disapplying the statutory pre-emption rights and replacing them with near identical rights. In the UK, for example, issuers usually disapply statutory pre-emption rights to facilitate the treatment of fractions, exclude certain overseas shareholders from the offer and avoid the "Gazette route" but comply with the pre-emptive requirements of the Listing Rules. Accordingly, in its October 2011 *Final Report*, ESMA advised the Commission to implement art.7.2(g) in a broad manner rather than in a strict manner that would exclude issuers using the replacement technique. Its advice was accompanied by a proposed definition of "near identical rights"—such definition did not extend to non-compensatory open offers. Regulation 486/2012 regarding the format and content of the prospectus[18] follows ESMA's advice by inserting the following new definition of "rights issue" in art.2(13) of the existing PD Regulation:

> "'Rights issue' means any issue of statutory pre-emption rights which allow for the subscription of new shares and is addressed only to existing shareholders. Rights issue also includes an issue where such statutory pre-emption rights are disabled and replaced by an instrument or a provision conferring near identical rights to existing shareholders when those rights meet the following conditions:
>
> (a) shareholders are offered the rights free of charge;
> (b) shareholders are entitled to take up new shares in proportion to their existing holdings, or, in the case of other securities giving a right to participate in the share issue, in proportion to their entitlements to the underlying shares;
> (c) the rights to subscribe are negotiable and transferable or, if not, the shares arising from the rights are sold at the end of the offer period for the benefit of those shareholders who did not take up those entitlements;
> (d) the issuer is able, as regards the entitlements referred to in point (b), to impose limits or restrictions or exclusions and make arrangements it considers appropriate to deal with treasury shares, fractional entitlements and requirements laid down by law or by a regulatory authority in any country or territory;

---

[18] Regulation 486/2012 amending Regulation 809/2004 as regards the format and the content of the prospectus, the base prospectus, the summary and the final terms and as regards the disclosure requirements [2012] OJ L150/1 art.1(2).

(e) the minimum period during which shares may be taken up is the same as the period for the exercise of statutory pre-emption rights laid down in Article 29(3) of Council Directive 77/91/EEC; and

(f) the rights lapse at the expiration of the exercise period."

Regulation 486/2012 introduced a new para.3 in art.21 of the PD Regulation, giving a choice to issuers seeking admission to trading of shares issued in the context of a rights issue to draw up a prospectus in accordance with the minimum disclosure requirements contained in new proportionate disclosure schedules set out in new Annexes XXIII and XXIV to the PD Regulation instead of the full disclosure schedules set out in the existing Annexes I and III.

The proportionate disclosure schedules for rights issues contained in Annexes XXIII and XXIV follow ESMA's advice in its October 2011 *Final Report*:

- certain disclosures required by Annexes I and III of the existing PD Regulation which duplicate mandatory disclosures already made available to the market on an ongoing basis pursuant to the Transparency Directive and MAR do not appear in the proportionate disclosure schedules. These include, most significantly, disclosures on: selected financial information, the history and development of the issuer, significant subsidiaries, property, plant and equipment, operating and financial review, capital resources, research and development, number of employees, share capital history, memorandum and articles of association and certain documents on display and holdings;
- certain of the remaining disclosure requirements contained in Annexes I and III were redrafted to require only historical financial information for the last financial year and basic information on the issuer's activities and markets together with an update on any significant event since publication of the last audited financial statements; and

- the prospectus must include at the beginning a statement indicating clearly that the rights issue is addressed to shareholders of the issuer and that the level of disclosure of the prospectus is proportionate to that type of issue.

However, the proportionate disclosure regime does not affect liability standards in Member States, and issuers will also need to consider applicable disclosure and liability standards in other jurisdictions where shareholders may be located, such as the US. Accordingly, in practice, the proportionate disclosure regime has been rarely used and is only likely to be used in relation to small rights issues and/or rights issues with no US element (i.e. made in reliance on reg.S under the US Securities Act 1933, as amended).

4.9 Takeovers

The position under the current regime is as follows. It should be possible to structure loan notes so that they are not "transferable securities" (s.102A of the FSMA defines "transferable securities" as meaning, in summary, anything which is a transferable security for the purpose of the EU Markets in Financial Instruments Directive 2014/65)[19] and therefore remain outside the prospectus regime. So far as shares are concerned, there is an exemption from the requirement for a prospectus in the case of a takeover by way of exchange offer or a merger, but this only applies if a document containing information that is regarded by the competent authority as equivalent to that required in a prospectus is made available. The up to 20% exemption applies in relation to the admission of shares to trading but not in respect of public offers. Takeovers and mergers involving new shares are therefore likely to require the production of a prospectus or equivalent document. Where, however, shares are being issued pursuant to a scheme of arrangement, the market consensus is typically that it would not involve a public offer since there would be no offer and no acceptance of an offer by the offeree shareholders.

---

[19] Directive 2014/65 on markets in financial instruments and amending Directive 2002/92 and Directive 2011/61 [2014] OJ L173/349.

On that basis, there would be no requirement for a prospectus or equivalent document if the new shares to be admitted to trading qualify for the up to 20% exemption.

The UKLA seems to regard the requirement for the document to be "equivalent" as a requirement that it should contain all, or substantially all, the information that would be required in a prospectus; and the Prospectus Rules require the submission of a cross-reference list showing where each of the disclosure requirements that would apply for a prospectus is satisfied. It might, therefore, be thought that there is no great difference in the work involved in producing an equivalent document from that involved in producing a prospectus. Moreover, an "equivalent document" would not benefit from EU passporting rights or the s.90(12) of the FSMA exclusion of liability for the summary, discussed above.

As noted in s.4.7 above, however, s.87Q(4) of the FSMA confers on investors rights of withdrawal following the publication of a supplementary prospectus. These rights go beyond the rights of withdrawal available under the City Code on Takeovers and Mergers (the City Code). Under the City Code, withdrawal rights normally cease to be available after an offer has become or been declared unconditional as to acceptances. The Takeover Panel Executive (the Executive) has expressed concern that, if withdrawal rights arise after an offer is unconditional as to acceptances but is not yet wholly unconditional, there could be material implications if the acceptance level falls below 50% as a result of the exercise of withdrawal rights. While the interpretation of s.87Q(4) of the FSMA is ultimately a matter for the courts, the Executive notes that it has received legal advice that this section can be interpreted to mean that the period for withdrawal by an acceptor ends once the offer has become or been declared wholly unconditional and the relevant securities have been conditionally allotted to the acceptor. This view is shared by the UKLA. The Executive recommends that bidders intending to use a prospectus should consider adding an additional condition or term to their offers so that the offer will not continue to be unconditional if the bidder has no longer achieved the 50% minimum acceptance threshold. Bidders who might need to include such a provision are advised to consult the Executive in advance. The Executive also suggests that offerors should organise matters so that the offer becomes or is declared unconditional as to acceptances and wholly unconditional at the same time. In light of the uncertainty surrounding withdrawal rights, issuers may favour the use of an equivalent document, particularly where the offer is a hostile one, unless there are compelling reasons for wanting to benefit from the passport in relation to other Member States.

On the basis of the UKLA's stated position on equivalence, it seems likely that the UKLA would apply the same approach to "equivalent documents" as well, with the result that the offeror and its directors would need to take responsibility for the whole document. Nothing in the Prospectus Rules would, however, prevent the offeree and its directors accepting responsibility for their parts of the document in parallel with the offeror and its directors.

On 13 July 2018, ESMA published a consultation on exempt documents published for offer or admission connected to a takeover, merger or division (ESMA, Consultation Paper on "Draft technical advice on minimum information content for prospectus exemption", ESMA31-62-962 (13 July 2018)).

4.10   Concluding thoughts

Section 90 of the FSMA confers an express right of compensation on an investor who has acquired any securities which are the subject of a prospectus or supplementary prospectus and who has suffered a loss as a result of any untrue or misleading statement in the document. It also provides a right of compensation where the loss occurs as the result of the omission of any matter required to be included. Those responsible for the prospectus are liable to pay the compensation but their liability to do so is excluded in a variety of circumstances, based largely on the principle that no liability should attach to them if they have acted reasonably.

The breadth of s.90 is of considerable importance, not only because the right to compensation extends to purchasers of the relevant securities in the market as well as those who initially apply for them under an offer, but also because there is no requirement that the investor suffering the loss should actually have relied on the prospectus, as long as the loss resulted from an error or omission within said section. It is not necessary, therefore, for an investor to have read the prospectus in order for him to avail himself of whatever remedies s.90 may offer him.

When one looks at the amount of material which has been contained in listing particulars and prospectuses in recent times, that must be quite a comforting thought from an investor's point of view.

Although the Prospectus Directive regime has given some impetus to the efforts to make listing documents more user-friendly, in view of the emphasis on the summary, the identification of risk factors and the requirement to present information in a form which is comprehensible and easy to analyse, prospectuses have not become any shorter and, if anything, continue to grow in length.

Chapter 5

Financial Information

Linda Main
Partner, KPMG LLP

5.1 Introduction

This chapter deals with the requirements for financial information in prospectuses or circulars as set out in the UK Listing Authority (UKLA) Prospectus Rules (PRs) and Listing Rules (LRs) in relation to issuers with a premium listing of their equity shares. In addition, the following practical points are covered:

(1) historical financial information requirements for new applicants;
(2) historical financial information requirements for Class 1 circulars;
(3) pro forma statements;
(4) profit forecasts and estimates;
(5) working capital;
(6) statement of capitalisation and indebtedness;
(7) financial position and prospects procedures;
(8) significant change in financial and trading position; and
(9) routine obligations to publish financial information.

5.2 Historical financial information requirements

5.2.1 *Circumstances requiring historical financial information*

The historical financial information provides the basis for one of the key parts of most prospectuses or acquisition circulars; that is, the trading record of the company in question. It is, of course, that trading record, together with any forecast or pro forma statement, which underpins the evaluation process.

The general requirements for the contents of a prospectus are recorded in Ch.2 of the Prospectus Rules. Detailed requirements for the contents of a prospectus in connection with an equity issue are set out in Annexes I–III of Regulation 809/2004 of the European Commission (Prospectus Directive Regulation).[1] The content of a Class 1 circular is set out in LR 13. A general duty of disclosure of financial information in a prospectus is included in s.87 of the Financial Services and Markets Act 2000 (FSMA). Listing Rule 6 sets out additional requirements for the premium listing of equity securities. Listing Rule 14 sets out the requirements for the standard listing of equity securities. Additional and modified requirements for premium listing of certain types of investment companies are set out in LRs 15 and 16. Finally, the European Securities and Markets Authority (ESMA) has set out recommendations for the consistent implementation of the Prospectus Directive Regulation. This guidance is contained in the ESMA update 2011/81.[2]

A requirement for the provision of historical financial information arises in two main circumstances:

---

[1] Regulation 809/2004 implementing Directive 2003/71 as regards information contained in prospectuses as well as the format, incorporation by reference and publication of such prospectuses and dissemination of advertisements [2004] OJ L149/3.

[2] ESMA, *ESMA update of the CESR recommendations: The consistent implementation of Regulation 809/2004 implementing the Prospectus Directive*, ESMA/2011/81 (23 March 2011).

(1) when an application is being made for the shares of a company to be admitted to the Official List (either as a new applicant or a further issue of shares by an existing listed company); and

(2) for inclusion in a Class 1 circular issued in respect of an acquisition or disposal by a company with a premium listing.

5.2.2 *New applicant*

The prospectus of a new applicant must include audited historical financial information covering the latest three financial years and an audit report in respect of each year. The last two years' audited historical financial information must be presented and prepared in a form consistent with that which will be adopted in the issuer's next published annual financial statements, having regard to accounting standards and policies and legislation applicable to such annual financial statements. This can require careful consideration where new accounting standards are being introduced as the correct approach may depend on whether or not they are intended to be applied retrospectively or prospectively.

New applicants incorporated in the EU must prepare their financial statements using International Financial Reporting Standards (IFRS). Third-country issuers must also prepare their financial statements using IFRS except that, in certain circumstances, they may do so in accordance with certain approved Generally Accepted Accounting Principles (GAAPs). This is discussed further at s.5.2.6 below ("Accounting standards").

For the new applicant to be suitable for a premium listing, the historical financial information must have been reported on by the auditors without modification (LR 6.1.3(1)(e)) and the latest balance sheet must be no more than six months before the date of the prospectus.

The UKLA may modify or dispense with the requirement for a company to have three years' historical financial information if it is satisfied that it is desirable in the interests of investors and that investors have the necessary information available to arrive at an informed judgement about the new applicant and the equity shares for which listing is sought (LR 6.1.13).

The content of the three-year history for a new applicant should include income statements, statements of financial position, statements of changes in equity, cash flow statements, accounting policies and full notes consistent with that required by the applicable accounting standards.

Where a company's annual accounts for a three-year period prior to listing do not require material adjustment in order for them to present the historical record of the group in accordance with the listing requirements, reproducing the audited annual accounts in the prospectus will, in principle, be sufficient. However, where material changes are required to present the historical record in accordance with the listing requirements (e.g. to bring the most recent two years into line with the basis to be applied in the next published financial statements), the financial information covering the last two financial years will need to be restated. The restated financial information will need to be reported on and hence work to support this opinion, performed in accordance with the UK Auditing Practices Board's Standards for Investment Reporting (SIR) 2000 (revised), will need to be undertaken.

If the last two years only are restated, it may be appropriate for the first of the two years to be presented on both the original basis and the restated basis in order to bridge the gap between the first and third years of the track record. In practice, the ESMA guidance suggests presenting both the original basis and restated basis for the year in question on the face of the historical financial information where the formats are sufficiently comparable. If this is not the case, then the guidance suggests presenting the historical financial information prepared on the original basis on separate pages.

5.2.3   Class 1 circulars

A Class 1 transaction is defined as one in which the size of the company, business or assets being acquired or disposed of represents 25% or more of the listed company by reference to any of the class tests set out in Annex 1 to LR 10.

In the case of a Class 1 acquisition by a listed company of an interest in an undertaking which will result in consolidation of the assets and liabilities of that undertaking, a financial information table for that undertaking is required.

The contents of this financial information table are set out in LR 13.5. The information which is required must be given in respect of a period of three years up to the end of the latest financial period for which the undertaking or its parent has prepared audited accounts. For each of the periods reported on, the financial information table must include the following:

(1)   a statement of financial position and its explanatory notes;
(2)   an income statement and its explanatory notes;
(3)   a cash flow statement and its explanatory notes;
(4)   a statement showing either all changes in equity or changes in equity other than those arising from capital transactions with owners and distributions to owners;
(5)   the accounting policies; and
(6)   any additional explanatory notes.

In the case of a Class 1 acquisition, this financial information table must be accompanied by a reporting accountant's opinion (of which there are two different types depending on the circumstances). The reporting accountant's opinion (referred to elsewhere in this chapter as an "accountant's report") sets out:

(1)   whether, for the purposes of the Class 1 circular, the historical financial information table gives a true and fair view of the financial matters set out in it; and

(2) whether the historical financial information table has been prepared in a form that is consistent with the accounting policies adopted in the listed company's latest annual accounts.

In the case of a disposal, there is no requirement to issue a reporting accountant's opinion in respect of businesses which are to be sold, although the latest statement of financial position and last three years' income statements must be provided in the circular in the form of extracts from previously audited accounts. If audited accounts have not been prepared for the business being disposed of, the information must be extracted from the consolidation schedules that underlie the listed company's audited consolidated accounts.

5.2.4 Contents of the accountant's report

The format of the accountant's report for a new applicant or a Class 1 acquisition is set out in the SIR 2000 which was revised in March 2011. An unqualified accountant's report is typically worded as set out below. The report for inclusion in a Class 1 circular is very similar, with appropriate modification to reflect the applicable regulations and the need to comment on consistency with the acquirer's policies:

> "We report on the financial information [set out in paras ... to ... which comprises], for the [specify periods]. This financial information has been prepared for inclusion in the [prospectus] dated ... of ABC plc on the basis of the accounting policies set out in paragraph [...]. This report is required by [Relevant Regulation] and is given for the purpose of complying with that [paragraph] and for no other purpose. [We have not audited or reviewed the financial information for the [26 weeks ended ...] [which has been included for comparative purposes only and accordingly do not express an opinion thereon.][3]

---

[3] Relevant where interim financial information is included in the Historical Financial Information and reported upon. The comparative information is also presented but not reported upon.

Responsibilities

The Directors of [ABC Plc] are responsible for preparing the financial information in accordance with International Financial Reporting Standards as adopted by the European Union.

It is our responsibility to form an opinion on the financial information and to report our opinion to you.

Basis of opinion

We conducted our work in accordance with Standards for Investment Reporting issued by the Auditing Practices Board in the United Kingdom. Our work included an assessment of evidence relevant to the amounts and disclosures in the financial information. It also included an assessment of significant estimates and judgments made by those responsible for the preparation of the financial information and whether the accounting policies are appropriate to the entity's circumstances, consistently applied and adequately disclosed.

We planned and performed our work so as to obtain all the information and explanations which we considered necessary in order to provide us with sufficient evidence to give reasonable assurance that the financial information is free from material misstatement whether caused by fraud or other irregularity or error.

Opinion on financial information

In our opinion, the financial information gives, for the purposes of the [prospectus] dated ..., a true and fair view of the state of affairs of [ABC Plc]/[XYZ Ltd] as at [specify dates] and of its profits, cash flows and [recognised gains and losses] [changes in equity] for the [specify periods] in accordance with International Financial Reporting Standards as adopted by the European Union [and has been

193

prepared in a form that is consistent with the accounting policies adopted in [ABC Plc's] latest annual accounts.[4]

Declaration[5]

For the purposes of [Prospectus Rule 5.5.3R(2)(f) and 5.5.4R(2)(f),] we are responsible for [this report as part] of the [prospectus] and declare that we have taken all reasonable care to ensure that the information contained in [this report] is, to the best of our knowledge, in accordance with the facts and contains no omission likely to affect its import. This declaration is included in the [prospectus] in compliance with [Item 1.2 of Annex 1 to the Prospectus Regulation[6] and Item 1.2 of Annex 3 to the Prospectus Regulation].

Yours faithfully

Reporting accountant."

5.2.5   Qualified audit report

There are requirements under the Companies Act 2006 and Prospectus Directive Regulation (Annex I, para.20.4.1) to give details of any audit qualifications. For Companies Act purposes, such details form part of the statement under s.435 of the Companies Act 2006 that the historical financial information does not constitute the company's statutory accounts and that such statutory accounts have been filed with the Registrar of Companies. This statement forms a paragraph within the statutory information section of the document in question, which is usually the last section.

The reporting accountant's opinion should be arrived at independently of any previous audit opinions given on the

---

[4]   Relevant for Class 1 acquisition circulars.
[5]   Relevant for a prospectus but not a circular.
[6]   Regulation 809/2004 implementing Directive 2003/71 as regards information contained in prospectuses as well as the format, incorporation by reference and publication of such prospectuses and dissemination of advertisements [2004] OJ L149/3.

financial statements which form the basis for the historical financial information to be reported on. It is not part of the reporting accountant's role to explain why their opinion differs from the opinion of the auditor (where this is the case). The directors of the issuer will be required to disclose details of the qualifications or disclaimers contained in audit reports prepared by the statutory auditor and the reporting accountant considers the disclosures made. If he/she is not satisfied with the disclosures, the reporting accountant should discuss the matter with the directors and ensure appropriate information is included by the issuer or is included in the accountant's report.

5.2.6 Accounting standards

For new applicants, the Prospectus Directive Regulation (Annex I, para.20.1) requires that the historical financial information be drawn up in accordance with Regulation 1606/2002,[7] if applicable. This regulation requires a company listed on a regulated exchange to prepare its consolidated financial statements using IFRS as adopted in the EU. For third-country issuers, the Prospectus Directive Regulation also permits the historical financial information to be drawn up in accordance with the national accounting standards of the third country, if those standards are equivalent to IFRS as adopted in the EU. From 1 January 2009, Regulation 1289/2008[8] establishes that, except as noted below, third-country issuers must present their historical financial information in accordance with one of the following:

(1) IFRS as per Regulation 1606/2002;
(2) IFRS provided that the notes to the financial statements contain an explicit and unreserved statement that the

---

[7] Regulation 1606/2002 on the application of international accounting standards [2002] OJ L243/1.
[8] Regulation 1289/2008 amending Regulation 809/2004 implementing Directive 2003/71 as regards elements related to prospectuses and advertisements [2008] OJ L340/17.

financial statements comply with IFRS in accordance with International Accounting Standard (IAS) 1 Presentation of Financial Statements; and

(3) GAAPs of Japan, the US, Canada, the People's Republic of China and the Republic of Korea as these have been granted equivalence to IFRS by the European Commission.

In the case of Class 1 acquisitions, the Listing Rules require the financial information table on the target to be prepared in a form that is consistent with the accounting policies adopted in the issuer's latest annual consolidated accounts (LR 13.5.4) (except where the target is admitted to trading on a recognised investment exchange or has securities listed on an overseas investment exchange or admitted to trading on an overseas regulated market, in which event the financial information table will reflect the target's accounting policies and be accompanied, if necessary, by a reconciliation to the issuer's accounting policies).

5.2.7 *Liaising with the UK Listing Authority*

For the purpose of a prospectus for a new applicant, the Prospectus Directive Regulation sets out the full requirements and the UKLA has no ability to require additional information. However, in the case of a Class 1 circular, the UKLA may dispense with or modify the Listing Rules or require further information to be included. Communication between the directors of the issuer and the UKLA is conducted through the sponsor appointed for the transaction. Where the queries raised by the UKLA are easily resolved, this presents no problem, but, for specific queries on the historical financial information and the reporting accountant's ability to report on it, it can be helpful to involve the accountants in the discussion so that misunderstandings can be avoided.

5.2.8 *Adjustments from previously audited figures*

The directors of the issuer may make adjustments to restate previously audited historical financial information which fall broadly into three categories:

(1) to present the financial information for all years on the basis of consistent, acceptable and appropriately applied accounting policies, in accordance with the applicable requirements;
(2) to correct errors; and
(3) to record adjusting post balance sheet events where appropriate.

The directors should only seek to make adjustments insofar as necessary to achieve the objectives set out above. The directors do not seek to replace accounting policies, accounting estimates or valuation adjustments with those selected by themselves. They consider whether the specific application of the basis of accounting originally adopted falls within an acceptable range of alternatives and, if not, may conclude that an error has occurred which may need to be adjusted. Furthermore, adjustments should not be made in order for the track record to be more consistent with the entity's expected operations or structure following the transaction. Such adjustments would anticipate future events and are not consistent with the principle that the historical financial information should record the events which actually occurred during the period of the historical financial information.

Some examples of the circumstances where adjustments can be made are to:

(1) ensure that the same accounting policies have been applied throughout the period covered by the information (e.g. if new accounting standards have been introduced during the period);
(2) ensure that the accounting policies are consistent with those which will be in use in the next set of annual financial statements; and

(3) correct a failure to comply with an accounting standard.

The adjustments are made by the directors to arrive at the restated financial information group being reported upon, which may often have changed its composition within the period covered by the report. The question therefore arises as to how the relevant historical financial information should be prepared.

In the case of a new issue, the primary objective is to give a fair presentation of the results of the business being floated and which has been managed by the people concerned. It is not uncommon for entrepreneurs to have been operating separate companies previously which may then be brought together to form a group for flotation. Clearly, whatever the form of reconstruction, it is likely to assist in an understanding of the historical record of the business to combine the results of the separate enterprises as if they had been part of a group throughout the three-year period. Other businesses may have been acquired and the management of them may now form part of the central management of the enlarged group. In these circumstances, there may be a desire to bring in the results of such businesses throughout the period. However, the only circumstances in which the UKLA will permit the presentation of combined or aggregated figures is where the component parts of a group have been under common ownership and control throughout the period but did not form a group for accounting purposes.

The Listing Rules make it clear that, in a Class 1 circular where the target company has itself made acquisitions which would have been classified at the date of acquisition as Class 1 in relation to the issuer, financial information on that undertaking must be given covering a minimum of three years (including in respect of the pre-acquisition period) in the form of a separate financial information table (LR 13.5.1). There are obviously potential practical problems with this approach, such as the need to obtain access to records held by the previous owner.

The application of the same accounting policies throughout the period is, in theory, a relatively simple matter but it can give rise to practical complications if the information necessary to enable the accounts of previous years to be restated on the current policies is not easily available. The important issue is the question of materiality and what the directors may have to do is to decide whether they believe that, whilst the figures cannot be computed precisely, reasonable estimates can nevertheless be arrived at which are acceptable and which enable a true and fair opinion to be given by the accountants.

The question of considering errors is more difficult. There can well be circumstances in which the directors will say that the figures they are looking at are clearly wrong and were clearly wrong at the time. This is the important question. The directors always have to avoid the excessive use of hindsight. In preparing the financial information, the directors have to put themselves in the position of judging whether or not the view taken on a particular issue was reasonable at the time, even though subsequent events may cause one to take a different view.

It is an unavoidable part of accounts preparation that estimates have to be made. Each year's accounts contain the adjustments made to the previous year's estimates as well as the estimates made at that year end. Subject to the overriding need to present a true and fair view, it is not the purpose of the restated historical financial information to substitute more accurate information subsequently ascertained in place of reasonable estimates made at the time.

Part of the reporting accountant's responsibility will be to consider the judgements made by the directors in this regard.

5.2.9 Modified opinions

Circumstances can obviously arise where it is not possible to give a clean opinion on a company's figures. If this is in respect of a company seeking to come to the market, it will, in all probability, be fatal. Those who are thinking about a listing should take note of this because what at the time may appear to be an innocuous audit qualification may cause a delay in flotation plans. Similarly, an emphasis of matter, for example, in relation to a significant uncertainty in the auditors' report, has the same consequences as a qualification.

In the case of acquisitions, reporting on an entity that has not been subject to audit clearly presents problems. In some respects, time is a great auditor and it may be possible to carry out sufficient work to enable an opinion to be given, but this will depend upon the nature of the business and the records maintained. However, the lack of physical checking and evaluation of stock may prove insuperable in some businesses.

This situation can arise, for instance, where a division is acquired from another company or where a company is acquired in an overseas country where there is no requirement for all companies to be subject to full scope audits. If the reporting accountant concludes that it is not possible to report without modification for the purpose of a Class 1 circular, the circular must set out all material matters, including the reasons for the modification and a quantification of the effects if both relevant and practicable.

In the absence of reliable evidence relating to significant accounts and balances, it may not be possible to form an opinion on the financial information. In cases where a disclaimer of opinion needs to be given on the information for the entire period, the reporting accountant should not agree to be associated with financial information.

5.3 Pro forma figures

Pro forma financial information may be included in a number of circumstances, for example, where a group is coming together for the first time or where an issuer is making a significant acquisition or disposal. Pro forma statements of net assets may also be included to show the effect of funds raised on flotation on the gearing of the company. A description of the effect on the issuer's assets and liabilities and earnings, normally in the form of pro forma financial information, is required in a prospectus in the case of significant gross change (i.e. where there has been a variation of more than 25% relative to one or more indicators of the size of the issuer's business). Indicators of size are not defined but guidance suggests that this includes total assets, revenue and profit or loss. Pro forma information is covered by Annex II of the Prospectus Directive Regulation.

All pro forma information in a prospectus or circular must be publicly reported on by the reporting accountant. The sources must be stated and, if applicable, the financial statements of the acquired businesses must be included in the prospectus.

The adjustments which can be made to the historic information must be:

(1) clearly shown and explained;
(2) directly attributable to the transaction concerned;
(3) factually supportable; and
(4) in the case of a pro forma profit statement or cash flow, distinguish between those expected to have a continuing impact and those which will not.

The Auditing Practices Board (APB) has published a standard (Standards for Investment Reporting (SIR) 4000) providing standards and guidance for the provision of reports on pro forma financial information. The Institute of Chartered Accountants in England and Wales (ICAEW) published a Technical Release in 2015 (Tech 01/15CFF) entitled *Guidance for preparers of pro forma financial information* which provides further detail on the interpretation of the Prospectus Regulation requirements.

5.4 Profit forecasts and estimates

A profit forecast may be included in a prospectus where, for example, some time has elapsed since the end of the last period for which results are included, or where the directors or sponsor consider that the actual results for the current period may differ from that which might be deduced from the historic trend or if a listed company has an outstanding profit forecast at the date of the document.

It is also important to remember that the UKLA may consider a form of words to be a forecast even if it does not specifically mention a figure and does not use the word "profit". For this reason, great care must be taken when drafting documents to avoid inadvertently giving a forecast.

When a forecast or estimate is included in the prospectus, there must be a published report by the reporting accountants. A report is not required where financial information relates to the previous financial year and only contains non-misleading figures substantially consistent with the final figures to be published in the next annual audited financial statements for the previous financial year and the explanatory information necessary to assess the figures, provided that the prospectus includes all of the following statements (Prospectus Directive Regulation Annex I s.13.2):

(1) the person responsible for this financial information, if different from the one who is responsible for the prospectus in general, approves that information;
(2) independent accountants or auditors have agreed that this information is substantially consistent with the final figures to be published in the next annual audited financial statements; and
(3) this financial information has not been audited.

The APB has published a standard (SIR 3000) providing standards and guidance for the provision of reports on profit forecasts.

The wording surrounding a profit forecast or estimate generally includes the words "subject to unforeseen circumstances". This is important wording, particularly for estimates, in order to cover the possibility of adjusting post balance sheet events.

The language of the accountant's report on a profit forecast or estimate carefully points out that the forecast or estimate is the directors' responsibility. This must be understood, most particularly by the directors. It is important to be aware that the accountant's opinion is solely directed at the preparation of the forecast.

The assumptions underlying a profit forecast or estimate must:

(1) distinguish between those which the members of the administrative, management or supervisory bodies can influence and those which are exclusively outside the influence of these members;
(2) be readily understandable by investors; and
(3) be specific and precise and not relate to the general accuracy of the estimates underlying the forecast.

The Listing Rules include a requirement to reproduce any profit forecast or estimate in the annual report, to set out the actual figures and to provide an explanation if the actual figures differ by 10% or more from the profit forecast or estimate (LR 9.2.18).

5.5 Working capital

The Prospectus Rules (Annex III s.3.1) and Listing Rules require the issuer to make a statement in the prospectus, or circular relating to a Class 1 transaction, that in its opinion the working capital available to the group is sufficient for its present requirements or, if not, how it proposes to provide the additional working capital thought by the issuer to be necessary. Present requirements are interpreted to mean a minimum of 12 months from the date of the prospectus. In the case of a new applicant, the working capital statement must be without qualification (LR 6.1.16).

The Listing Rules make it clear that in the case of an acquisition the statement must be on the basis of the enlarged group, except (initially) a takeover offer which is not recommended, and on the basis that the disposal has taken place in the case of a disposal.

The company's sponsor must confirm to the UKLA that they are satisfied that the directors of the issuer have a reasonable basis on which to conclude that the working capital available to the issuer and its group is sufficient for at least the next 12 months from the date of publication of the prospectus or Class 1 circular (as applicable). The sponsor will undertake its own due and careful enquiry into the directors' conclusion, including seeking a comfort letter from the reporting accountants.

The comfort will take the form of a private letter from the reporting accountants to the company and the sponsor. In order for the reporting accountant to be able to provide comfort, it is necessary for the company to prepare a Board Memorandum setting out the cash flow projections and the assumptions which underlie them. Whether or not a report is being given on a profit forecast, any profit forecast will need to be considered as this, of course, has a direct bearing on the cash forecast. The level of detailed work performed by the reporting accountant will vary, to a certain extent, depending upon the margin between the facilities available and the requirements shown by the forecast. The period has to be a minimum of the next 12 months, although in practice a longer period may need to be covered and in particular it is necessary to consider any known circumstances beyond that time.

5.6 Statement of capitalisation and indebtedness

A new applicant is required to present a statement of capitalisation and indebtedness (distinguishing between guaranteed and unguaranteed, secured and unsecured indebtedness) as of a date no earlier than 90 days prior to the date of the document (PR Annex III s.3.2). The information should be computed on the basis of the consolidated accounts of the issuer.

The information, so far as it relates to capitalisation, should be derived from the last published financial information of the issuer but, if this information is more than 90 days old and there has been a material change, the issuer should provide more up-to-date information. If any of the capitalisation information is older than 90 days but there is no material change then this fact should be stated.

There is no specific reporting by the sponsor on this matter, this being a statement required by the Prospectus Directive Regulation and, therefore, the responsibility of those who take responsibility for the prospectus (i.e. the directors). The company and sponsor may request the reporting accountants to perform procedures in relation to the balances which make up the statement and to report the findings from those procedures.

The ESMA guidance includes details on how capitalisation and indebtedness information is expected to be presented.[9]

5.7 Significant change in financial and trading position

The issuer must include a description of any significant change in the financial or trading position of the group which has occurred since the end of the last financial period for which

---

[9] ESMA, *ESMA update of the CESR recommendations: The consistent implementation of Regulation 809/2004 implementing the Prospectus Directive*, ESMA/2011/81 (23 March 2011).

either audited financial information or interim financial information has been published, or provide an appropriate negative statement. The company and sponsor generally request the reporting accountants to perform procedures in relation to the significant change statement.

5.8 Financial position and prospects procedures

For new applicants seeking a premium listing, the Listing Rules include a requirement for the sponsor to confirm that the directors have established procedures which provide a reasonable basis for them to make proper judgements on an ongoing basis as to the financial position and prospects of the issuer (LR 8.4.2(4)).

The reporting accountants are usually asked to provide comfort to the sponsor in this area.

The ICAEW published a Technical Release in 2014 (Tech 14/14CFF) entitled *Guidance on financial position and prospects procedures* which is aimed at directors and reporting accountants and sets out how they might establish and report on the procedures.

5.9 Annual accounts, preliminary statements and interim reports

Once listed, a company must satisfy the demands for continuing financial information. The principal requirements are contained in Ch.9 of the Listing Rules and Ch.4 of the Disclosure and Transparency Rules (DTRs). The DTRs implement the requirements of the EU Transparency Directive.[10]

---

[10] Directive 2013/50 amending Directive 2004/109 on the harmonisation of transparency requirements in relation to information about issuers whose securities are admitted to trading on a regulated market, Directive 2003/71 on the prospectus to be published when securities are offered to the public or admitted to trading and Directive 2007/14 laying down detailed rules for the implementation of certain provisions of Directive 2004/109 [2013] OJ L294/13.

In addition to its annual accounts, a company must release a statement of half-year results to the market. Under the DTRs, preliminary statements of annual results are not a requirement but, if companies choose to issue such a statement, they should comply with the requirements of the Listing Rules on preparation and issuance.

The annual accounts, for domestic companies, must contain all the information required by the Companies Act 2006 and the IFRS but must also include a variety of additional disclosures as specified by the UKLA and the DTRs. The DTRs require annual reports to be published within four months of the year end. Both the annual accounts and statements of half-yearly results must contain a "responsibility statement" prepared by the board directors confirming: (1) that the financial statements give a true and fair view; and (2) that their management report includes a fair review of the business and describes the principal risks and uncertainties it faces.

Under the DTRs, half-yearly statements must be published within three months of the half-year end and must comply with IAS 34 Interim Financial Reporting.

The DTRs stipulate that both the annual statements and statements of half-yearly results include a mandatory forward-looking section.

Chapter 6

Continuing Obligations

Joseph Newitt and Greg Stonefield
Partners, KWM Europe LLP

6.1 Introduction

6.1.1 General

This chapter describes the continuing obligations of a company with a premium listing of equity shares on the Official List maintained by the Financial Conduct Authority (FCA). These obligations are contained in the Disclosure Guidance and Transparency Rules (formerly the Disclosure and Transparency Rules) (DTRs), the Listing Rules (LRs) and, from 3 July 2016, in the EU Market Abuse Regulation (2014/596) (EU MAR).[1] It also covers the requirements for a listed company seeking a cancellation of its listing and the enforcement powers of the FCA in relation to breaches of the DTRs, the LRs and EU MAR.

Some of these continuing obligations, including the rules relating to transactions (LR 9.5), significant transactions (LR 10), related party transactions (LR 11) and periodic financial information (LRs 9.7A, 9.8 and DTR 4), are not considered in this chapter as they are covered elsewhere in this book (in particular, see Ch.7 below on transactions, significant transactions and related party transactions, and Ch.5 above on periodic financial reporting). In addition, the rules relating to corporate governance set out in Ch.7 ("Corporate Governance") of the DTRs are not considered as corporate governance matters generally are outside the scope of this chapter.

---

[1] Regulation 2014/596 on market abuse (market abuse regulation) and repealing Directive 2003/6 and Directives 2003/124, 2003/125 and 2004/72 [2014] OJ L173/1.

The Official List comprises two listing segments: "premium listing" and "standard listing". Only equity shares may be admitted to premium listing. A premium listing requires compliance with both EU directive minimum requirements and with certain additional (or "super-equivalent") listing requirements. Other types of security (e.g. global depositary receipts) may be admitted to standard listing. A standard listing only requires compliance with EU directive minimum requirements. Both UK and overseas issuers have a choice between seeking a premium or a standard listing.

This chapter focuses on the continuing obligations of issuers with a premium listing of equity shares. However, the main continuing obligations of issuers with a standard listing of equity shares are described in s.6.6 below.

6.1.2 Scope of the relevant rules

6.1.2.1 Scope: General

The introduction of the DTRs was driven primarily by the implementation in the UK of the Market Abuse Directive (2003/6) and the Transparency Directive (2004/109).[2] The Market Abuse Directive made it clear that the issuer disclosure regime plays an important role in preventing market abuse by ensuring that the market operates on the basis of prompt and fair disclosure of information to the public. The Transparency Directive reinforced this and seeks to enhance transparency in EU capital markets through a common framework requiring:

(1) issuers to produce periodic financial reports (comprising an annual report and a half yearly report) and to disseminate regulated information;

(2) vote holders to disclose major holdings of voting rights; and

---

[2] Directive 2003/6 on insider dealing and market manipulation (market abuse) [2003] OJ L96/16; Directive 2004/109 on the harmonisation of transparency requirements in relation to information about issuers whose securities are admitted to trading on a regulated market and amending Directive 2001/34 [2004] OJ L390/38.

(3) Member States to establish central mechanisms for storing and sharing regulated information.

These requirements are reflected in the subject areas covered by the DTRs.

6.1.2.2   Scope: Changes following the EU Market Abuse Regulation

The EU MAR repealed the Market Abuse Directive with effect from 3 July 2016. The EU MAR is an EU regulation which means that, unlike the Market Abuse Directive, it applies directly in the UK without the need for any domestic implementing legislation. Instead, changes have been made to the UK's existing domestic regime to ensure that UK national law does not conflict with the EU MAR. The two main areas of change have been to the *FCA Handbook* and the Financial Services and Markets Act 2000 (FSMA).

The FCA's approach to amending the *FCA Handbook* has been:

(1) where the *Handbook* copied out parts of domestic legislation (such as part of the FSMA) and that legislation has been repealed, then the copied out section has been deleted and replaced with a signpost to the relevant articles of the EU MAR;
(2) similarly where there was a provision which is now sufficiently addressed by an equivalent provision in the EU MAR, it has been deleted and replaced with a signpost to the relevant article in the EU MAR;
(3) if there is not an equivalent provision in the EU MAR and the *Handbook* provision provides clarification on the interpretation of a concept in the EU MAR, those provisions have been maintained so long as they are compatible with EU law; and
(4) in other cases, to make minor conforming changes to the wording of the provisions to make them consistent with the EU MAR terminology but with no changes to the intention of the provision.

The FCA published a number of consultation papers and policy statements in relation to the changes including Consultation Paper (CP) 15/35 (consultation on changes related to the implementation of the Market Abuse Regulation), CP 15/38 (provisions to delay disclosure of inside information within the FCA's Disclosure Guidance and Transparency Rules), CP 16/13 (proposed changes to DTR 2.5 on delay in disclosure of inside information) and Policy Statement (PS) 16/13 (implementation of the Market Abuse Regulation). These provide helpful background to the amendments.

Her Majesty's (HM) Treasury is separately responsible for any changes required to primary or secondary legislation. The necessary changes to the FSMA and other impacted legislation have been made through the Financial Services and Markets Act 2000 (Market Abuse) Regulations 2016 (SI 2016/680) (2016 Regulations).

Looking ahead, if the UK leaves the EU on Friday 29 March 2019, the European Union (Withdrawal) Bill, should it become law, will onshore the EU MAR as it exists just before exit day. This will create a new UK law to which modifications are likely to be made by HM Treasury to make it operable as a new piece of UK legislation. We could eventually even see the approach to how the obligations on issuers to disclose inside information are documented come full circle in that the references are set out again in full in the *FCA Handbook*. However, at least for the moment, this is still a little way off.

6.1.2.3   Scope: Listing Rules

The LRs apply to issuers of securities admitted (or seeking admission) to the Official List. Essentially, the LRs contain rules and guidance on the eligibility criteria for new applicants, the listing application process, the continuing obligations of listed issuers (in addition to those set out in the DTRs), the sponsor regime and the suspension and cancellation of listing.

Certain rules (for example, the Premium Listing Principles (set out in Ch.7 ("The Listing Principles and Premium Listing

Principles") below of the LRs) and the continuing obligations contained in Ch.9 ("Continuing obligations") below) only apply to issuers which have a premium listing of equity shares.

The DTRs have wider application than the LRs. The DTRs apply to issuers whose securities are admitted (or seeking admission) to trading on a regulated market. Regulated markets in the UK include not only the Main Market of the London Stock Exchange (LSE) but also markets such as NYSE Euronext London and the London International Financial Futures and Options Exchange (LIFFE). In addition, as described in s.6.1.2.4 below, certain elements of the DTRs also apply to issuers incorporated in the UK which have securities admitted to trading on markets which are not "regulated markets". However, certain issuers are not required to comply with particular DTRs, either because they are already subject to corresponding requirements derived from EU law in their own home Member State (e.g. European Economic Area (EEA) issuers in the case of DTRs 5 and 6) or because the laws of their country of incorporation have been declared to contain equivalent obligations to those contained in the DTRs (e.g. for non-EEA issuers incorporated in certain jurisdictions in the case of DTR 5).

The Listing Principles (contained within the LRs) are intended to ensure that the spirit, as well as the letter, of the DTRs and the LRs is adhered to.

6.1.2.4   Scope: Disclosure Guidance and Transparency Rule 5

Disclosure Guidance and Transparency Rule 5 (relating to vote holder and issuer notification) applies to issuers of shares admitted to trading on a "regulated market" whose home Member State is the UK (DTR 5.1.1R(1)). The home Member State for an issuer of shares is the EEA state chosen by the issuer from either: (1) the state in which the issuer has its registered office; or (2) the state in which its securities are admitted to trading on a regulated market. The EEA states consist of the EU states together with Norway, Iceland and Liechtenstein. "Regulated markets" are defined by reference to the EU Markets in Financial Instruments Directive (2004/39).[3] The Main Market of the LSE is a regulated market.

Disclosure Guidance and Transparency Rule 5 also applies to UK-incorporated companies with shares admitted to trading on a market (not being a regulated market) that is a "prescribed market". A "prescribed market" is a market prescribed by the Treasury in the Financial Services and Markets Act 2000 (Prescribed Markets and Qualifying Investments) Order 2001 (SI 2001/996) (as amended). This includes any market established under the rules of a UK-recognised investment exchange (such as AIM).

Issuers falling within the above two paragraphs are referred to as "UK issuers" in this chapter.

Non-UK incorporated issuers whose shares are admitted to trading on a "prescribed market" (not being a regulated market) are not required to comply with DTR 5 (see the UK Listing Authority (UKLA) Technical Note on Scope and application of vote holder and issuer notification rules (UKLA/TN/541.1)).

An issuer which is not a UK-incorporated company, whose shares are admitted to trading on a regulated market and whose home Member State is the UK, must comply with the requirements of DTR 5 applicable to what are termed "non-UK issuers" (DTR 5.1.1R(2)) (i.e. the Transparency Directive minimum disclosure requirements) unless the laws of its jurisdiction of incorporation are deemed equivalent.

Issuers incorporated in another EEA state whose home Member State is not the UK do not have to comply with DTR 5 as they are required to comply with corresponding requirements in their home Member State (see UKLA/TN/541.1).

---

[3] Directive 2004/39 on markets in financial instruments amending Directives 85/611 and 93/6 and Directive 2000/12 and repealing Directive 93/22 [2004] OJ L145/1.

An issuer whose registered office is in a non-EEA state whose relevant laws are considered equivalent by the FCA is exempted from the corresponding obligations in DTR 5 (DTR 5.11.4R). The shareholder notification requirements in DTR 5.1.2R also do not apply to shareholders in respect of the shares of an issuer which has its registered office in a non-EEA state whose laws are considered to be equivalent to those imposed by DTR 5 (see the FCA's "Equivalence of non-EEA regimes").[4] The FCA currently considers the laws of Israel, Japan, Switzerland and the US to be equivalent for this purpose.

This equivalency exemption will not generally affect a non-EEA issuer's obligation to comply with other continuing obligations (DTR 5.11.5G). However, the FCA is currently satisfied that issuers of shares admitted to trading on a regulated market in the UK that are incorporated in Switzerland will be exempt from certain information requirements of DTR 6 (see the FCA's "Equivalence of non-EEA regimes").

In relation to issuers of global depositary receipts (GDRs), the FCA has stated that it would not normally expect such issuers to fall within DTR 5 unless the issuer's shares are also admitted to trading on a regulated market (see UKLA/TN/541.1).

6.1.3 The FCA Handbook and the UKLA Knowledge Base

The rules follow the *FCA Handbook* style and format, namely that guidance on the DTRs and LRs is included next to the relevant rule(s) rather than in a separate manual. Guidance is denoted in relation to a particular paragraph of the DTRs and LRs by the suffix "G", with the suffix "R" used to denote the rule itself.

The rules are supplemented by the FCA's technical and procedural notes contained in the UKLA Knowledge Base, which represent the FCA's most up-to-date and formal guidance, and the FCA newsletter, *Primary Market Bulletin*.

---

[4] FCA, "Equivalence of non-EEA regimes" (2016; updated 2017) available at: *https://www.fca.org.uk/markets/ukla/regulatory-disclosures/equivalence-non-eea-regimes* [Accessed 8 June 2018].

The UKLA had previously issued informal commentary on relevant issues in the *List!* newsletters issued by the Financial Services Authority (FSA). From October 2010, *List!* was gradually replaced by technical and procedural notes ("2010 UKLA Technical Notes") published by the FSA, which brought together some existing and updated articles that had appeared in *List!*. In December 2012, the UKLA announced in the 4th edition of *Primary Market Bulletin* the introduction of the Knowledge Base, comprising of 80 formal guidance notes divided into procedural notes and Technical Notes on the LRs, Prospectus Rules and DTRs. Most of the technical and procedural notes cited in this chapter can be found in the Knowledge Base. As a result of the Legal Cutover (Financial Conduct Authority Non-Handbook Guidance) Instrument 2013 (FCA 2013/32), published by the FCA on 27 March 2013, the technical and procedural notes contained in the Knowledge Base from 1 April 2013 constitute formal FCA guidance.

Where informal commentary contained in the pre-existing 2010 UKLA Technical Notes has not been replicated in the Knowledge Base, this chapter may refer to the UKLA Technical Note on the DTRs ("DTR Technical Note 2010") and the UKLA Technical Note on the LRs ("LR Technical Note 2010").[5] The latter do not constitute formal FCA guidance.

6.1.4 Regulatory Information Services

Under both the DTRs and the LRs, listed companies are required to disclose/notify certain information to a regulatory information service (RIS). The RISs are primary information providers which have been approved by the FCA to disseminate the full text of regulatory announcements on behalf of listed companies by passing them on to news vendors and equivalent organisations (known as information society services) established in another EEA state.

---

[5] UKLA , Technical Note on the DTRs (2010) available at: *http://www.fsa.gov.uk/pubs/ ukla/listing_rules.pdf*; UKLA, Technical Note on the LRs (2010) available at: *http://www.fsa.gov.uk/pubs/ukla/disclosure_transparency.pdf* [Both accessed 12 July 2018].

If an issuer is admitted to trading on a regulated market it must also disclose any inside information it is required to make public under the EU MAR via a RIS as a result of being subject to the Transparency Directive. Neither the EU MAR nor Regulation 2016/1055 (laying down implementing technical standards with regard to the technical means for appropriate public disclosure of inside information and for delaying the public disclosure of inside information)[6] require an issuer to notify information via a RIS. This is because the EU MAR, unlike the Transparency Directive, will also apply to issuers admitted to trading on, for example, multilateral trading facilities (MTFs), and not just issuers admitted to trading on regulated markets. Regulation 2016/1055 does, however, require that information is made public via a mechanism which in effect has the same characteristics as a RIS and publication on the issuer's website or social media alone is not sufficient.

6.1.5 Other relevant regulation

In addition to their continuing obligations under the DTRs, the LRs and EU MAR, listed companies must meet the ongoing disclosure requirements contained in the Admission and Disclosure Standards of the LSE (or the rules of any other recognised investment exchange on which their shares are admitted to trading). Listed companies which are involved in a transaction governed by the City Code on Takeovers and Mergers (Takeover Code) must also comply with the rules of the Takeover Code, for example, relating to secrecy and the content and timing of announcements.

---

[6] Regulation 2016/1055 laying down implementing technical standards with regard to the technical means for appropriate public disclosure of inside information and for delaying the public disclosure of inside information in accordance with Regulation 596/2014 [2016] OJ L173/47.

6.2 The Disclosure Guidance and EU Market Abuse Regulation

6.2.1 Background

Prior to the EU MAR coming into effect, issuers whose securities were admitted (or seeking admission) to trading on a regulated market in the UK were subject to the Disclosure Rules. The Disclosure Rules were contained in Chs 2 ("Disclosure and control of inside information by issuers") and 3 ("Transactions by persons discharging managerial responsibilities and their connected persons") of the DTRs. These provisions have been amended to take account of the EU MAR. Disclosure Guidance and Transparency Rules 2 and 3 now provide guidance only and, together with DTR 1, have been renamed the *Disclosure Guidance*.

Issuers are instead subject to the disclosure obligations in the EU MAR. These obligations are primarily contained in arts 17, 18 and 19 of the EU MAR which are collectively referred to in the *FCA Handbook* as the "disclosure requirements".

6.2.2 Scope and purpose of the Disclosure Guidance

Chapter 1 ("Introduction") of the DTRs used to contain general rules relating to the application and purpose of the Disclosure Rules. As the purpose of DTRs 1, 2 and 3 following the EU MAR coming into effect is only to provide guidance on aspects of the EU MAR disclosure requirements, these operative provisions have been deleted from DTR 1. In certain cases, where the operative provisions are not replicated in the EU MAR itself, they have been reintroduced through other legislation.

Provisions which used to form part of DTR 1 and which have now been rehoused include:

(1) the obligations on issuers, persons discharging managerial responsibilities (PDMRs) and connected persons to provide to the FCA all information which it considers

appropriate to protect investors, ensure the smooth operation of the market or to verify whether the Disclosure Rules are being and have been complied with (formerly DTR 1.3.1R); and

(2) the FCA's right to require the publication of, or to publish itself, information which it considers appropriate to protect investors or to ensure the smooth operation of the market (formerly DTR 1.3.3R).

Both of these requirements have instead been inserted directly into the FSMA by the 2016 Regulations (s.122A and B).

Disclosure Guidance and Transparency Rule 1 now only includes very limited guidance. This guidance includes:

(1) that early consultation with the FCA is recommended if there is doubt as to the application of the disclosure requirements (DTR 1.2.4G); and

(2) provisions for making announcements when a RIS is not open for business (DTR 1.3.6R).

Chapter 1 of the DTRs also used to set out the FCA's right to require the suspension of trading of a financial instrument if it determined that there were reasonable grounds to suspect non-compliance with the Disclosure Rules (DTR 1.4.1R). Going forwards, the FCA instead has this right under s.122I of the FSMA which was inserted into the FSMA by the 2016 Regulations.

Other sanctions and enforcement rights are dealt with in more detail at the end of this chapter at s.6.9.2 below.

6.2.3 *Disclosure and control of inside information*

6.2.3.1 *General*

Following the EU MAR coming into effect, art.17 of the EU MAR contains the key general disclosure obligation for issuers whose securities are admitted (or seeking admission) to trading on a regulated market in the UK. It replaces the general disclosure obligation previously in Ch.2 ("Disclosure and control of inside information by issuers") of the DTRs.

Issuers should also have regard to Listing Principle 1 and, if relevant, Premium Listing Principle 6 (see ss.6.4.2.5 and 6.4.2.12 below). These require listed companies to:

(1) take reasonable steps to establish and maintain adequate procedures, systems and controls to enable them to comply with their obligations under the LRs, the EU MAR disclosure requirements and the transparency rules (including, in particular, its obligation to disclose information to the market in a timely and accurate manner (LR 7.2.1R)); and

(2) to communicate information to holders and potential holders of their listed equity shares in such a way as to avoid the creation or continuation of a false market in those shares (LR 7.2.1AR).

6.2.3.2   *Disclosure of inside information*

Subject to the limited ability to delay disclosure (see s.6.2.3.6 below), an issuer is required to inform the public as soon as possible of any "inside information" which directly concerns the issuer (art.17(1) of the EU MAR).

6.2.3.2.1   Definition of inside information

"Inside information" is defined in art.7 of the EU MAR as information of a *precise nature* which:

(1) has not been made public;
(2) relates, directly or indirectly, to one or more issuers or to one or more *financial instruments*; and
(3) if it were made public, would be likely to have a *significant effect* on the prices of those financial instruments or on the price of related derivative financial instruments.

6.2.3.2.2 Relevant financial instruments

One of the key effects of the EU MAR is to significantly extend the scope of instruments that fall within the market abuse regime. As a result, the scope of financial instruments caught by the disclosure requirements is also wider. The definition of "financial instruments" which applies in the EU MAR is the definition from MIFID II (art.4(1)(15) of Directive 2014/65)[7] and includes, among other things, shares, GDRs, transferable debt securities, money-market instruments, forward interest-rate agreements, currency and equity swaps and commodity derivatives.

6.2.3.2.3 The reasonable investor test

Prior to the EU MAR coming into effect, guidance on how to identify inside information was provided in the DTRs (DTRs 2.2.3G–2.2.8G). The test for disclosure was essentially whether or not the relevant information is price sensitive. In determining the likely price significance of information, the guidance given to an issuer was to assess whether the information in question would be likely to be used by a reasonable investor as part of the basis of his investment decisions and would, therefore, be likely to have a significant effect on the price of the issuer's financial instruments.

Article 7(4) of the EU MAR has maintained and reinforced the reasonable investor test. It provides that information which, if it were made public, would be likely to have a significant effect on the prices of financial instruments "shall mean" information a reasonable investor would be likely to use as part of the basis of its investment decisions.

The FCA has also retained and confirmed the guidance in DTR 2.2.5G that an issuer may wish to take account of the following factors when considering whether the information in question would be likely to be used by a reasonable investor as part of the basis of their investment decisions:

---

[7] Directive 2014/65 on markets in financial instruments and amending Directive 2002/92 and Directive 2011/61 [2014] OJ L173/349.

(1) the significance of the information will vary widely from issuer to issuer depending on a variety of factors such as the issuer's size, recent developments and market sentiment about both the issuer and the sector in which it operates; and

(2) the likelihood that a reasonable investor will make investment decisions relating to the relevant financial instrument to maximise his economic self-interest.

In addition, any such assessment may need to take into consideration the anticipated impact of the information in light of the issuer's activities generally, the reliability of the source of the information and other market variables likely to affect the relevant financial instrument in the given circumstances (DTR 2.2.6G). Information which is likely to be considered relevant to a reasonable investor's decision includes information which affects:

(1) the assets and liabilities of the issuer;
(2) the performance, or the expectation of the performance, of the issuer's business;
(3) the financial condition of the issuer;
(4) the course of the issuer's business;
(5) major new developments in the business of the issuer; and
(6) information previously disclosed to the market.

The reasonable investor test is one which the FCA has previously applied in practice. It was considered by the Upper Tribunal in its decision to uphold an enforcement decision by the FSA to fine Mr David Massey for market abuse (Upper Tribunal decision, *Massey*, February 2011).[8] Although it was a market abuse offence rather than a breach of the then Disclosure Rules, the same definition of "inside information" applied to each. In that case, Mr Massey knew of the company's intention to issue discounted shares to the market. He short-sold shares in the company at the trading price (8p). Almost immediately after, he subscribed for newly issued

---

[8] *Massey v Financial Services Authority* [2011] UKUT 49 (TCC); [2011] Lloyd's Rep. F.C. 459.

shares of the company at the discounted price (3.5p) to fill the short sale. In so doing, he made a net profit of just over £100,000.

The Upper Tribunal found that it was unlikely that the new issue, when announced, would have a "significant" effect (in the ordinary sense) on the price of the company's shares. However, because the information was of a kind that a reasonable investor would be likely to use as part of the basis of his investment decision, the Upper Tribunal concluded that the information was price-sensitive. The case suggested that if the information was relevant to a "reasonable investor", the information would meet the "significant price effect" criterion in the definition of "inside information" at the time under s.118C of the FSMA (repealed by the 2016 Regulations).

However, the Upper Tribunal's conclusion in *Massey* must now be viewed in light of its subsequent comments in Upper Tribunal decision, *Hannam*, October 2013.[9] The Upper Tribunal in *Hannam* commented that

> "it is not at all clear to us why the tribunal [in *Massey*] put the matter the way it did in expressing sympathy with Mr Massey's view: earlier on in its decision it had concluded on the facts that the announcement of the placing would be likely to have a significant effect on the price, which would fall".

6.2.3.2.4   No percentage threshold

The FCA has also retained its guidance which makes it clear that an issuer must be mindful that there is no figure (percentage change or otherwise) which can be set for any issuer when determining what constitutes a significant effect on the price of the financial investments (DTR 2.2.4G(2)) as this will vary from issuer to issuer.

---

[9]   *Hannam v Financial Conduct Authority* [2014] UKUT 233 (TCC); [2014] Lloyd's Rep. F.C. 704.

The FCA has previously noted that some market practitioners regard 10% as the relevant threshold for impact on the price of an issuer's financial instruments, or for assessing whether a variation in underlying financial information (e.g. operating profits or projected operating profits), triggers a corresponding requirement to make an announcement under the Disclosure Rules. The FCA has commented that this is not the case and that the guidance in DTRs 2.2.4G(2) and 2.2.6G should be followed (Technical Note on Assessing and handling inside information (UKLA/TN/521.1)). In its second set of Level 3 guidance, the Committee of European Securities Regulators (CESR) was also clear that fixing a threshold for price movements in financial instruments or quantitative criteria alone are not a suitable way of determining whether information is likely to have a significant effect on price.

In its enforcement decision relating to Woolworths Group Plc ("Woolworths") (see s.6.9.2.2 below), the FSA reiterated that there is no set percentage or other figure which determines whether or not there is a "significant effect" on the share price and it will vary from issuer to issuer (FSA, Final Notice to Woolworths Group Plc (11 June 2008)). In that case, the variation of a supply contract with Tesco Stores Ltd, which resulted in a reduction of over 10% in Woolworths' anticipated profits for the relevant financial year, was considered inside information which should have been disclosed as soon as possible. On the day the information was announced, Woolworths' share price fell by just over 12%. The case is interesting in that previous enforcement proceedings brought by the FSA had involved far greater price movements.

6.2.3.2.5 Information of a precise nature

An essential element of information being inside information is that it is "of a precise nature". Article 7(2) of the EU MAR provides that information will be deemed to be of a precise nature if

"it indicates a set of circumstances which exists or which may reasonably be expected to come into existence, or an event which has occurred or which may reasonably be expected to occur, where it is specific enough to enable a conclusion to be drawn as to the possible effect of that set of circumstances or event on the prices of the financial instruments".

This was highlighted in the FCA's enforcement decision relating to the late disclosure of inside information by Tejoori Ltd ("Tejoori") and the FCA's comments as to when Tejoori's disclosure obligation arose.[10] The decision was also notable as it was the first fine that the FCA has imposed on an AIM company for late disclosure following the EU MAR coming into effect.

Tejoori was an investment company whose shares were traded on AIM. In early 2016, Tejoori had two material investments, one of which was a shareholding in BEKON Holding AG ("BEKON"). On 12 July 2016, Tejoori was notified by BEKON about a compulsory acquisition of its shares by Eggersmann Gruppe GmbH & Co KG ("Eggersmann"). This was due to a drag-along provision which allowed the majority shareholders to require other shareholders to sell in the event of a takeover. The acquisition required Tejoori to sign a share purchase agreement and to sell its BEKON shares to Eggersmann for no initial consideration and with only a possibility of receiving deferred consideration that was materially lower than the value Tejoori had placed on its investment in its financial statements.

Tejoori's BEKON shares were ultimately transferred to Eggersmann on 10 August 2016 with both BEKON and Eggersmann issuing press releases announcing the acquisition the following day. The press releases made no reference to Tejoori so the market was unaware of the terms, including the consideration paid to Tejoori by Eggersman. In the absence of these details, the market speculated about the consideration that may have been paid to Tejoori. The speculation regarded the sale as a positive development for Tejoori and its share price rose 38% over the course of 22 and 23 August 2016.

---

[10] FCA, Final Notice to Tejoori Ltd (13 December 2017).

The LSE contacted Tejoori's Nomad on 23 August 2016 to query the sudden share price rise. Tejoori informed its Nomad that it did not hold any inside information and that it had not sold its shares in BEKON. This was based on a misunderstanding of the legal effect of the share purchase agreement. Only after consulting with Tejoori's German legal advisers was the correct position established. Tejoori ultimately released an announcement on 24 August 2016 and its share price closed down 13% on the day.

The FCA concluded that Tejoori breached art.17(1) of the EU MAR because it did not release an announcement about its shareholding in BEKON as soon as possible after being informed on 12 July 2016 that there was a reasonable expectation that it would be required to sell its shares in BEKON for no initial consideration and with only a possibility of receiving deferred consideration that was materially lower than Tejoori's valuation of its investment.

6.2.3.2.6   Seeking advice

In this context, it is the issuer and its advisers who are best placed to make an initial assessment of whether particular information amounts to inside information (DTR 2.2.7G). However, in its 2009 enforcement decision relating to Wolfson Microelectronics Plc (see s.6.9.2.2 below),[11] the FSA highlighted that a company should not rely exclusively on advice from its investor relations advisers in determining whether a disclosure obligation has arisen as it is neither legal advice nor advice from the company's corporate brokers.

In seeking advice from its advisers, an issuer must ensure that it keeps them fully informed in order to allow them to provide appropriate advice in respect of its disclosure obligations. The importance of doing so was highlighted in the FSA's 2011 enforcement decision in relation to JJB Sports Plc ("JJB")[12] for

---

[11]   FSA, Final Notice to Wolfson Microelectronics Plc (19 January 2011).
[12]   FSA, Final Notice to JJB Sports Plc (25 January 2011).

its failure to disclose promptly to the market the true price that it paid for two acquisitions, in breach of what was then DTR 2.2.1R and Listing Principle 4.

JJB acquired a retail chain for which it agreed to pay to the seller £5 million in cash plus the value of the seller's in-store stock. JJB announced the acquisition within 24 hours of the agreement being signed as well as the cash consideration for the deal. However, it failed to announce that it was liable to pay for the seller's stock, which was valued at approximately £10 million. JJB subsequently acquired another retail chain. The consideration payable by JJB to the seller under the share purchase agreement was £1 but JJB had also agreed to settle the target's bank overdraft. JJB announced the acquisition of the retailer for £1 but did not announce its obligation to settle the overdraft, which was estimated at the time to be nearly £6 million.

Following the acquisitions, JJB made several announcements concerning its financial position but did not, in so doing, disclose the true cost of these acquisitions. These liabilities were only publicly disclosed nine months later when JJB released its interim results. Following the release of the results, the company's share price fell approximately 49.5%.

The FSA imposed a financial penalty on JJB (see s.6.9.2.2 below) on the basis that its delay in disclosing the full cost of the acquisitions had led to the creation and continuation of a false market in JJB's shares. The full purchase price for the acquisitions was also inside information and should have been announced under DTR 2. Although JJB consulted with its brokers in respect of the relevant announcements, it had not expressly sought their view as to whether it was required to announce the omitted information.

6.2.3.2.7   Monitoring changes

The directors of an issuer should carefully and continuously monitor whether changes in the circumstances of the issuer are such that an announcement obligation has arisen under art.17

227

of the EU MAR (DTR 2.2.8G). This guidance is consistent with Listing Principle 1 (see s.6.4.2.5 below) which requires listed companies to take reasonable steps to establish and maintain adequate procedures, systems and controls to enable them to comply with their obligations under the LRs, the EU MAR disclosure requirements and the transparency rules.

The FCA has noted previously that in some circumstances announcements by industry regulators, trade associations, government departments and other bodies could amount to inside information. To avoid a breach of their disclosure obligations, issuers should have an agreed understanding with any such relevant organisations regarding the sensitivity of such statements and their impact on the market so that they can make announcements to the market where appropriate (Technical Note on Assessing and handling inside information (UKLA/TN/521.3)).

6.2.3.2.8   Content of notification

The European Securities and Markets Authority (ESMA) published draft technical standards in September 2015 (*Final Report: Draft technical standards on the Market Abuse Regulation*, ESMA/2015/1455 (2015)) on a number of aspects of the EU MAR. These included in Annex XII draft implementing technical standards on the technical means for appropriate public disclosure of inside information. These draft technical standards have been adopted by the Commission in Regulation 2016/1055 (laying down implementing technical standards with regard to the technical means for appropriate public disclosure of inside information and for delaying the public disclosure of inside information). Article 2(1)(b) of the Regulation 2016/1055 sets out certain information which any disclosure of inside information should clearly identify. One requirement which should be noted is that the relevant announcement should clearly identify that the information communicated is inside information. While practices are still developing, a number of issuers have satisfied this obligation by including rubric in the announcement along the following or similar lines: "information contained in this announcement is deemed by the Company to constitute inside information for the purposes of Article 7 of the Market Abuse Regulation 596/2014".

6.2.3.2.9   Other considerations and possible offences

The general disclosure obligation in art.17(1) of the EU MAR should also be considered in the context of:

(1)   s.90 of the Financial Services Act 2012 (as amended by the 2016 Regulations), which provides that a person who does any act or engages in any course of conduct which creates a false or misleading impression as to the market in, or the price or value of, relevant instruments commits a criminal offence if certain conditions are met; and

(2)   arts 14 and 15 of the EU MAR, which prohibit market abuse.

A failure to announce inside information under art.17(1) of the EU MAR may create a false or misleading impression for the purpose of s.90 of the Financial Services Act or constitute market abuse for the purpose of art.14 or art.15 of the EU MAR.

6.2.3.3   *Misleading information*

6.2.3.3.1   General

An issuer must take all reasonable care to ensure that any information which it notifies to a RIS is not misleading, false or deceptive, and does not omit anything likely to affect the import of the information (DTR 1A.3.2).

An issuer must not combine (in a manner likely to be misleading), the disclosure of inside information in a RIS announcement with the marketing of its activities (art.17(1) of the EU MAR).

The FSA has also previously stated that regulatory announcements should be written so that the key content of the message is given due prominence. For example, where issuers make announcements primarily to update the market on trading prospects, this information should be clearly visible, readily understandable by the reasonable investor and not relegated to the final paragraphs of the announcement. The announcement headline should reflect the information that has the greatest significance (see the DTR Technical Note 2010 under the heading "Regulatory announcements" in the section on DTR 1.3.5R).

6.2.3.3.2   Enforcement

The following are examples of where the FSA has taken enforcement action in respect of misleading disclosures, both under the pre and post-1 July 2005 regimes.

In December 2003, the FSA publicly censured SFI Group Plc ("SFI") for failing to take reasonable care to ensure that its preliminary results announcement issued on 30 July 2002 was not false or misleading.[13] The FSA concluded that SFI's announcement presented:

> "… an overstated and over-optimistic view of SFI's financial results and future prospects, not only as at July 30, 2002, but also in relation to the results for the two financial years prior to that date".

The FSA further concluded that persistent accounting systems and control failures (eventually identified by SFI in November 2002) had caused the announcement to be false and misleading. As a result of such failures, the FSA determined that SFI had failed to take reasonable care to ensure that the announcement was not misleading or false.

The FSA's public censure of The Big Food Group Plc in April 2002 also included a criticism of its public disclosure of the synergies achievable from its acquisition of Booker Plc in June 2000.[14] On 13 December 2000, the company announced that management was "confident that all expected benefits of the

---

[13]   FSA, Final Notice to SFI Group Plc (11 December 2003).
[14]   FSA, Disciplinary Decision—The Big Food Group Plc (26 April 2002).

merger with Booker are real and achievable".[15] The FSA concluded that the information available within the company indicated that the synergy benefits of the merger were likely to be at least 25% below the company's original forecast and market expectations. It concluded that the statement was misleading and a serious breach of the pre-1 July 2005 Listing Rules.

In March 2013, the FSA imposed a fine of more than £2.4 million on Lamprell Plc ("Lamprell") for breaches of DTRs 1.3.4R and 2.2.1R, among other breaches. In early 2012, the company's financial position started to deteriorate but, due to inadequate systems and controls in respect of financial oversight of the business, the company could not adequately assess its financial performance against budget and market expectations. Consequently, it was not until 16 May 2012 that the company issued a profit warning, which resulted in a 57% drop in its share price on the same day. The FSA found that Lamprell had failed to take all reasonable care to ensure that the information notified by it to a RIS did not omit anything likely to affect the import of the information. It also concluded that the company should have, at the least, issued a holding statement putting the market on notice of a potential material change to its expected financial performance, when the company's senior management possessed sufficient information by 29 April 2012. Consequently, the delay of 17 days to release any information to the market meant that the company failed to meet its obligation to notify a RIS as soon as possible of inside information which directly concerned it.

The FCA may also take criminal proceedings in relation to misleading impressions under ss.89–90 of the Financial Services Act. In August 2005, the FSA secured its first conviction for an offence of making a misleading statement contrary to s.397 of the FSMA (the predecessor to ss.89–90 of the Financial Services Act). The chief executive and finance director of AIT Group Plc ("AIT"), a provider of customer relationship management software, released an announcement stating that

---

[15] Paragraph 10 of the FSA, Disciplinary Decision—The Big Food Group Plc (26 April 2002).

AIT had met market expectations in May 2002.[16] The figures in the announcement were dependent on AIT's ability to recognise revenue from various contracts, none of which actually existed. Instead, they were governed by side letters and revenue recognition from these arrangements was subject to certain conditions being met. The FSA took criminal action against the chief executive and finance director as a result of the misleading announcement under s.397 of the FSMA and they each received prison sentences. Compensation orders were also made in favour of those who relied upon the misleading announcement.

6.2.3.3.3 Issuer statutory civil liability regime

Under s.90A of and Sch.10A to the FSMA, an issuer whose securities are, with the consent of the issuer, admitted to trading on a securities market (where that market is situated or operated in the UK or where the UK is the issuer's home Member State) is liable to pay compensation to investors in respect of losses suffered as a result of any untrue or misleading statement, or omission of any matter required to be included, in any information published by the issuer to which the regime applies. In practice, this means information published by an issuer under Ch.4 ("Periodic Financial Reporting") of the DTRs (i.e. an issuer's annual financial report and half-yearly financial report) and all RIS announcements by an issuer under the DTRs and the disclosure requirements.

As a result, an investor who acquires, continues to hold or disposes of such an issuer's securities can claim compensation for loss arising as a result of any untrue or misleading statement, or omission of a matter required to be included, in published information. Any such claim is subject to the following conditions:

(1) the investor's loss arose in reliance on the information in question and at a time when, and in circumstances in which, it was reasonable for him to rely on it; and

---

[16] *R. v Bailey* [2005] EWCA Crim 3487; [2006] 2 Cr. App. R. (S.) 36.

(2) a director (or another PDMR) of the issuer knew, or was reckless as to whether, the statement was untrue or misleading, or knew the omission to be a dishonest concealment of a material fact.

Under this regime, such an issuer will be liable to pay compensation to investors who suffer loss as a result of any dishonest delay by a PDMR of the issuer in the publication of information to which the regime applies. A PDMR's conduct is regarded as dishonest if (and only if) it is regarded as dishonest by persons who regularly trade in the securities market in question and the PDMR was aware (or must be taken to have been aware) that it was so regarded (paras 5 and 6 of Sch.10A to the FSMA).

Separately, the FCA also has the power under s.384 of the FSMA to require a person who has engaged in market abuse to compensate those persons suffering a loss or otherwise adversely affected as a result of the market abuse. The FCA exercised this power for the first time in relation to a listed company when in March 2017 it ordered that Tesco pay compensation to certain Tesco shareholders and bondholders following the FCA's finding that Tesco had committed market abuse in relation to a trading update published in August 2014.[17]

On 29 August 2014, Tesco Plc published a trading update which contained a statement as to its expected trading profit for the half-year. In producing that update, Tesco Plc relied on information provided to it by its subsidiary, Tesco Stores Ltd, which was not correct. On 22 September 2014, Tesco Plc published a further trading update in which it announced that it had "identified an overstatement of its expected profit for the half year, principally due to the accelerated recognition of commercial income and delated accrual of costs".[18]

---

[17] FCA, Final Notice to Tesco Plc and Tesco Stores Ltd (28 March 2017).
[18] Paragraph 2.2 of the FCA Final Notice to Tesco Plc and Tesco Stores Ltd (28 March 2017).

The FCA found that the trading update published in August gave a false or misleading impression as to the value of Tesco Plc's shares and publicly traded bonds issued by other Tesco group companies. As a result, the FCA considered that Tesco had engaged in market abuse even though the FCA did not suggest that the Tesco Plc board knew that the information was false or misleading.

6.2.3.4   When to disclose inside information

Subject to the limited ability to delay disclosure (see s.6.2.3.6 below), an issuer is required to inform the public of inside information "as soon as possible" (art.17(1) of the EU MAR).

"As soon as possible" was also the test under the former DTR 2.2.9G(1) prior to the EU MAR coming into effect. Under the pre-1 July 2005 regime for the disclosure of information (which was set out in the LRs), an issuer was required to disclose price-sensitive information "without delay". The FSA has previously stated that it did not believe that the change from "without delay" to "as soon as possible" allowed an issuer a longer period within which to make required disclosures to the market (para.4.51 of HM Treasury and the FSA's joint Consultation Document of June 2004 on "UK Implementation of the EU Market Abuse Directive" (2004 Consultation Paper)).

The leading FSA enforcement decision on the meaning of "without delay" under the pre-1 July 2005 regime related to Marconi Plc ("Marconi").[19] In April 2003, Marconi was censured by the FSA for a breach of the LRs when it failed to make an announcement "without delay" of a change in its expected performance for the half-year ended 30 September 2001 and the full-year ended 31 March 2002. The change to Marconi's expectation of performance had been agreed by Marconi's chief executive and chief financial officer in the afternoon of 2 July 2001 but an announcement was not made until after the market had closed on 4 July 2001, once the matter had been discussed at a pre-arranged board meeting.

---

[19] FSA, Final Notice to Marconi Plc (11 April 2003).

On 5 July 2001, there was a 25-fold increase in the volume of Marconi's securities traded and a 54% fall in its share price. The FSA considered that, once the change in expected performance had been agreed on the afternoon of 2 July 2001, Marconi should immediately have taken steps to bring forward its board meeting to a time no later than the afternoon of 3 July 2001 and that it should then have been in a position to release an announcement to the market by, at the latest, the evening of 3 July 2001.

The case shows that, while a small delay may have been acceptable so as to enable the preparation of a clear statement which was not misleading, the FCA will monitor very closely the steps taken to release an announcement once it becomes clear that some form of notification to the market is required.

The Marconi case also made it clear that, under the pre-1 July 2005 regime, the FSA was unlikely to regard the unavailability of directors to attend a board meeting as a sufficient excuse to delay the decision to release an announcement. The FCA similarly confirmed that, under the pre-EU MAR regime, the inability of the issuer to convene a full board meeting is unlikely to be viewed as a legitimate reason for delaying disclosure (UKLA/TN/521.3). Although the overall policy for the identification, control and dissemination of inside information is the responsibility of the issuer's board of directors, this responsibility can be delegated to a smaller number of directors who can react quickly. Premium Listing Principle 1 and Listing Principle 1, which require a listed company to take steps to enable its directors to understand their responsibilities and obligations as directors and to establish systems and controls to enable it to comply with its obligations under the LRs, the transparency rules and the EU MAR disclosure requirements (see ss.6.4.2.5 and 6.4.2.7 below), are also relevant here (UKLA/TN/521.3).

The disclosure obligations are continuous and apply in a variety of situations. The FCA's view has previously been that in "close periods" (i.e. the period before any regular results announcement when the directors and PDMRs of an issuer are not permitted to deal in the relevant company's shares without prior clearance), inside information must still be disclosed where necessary regardless of whether the issuer wishes to be pro-active in its investor communications during these periods (former Technical Note on Close periods (UKLA/TN/505.1)). If issuers elect not to publish preliminary statements of annual results, they are still required to publish inside information as soon as possible (Technical Note on Preliminary statement of annual results (UKLA/TN/502.2)).

The FCA has historically permitted an issuer to announce updates on their trading and financial performance at an annual general meeting (AGM), provided the issuer complies with the general disclosure obligations, which may include making a simultaneous public announcement (UKLA/TN/ 521.3). However, disclosure of inside information, including information relating to financial performance, must not be delayed to coincide with the announcement of a periodic financial report (Technical Note on Periodic financial information and inside information (UKLA/TN/506.1)).

6.2.3.5   Holding announcements

Where an issuer is faced with an unexpected and significant event, a short delay may be acceptable if it is necessary to clarify the situation prior to the release of a full announcement. In such situations, a holding announcement should be used where the issuer believes there is a danger of inside information leaking before the facts and their impact can be confirmed. The holding announcement must detail as much of the subject-matter as possible, set out the reasons why a fuller announcement cannot be made and include an undertaking to announce further details as soon as possible (DTR 2.2.9G(2)).

If an issuer is in any doubt as to the timing of any announcement which is required by the DTRs, it is required to consult the FCA at the earliest opportunity (DTR 2.2.9G(4)).

6.2.3.6 *Delaying disclosure of information*

An issuer may only delay disclosure of inside information in limited circumstances, namely where:

(1)   immediate disclosure is likely to prejudice the legitimate interests of the issuer;
(2)   the delay is not likely to mislead the public; and
(3)   the issuer is able to ensure the confidentiality of the information (art.17(4) of the EU MAR).

In accordance with art.17(11) of the EU MAR, ESMA has issued guidelines (*MAR Guidelines: Delay in the disclosure of inside information*, ESMA/2016/1478 (2016)—"ESMA Guidelines") to establish a non-exhaustive and indicative list of:

(1)   legitimate interests of the issuer that are likely to be prejudiced by immediate disclosure of inside information; and
(2)   situations in which delay of disclosure is likely to mislead the public.

The ESMA Guidelines are based on Recital 50 of the EU MAR and the CESR's second set of Level 3 guidance (CESR/06-5026).

The Guidelines provide three example situations as to where disclosure of inside information is likely to mislead the public (and therefore immediate disclosure is always necessary and mandatory):

(1)   the information is materially different from a previous public announcement of the issuer on the matter the information relates to;
(2)   the information is regarding the fact that the issuer's financial objectives are not likely to be met, where such objectives were previously announced; and
(3)   the information is in contrast with the market's expectations where such expectations are based on signals that the issuer has previously sent to the market.

Issuers will need to be watchful on this last point when inside information arises to check whether it could be said to contrast with any signals already given.

The example situations provided of where immediate disclosure of the inside information is likely to prejudice the issuer's legitimate interests include:

(1)   the issuer is conducting negotiations, where the outcome of such negotiations would likely be jeopardised by immediate public disclosure;

(2)   the financial viability of the issuer is in grave and imminent danger, although not within the scope of the applicable insolvency law, and immediate public disclosure of the inside information would seriously prejudice the interests of existing and potential shareholders by jeopardising the conclusion of the negotiations designed to ensure the financial recovery of the issuer;

(3)   the issuer has developed a product or invention and the immediate public disclosure of that information is likely to jeopardise the intellectual property rights of the issuer;

(4)   the issuer is planning to buy or sell a major holding in another entity and the disclosure of such an information would likely jeopardise the implementation of such plan; or

(5)   a transaction previously announced is subject to a public authority's approval and such approval is conditional upon additional requirements where the immediate disclosure of those requirements will affect the ability for the issuer to meet them and therefore prevent the final success of the deal or transaction.

The ESMA Consultation Paper on "Draft guidelines on the Market Abuse Regulation" (ESMA/2016/162) published when ESMA was consulting on the draft guidelines emphasises that:

(1)   this list is not meant to be exhaustive and issuers may be in other situations where they have legitimate interests to delay disclosure;

(2)   the possibility to delay represents an exception to the general rule of disclosure and therefore should be narrowly interpreted; and

(3)   the list is indicative and each situation should be assessed on a case by case basis.

Disclosure Guidance and Transparency Rule 2.5 (delaying disclosure of inside information) has been amended in light of both the EU MAR and the ESMA Guidelines.

The guidance in DTR 2.5.2G states that: (1) delaying disclosure of inside information will not always mislead the public (although a developing situation should be monitored so that if circumstances change an immediate disclosure can be made); and (2) investors understand that some information must be kept confidential until developments are at a stage where an announcement can be made without prejudicing the legitimate interests of the issuer, has been retained. As has the guidance which previously formed the first part of DTR 2.5.5G, it is for the issuer in the first instance to make an assessment of whether or not it has a legitimate interest which would be prejudiced by the disclosure of certain inside information.

Following the publication of the ESMA Guidelines, the illustrative situations previously in DTR 2.5.3G as to when an issuer may have legitimate interests to delay disclosure have now understandably been deleted. As the guidance previously stated in DTR 2.5.5G, the FCA considers that, other than such matters, there are unlikely to be circumstances where delay would be justified. However, when publishing the amendment to DTR 2.5.5G, the FCA emphasised that, even though the list in the ESMA Guidelines is non-exhaustive and indicative, it is the FCA's and ESMA's expectation that art.17(4) of the EU MAR should be narrowly interpreted and that all the conditions set out in art.17(4) must be met in order to legitimately delay the disclosure of inside information.

Issuers should be careful to distinguish between an event that gives rise to inside information (e.g. the loss of an important contract), which requires disclosure as soon as possible under art.17(1) of the EU MAR, and subsequent events (e.g. attempts to renegotiate that contract) that may benefit from the provisions allowing for the delay of an announcement. In its enforcement decision relating to Wolfson Microelectronics Plc (see s.6.9.2.2 below)[20] and in its technical guidance (UKLA/ TN/521.3), the FCA has previously reiterated that an issuer cannot "offset" negative news (e.g. loss of a major contract) against positive news (e.g. increased sale of other products) in order to justify delaying or withholding disclosure of the negative news. The FSA has also previously found in its enforcement decision relating to Entertainment Rights Plc (see s.6.9.2.2 below) that the fact that there may have been opportunities to mitigate the damaging impact of the negative news (in this case a variation of an agreement which would result in a reduction of profits) did not justify the delay in disclosing the negative news.[21]

Similarly, in its enforcement decision relating to Photo-Me International Plc ("PMI") in June 2010 (see s.6.9.2.2 below),[22] the FSA has previously taken the view that it is not acceptable for issuers to announce good news which is likely to have a positive impact but to withhold bad news on the same matter which is likely to have an adverse impact. In September 2006, PMI had announced that it expected to benefit substantially from growing sales of minilabs and from the securing of certain new contracts. Several months later, PMI made a further announcement that it had secured a contract with a buyer and that it continued "to be in discussion with other large US chains". At that stage, PMI had been in advanced negotiations with a large US retailer, Albertsons.

In January 2007, PMI was advised that it was no longer in exclusive negotiations with Albertsons. Also, in February 2007, one of PMI's directors was sent an email which included a document showing that sales of minilabs for the month of January had dropped by 40%, as compared with expected figures. It was only in March 2007 that PMI issued a profit

---

[20] FSA, Final Notice to Wolfson Microelectronics Plc (19 January 2009).
[21] FSA, Final Notice to Entertainment Rights Plc (19 January 2009).
[22] FSA, Final Notice to Photo-Me International Plc (21 June 2010).

warning relating, in large part, to an expected sales shortfall in minilabs. It also announced that the board did not expect to win the Albertsons contract.

The FSA decided that in both January and February 2007, PMI had inside information which should have been disclosed to the market and that its delay in doing so had created a false market in its shares. In the FSA's view, PMI's previous announcements had created an expectation in the market that it would benefit substantially from strong minilab sales and the company's loss of confidence that the Albertsons contract would be secured should have been disclosed in January 2007.

The FSA also found that the failure of a board member to open an email attachment and to consider the available information did not excuse the delay in disclosing that information to the market. It took the view that, if a company was in possession of inside information, a failure to consider or identify that information did not preclude a breach of what was then DTR 2.2.1R.

In the context of results announcements, the FSA commented in the DTR Technical Note 2010 that, as the release of results is a crucial communication of information to the market, it expects issuers always to work towards announcing their results as soon as possible, treating them with similar sensitivity as they would treat other inside information. Issuers should not delay the announcement in order to make preparations for the announcement of results, such as presentations to analysts or webcasts unless such preparations can legitimately occur alongside the efforts to release results quickly. The announcement of material information which does not relate to the performance of the company (e.g. a change in dividend policy, a change of strategy or a change of senior management) can only be delayed where confidentiality is maintained and the issuer has legitimate reasons for the delay. Generally, it would not be acceptable to delay an announcement where a decision regarding material information had clearly been made but not yet been formally approved by the board (DTR Technical Note 2010 under the heading "Timing of results announcements" in the section on DTR 2.2.3G).

This being said, it has been the general practice in the UK for issuers to publish results in accordance with a planned and often disclosed timetable. An area of debate since the EU MAR came into effect is the basis on which issuers are able to keep to their planned results timetable. Reasons suggested have included that: results in line with expectations are not inside information; the results are not inside information until they have been approved by the board; any slight delay is still consistent with the requirement to publish "as soon as possible"; and any delay is permitted under art.17(4) of the EU MAR.

The FCA announced in the June 2018 edition of its 19th *Primary Markets Bulletin* that it has launched a consultation on a proposed update to the existing Technical Note on Periodic financial information and inside information (UKLA/TN/506.1). The proposed draft guidance provides that issuers should not consider that information to be included in periodic financial reports will always or never constitute inside information. Issuers should asses on an ongoing and case-by-case basis and begin from the assumption that information relating to financial results could constitute inside information. The draft guidance further proposes that if the information does include inside information then publication may potentially be delayed under art.17(4) of the EU MAR where the issuer is in the process of preparing a periodic financial report and immediate public disclosure of information to be included in the report would impact on the orderly production and release of the report and could result in the incorrect assessment of the information by the public". Once the consultation has closed, issuers should watch for the final version of any update to the Technical Note.

ESMA has published guidance in the form of the ESMA Questions and Answers on the EU MAR[23] as to an issuer's obligations where it has delayed a disclosure of information in accordance with art.17(4) of the EU MAR but, due to subsequent circumstances, that information loses the element of price sensitivity and therefore its inside nature. ESMA's view is that in this situation the information ceases to be inside information and thus is considered outside the scope of art.17(1) of the EU MAR. Therefore, the issuer is neither obliged to publicly disclose that information nor to inform the competent authority in accordance with art.17(4) (see below) that disclosure of such information was delayed. However, given the information had been inside information for a period of time, the issuer had to comply with all relevant obligations relating to the drawing up and updating of insider lists and the maintenance of the information relating to the delay of disclosure while it still was inside information.

6.2.3.7 *Requirement to notify*

One new obligation imposed by the EU MAR is that, where an issuer has delayed the disclosure of inside information in accordance with art.17(4), the issuer must, immediately after the information is subsequently disclosed to the public, inform the competent authority (the FCA) that disclosure of the information was delayed.

The issuer is also required to provide a written explanation as to how the conditions for delaying were met. However, the EU MAR allows Member States the flexibility to determine whether this explanation: (1) must always be provided at the same time the competent authority is not notified of the delay; or (2) only if the competent authority requests an explanation. In the UK, the current position is that an issuer is only required to provide an explanation if the FCA requests one (s.4(1) of the 2016 Regulations).

---

[23] ESMA, "Questions and Answers: On the Market Abuse Regulation (MAR)", ESMA70-145-111 (23 March 2018).

In order to ensure uniform application of the requirements to notify and provide explanations, ESMA was required to develop draft implementing technical standards which the European Commission could then adopt. ESMA published draft technical standards in September 2015 (ESMA/2015/1455). These have now been implemented by the 2016/1055 (laying down implementing technical standards with regard to the technical means for appropriate public disclosure of inside information and for delaying the public disclosure of inside information). The draft implementing standards clarified that ESMA had decided not to impose common templates for notification of delays. Instead, Regulation 2016/1055 sets out the list of information which is required to be included in any notification and an obligation on issuers to record and maintain information regarding the delay of disclosure.

The commentary to the technical standards specifies:

(1)   that issuers are expected to have in place a minimum level of organisation and a process to conduct a prior assessment as to whether information is inside information, whether its disclosure needs to be delayed and for how long;

(2)   there should be a person or persons appointed within the issuer responsible for making the decision. This person should be clearly identified within the issuer and should have the necessary decision making power; and

(3)   before taking a decision allowing the delay of publication of inside information, this person should conduct an assessment on whether the three conditions in art.17(4) for delaying are fulfilled. Given the requirement for the issuer to be able to provide a written explanation concerning the delay, these decisions and information should be recorded together with the relevant reasons supporting such decisions.

Each of these will be required in order to enable an issuer to comply with art.4(1) of Regulation 2016/1055. Notably, Regulation 2016/1055 also requires an issuer to record and maintain details of dates and times when the inside information first existed within the issuer. This may not always be easy for an issuer to know or be able to discover.

Any notification to the FCA of a delay in disclosure should be made on the "delay disclosure notification form" which is available on the FCA's website.

6.2.3.8   Selective disclosure

Other than in situations where disclosure of inside information is delayed in accordance with art.17(4) of the EU MAR, an issuer must ensure that inside information is not disclosed on a selective basis. Selective disclosure cannot be made to any person simply because they owe the issuer a duty of confidentiality. Depending on the circumstances, an issuer may be justified in disclosing inside information to certain recipients (in addition to its employees) who require the information to perform their functions. The latter may include:

(1)   the issuer's advisers and advisers of any other persons involved in the matter in question;
(2)   persons with whom the issuer is negotiating, or intends to negotiate, any commercial, financial or investment transaction;
(3)   employee representatives or trade unions acting on their behalf;
(4)   any government department, the Bank of England, the Competition Commission or any other statutory or regulatory body or authority;
(5)   major shareholders of the issuer;
(6)   the issuer's lenders; and
(7)   credit rating agencies (DTR 2.5.7G(2)).

Selective disclosure to any or all of the persons listed above may not be justified in every circumstance where an issuer delays disclosure in accordance with art.17(4) of the EU MAR. An issuer should also bear in mind that the wider the group of recipients of inside information, the greater the likelihood of a leak, which will trigger the requirement for public disclosure of the information under art.17(8) of the EU MAR (see s.6.2.3.11 below) (DTR 2.5.9G).

Where an issuer relies on art.17(4) of the EU MAR to delay the disclosure of inside information and makes selective disclosure to permitted recipients, it must prepare a holding announcement (see s.6.2.3.5 below) to be issued in the event of an actual or likely breach of confidence (DTR 2.6.3G). This requirement is designed to ensure that an announcement can be released as soon as possible if there is a breach of confidentiality.

If an issuer is considering making a selective disclosure of information it should carefully consider the new rules relating to market soundings in art.11 of the EU MAR. These rules are outside the scope of this chapter but apply where information is communicated prior to the announcement of a transaction in order to gauge the interest of potential investors in a possible transaction and the conditions relating to it such as potential size or pricing. The EU MAR rules on market soundings are supplemented by Regulation 2016/960 (with regard to regulatory technical standards for the appropriate arrangements, systems and procedures for disclosing market participants conducting market soundings)[24] and the ESMA guidelines on market soundings and delay of disclosure of inside information (*Final Report: Guidelines on the Market Abuse Regulation—market soundings and delay of disclosure of inside information,* ESMA 2016/1130 (2016)).

Under art.6 of the EU MAR and art.5 of the Regulation 2016/960 where information that has been disclosed in the course of market soundings ceases to be inside information, the issuer is required to inform the recipient of this as soon as possible. Where market soundings have been taken in respect of matters contained in an announcement, issuers generally include a statement along the following lines:

---

[24] Regulation 2016/960 supplementing Regulation 596/2014 with regard to regulatory technical standards for the appropriate arrangements, systems and procedures for disclosing market participants conducting market soundings [2016] OJ L160/29.

"Market soundings were taken in respect of the matters contained in this announcement, with the result that certain persons became aware of such inside information. Upon publication of this announcement, this inside information is now considered to be in the public domain and such persons shall therefore cease to be in possession of inside information."

6.2.3.9   *Dealing with rumours*

If there is press speculation or market rumour regarding an issuer, an issuer should assess whether a disclosure obligation arises under art.17(1) of the EU MAR. To do this, an issuer must assess carefully whether the speculation or rumour has given rise to a situation where the issuer has inside information (DTR 2.7.1G).

Where disclosure of inside information has been delayed in accordance with art.17(4) of the EU MAR and the confidentiality of that inside information is no longer ensured, the issuer must disclose that inside information to the public as soon as possible. This includes situations where a rumour explicitly relates to that inside information and the rumour is sufficiently accurate to indicate that the confidentiality of that information is no longer ensured (art.17(7) of the EU MAR). The FCA may contact an issuer or its adviser to discuss the matter but the issuer should not wait until it is contacted to consider whether inside information should be notified. If required, the FCA may seek to establish the truth of a story and the presence (or likelihood) of a related significant price movement and may seek an opinion from the issuer or advisers and challenge opinions received (Technical Note on Delaying disclosure/dealing with leaks and rumours (UKLA/TN/520.2)).

In the DTR Technical Note 2010, the FSA commented that evidence that a breach of confidence had occurred would vary from case to case and an issuer would have to use its own judgement, usually in consultation with its advisers. The FSA gave the example of a large multinational issuer that was known to have been in talks with a number of potential US partners in the past. Such an issuer was not necessarily obliged to respond to a rumour that it was once again in talks with a US company, even if it was actually in talks. However, if the rumour contained more concrete information, such as the name of the other party, dates of meetings, details of any proposed structure or the amount of any consideration, then this would suggest that there had been a breach of confidence and an announcement would be required as soon as possible. An issuer should not wait until substantially the entire deal was revealed in the press before making an announcement. As soon as there was any indication that there had been a leak, or that a leak was likely, or if there were details contained in the rumour that suggested a breach of confidence had occurred, the issuer should make an announcement as soon as possible (DTR Technical Note 2010 in the section on DTR 2.6.2R).

If a leak occurs and a full announcement is not possible, any holding announcement should be meaningful and, at minimum, reflect the extent to which a leak or rumour is truthful. If, in the FCA's view, the holding announcement does not sufficiently reflect the leak, it may be challenged (Technical Note on Delaying disclosure/dealing with leaks and rumours (UKLA/TN/520.2)).

The knowledge that press speculation or market rumour is false is not likely to amount to inside information (although the FSA has stated in the past that there is a possibility that the issuer's knowledge that a particular piece of information is false could, in very limited circumstances, amount to inside information) (DTR Technical Note 2010 under the heading "Press speculation and market rumours" in the section on DTR 2.7). Even if it does, the FCA expects that in most cases an issuer would be able to delay disclosure in accordance with art.17(4) or (5) of the EU MAR (DTR 2.7.3G). Therefore, an issuer should be able either not to respond or to maintain a consistent "no comment" approach to false press speculation or market rumour. FSA commentary indicates that, while an issuer is not usually required to make a negative statement denying a wholly unfounded rumour, if it does it should consider doing so by making a formal announcement rather than just doing so in a single publication. This should ensure that the whole market is informed rather than just the readers of a single newspaper or newswire service (DTR Technical Note 2010 under the heading "Press speculation and market rumours" in the section on DTR 2.7).

Section 4 of the second set of CESR guidance (CESR/06-5026— see s.6.2.3.2.6 above) also clarified that issuers are under no obligation to respond to either speculation or market rumours that are without substance, or to equivalent information in publications. Only where the information contained in the rumour or publication relates explicitly to a piece of information that is inside information within the issuer and it is clear that a leak has occurred does the disclosure obligation arise. It is emphasised that such circumstances should be the exception rather than the rule and should be examined by the issuer on a case-by-case basis.

The inaccuracy of some aspects of a rumour may not in themselves be justification for non-disclosure (UKLA/TN/ 520.2). An example may be inaccuracies in a rumour as to the size or pricing of a capital raising, which may not of themselves negate the obligation to announce the existence of a (planned) capital raising.

6.2.3.10 *Communication with analysts and other third parties*

Many issuers do provide unpublished information to third parties such as analysts, employees, credit rating agencies, finance providers and major shareholders, often in response to queries. The fact that information is unpublished does not in itself make it inside information. However, unpublished information which amounts to inside information is only permitted to be disclosed in accordance with the requirements of the EU MAR (DTR 2.2.10G), including the new rules relating to market soundings in art.11 of the EU MAR (see s.6.2.3.8 above).

The FCA recognises that analysts play a constructive role in helping the market understand and value an issuer's securities.

In the DTR Technical Note 2010, the FSA gave advice on good practice concerning the way in which an issuer's relationships with analysts should be conducted. This included the following:

(1) companies should have a clear policy about the extent to which they should answer analysts' questions. For example, issuers can explain information already in the public domain or discuss the markets in which they operate;

(2) issuers should decline to answer analysts' questions where, individually or cumulatively, the answers would provide inside information;

(3) although an issuer is not generally obliged to correct analysts' forecasts, it should consider making an announcement to correct significant errors that have come to its attention, which in its view have led to a widespread and serious misapprehension in the market. Knowledge that a forecast is inaccurate is more likely to amount to inside information if an issuer is covered only by a small number of analysts;

(4) if an analyst sends an issuer a draft report for comment, the issuer can choose whether to respond and is not obliged to correct incorrect statements or assumptions. If an issuer chooses to comment, it should take care not to disclose inside information;

(5) in respect of meetings with analysts, issuers should consider establishing internal procedures to reduce the risk that they may be mistakenly accused of providing inside information to analysts at such meetings. These procedures could include, for example, ensuring that more than one company representative is present during the meeting and that an accurate record of all discussions is kept, or opening analysts' briefings so as to include the press, and possibly the public, albeit in a non-participating capacity (e.g. via telephone lines or on the company's website); and

(6) employees meeting analysts during visits to an issuer's premises should be briefed on the extent and nature of the information which they can communicate.

In *Market Watch* Issue No.30 (November 2008), the FSA acknowledged the analyst's role and clarified that statements which are clearly an expression of an individual's or a firm's opinion, such as an analyst's view of the prospects of a company, are unlikely to be considered a rumour.

6.2.3.11 Control of inside information

In order to minimise the possibility of an unauthorised leak of inside information, an issuer should establish effective arrangements to deny access to inside information to persons other than those who require it for the exercise of their functions within the issuer (DTR 2.6.1R).

Market Watch Issue No.27 (June 2008) included the "Principles of Good Practice for the Handling of Inside Information" ("Principles for Handling Inside Information") drawn up by an industry working group. The main objective of the Principles for Handling Inside Information was to increase awareness by non-regulated firms of the ways to protect inside information and to set out voluntary policies and practices such firms could adopt. However, the FSA noted that they could also provide assistance to other market participants as well (by implication, including issuers and their advisers). The Principles for Handling Inside Information covered:

(1) policies and procedures;
(2) awareness and training;
(3) "need to know" and other information controls;
(4) passing price-sensitive information to third parties;
(5) information technology security; and
(6) personal dealing policies.

In the DTR Technical Note 2010, the FSA advised issuers that areas of responsibility for communication with analysts, investors and the media should be clearly defined. If the issuer's communications policy and the identity of the key employees who are responsible for the implementation of that policy are clearly identified to staff, senior management should be better able to control the dissemination of information and reduce the chance of unauthorised or careless disclosure (DTR Technical Note 2010, under the heading "A framework for handling inside information" in the section on DTR 2.2.3G).

In *Market Watch* Issue No.37 (September 2010), the FSA set out its key findings from its investigation into potential disclosures of inside information to the media prior to certain announcements and provided a list of best practice recommendations.

6.2.3.12   *Publication of information on internet sites*

In addition to announcing inside information via a RIS, an issuer must post on its website all inside information which it is required to disclose publicly under art.17(1) of the EU MAR. The issuer must then maintain this information on its website for at least five years (art.17(1) of the EU MAR).

6.2.3.13   *Notification when a regulatory information service is not open for business*

If an issuer is required to make inside information public at a time when a RIS is not open for business, it must distribute the information as soon as possible to:

(1)   not less than two national newspapers in the UK;
(2)   two newswire services operating in the UK; and
(3)   a RIS for release as soon as it opens (DTR 1.3.6G).

The FSA had previously noted that issuers must not use the "Friday Night Drop" to delay disclosure, i.e. delaying disclosure of inside information until Friday evening when RISs have closed for business so that information can only be released on Monday morning (DTR Technical Note 2010 under the heading "Selective disclosure"). More generally, issuers should not provide inside information to third parties such as journalists, under an embargo, which would seek to prevent those parties using the information until it has been released to a RIS since there is a potential loss of control over the information as soon as the disclosure is made (UKLA/TN/ 520.2).

6.2.3.14   Equivalent information

Prior to the implementation of the EU MAR, the DTRs used to provide that an issuer with financial instruments admitted (or to be admitted) to trading on more than one regulated market or listed on any other overseas exchange needs to ensure that the disclosure of inside information is synchronised as closely as possible in all jurisdictions (formerly DTR 2.4.1R). If the rules of another regulated market or overseas stock exchange require an issuer to disclose inside information at a time when a RIS is not open for business, an issuer was required to disclose the information in accordance with DTR 1.3.6G (see s.6.2.3.13 above) at the same time as it is released to the public in the other jurisdiction (formerly DTR 2.4.2R). The FCA has deleted the former DTRs 2.4.1R and 2.4.2R on the basis that art.17(10) of the EU MAR allows the Commission to adopt implementing technical standards in the technical means for appropriate public disclosure of inside information.

6.2.4   Insider lists

6.2.4.1   Requirement to draw up insider lists

An issuer or any person acting on behalf of an issuer or on its account must:

(1)   draw up a list of all persons who have "access to inside information" and who are working for them under a contract of employment or otherwise performing tasks through which they have access to inside information; and
(2)   promptly update the insider list (art.18(1) of the EU MAR).

Insider lists must be promptly updated when there is a change in the reason why a person is already on the list, when any person who is not already on the list is provided with access to inside information and when a person already on the list no longer has access to inside information. Each update must specify the date and time when the change triggering the update occurred (art.18(4) of the EU MAR).

In this context, "access to inside information" is a key concept. Clearly, the phrase could be interpreted extremely widely to include secretarial, administrative and IT staff who potentially have access to inside information. In the DTR Technical Note 2010, in the section on DTR 2.8 as it then was, the FSA indicated that, in relation to advisers to issuers, staff needed only to be included on an insider list if they met the following two tests that:

(1) they have access to inside information; and
(2) they are acting on behalf of the issuer.

The FSA further considered that, for advisers, normally only members of deal teams and client-facing staff should be included on insider lists (provided they have access to inside information). The FSA cited the example of a person employed to photocopy documents, or who acts in a "control room" type function, as a person who would not be required to be included on an insider list as, despite in theory having access to inside information, he/she would not be acting on behalf of the issuer. Similarly, an adviser's senior management or secretaries employed in a general capacity rather than attributed to a particular client would not need to be included unless they were clearly working on an assignment for an issuer.

As part of its efforts to harmonise the application of the Market Abuse Directive across the EU (before it was repealed by the EU MAR), the CESR published its third set of Level 3 guidance on the implementation of the Market Abuse Directive (CESR/09-219) in May 2009. The CESR suggested that persons included on insider lists should be those with access to inside information about the relevant issuer as a result of their activities or duties within the issuer, as opposed to those who obtain access by some other means (e.g. by accident) of which the issuer is not aware. According to the CESR, the focus should be on access (either regular or occasional) of persons to the inside information, rather than on the legal distinction between regular and occasional insiders.

Insider lists must be kept for at least five years from the date on which they are drawn up or updated, whichever is the latest (art.18(5) of the EU MAR).

6.2.4.2   *Content of insider lists*

To ensure that national differences do not exist with regard to the data included in insider lists, ESMA was required under the EU MAR to develop implementing technical standards which the Commission could then adopt. ESMA published draft technical standards in September 2015 (ESMA/2015/1455). These were then adopted under Regulation 2016/347 (laying down technical standards with regard to the precise format of insider lists).[25] Regulation 2016/347 sets out a template insider list which includes the following items: name; company name and address; work direct line and work mobile; function and reason for being an insider; date and time at which person obtained inside information; date and time at which person ceased to have information; date of birth; national identification number (where applicable); personal home and mobile telephone numbers; and personal full address.

Prior to the EU MAR coming into effect, it had been usual for issuers to maintain one insider list for those persons within the company who have regular access to inside information and then further ad hoc or transaction-specific lists containing the names of other relevant persons. This practice was partially recognised in the DTR Technical Note 2010. Regulation 2016/347 envisages that there will be just one insider list of the issuer but that this can be made up of a permanent insider section and different deal specific, event-based sections. All of the sections together will form the whole insider list.

If requested, an issuer must provide an insider list to the FCA as soon as possible (art.18(1)(c) of the EU MAR). The insider list must be provided in the form set out in the Regulation

---

[25] Regulation 2016/347 laying down implementing technical standards with regard to the precise format of insider lists and for updating insider lists in accordance with Regulation 596/2014 [2016] OJ L65/49.

2016/347. No guidance is given as to what "as soon as possible" means in this context but issuers should ensure that they have appropriate procedures in place so that insider lists can be produced at short notice, most likely within 24 hours of a request.

6.2.4.3   *Acknowledgement of legal and regulatory duties*

Issuers or any person acting on their behalf or on their account must take all reasonable steps to ensure that any person on the insider list acknowledges in writing the legal and regulatory duties entailed and is aware of the sanctions applicable to insider dealing and unlawful disclosure of inside information (art.18(2) of the EU MAR).

To comply with these requirements, issuers should consider appropriate training for their employees and the inclusion of appropriate wording in employee service agreements. Issuers may also wish to have regard to the Principles for the Handling of Inside Information set out in *Market Watch* Issue No.27 (see s.6.2.3.11 above) in determining how to comply with these requirements. In relation to advisers' insider lists, these requirements are likely to be addressed by including appropriate language in the relevant engagement letters.

6.2.4.4   *Issuer ultimately responsible*

Where another person acting on behalf or on account of the issuer assumes the task of drawing up and updating the insider list, the issuer remains fully responsible for compliance with art.18 of the EU MAR (art.18(2) of the EU MAR). The issuer must also ensure that it always retains a right of access to the insider list. However, the ESMA Questions and Answers on EU MAR clarify that this is only in respect of the issuer's insider list. The issuer is not responsible for the fulfilment of the insider list requirements of persons acting on its behalf or account (e.g. advisors and consultants) who are personally responsible for the obligation to draw up, update and provide to the relevant national competent authority on request their own insider list.

6.2.5 Transactions by persons discharging managerial responsibilities

6.2.5.1 Scope

Article 19 of the EU MAR sets out the notification requirements of issuers, PDMRs and persons closely associated with them in respect of dealings by PDMRs and their persons closely associated with them in the shares or debt instruments (or related derivatives or other financial instrument(s)) of an issuer.

Article 19 is without prejudice to the right of Member States to provide for notification obligations other than those referred to in it.

6.2.5.2 Notification of transactions by persons discharging managerial responsibilities

PDMRs and persons closely associated with them must notify the issuer in writing of all transactions conducted on their own account in the shares or debt instruments (or derivatives or other related financial instrument(s)) of the issuer. The notification must be made promptly and no later than three business days after the transaction occurred (art.19(1) of the EU MAR).

The requirement to notify applies to every transaction. To limit the burden:

(1) a PDMR or closely associated person is able to send a single notification listing and detailing multiple transactions carried out, as long as the three working day deadline for notifying each of the transactions is complied with; and

(2) notifications are only required once a total transaction threshold of €5,000 has been reached within a calendar year. The FCA can decide to increase this threshold to €20,000 but for the moment has maintained it at €5,000 (DTR 3.1.2B).

The ESMA Questions and Answers on the EU MAR helpfully clarify that, if transactions are carried out in a currency other than the euro, then the exchange rate to be used to determine if the threshold is reached is the official daily spot foreign exchange rate applicable at the end of the business day when the transaction is conducted. They also clarify that, when calculating whether the threshold is reached, you do not aggregate the transactions carried out by a PDMR with any transaction carried out by a closely associated person to that PDMR.

In addition to notifying the issuer, the person making the notification must also notify the competent authority of the Member State where the issuer is registered (or, if it is not registered in a Member State, its home Member State and, failing that, the competent authority of the trading venue).

The notification must contain the name of the person dealing in the relevant financial instrument, the reason for the responsibility to notify, the name of the issuer, a description of the financial instrument, the nature of the transaction (i.e. whether it was an acquisition or disposal), and the date, place, price and volume of the transaction (art.19(6) of the EU MAR).

As with insider lists, in order to ensure consistency, ESMA was required to develop draft implementing standards for the Commission to adopt concerning the format and template in which the information is to be notified and made public. In earlier consultations, it was envisaged that the template would comprise two sections. One section which would be made public and another more detailed section which would not. In the implementing standards adopted by the Commission under Regulation 2016/523 (laying down implementing technical standards with regard to the format and template for notification and public disclosure of managers' transactions),[26] the template has been simplified so that it still retains the

---

[26] Regulation 2016/523 laying down implementing technical standards with regard to the format and template for notification and public disclosure of managers' transactions in accordance with Regulation 596/2014 [2014] OJ L88/19.

information needed by competent authorities while at the same time being suitable for publication in full.

Any notification to the FCA should be made on the PDMR notification form published on its website. The FCA has also published a guide to completing the PDMR notification form.

The EU MAR and the DTRs do not define the meaning of "transactions conducted on own account". In the former Technical Note on Transactions by persons discharging managerial responsibilities and their connected persons (UKLA/TN/540.1), the FCA provided guidance on what is meant by "on own account".

This provided that transactions that were unlikely to be considered to be "on own account" included those over which the PDMR did not have any control nor give any instruction or consent. Examples included the automatic vesting of an option, and dealings by an employee benefit trust in respect of an employee share scheme, for the benefit of all participants including the PDMRs, where the PDMRs have not instructed the dealings. The FCA added that it was not possible to provide a definitive test for transactions that are "on own account" as each transaction by a PDMR should be assessed on a case-by-case basis as to whether it was conducted "on own account". This guidance has been withdrawn and the question must now be considered in light of certain specific examples of dealings which are required to be disclosed listed in art.19(7) of the EU MAR and art.10 of Regulation 2016/522 (as to types of notifiable managers/transaction).[27]

In particular, it should be noted that art.10 of Regulation 2016/522 specifically requires the notification of the acceptance or exercise of a stock option, including a stock option granted to managers or employees as part of their remuneration package. Further guidance is also given in the ESMA Questions

---

[27] Regulation 2016/522 supplementing Regulation 596/2014 as regards an exemption for certain third countries public bodies and central banks, the indicators of market manipulation, the disclosure thresholds, the competent authority for notifications of delays, the permission for trading during closed periods and types of notifiable managers' transactions [2016] OJ L88/1.

and Answers on EU MAR as when shares received as part of a remuneration package are required to be notified and the relevant price.

Under DTR 3, PDMRs and their connected persons were required to disclose the grant of security over shares (or other related financial instrument(s)) of the issuer. This is confirmed by art.19(7)(a) of the EU MAR which specifically refers to the pledging or lending of financial instruments. Recital 58 states that it is necessary to clarify that the obligation to publish the managers' transactions also includes the pledging or lending of financial information, as the pledging of shares can result in a material and potentially destabilising impact on the company in the event of a sudden, unforeseen disposal.

6.2.5.3   Who is a person discharging managerial responsibilities?

PDMRs are not limited to directors but also include senior executives of the issuer who:

(1)   have regular access to inside information relating, directly or indirectly, to the issuer; and
(2)   have the power to make managerial decisions affecting the future development and business prospects of the issuer (art.3(1)(25) of the EU MAR).

It is likely, therefore, that in order to be a PDMR a person must be a senior decision-maker, for example, a member of an executive committee, rather than a line manager. The definition is similar to the former definition in s.96B(1) of the FSMA. In that context, prior to the EU MAR taking effect, the FCA was of the view that those having the power to make managerial decisions which affect the future development and business prospects of the issuer, such as members of the board of directors, are clearly PDMRs. On the other hand, those that offer analysis or information to enable others ultimately to make a managerial decision may not be PDMRs, even where they give informed recommendations. Where the classification is not clear-cut, the FCA has previously suggested that companies should consider how much influence or responsibility a person has in managerial decision-making. For example, company secretaries who deal solely with administration and general counsel who offer their company legal advice are usually not classified as PDMRs (former UKLA/TN/540.1).

An individual may be a "senior executive" as defined in art.3(1)(25)(b) of the EU MAR irrespective of the nature of (or absence of) any contractual arrangements between the issuer and the individual (DTR 3.1.2AG).

It is impossible to estimate how many PDMRs there should be, on average, across the broad spectrum of listed companies. Some issuers may not in fact have any PDMRs outside of the board of directors. The FCA has previously advised that companies must determine the existence of PDMRs based on a consideration of the functions and responsibilities of their employees. If a managerial decision affecting the future development and business prospects of an issuer is ratified by the issuer's board of directors, the non-board members recommending the action may nevertheless be PDMRs. However, in those cases where the decision is clearly made by the board members and not senior management, a non-board member is unlikely to be a PDMR (former UKLA/TN/540.1).

A "person closely associated" with a PDMR means:

(1) a spouse, or a partner considered to be equivalent to a spouse in accordance with national law;
(2) a dependent child, in accordance with national law;
(3) a relative who has shared the same household for at least one year on the date of the transaction concerned; or
(4) a legal person, trust or partnership, the managerial responsibilities of which are discharged by a person discharging managerial responsibilities or by a person referred to in (1), (2) or (3) which is directly or indirectly controlled by such a person, which is set up for the benefit of such a person, or the economic interests of which are substantially equivalent to those of such a person (art.3(1)(26) of the EU MAR).

6.2.5.4 *Notification of transactions by issuers to a regulatory information service*

An issuer is required to ensure that information which is notified to it in accordance with art.19 is made public. In the case of an issuer admitted to trading on a regulated market, this means notifying a RIS. The notification must be made promptly and by no later than three business days after the relevant transaction (art.19(3) of the EU MAR).

From a practical point of view, issuers should establish the identity of PDMRs within their organisation and ensure that they understand, and comply with their obligations, and should make the relevant disclosures to the market.

6.3 The Transparency Rules

6.3.1 *Background*

With the implementation of the Transparency Directive, Chs 4–6 were added to the DTRs, together with a new Ch.1A ("Introduction (Transparency rules)") that sets out general rules relating to the application and purpose of the Transparency Rules (DTRs 1A.1.1G–1A.1.4G). Chapter 1A contains provisions relating to:

(1) the FCA's rights to modify or dispense with the Transparency Rules (DTRs 1A.2.1R–1A.2.3G);
(2) the importance of early consultation with the FCA in relation to the Transparency Rules (DTR 1A.2.4G);
(3) the FCA's right to publish information itself to protect investors or to ensure the smooth operation of the market (DTR 1A.3.1R);
(4) the overriding obligation to avoid misleading announcements (DTR 1A.3.2R); and
(5) the making of announcements when no RIS is open for business (DTR 1A.3.3R—see s.6.2.3.13 below for further detail).

6.3.2 Notification of voting rights

6.3.2.1 Introduction

Chapter 5 ("Vote Holder and Issuer Notification Rules") of the DTRs contains the UK transparency rules which deal with disclosure of control over, or access to, voting rights attached to shares. The rules set out in DTR 5 apply to direct shareholdings, indirect interests (such as access to voting rights), financial instruments which give the holder the right to acquire shares with voting rights and financial instruments which are referenced to the shares of a UK issuer and have a similar economic effect to qualifying financial instruments.

Subject to certain exemptions, DTR 5 requires a person to notify relevant categories of issuers of the percentage of voting rights he holds as a shareholder, or is deemed to hold through his direct or indirect holding of certain financial instruments described at s.6.3.2.4 below, if the percentage of such voting rights reaches, exceeds or falls below specified thresholds (DTR 5.1.2R). Voting rights must be calculated on the basis of all the shares to which voting rights are attached even if exercising these rights is suspended (see the Technical Note on Issuer's obligations (UKLA/TN/542.2)). If the notification relates to shares admitted to trading on a "regulated market", such a person must also file a copy of the notification with the FCA at the same time as the issuer is notified (DTR 5.9). As soon as possible, and in any event, by no later than the trading day following receipt of such a notification, a UK issuer is required then to notify the wider market (DTR 5.8.12R(1)).

As mentioned in s.6.1.2.4, Ch.5 ("Vote Holder and Issuer Notification Rules") of the DTRs does not apply to holders of securities of EEA issuers incorporated in another EEA state whose home Member State is not the UK. These issuers are required to comply with the corresponding transparency requirements of their home Member State.

In addition, the FCA currently considers the laws in the US, Japan, Israel and Switzerland as being "equivalent" regimes for the purposes of DTR 5. This means that issuers incorporated in these countries (as well as their major shareholders) are not required to comply with DTR 5. The FCA publishes a list of equivalent regimes and the FSA had previously indicated that this list would continue to be updated as further equivalence exercises were completed.

6.3.2.2 *Notification thresholds*

Disclosure Guidance and Transparency Rule 5 focuses on control over, or access to, "voting rights" attached to shares.

In relation to UK issuers, persons are required to inform the issuer (and the FCA, where such issuer's shares are admitted to trading on a regulated market) if:

(1) they have notifiable holdings of voting rights (this includes direct holdings (holdings of shares with voting rights attached), indirect holdings (those with access to voting rights) and holdings of certain types of financial instruments (described at s.6.3.2.4 below)), where such holdings (or a combination thereof) represent 3% or more of the issuer's total voting rights as a result of an acquisition or disposal of shares or financial instruments; and

(2) if their holdings change so as to reach, exceed or fall below every 1% above 3% (up to 100%) of the issuer's total voting rights (DTR 5.1.2R).

Subject to the equivalency exemptions described in s.6.3.2.1 above, issuers which are not UK-incorporated companies whose shares are admitted to trading on a regulated market and whose home Member State is the UK must comply with the requirements of DTR 5 applicable to what are termed "non-UK issuers" by the FCA (i.e. the Transparency Directive minimum disclosure requirements). This means that a notification is required where the percentage of voting rights held or deemed to be held reaches, exceeds or falls below 5%, 10%, 15%, 20%, 25%, 30%, 50% and 75%. In relation to non-UK issuers, there is no requirement to disclose holdings of financial instruments with similar economic effect (described in s.6.3.2.4.2 below).

The following holdings of qualifying investment managers are notifiable at thresholds of 5% and 10% and above (but not at the lower threshold of 3% and above):

(1) voting rights attaching to shares forming part of the property belonging to another which that person lawfully manages under an agreement in, or evidenced in, writing;

(2) voting rights attaching to shares which may be exercisable by a person in his capacity as the operator of an "authorised unit trust scheme", an "authorised contractual scheme", a "recognised scheme" or a Undertakings for Collective Investment in Transferable Securities (UCITS) scheme; and

(3) voting rights attaching to shares which may be exercisable by an investment company with variable capital (DTR 5.1.5R).

In all cases, the total voting rights are calculated on the basis of the issuer's most recent disclosure under DTR 5.6.1R (month-end disclosure) (subject to any material change disclosure under DTR 5.6.1AR), disregarding treasury shares (DTR 5.8.8R). To assist vote holders in calculating their percentage holdings, issuers are required to disclose the total number of voting rights and capital for each class of shares, setting out the numbers of voting rights attaching to treasury shares, in the following circumstances: (1) at the end of each month where there has been a change (DTR 5.6.1R); and (2) by the end of the next business day following a material increase or decrease to its total voting rights (DTR 5.6.1AR). It is up to the issuer to determine whether a change is material, although the FCA considers that an increase or decrease of 1% or more is likely to be material for these purposes. Voting rights must be calculated on the basis of all shares to which voting rights are attached, even if the exercise of such rights is suspended.

Some entities, individuals or types of holdings are either fully or partially exempt from the notification requirements, subject to certain conditions being met. These include, amongst others: managers of lawfully managed investments (except at the thresholds of 5% and 10% and above); stock lenders and borrowing intermediaries; shares acquired for the sole purpose of clearing and settlement; custodians or nominees of holdings; collateral takers; and market makers (for holdings below 10%), credit institutions or investment firms for holdings of up to 5% in their trading books (DTR 5.1.3R).

6.3.2.3 *Indirect holders*

A person is an indirect holder of shares to the extent that he is entitled to acquire, to dispose of, or to exercise voting rights in respect of such shares. Disclosure Guidance and Transparency Rule 5.2.1R lists examples of where a person is deemed an indirect holder of shares. Apart from those indicated, the FCA does not expect there to be any other significant categories of indirect holders. These examples are also relevant in determining whether a person is an indirect holder of qualifying financial instruments which result in an entitlement to acquire shares (DTR 5.2.3G). The examples include, among others: voting agreements; temporary transfers of voting rights; shares held as collateral where the holder is entitled to, and has declared his intention to, exercise the voting rights; holders having a life interest in shares; voting rights held by an undertaking controlled by the holder; and voting rights held by a proxy holder at its discretion.

A person must aggregate all direct and indirect holdings held as a shareholder with all voting rights held as a result of direct and indirect holdings of relevant "financial instruments". A person may have to make a notification if the overall percentage level of his voting rights remains the same but there is a notifiable change in the percentage level of one or more of the categories of voting rights held (see DTR 5.7.2G and the Technical Note on Aggregation of holdings (UKLA/TN/ 551.2)).

The FCA has confirmed that, in relation to cases where the chairman is appointed proxy and his total holdings as a result pass the relevant threshold and become notifiable, the chairman will only be required to make a disclosure once all the proxies have been received. An interest is only notifiable where a proxy is granted entitling a proxy holder to decide with discretion how the votes are cast. When calculating this position, the proxy holder should include his own holdings as well as the proxies he has received (DTRs 5.8.4R(3) and 5.8.5G). A proxy giver is not required to notify a disposal of voting rights once the proxy expires so long as the Form TR-1 (notification form) makes it clear what the position will be once the proxy has expired. It is suggested that the additional information box be filled out to show clearly what voting rights will be returned to the proxy giver (an example form can be found in the Technical Note on Shareholder obligations (UKLA/TN/543.2)).

Holdings of parent and controlled undertakings are to be aggregated under DTR 5.2.1R unless they fall within the exceptions set out in DTRs 5.4.1R and 5.4.2R which relate to parents of management companies and investment firms which manage investments and which operate independently from their parent company.

6.3.2.4   *Financial Instruments*

6.3.2.4.1   Financial instruments

Chapter 5 of the DTRs catches certain financial instruments if they: (1) give the holder, under a formal agreement, an unconditional right or the discretion to acquire on maturity the underlying shares of an issuer admitted to trading on a regulated or prescribed market; or (2) are referenced to shares referred to in the aforementioned point and with economic effects similar to that of the financial instruments referred to in (1) (whether or not they confer a right to a physical settlement) (DTRs 5.3.1R(1)(a)(b) and 5.3.3G). An indicative list of financial instruments that are subject to the notification requirements is published by ESMA (ESMA 2015/1598). These instruments include options, futures and swaps. Instruments which entitle a holder to receive shares only upon satisfaction of certain conditions, such as the price of the underlying share reaching a certain level at a certain moment in time, are not included. Similarly, instruments that allow the instrument issuer or a third party to elect whether to give shares or cash to the instrument holder on maturity are not caught (DTR 5.3.3G).

The number of voting rights must be calculated by reference to the full notional amount of shares underlying the financial instrument (DTR 5.3.3AR).

6.3.2.4.2 Instruments having a similar economic effect to financial instruments

In 2009, a broader disclosure regime was introduced in the UK requiring the disclosure of substantial economic interests in shares of UK issuers (DTR 5.3.1R(1)(b)). For example, economic interests held through derivatives such as contracts for differences (CFDs) (see the FSA publication PS 09/03: "Disclosure of Contracts for Difference").

These instruments are referred to in the DTRs as instruments having a similar economic effect to (but which are not) financial instruments (DTR 5.3.1R(1)(b)). A financial instrument has a similar economic effect to a financial instrument if its terms are referenced, in whole or in part, to an issuer's shares and the holder of the financial instrument has, in effect, a long position on the economic performance of the shares, whether the instrument is settled physically or in cash. Again, an indicative list of such instruments is published by ESMA ("Indicative list of financial instruments that are subject to notification requirements according to Article 13(1b) of the revised Transparency Directive", ESMA 2015/1598 (2015)). These instruments include CFDs, cash-settled call options and the writing of put options. Convertibles and warrants which give the holder the rights to acquire shares which have not yet been issued are also caught (see para.2.6 of PS 09/03).

In relation to "long" financial instruments not having a linear, symmetrical pay-off profile in line with the underlying share (as described in DTR 5.3.3C) and including, for example, cash-settled options, disclosure of the financial instruments is required on a delta-adjusted basis. Financial instruments with a similar economic effect held in the trading book of a credit institution or investment firm benefit from an exemption up to 5% (DTR 5.1.3R(4)(b)). The FCA has also clarified that the market makers' and asset managers' partial exemptions extend to shares held through long economic CFDs and qualifying financial instruments (see the Technical Notes on Market makers (UKLA/TN/548.2) and on Asset managers (UKLA/TN/549.2)).

In relation to UK issuers, holdings of financial instruments with "similar economic effect", along with holdings of shares and financial instruments in the same issuer, need to be aggregated and disclosed when the overall percentage holding reaches, exceeds or falls below an initial threshold of 3% and each percentage point above that.

6.3.2.5   Notifiable Interests

Vote holder notification may be triggered in the following situations:

(1)   where the holder has made an acquisition or disposal of shares with voting rights attached or qualifying financial instruments or financial instruments with a similar economic effect falling within the scope of DTR 5;

(2)   there can be a notifiable change in the composition of holdings, even if the holder's overall percentage holding remains the same (DTRs 5.1.2R(2) and 5.7.2G). This can occur where, for example, a holder exercises options and receives shares, thereby changing the composition of his holdings in the issuer. For example, if a holder has, in relation to a UK issuer, total direct share holdings of 3% and holdings of financial instruments of 6%, giving a total holding of 9%, if the holder's direct holdings increase by 3% and his holdings in financial instruments decrease by

3% (e.g. following the exercise of an option), the holder will have to notify the issuer even though his total holding is still 9%. This is because there has been a notifiable change of more than 1% in the composition of his holdings (see the Technical Note on Shareholder obligations (UKLA/TN/543.2); and

(3) where there is a change in the total voting rights of the issuer, which impacts on a holder's percentage holding in an issuer. This can occur if, for example, an issuer issues more shares, diluting interests, or buys back shares, concentrating interests. For example, if a UK issuer has 2,000 shares with voting rights in issue and a shareholder holds 120 shares with voting rights, then that shareholder holds 6% and must disclose (as this is above the 3% minimum disclosure threshold). If the UK issuer then issues a further 1,000 shares with voting rights, although the shareholder still owns 120 shares, his percentage of voting rights has fallen to 4%, triggering a disclosure obligation (as the interest has changed by more than 1%) (see the Technical Note on Changes in holdings (UKLA/TN/545.2)).

The Technical Notes provided by the FCA in its Knowledge Base on the rules in DTR 5 give helpful examples on calculating notifiable holdings. The examples cover changes in the composition of holdings, aggregation of holdings and changes in voting rights.

6.3.2.6 *Company acquiring own shares*

If an issuer of shares acquires or disposes of its own shares, it must make public the percentage of voting rights attributable to those shares it holds as a result of the transaction as a whole, as soon as possible, but not later than four trading days following such acquisition or disposal, where that percentage reaches, exceeds or falls below the thresholds of 5% or 10% of the voting rights (DTR 5.5.1R). The percentage is to be calculated on the basis of the total number of shares to which voting rights are attached (DTR 5.5.2R) and so treasury shares are not to be counted.

However, on a purchase of own shares, UK issuers can either:

(1) buy back their shares and hold these in treasury; or
(2) buy back their shares and cancel them.

Under the first alternative, it could therefore be possible for an issuer to make a series of purchases and disposals over a period of time, which would be notifiable according to the thresholds set out in DTR 5.5.1R. Also, there is a separate requirement for issuers to disclose the total number of shares held in treasury, either at the end of any calendar month if there has been an increase or decrease in treasury shares (DTR 5.6.1R(2)), or following a material increase or decrease in the total number of shares held in treasury (DTR 5.6.1AR).

Under the second alternative, as the shares are cancelled, the number of shares held by the issuer does not change as a result of the transaction so no notification under DTR 5.5.1R is required. However, where an issuer purchases and cancels its own shares and the cancellation has the indirect effect of altering the proportion of shares held in treasury, such that the proportion reaches, exceeds or falls below the 5% and 10% threshold, this would trigger a disclosure obligation under DTR 5.5.1R (see the Technical Note on Issuer's obligations (UKLA/TN/542.2)).

There are additional requirements in relation to a listed company that purchases its own shares in LR 12.4.6R (see s.6.5.2.3 below). In addition, certain provisions of the Companies Act 2006 govern the acquisition and holding of shares by a listed company (see, for instance, ss.658–669, 724 and 726–732 of the Companies Act 2006).

6.3.2.7 Filing of major shareholder notifications

The Technical Note on Shareholder obligations (UKLA/TN/543.2) under the heading "Filing notifications" provides guidance on the filing of major shareholder notifications. Where the issuer is admitted to trading on a regulated market, these should be filed with the FCA in electronic format using the TR-1 form, including the Annex which contains specific investor contact information. However, shareholders are not required to send the Annex to the relevant issuer and, if the Annex is received, issuers should ensure that this contact information is not disseminated to the market.

On receipt of a major shareholding notification, issuers have three options as to how they disseminate this information to a RIS:

(1) forward the TR-1 form to a RIS (excluding the Annex);
(2) forward the information on an electronic version of the TR-1 form (excluding the Annex) possibly obtained from their chosen RIS provider; or
(3) make the announcement in a text-free format.

Under DTR 5.1.4R(2), a market maker relying on an exemption for shares held by it, in that capacity, must notify the competent authority of the issuer's home Member State. In the past, notification has been by email. However, in line with the European Commission's stated objective of standardising notification forms and suggestions from market participants, the FCA encourages market makers to use Form TR-2 rather than notify the FCA by email. Notifications should be made when a market maker intends either to conduct or cease market making activities in relation to an issuer (see UKLA/TN/543.2).

Forms TR-1 and TR-2 are both available on the FCA website.

The obligation imposed by DTR 1A.3.2R, under which an issuer must take all reasonable care to ensure that any information it notifies to a RIS is not misleading, false or deceptive and does not omit anything likely to affect the import of the information, does not apply to an issuer's obligation under DTR 5.8.12R to make public the information contained in a vote holder notification made to it under DTR 5.1.2R (DTR 1A.3.2AR). This rule clarifies that issuers are not required to verify the information contained in the notifications received from substantial shareholders before disclosing such information to the market.

6.3.2.8 *Notification deadlines*

As described above, the notification regime places obligations on vote holders and issuers. Vote holders are required to notify the issuer and, in some cases, the FCA, within certain periods. Issuers are then required to notify the market within certain periods. The various periods depend on the type of issuer, when the vote holder learns of the transaction (or is deemed to have learned of it) and when settlement of the relevant transaction occurs.

The notification to a UK issuer by the vote holder must be made as soon as possible and in any event within two trading days (DTR 5.8.3R). A UK issuer must, in relation to shares admitted to trading on a regulated market, make a notification to the market as soon as possible and in any event by the end of the next trading day following receipt of the notification (DTR 5.8.12R).

A UK issuer whose shares are admitted to trading on a prescribed (but not a regulated) market must make a notification to the market as soon as possible and in any event within three trading days following receipt of the notification (DTR 5.8.12R). Note that, in relation to UK issuers whose shares are admitted on AIM (a prescribed market), the notification to the market must be made "without delay", notwithstanding the time limits in the DTRs (see r.17 of the AIM Rules for Companies (July 2016) and its guidance notes).

The notification by the vote holder to a non-UK issuer whose shares are admitted to trading on a regulated market and whose home Member State is the UK (whose domestic regime is not deemed "equivalent" for these purposes by the FCA) must be made as soon as possible and in any event within four trading days (DTR 5.8.3R). Such a non-UK issuer must make a notification to the market as soon as possible and in any event within three trading days following receipt of the notification (DTR 5.8.12R).

The notification periods during which a notification must be made by the vote holder to the issuer start on the date the vote holder learns of the relevant acquisition or disposal, should have learned of it (having regard to the circumstances) or is informed of a disclosed change to an issuer's total voting rights. If the vote holder is a party to, or has instructed, the transaction, he/she will be deemed to have knowledge of the transaction no later than two trading days following the transaction in question. If a transaction is conditional upon the approval by public authorities or future uncertain events outside the control of the parties, the vote holder is deemed to have learned of the transaction only when the relevant approvals are obtained or the event happens (DTR 5.8.3R).

Furthermore, an acquisition or disposal of shares is considered effective upon execution of the relevant transaction, unless the transaction provides for settlement to be subject to conditions which are beyond the control of the parties, in which case the acquisition or disposal will be considered effective on settlement (DTR 5.1.1R(4)).

In August 2011, the FSA issued its first notice for breach of DTR 5.[28] It fined Sir Ken Morrison, the former chairman of Wm Morrison Supermarkets Plc, £210,000 for breach of DTR 5.8.3R. Between 16 September 2009 and 21 June 2010, Sir Ken's voting rights in Wm Morrison Supermarkets Plc had reduced from 6.07% to 0.9% as a result of a number of separate transactions but these were only disclosed to the company in 2011. This meant that the company was not in a position to update the market in accordance with DTR 5.8.12R(1) and meant that Sir Ken's shareholding was incorrectly stated in the company annual report of 31 January 2010. The FSA considered the failings to be serious due to Sir Ken's prominent position and the significant delay in him eventually making the required notification.

---

[28] FSA, Final Notice to Sir Ken Morrison (16 August 2011).

6.3.2.9   Notifications relating to capital

When disclosing transactions in its own shares, an issuer must notify the market as soon as possible and in any event within four trading days after the transaction where that percentage reaches, exceeds or falls below the thresholds of 5% or 10% of the voting rights (DTR 5.5.1R). An issuer must also notify the market by the end of the next business day after a material change in its total number of voting rights and, in any event, at the end of the calendar month in which there has been a change (DTRs 5.6.1R and 5.6.1AR). This is so that vote holders can calculate whether the change has resulted in a notifiable change to their own voting rights (e.g. via dilution or concentration).

6.3.3   Disclosure Guidance and Transparency Rule 6

6.3.3.1   Scope

Chapter 6 ("Continuing obligations and access to information") of the DTRs contains a number of continuing obligations, several of which were contained in Ch.9 ("Continuing obligations") of the Listing Rules before implementation of the Transparency Directive on 20 January 2007.

Disclosure Guidance and Transparency Rule 6.1 applies to an issuer whose home Member State is the UK (DTR 6.1.1R) save that:

(1)   an issuer whose registered office is in a non-EEA state whose relevant laws are considered to be equivalent by the FCA is exempt from DTRs 6.1.3R, 6.1.4R, 6.1.5(1)–(3)R, 6.1.6R, 6.1.9R and 6.1.3–6.1.13 (DTR 6.1.16R). The FCA website page dealing with the equivalence of non-EEA regimes for the purpose of the Transparency Directive[29] states that it is satisfied that issuers of shares admitted to trading on a regulated market in the UK that are

---

[29]   FCA, "Equivalence of non-EEA regimes" (last updated 22 August 2017) available at: *https://www.fca.org.uk/markets/ukla/regulatory-disclosures/equivalence-non-eea-regimes* [Accessed 12 July 2018].

incorporated in Switzerland will be exempt from the majority of the aforementioned DTR provisions; and

(2) DTRs 6.1.3R–6.1.8R (equality of treatment, exercise of rights by holders, exercise of rights by proxy, appointment of financial agent and electronic communications) and 6.1.12R–6.1.15R (information about meetings, issue of new shares and payments of dividends, and information about meetings and payment of interest—debt security issuers) do not apply to issuers of convertible securities, preference shares and depositary receipts (DTR 6.1.19R).

6.3.3.2 Disclosure Guidance and Transparency Rule 6.1.3: Equality of treatment

An issuer of shares must ensure equal treatment for all holders of shares who are in the same position. An issuer of debt securities must ensure that all holders of debt securities ranking pari passu are given equal treatment in respect of the rights attaching to those debt securities.

6.3.3.3 Disclosure Guidance and Transparency Rule 6.1.4: Exercise of rights by holders

An issuer must ensure that all the facilities and information necessary to enable holders of shares or debt securities to exercise their rights are available in the home Member State and that the integrity of the data is preserved.

6.3.3.4 Disclosure Guidance and Transparency Rule 6.1.5: Exercise of rights by proxy

Shareholders and debt security holders must not be prevented from exercising their rights by proxy, subject to the law of the country in which the issuer is incorporated. Proxy forms must be made available to persons entitled to vote, either together with notice of the meeting, or after its announcement.

6.3.3.5 *Disclosure Guidance and Transparency Rule 6.1.6: Appointment of a financial agent*

An issuer of shares or debt securities must designate, as its agent, a financial institution through which shareholders or debt securities holders may exercise their financial rights.

6.3.3.6 *Disclosure Guidance and Transparency Rules 6.1.7 and 6.1.8: Electronic communications*

An issuer may use electronic means to convey information to shareholders or debt security holders (DTR 6.1.7G). The decision to use electronic means must: (1) be taken in a general meeting; (2) may not depend on residence of the security holder; and (3) identification arrangements must be put in place so that the shareholders, debt security holders or other persons entitled to exercise or to direct the exercise of voting rights are effectively informed (DTR 6.1.8R). An issuer will have to request the consent, in writing, of shareholders, debt security holders or other persons for the use of electronic means and, if they do not object within a reasonable time, their consent will be deemed as given. However, the procedure for obtaining consent to send documents electronically in the DTRs does not apply where Sch.5 to the Companies Act 2006 applies (in which case, the procedure set out in Sch.5 to the Companies Act 2006 applies). Under the Companies Act 2006, a company subject to the Act will not be able to request consent more than once in every 12-month period in relation to website communications (Sch.5 Pt 4 s.10(4)(b) of the Companies Act 2006).

6.3.3.7 *Disclosure Guidance and Transparency Rules 6.1.9 and 6.1.10: Information about changes in rights attaching to securities*

An issuer of shares must, without delay, disclose to the public any change in the rights attaching to its various classes of shares, including changes to the rights attaching to derivative securities issued by the issuer giving access to the shares of that issuer (DTR 6.1.9R). Similar obligations exist in relation to

277

issuers of securities other than shares admitted to trading on a regulated market (DTR 6.1.10R).

6.3.3.8 *Disclosure Guidance and Transparency Rules 6.1.12 and 6.1.13: Information about meetings, issue of new shares and payment of dividends—share issuers*

An issuer of shares must inform holders of the place, time and agenda of meetings, its total number of shares and voting rights, and of holders' rights to participate in meetings (DTR 6.1.12R). An issuer of shares must also publish notices or distribute circulars giving information on the allocation and payment of dividends and the issue of new shares, including information on any arrangements for allotment, subscription, cancellation or conversion (DTR 6.1.13R).

Disclosure Guidance and Transparency Rule 6.1.14R contains similar obligations for issues of debt securities.

6.3.3.9 *Disclosure Guidance and Transparency Rule 6.2: Filing information with the FCA*

Disclosure Guidance and Transparency Rule 6.2 applies to:

(1) issuers whose transferable securities are admitted to trading and whose home Member State is the UK; and
(2) to a person who, without the issuer's consent, has requested admission of its transferable securities to trading on a regulated market.

An issuer that discloses regulated information must, at the same time, file that information with the FCA (DTR 6.2.2R) but may comply with this requirement by announcing via a RIS in accordance with DTR 6.3 (DTR 6.2.3G).

There are detailed provisions relating to the language of announcements in DTRs 6.2.4R–6.2.8R.

6.3.3.10 *Disclosure Guidance and Transparency Rule 6.3: Dissemination of information*

Disclosure Guidance and Transparency Rule 6.3 applies to the same parties to whom DTR 6.2 applies (see s.6.3.3.9 above) and also to transferable securities admitted to trading only in the UK which is the "Host State" and are not admitted in the "Home State" (DTR 6.3.1R). It governs the way in which regulated information must be disseminated and sets out minimum standards in relation to such dissemination (DTRs 6.3.2R and 6.3.3R(1)). An issuer or person must use a RIS for the disclosure of regulated information to the public and must ensure that the RIS complies with the minimum standards contained in DTRs 6.3.4R–6.3.8R (DTR 6.3.3R(2)).

Regulated information must be disseminated in a manner ensuring that it is capable of being disseminated to as wide a public as possible and as close to simultaneously as possible in the home Member State and in other EEA states (DTR 6.3.4R). Information disclosed in a non-EEA state which may be of importance to the public in the EEA must be disclosed in compliance with DTRs 6.2 and 6.3 (DTR 6.3.10R).

Certain special rules apply to periodic financial reporting (see Ch.5 above for further details) but other "regulated information" must be released in full unedited text (DTR 6.3.5R(1)) and must clearly identify the relevant issuer, the subject-matter and the time and date of the announcement (DTR 6.3.7R), must comply with various security requirements (DTR 6.3.6R) and no specific cost for dissemination may be charged to investors for its release (DTR 6.3.9R). "Regulated information" is defined as all information which an issuer, or any other person who has applied for the admission of financial instruments to trading on a regulated market without the issuer's consent, is required to disclose under the Transparency Directive, certain provisions of the EU MAR, the Listing Rules and the DTRs.

6.3.4 Short selling

On 1 November 2012, the European short selling regime became applicable across the EU, including the UK, superseding the previous UK provisions on short selling. The EU Short Selling Regulation (Regulation 236/2012) and its associated Delegated Regulations and Implementing Regulation (the "Short Selling Regulation")[30] is directly applicable law in all EU Member States (and is applicable in the other EEA states), although some powers are provided to, and some obligations are placed on, national regulators. The FCA has published information in relation to those powers and obligations under its web page "Short Selling Regulation".

In summary, the Short Selling Regulation restricts uncovered short sales of shares and EU sovereign debt instruments; prohibits the entry into uncovered sovereign credit default swaps; and requires investors to notify the relevant national regulator (e.g. the FCA in the UK) of significant "net short positions" in EU sovereign debt instruments and shares

---

[30] Regulation 236/2012 on short selling and certain aspects of credit default swaps [2012] OJ L86/1. Regulation 826/2012 supplementing Regulation 236/2012 with regard to regulatory technical standards on notification and disclosure requirements with regard to net short positions, the details of the information to be provided to the European Securities and Markets Authority in relation to net short positions and the method for calculating turnover to determine exempted shares [2012] OJ L251/1; Regulation 918/2012 supplementing Regulation 236/2012 on short selling and certain aspects of credit default swaps with regard to definitions, the calculation of net short positions, covered sovereign credit default swaps, notification thresholds, liquidity thresholds for suspending restrictions, significant falls in the value of financial instruments and adverse events [2012] OJ L274/1; Regulation 919/2012 supplementing Regulation 236/2012 on short selling and certain aspects of credit default swaps with regard to regulatory technical standards for the method of calculation of the fall in value for liquid shares and other financial instruments [2012] OJ L274/16; Regulation 827/2012 laying down implementing technical standards with regard to the means for public disclosure of net position in shares, the format of the information to be provided to the European Securities and Markets Authority in relation to net short positions, the types of agreements, arrangements and measures to adequately ensure that shares or sovereign debt instruments are available for settlement and the dates and period for the determination of the principal venue for a share according to Regulation 236/2012 on short selling and certain aspects of credit default swaps [2012] OJ L251/11.

admitted to a "trading venue" (i.e. a "regulated market" (such as the LSE Main Market) or a "multilateral trading facility" (such as AIM)) in the EEA.

As regards the UK disclosure position relating to shares, a private share notification must be made to the FCA when the net short position in shares reaches 0.2% of the issued share capital of the company concerned and again at each 0.1% increment after that. This is in relation to both increases and decreases of the position (including each time the position drops from 0.2% or above to below 0.2%). A share notification form needs to be completed and emailed to: privatedisclosureSSR@fca.org.uk.

A public share notification must be made to the FCA when the net short position of shares reaches 0.5% of the issued share capital of the company concerned and again at each 0.1% increment after that. This is in relation to both increases and decreases of the position (including each time the position drops from 0.5% or above to below 0.5%). A share notification form needs to be completed and emailed to: publicdisclosureSSR@fca.org.uk.

Certain shares are exempt from the notification and disclosure requirements in the Short Selling Regulation where they are principally traded in third countries outside the EEA. A list of exempted shares is published by the ESMA on its website.

The FCA has powers to consider the imposition of measures to prohibit or restrict short selling or otherwise limit transactions in a financial instrument on a trading venue where there is a significant price fall during a single trading day. Guidance on the use of these powers is contained in the FCA's *Financial Stability and Market Confidence Sourcebook* (FINMAR). The FCA will assess whether the price fall is, or may become, disorderly and if the measures to prohibit, restrict or limit the transactions would prevent further disorderly decline (FINMAR 2.5.1G). If the FCA considers there to be a legitimate cause for the price fall, there is no cause for it to intervene (FINMAR 2.5.3.G). These measures will not normally apply to persons benefitting from either the market maker exemption or the authorised primary dealer exemption (FINMAR 2.5.5.G). Guidance in relation to these exemptions can be found in FINMAR 2.6.

6.4 The Listing Rules

6.4.1 Introduction

The Listing Rules contain rules and guidance for issuers of securities admitted (or seeking admission) to the Official List.

Sections 6.4.2–6.4.3 of this chapter focus on the Listing Principles (contained in Ch.7 ("Listing Principles and Premium Listing Principles") of the Listing Rules) and the additional continuing obligations (contained in Ch.9 ("Continuing obligations") of the Listing Rules) which an issuer with a premium listing of equity shares must observe in addition to those contained in the DTRs and Prospectus Rules and in Chs 10 ("Significant transactions: Premium listing") and 11 ("Related party transactions: Premium listing") of the Listing Rules, which are covered elsewhere in this book.

6.4.2 Listing Principles and Premium Listing Principles

6.4.2.1 General

The Listing Principles contained in LR 7.2.1R apply to all listed companies with a listing of equity shares (LR 7.1.1(1)R). In addition, the Premium Listing Principles contained in LR 7.2.1AR apply to all listed companies with a premium listing of equity shares (LR 7.1.1(2)R). They are intended to ensure that listed companies pay due regard to the fundamental role they play in maintaining market confidence and ensuring fair and orderly markets (LR 7.1.2G).

There is limited guidance in the Listing Rules on the interpretation and application of the Listing Principles or the Premium Listing Principles (with the exception of Listing Principle 1 (see s.6.4.2.5 below)). The FCA's stated objective is to ensure that they are interpreted in a common sense way in accordance with their everyday meaning, rather than in a restrictive or legalistic manner.

6.4.2.2 Relationship with specific Listing Rules and Disclosure Guidance and Transparency Rules

When the FSA consulted on the introduction of the Listing Principles, market respondents expressed concern over the broad terms in which they were drafted and, with the exception of what are now Listing Principle 1 and Premium Listing Principle 1 (see ss.6.4.2.5 and 6.4.2.7 below), the fact that they were not objectively verifiable. Generally, the Listing Principles and the Premium Listing Principles require listed companies, for example, to "take reasonable steps", or to establish "adequate" procedures or systems, rather than imposing absolute obligations. This may mean that conduct which does not breach a specific rule may nonetheless be treated by the FCA as a breach of a more general Listing Principle or Premium Listing Principle. In response to these concerns, the FSA stated that the Listing Principles were not meant to introduce different standards, or to impose new requirements, from those under the Listing Rules.

The Listing Principles and the Premium Listing Principles are designed to assist listed companies in identifying their obligations and responsibilities under the Listing Rules, the DTRs and corporate governance rules and should be read in conjunction with the relevant rules and guidance which underpin the Listing Principles and the Premium Listing Principles (LR 7.1.3G).

6.4.2.3 Enforcement of the Listing Principles and of the Premium Listing Principles

The Listing Principles and the Premium Listing Principles form part of the Listing Rules and are enforceable in the same way as the Listing Rules. They can be enforced against listed companies and their directors by the FCA but not by third parties such as investors or consumers.

The FCA has stated that most enforcement proceedings are likely to be based on a breach of a specific rule but that it may bring proceedings based on a breach of a Listing Principle or a Premium Listing Principle alone where an issuer deliberately circumvents the rules (para.3.17 of the FSA's CP 04/16: "The Listing Review and Implementation of the Prospectus Directive"). In the Technical Note on Compliance with the Listing Principles and Premium Listing Principles (UKLA/TN/203.2), the FCA reiterated that it is prepared to take enforcement action on the basis of the Listing Principles alone. Examples of when it might be appropriate to discipline a listed company based on a breach of the Listing Principles or the Premium Listing Principles alone are given in DEPP 6.2.18G of the FCA's *Decision Procedure and Penalties Manual* (DEPP) (LR 7.1.4G). These are:

(1) where there is no detailed Listing Rule which prohibits the behaviour in question but the behaviour clearly contravenes a Listing Principle or, if applicable, a Premium Listing Principle; and

(2) where a listed company has committed a number of breaches of detailed rules which individually may not merit disciplinary action but the cumulative effect of which indicates a breach of a Listing Principle or, if applicable, a Premium Listing Principle.

On 28 March 2012, the FSA publicly censured Cattles Plc[31] for disseminating information likely to give a false or misleading impression to the market as to the value of Cattles' shares in breach of s.118(7) of the FSMA and for breaches of LR 1.3.3R and of the Listing Principles.

On 26 April 2012, the FSA fined Exillon Energy Plc £292,950 for failing to identify payments made to its chairman as related party transactions. This was in breach of LRs 11.1.10R(2) and 11.1.11R(3) as well as what is now Listing Principle 1, which requires a listed company to take reasonable steps to establish and maintain adequate procedures, systems and controls to enable it to comply with its obligations. The fine was the first to

---

[31] FSA, Final Notice to Cattles Ltd (28 March 2012).

have been imposed by the FSA for a breach of the related party transaction rules and the first such decision relating to a company's failure to establish and maintain systems and controls necessary to comply with the Listing Rules.

On 14 February 2013, Nestor Healthcare Group was fined £175,000 by the FSA for breaches of the Listing Principles as well as LR 9.2.8R. The company had failed to take adequate steps to ensure that its board members and senior executives complied with the share dealing provisions of the Model Code.

On 13 January 2015, Reckitt Benckiser Group was fined £539,800 for failures to ensure compliance with the Model Code and to make required DTR notifications as well as for breaches of the Listing Principles.

The FSA has also taken enforcement action against a company for a breach of the Listing Principles alone. Notably, it imposed a fine of £14 million on Prudential Plc ("Prudential") on 27 March 2013 for failing to deal with the FSA in an open and co-operative way in relation to its proposed takeover of AIA Group Ltd in early 2010, in breach of what is now Listing Principle 2. On 12 February 2010, FSA officials had met Prudential executives to ask for details about the group's strategy in Asia and its plans for raising equity and debt capital. However, the FSA was not informed of Prudential's proposed acquisition until after it was leaked to the media on 27 February 2010. The FSA commented that they should have been informed at the "earliest opportunity to allow the FSA to decide whether to approve or reject the deal on regulatory grounds" (see the FSA Statement FSA/PN/031/2013). The case demonstrates that companies must ensure timely and proactive communication with the FCA, particularly in relation to significant plans or developments in the business.

In June 2015, the FCA found that Asia Resource Minerals plc (ASRM), formerly Bumi Plc, committed serious breaches of Listing Principle 2, LRs 8 and 11 and DTR 4 in the period 28 June 2011 to 19 July 2013.

ASRM was admitted to the premium section of the Official List on 28 June 2011. On 19 April 2013, the company notified the UKLA that it would be unable to publish its *2012 Annual Financial Report* (AFR) within the deadline set out in DTR 4, due to an ongoing review of the integrity of a number of items on the balance sheet of its subsidiary, PT Berau Coal Energy Tbk. This review included historic potential related party transactions. On 22 April 2013, the company's shares were suspended from trading for three months.

During the period from 28 June 2011 to 19 July 2013, ASRM failed to take reasonable steps to establish and maintain adequate procedures, systems and controls to enable it to comply with its obligations, in breach of Listing Principle 2. The company also breached LR 11 in respect of its treatment of related party transactions and LR 8 with regard to the need to consult a sponsor when proposing to enter a transaction that is, or may be, a related party transaction. The belated discovery and review of these transactions, along with other financial irregularities, led to ASRM's failure to publish the 2012 AFR within the four months required by DTR 4. ASRM's shares were returned from suspension in July 2013.

The FCA found that these failings were significant given that the structure of the company and that its subsidiary director relationships gave rise to an increased risk of the occurrence of related party transactions.[32] As a result of these failings, the FCA felt that investors did not have the level of protection that should have been provided under the LRs in respect of transactions with related parties.

ASRM agreed to settle at an early stage in the investigation and therefore qualified for a 30% reduction in penalty. Were it not for this discount, the FCA would have imposed a financial penalty of £6,644,641.

---

[32] Paragraph 2.7 of FSA, Final Notice to Asia Resource Minerals Plc (12 June 2015).

6.4.2.4 Practical effect

Listed companies must ensure that the relevant people within the organisation are aware of their broader responsibilities under the Listing Principles and, if applicable, the Premium Listing Principles, even where their conduct does not necessarily breach a specific LR or DTR and that they have the relevant systems and controls in place.

6.4.2.5 Listing Principle 1: A listed company must take reasonable steps to establish and maintain adequate procedures, systems and controls to enable it to comply with its obligations

Listing Principle 1 is intended to ensure that listed companies have adequate procedures, systems and controls in relation to:

(1) identifying whether any obligations arise under Chs 10 ("Significant transactions: Premium listing") and 11 ("Related party transactions: Premium listing") of the LRs (which concern significant transactions and related party transactions—see Ch.7 below); and

(2) the timely and accurate disclosure of information to the market (LR 7.2.2G).

In relation to the latter, a listed company should have adequate systems and controls to be able to:

(1) ensure that it can properly identify information which requires disclosure under the LRs, the DTRs or corporate governance rules in a timely manner; and

(2) ensure that any such information is properly considered by the directors and that such consideration encompasses whether the information should be disclosed (LR 7.2.3G).

Listed companies should maintain internal procedures, systems and controls sufficient to ensure the timely identification, escalation, consideration and (if necessary) disclosure of inside information and the identification of significant and related party transactions. Listed companies may choose to operate a disclosure committee to oversee the identification, control and announcement of inside information in a timely manner. The complexity of the systems and controls required will depend on the nature of the issuer and its business. The effectiveness of these procedures, systems and controls should be reviewed on a regular basis.

On 24 May 2012, the GC100, an association of general counsel and company secretaries of FTSE 100 companies, published guidelines for establishing adequate procedures, systems and controls to ensure compliance with the LRs (*GC100 Listing Rules Guidelines: Part I: Guidelines for establishing procedures, systems and controls to ensure compliance with the Listing Rules*). The guidelines recommended the adoption of compliance and financial reporting procedures to enable companies to meet their obligations under Listing Principle 1. The guidelines state that a company must be satisfied that its systems and procedures are designed to produce the right information flows, the information is directed to those responsible for taking informed decisions about inside information, these procedures and systems are clearly understood by those involved and their efficacy can be checked and a proper record is kept of relevant decisions made and actions taken.

In its enforcement decision relating to Marconi (see s.6.2.3.4 above) under the pre-July 1 2005 disclosure regime, the FSA criticised the systems and controls that Marconi had in place as being the reason for the failure to announce "without delay". In such a case, the FCA could now conclude that a company had breached Listing Principle 1, even though there was no breach of a specific provision of either the DTRs or the Listing Rules.

6.4.2.6 Listing Principle 2: A listed company must deal with the FCA in an open and co-operative manner

As noted above (see s.6.4.2.3), Listing Principle 2 allows the FCA to bring enforcement proceedings against an issuer if, among other things, it does not notify the FCA about relevant issues or developments in a timely manner.

6.4.2.7   *Premium Listing Principle 1: A premium listed company must take reasonable steps to enable its directors to understand their responsibilities and obligations as directors*

To ensure compliance with Premium Listing Principle 1, all directors of a premium listed company should receive training upon joining the board of the company on their responsibilities and obligations as directors and, if necessary, further training on changes to the relevant rules, including the DTRs and the LRs.

6.4.2.8   *Premium Listing Principle 2: A premium listed company must act with integrity towards holders and potential holders of its listed equity shares*

This Premium Listing Principle would probably cover, among other things, any statement the intention of which is to mislead shareholders.

6.4.2.9   *Premium Listing Principle 3: All equity shares in a class that has admitted to premium listing must carry an equal number of votes on any shareholder vote*

Each share within a premium listed class must have equal voting power. This is intended to prevent the listing of super-voting shares.

6.4.2.10   *Premium Listing Principle 4: Where a premium listed company has more than one class of equity shares admitted to premium listing, the aggregate voting rights of the shares in each class should be broadly proportionate to the relative interests of those classes in the equity of the premium listed company*

This is intended to deter the creation of artificial structures which involve multiple classes of equity shares with different voting powers primarily for the purpose of allowing control to rest with a small group of shareholders.

6.4.2.11 *Premium Listing Principle 5: A premium listed company must ensure that it treats all holders of the same class of its listed equity shares that are in the same position equally in respect of the rights attaching to those listed equity shares*

While establishing a general principle of equal treatment, Premium Listing Principle 5 gives some flexibility to issuers, who are prevented by the laws of another jurisdiction from treating all shareholders in exactly the same way, to treat some shareholders differently to others (e.g. by allowing the company to exclude certain shareholders from the right to participate in a capital raising).

6.4.2.12 *Premium Listing Principle 6: A premium listed company must communicate information to holders and potential holders of its listed equity shares in such a way as to avoid the creation or continuation of a false market in those listed equity shares*

This Premium Listing Principle overlaps with Ch.2 ("Disclosure and control of inside information by issuers") of the DTRs, the EU MAR and ss.89–90 of the Financial Services Act (misleading statements and impressions). It is intended to remind issuers that accurate and timely communication with the market is an important part of the UK regulatory regime and is not intended to alter the specific rules relating to disclosure.

6.4.3 *Listing Rules: Other continuing obligations*

Chapter 9 ("Continuing obligations") of the Listing Rules contains certain continuing obligations for companies with a premium listing of equity shares. These obligations are in addition not only to those set out in other chapters of the Listing Rules (e.g. Chs 10 ("Significant transactions: Premium listing") and 11 ("Related party transactions: Premium listing") which are dealt with in Ch.7 below) but also to those set out in the DTRs and the Prospectus Rules.

6.4.3.1 *Listing Rule 9.2: Requirements with continuing application*

Listing Rule 9.2 sets out a number of requirements which apply to companies at all times while they are listed. These include the following.

6.4.3.1.1 Admission to trading

Unless a specific exemption applies, to be listed a company's equity securities must be admitted to trading on a regulated market for listed securities operated by a recognised investment exchange and all other securities must be admitted to trading on a recognised investment exchange's market for listed securities (LR 9.2.1R).

6.4.3.1.2 Independent business

A listed company must carry on an independent business as its main activity at all times (LR 9.2.2(R). Guidance on factors that may indicate that a listed company is not carrying on an independent business is set out in LR 6.4.3(G).

An issuer may not satisfy the "independent business" requirement where:

(1) a majority of its revenue is attributable to business conducted directly or indirectly with a controlling shareholder (or any of its associates);
(2) it does not have strategic control over commercialisation of its product(s), its ability to earn revenue from it/them and/or freedom to implement its business strategy;
(3) it cannot demonstrate that it has access to financing other than from a controlling shareholder (or an associate of a controlling shareholder) (LR6.5.3(4)(G));
(4) it has granted or may be required to grant security over its business in connection with the funding of a controlling shareholder (or a member of that controlling shareholder's group) (LR6.5.3(1)(G));

(5) (except in relation to a mining company) it is unable to demonstrate that it exercises operational control over the business it carries on as its main activity. Factors that may indicate that an issuer does not satisfy the requirements include where it has a minority shareholding, its business consists primarily of holdings of shares in entities that it does not control, including entities where it is only able to exercise negative control or where its control is subject to contractual arrangements which can be altered without its agreement or could result in a temporary or permanent loss of control; or

(6) the controlling shareholder (or any of its associates) appears to be able to exercise improper influence over it ((LR 6.5.3(3)(G)).

6.4.3.1.3 Controlling shareholders

The Listing Rules contain provisions intended to strengthen minority shareholder rights and protections where a controlling shareholder does not maintain an appropriate relationship with a premium listed company. These require that, where a premium listed company has a controlling shareholder, it must enter into a "relationship agreement" with that shareholder containing provisions intended to ensure that: (1) all transactions with a controlling shareholder and its associates are conducted at arm's length and on normal commercial terms; (2) a controlling shareholder and its associates abstain from doing anything that would have the effect of preventing the company from complying with its obligations under the Listing Rules; and (3) neither the shareholder nor any of its associates will propose or procure the proposal of a shareholder resolution which is intended or appears to be intended to circumvent the proper application of the Listing Rules (LR 6.5.4R).

For this purpose, a controlling shareholder means any person who individually or together with any of their concert parties exercises or controls 30% or more of the votes able to be cast on all or substantially all matters at the company's general meeting.

The Listing Rules also require such companies to include in their annual report a statement by the directors that it has entered into a relationship agreement and that the company and the controlling shareholder have complied with the mandatory independence provisions in that agreement throughout the relevant financial year (LR 9.8.4R(14)(a) and (c)). Where an agreement with a controlling shareholder has not been entered into, or has been breached, the statement in the annual report must also confirm that the FCA has been notified and include a brief description of the reasons for failing to enter into the agreement (LR 9.8.4R(14)(b) and (d)). Where an independent director declines to support the statement of compliance by the board, this disagreement must also be disclosed in the annual report (LR 9.8.4AR).

If a premium listed company has a controlling shareholder but:

(1)   it does not have a relationship agreement in place;
(2)   the independence provisions in the relationship agreement are breached;
(3)   the controlling shareholder's obligation to procure compliance of a non-signing controlling shareholder and its associates with the obligations under the Listing Rules regarding the matters set out in s.6.4.3.1.3. above; or
(3)   if an independent director of the company declines to support a statement made by the board in the annual report regarding compliance with such obligations,

the company will become subject to "enhanced oversight measures" (LR 11.1.1AR). Essentially, this means that all transactions between the company and the controlling shareholder will be treated as related party transactions and will require prior independent shareholder approval regardless of their size (LR 11.1.1CR). These measures will continue to apply until the publication of the next annual report in which the board makes a clean compliance statement without any dissent from the independent directors (LR 11.1.1ER).

Where a company has a controlling shareholder, the election and re-election of its independent directors will require

293

separate approval by the shareholders as a whole and by the independent shareholders as a class (LR 9.2.2.ER). If either of these resolutions is not passed, the company may propose a further resolution which may be passed by a vote of the company's shareholders as a single class no earlier than 90 days and no later than 120 days from the date of the original vote (LR 9.2.2FR). A controlling shareholder would therefore still have the ability to block the appointment of an independent director.

6.4.3.1.4 Compliance with the Disclosure Guidance and Transparency Rules

A listed company should consider its obligations under the disclosure requirements (LR 9.2.5G).

A listed company not already required to comply with the obligations referred to under art.17 of the EU MAR must comply with those obligations as if the listed company were an "issuer" for the purposes of the DTRs subject to art.22 of the EU MAR (LR 9.2.6R).

A listed company that is not already required to comply with the Transparency Rules (or with the corresponding requirement imposed by another EEA state) must comply with Chs 4–6 of the DTRs as if it were an issuer for the purposes of the Transparency Rules (LR 9.2.6BR).

6.4.3.1.5 Compliance with the Model Code

Prior to the EU MAR coming into effect, LRs 9.2.7–9.2.10 contained a number of provisions requiring compliance with the Model Code annexed to Ch.9 ("Continuing Obligations") of the LRs. The purpose of the Model Code was to ensure that PDMRs and persons connected with them did not abuse, and did not place themselves under suspicion of abusing, any inside information which they may have had, especially in periods leading up to an announcement of the relevant listed company's results. The Model Code has been deleted in its entirety from the LR as the EU MAR now regulates dealings by PDMRs.

Equivalent provisions are set out in art.19(11) and (12) in the "Managers' Transactions" section of the EU MAR. The provisions are new on a European level. Article 19(11) provides that a PDMR shall not conduct any transactions on its own account or for the account of a third party directly or indirectly relating to the shares or debt instruments of the issuer during a closed period of 30 days before the announcement of an interim financial report or a year-end report which the issuer is obliged to make public under applicable law or regulations. An issuer may allow a PDMR to trade during a closed period under exceptional circumstances (or under an employee share scheme or where the beneficial interest does not change) under art.19(12).

Article 11 creates a new definition of "closed period". Under the Model Code, the restricted period was 60 days preceding announcement of the issuer's annual results; it will now be 30 days. There also appears to be no restriction on connected persons trading during closed periods as there was in the Model Code.

6.4.3.1.6   Contact details

The LRs require a listed company to provide the FCA with up-to-date contact details for at least one appropriate person nominated to act as the first point of contact for the FCA in relation to the company's compliance with the LRs and the DTRs (LR 9.2.11R). The contact person is expected to be knowledgeable about the company and the LRs applicable to it, capable of ensuring that appropriate action is taken on a timely basis and to be contactable by the FCA on business days between the hours of 07.00–19.00 (LR 9.2.12G).

The FCA expects many issuers to nominate their corporate brokers or sponsors to act as their contact point, particularly since most calls in relation to DTR matters are likely to be made before markets open.

6.4.3.1.7 Shares in public hands

At least 25% of the class of listed shares of a listed company must be in public hands in one or more EEA states at all times (LR 9.2.15R). This is known as the "free float" requirement. The FCA may accept a percentage lower than 25% if it considers that the market will operate properly with a lower percentage in view of the large number of shares of the same class and the extent of their distribution to the public (LR 6.14.5G(1)). For this purpose, the FCA may take into account shares of the same class that are held (even though they are not listed) in states that are not EEA states, the number and nature of public shareholders and, in relation to premium listed companies, whether the expected market value of the shares in public hands will exceed £100 million (LR 6.14.5G(2)).

6.4.3.1.8 Publication of unaudited financial information

Where a listed company has published any unaudited financial information in a Class 1 circular or in a prospectus, or any profit forecast or profit estimate, it must (subject to certain limited exceptions) reproduce that information in its next annual report and accounts, and must disclose in the annual report and accounts the actual figures for the same period covered by the information (LR 9.2.18R(1), (2)(a) and (b)). If there is a difference of 10% or more between the unaudited information, forecast or estimate and the actual figures, the company must provide an explanation for the difference (LR 9.2.18R(2)(c)).

The trigger for reproducing the relevant unaudited financial information, forecast or estimate and, if relevant, the explanation of variance, is when the listed company publishes financial information as required by LR 9.7A ("Preliminary statement of annual results, statement of dividends and half-yearly reports") and LR 9.8 ("Annual financial report"). It does not apply to pro forma financial information contained in a prospectus or any preliminary statements of annual results or half-yearly reports or quarterly reports reproduced with the unaudited financial information (LR 9.2.19G).

6.4.3.1.9   Externally managed companies

The discretion of the board to make strategic decisions on behalf of the company may not be limited or transferred to a person outside of the listed company's group and the board must have the ability to act on key strategic matters in the absence of a recommendation from such a person (LR 9.2.20R).

6.4.3.2   *Listing Rule 9.3: Continuing obligations—holders of securities*

Listing Rule 9.3 sets out a number of requirements with which a listed company must comply in relation to holders of its securities. Following implementation of the Transparency Directive, much of what was previously contained in LR 9.3 is now contained in DTR 6. The most important of the requirements which remain are set out below.

6.4.3.2.1   Proxy forms

Listed companies must ensure that (in addition to their obligations under the Companies Act 2006) a proxy form provides for at least three-way voting on all resolutions intended to be proposed (except that it is not necessary to provide proxy forms with three-way voting on procedural resolutions) and states that, if it is returned without an indication as to how the proxy holder shall vote on any particular matter, the proxy will exercise his discretion as to whether, and if so how, to vote (LR 9.3.6R).

However, it should be noted that para.E.2.1 of the UK Corporate Governance Code requires companies to include a "vote withheld" box on all general meeting proxy voting forms. The proxy form and any announcement of the results of a vote should make it clear that a "vote withheld" is not a vote in law and will not be counted in the proportion of the votes for and against the resolution.

6.4.3.2.2 Pre-emption rights

The principle of equality of treatment of holders of listed equity shares in Premium Listing Principle 5 and in DTR 6.1.3R is illustrated by the pre-emption rights for existing holders of securities on new issues of equity securities or the sale of equity shares out of treasury for cash (LR 9.3.11R). Pre-emption rights are designed to protect the interests of an existing shareholder by giving that shareholder the opportunity to participate in new issues of shares so as to maintain his proportionate shareholding. The pre-emption rights in the LRs reinforce, in the case of a UK-incorporated issuer, the statutory pre-emption rights under ss.561–573 of the Companies Act 2006 and, in the case of an overseas issuer, seek to replicate these statutory pre-emption rights. The pre-emption rights contained in LR 9.3.11R do not apply if they have been disapplied by shareholders' approval or to rights issues or open offers to the extent that pre-emption rights are disapplied in respect of fractional entitlements or shareholders who are excluded from the offer on account of the laws or regulatory requirements to which they are subject (LR 9.3.12(R)).

6.4.3.3 *Listing Rule 9.4: Documents requiring prior approval*

Listing Rule 9.4 requires a listed company to obtain the approval of its shareholders prior to the adoption of certain employee share schemes and long-term incentive schemes and to the granting of certain discounted option arrangements.

6.4.3.4 *Listing Rule 9.5: Transactions*

Listing Rule 9.5 sets out requirements relating to a number of types of transactions, including rights issues, open offers, vendor placings, reconstructions and refinancings and related ancillary issues (e.g. matters relating to documents of title).

These requirements are not covered in this section as they are dealt with in detail in Ch.3 above on transactions.

6.4.3.5 *Listing Rule 9.6: Notifications*

Listing Rule 9.6 requires a listed company to notify the market in certain specific circumstances. Following the implementation of the Transparency Directive, some of the requirements formerly dealt with in LR 9.6 are now dealt with in the DTRs (see s.6.3 above). However, some requirements remain, including the following.

6.4.3.5.1 Copies of documents

Although LR 9.6.1R still provides that listed companies must forward copies of a number of documents to the FCA for publication through the FCA's Document Viewing Facility, including all circulars, notices, reports and other documents to which the LRs apply (LR 9.6.1R), and two copies of all resolutions other than those concerning ordinary business passed at an AGM (LR 9.6.2R), on 1 September 2010, the Document Viewing Facility was discontinued and the National Storage Mechanism (NSM) was introduced. Issuers no longer have to forward copies of such documents to the FCA but must make them available for inspection on the NSM. On submission of a document to the NSM, an issuer must notify the market of this fact via a RIS announcement unless the full text of the document is provided to a RIS (LR 9.6.3R(1)). The RIS remains the mechanism for making information public and documents appearing on the NSM do not fulfil issuer's obligation to publish information via a RIS.

6.4.3.5.2 Notifications relating to capital

Listed companies must notify a RIS as soon as possible of certain information relating to their capital, including details of any proposed change in its capital structure (save that an announcement of a new issue may be delayed while marketing or underwriting is in progress), any redemption of listed shares and the results of new issues of equity securities or of a public offering of existing equity securities (LR 9.6.4R).

6.4.3.5.3 Board changes and information in respect of directors

A listed company must notify a RIS of any change to its board, including the appointment, resignation, removal, or retirement of a director and any important change to the role, functions or responsibilities of a director. The notification must be made as soon as possible and in any event by the end of the business day following the decision or receipt of notice about the change by the company (LR 9.6.11R).

When a new director is appointed to the board of a listed company, the company must notify a RIS of certain information in relation to that director, including details of all other directorships held by the director in publicly quoted companies in the previous five years (indicating whether or not he is still a director), any unspent convictions in relation to indictable offences, any insolvency procedure in relation to any company/partnership in which the director was a director/partner within 12 months preceding the commencement of the insolvency procedure and any public criticism of the director by any statutory or regulatory authorities as soon as possible following the decision to appoint the director, and in any event within five business days of the decision (LR 9.6.13R). It must also notify a RIS as soon as possible of any changes in this information, or any new directorships held by the director in any other publicly quoted company (LR 9.6.14R).

6.4.3.5.4 Lock-up arrangements

Listed companies must notify a RIS as soon as possible of details of any disposal of equity shares under an exemption under a lock-up arrangement which has previously been disclosed (e.g. in a prospectus) and changes to any lock-up arrangements previously disclosed (LRs 9.6.16R and 9.6.17R).

6.4.3.5.5   Shareholder resolutions, change of name and
            change of accounting reference date

A listed company must notify a RIS as soon as possible after a
general meeting of all resolutions passed by the company
(other than resolutions concerning ordinary business passed at
an AGM) (LR 9.6.18R). A listed company must also notify a RIS
as soon as possible of any change in its name or accounting
reference date (LRs 9.6.19R and 9.6.20R). In relation to a change
of name, a listed company must also inform the FCA in writing
of the change and, if such company is incorporated in the UK,
send the FCA a copy of the revised certificate of incorporation
(LR 9.6.19(3)R). If the effect of the change in accounting
reference date is to extend the company's accounting period to
more than 14 months, the company must prepare and publish a
second interim report in accordance with DTR 4.2 (LR 9.6.21R).

6.4.3.6   Listing Rules 9.7A and 9.8: Financial reporting

Listing Rules 9.7A and 9.8 set out rules on financial reporting
requirements. Following the implementation of the Transparency Directive, these are supplemented, and in some regards
replaced, by DTR 4. These requirements are dealt with in detail
in Ch.5 above.

6.5   Purchase of own securities and treasury shares

Chapter 12 ("Dealing in own securities and treasury shares:
Premium listing") of the LRs contains the rules which apply to
a company with a premium listing wishing to purchase or
redeem its own securities or sell or transfer treasury shares.
These rules do not apply to a transaction entered into: (1) in the
ordinary course of business by a "securities dealing business";
or (2) on behalf of third parties either by the company or any
member of its group; if the listed company has established and
maintains effective Chinese walls between those responsible
for any decision relating to the transaction and those in
possession of inside information relating to the listed company.

6.5.1 *Purchases from a related party*

If a listed company proposes to purchase its own equity shares or preference shares from a "related party", whether directly or through intermediaries, it must comply with the requirements of Ch.11 of the LRs ("Related party transactions: Premium listing"—see Ch.7 below for further details) unless:

(1) a tender offer is made to all holders of the class of securities; or
(2) in the case of a market purchase under a general authority granted by shareholders, it is made without prior understanding, arrangement or agreement between the company and the related party (LR 12.3.1R).

6.5.2 *Purchase of own equity shares*

6.5.2.1 *Purchases of less than 15%*

Unless a tender offer is made to all holders of the class, purchases by a listed company of less than 15% of any class of its equity shares (excluding treasury shares) pursuant to a general authority granted by shareholders may only be made if the price to be paid is not more than the higher of:

(1) 5% above the average market value of those shares for the five business days before the purchase is made; and
(2) that stipulated by art.5(6) of the EU MAR (see s.6.5.5 below) (LR 12.4.1R).

6.5.2.2 *Purchases of 15% or more*

Purchases by a listed company of 15% or more of any class of its equity shares (excluding treasury shares) pursuant to a general authority by the shareholders must be made by way of a tender offer to all shareholders of that class (LR 12.4.2R). Such purchases may now also be made other than by way of a tender offer provided that the full terms of the share buyback have been specifically approved by shareholders (LR

12.4.2AR). Special rules apply where a series of purchases made pursuant to a general authority amount to 15% or more in aggregate (LR 12.4.3G).

6.5.2.3 *Notifications*

Listed companies must notify a RIS as soon as possible of any decision by the board to submit to shareholders a proposal for the company to be authorised to purchase its own equity shares (LR 12.4.4R). However, this does not apply to a board decision to seek shareholder authority to renew an existing authority to purchase a company's own equity shares. The outcome of the shareholders' meeting must also be notified to a RIS as soon as possible (LR 12.4.5R). Any purchase must then be notified to a RIS as soon as possible and in any event no later than 07.30 on the business day following the day on which the purchase occurred (LR 12.4.6R). Such notification must contain the information prescribed in LR 12.4.6R. The notification requirements of DTR 5 must also be complied with (see s.6.3.2.6 below).

6.5.2.4 *Class consent*

If the listed company has on issue listed securities which are convertible into, exchangeable for, or carry a right to subscribe for, equity shares of the class proposed to be purchased, the approval of the holders of those securities must be obtained at a separate class meeting (prior to entering into the purchase agreement) unless the trust deed or terms of issue of those securities allow the company to purchase its own equity shares (LRs 12.4.7R and 12.4.8R). A circular convening such a class meeting must include (in addition to the requirements of Ch.13 of the Listing Rules ("Contents of circulars: Premium listing"— see Ch.7 below for further details) the additional information set out in LR 12.4.9R.

6.5.3 Purchase of securities other than equity shares

Less strict notification and other requirements apply in the case of a purchase by a company of its own securities convertible into its listed equity shares (LRs 12.5.1R–12.5.3R and 12.5.5R).

For purchases of warrants and options over a company's own equity shares, a circular to shareholders is required where, within a period of 12 months, a listed company purchases warrants or options over its own equity shares which, on exercise, convey the entitlement to equity shares representing 15% or more of the company's existing issued shares (excluding treasury shares) (LR 12.5.7R).

6.5.4 Provisions relating to shares held in treasury

Listing Rule 12.6.3R and LR 12.6.4R contain notification requirements in relation to transactions which involve treasury shares.

6.5.5 Safe harbour under the EU Market Abuse Regulation

The Market Abuse Directive created a safe harbour for share buy-backs (principally contained in Regulation 2273/2003 (Buy-Back and Stabilisation Regulation))[33] so that buy-backs which fell within the safe harbour (relating to volume and price) would not amount to market abuse. With effect from 3 July 2016, the EU MAR applies throughout the EU and a new safe harbour regime is set out in art.5. As with the Market Abuse Directive, the general prohibition on market manipulation and insider dealing will not apply to share buy-backs provided the conditions in art.5 (again relating to volume and price) are satisfied. In order to insure consistent application of the safe harbour, the Commission has adopted Regulation

---

[33] Regulation 2273/2003 implementing Directive 2003/6 as regards exemptions for buy-back programmes and stabilisation of financial instruments [2003] OJ L336/33.

2016/1052 (with regard to regulating technical standards for the conditions applicable to buy-back programmes and stabilisation measures).[34]

As the EU MAR has direct effect throughout the EU, ss.118–122 of the FSMA (which implemented a large part of the Market Abuse Directive, including the safe harbour) has been deleted by the 2016 Regulations.

Following the introduction of the EU MAR, as previously indicated by the FCA in its Policy Statement published on 28 April 2016 (PS 16/13), Annex 1 to Ch.1 of the *FCA Handbook* (which reproduces the Buy-Back and Stabilisation Regulation) has been deleted and art.5 of the EU MAR applies.

In addition to the market abuse regime, in considering any proposal to purchase its own securities, a listed company will also need to consider the Companies Act 2006, the insider dealing legislation, the views of the Investment Committees, the Takeover Code and any tax consequences.

6.6 Standard listing

Subject to certain exceptions, the key obligations of a company with a standard listing of equity shares are set out in Ch.14 ("Standard listing (shares)") of the LRs and specific provisions of the DTRs. The main continuing obligations of an issuer with a standard listing of equity shares are set out below.

---

[34] Regulation 2016/1052 supplementing Regulation 596/2014 with regard to regulatory technical standards for the conditions applicable to buy-back programmes and stabilisation measures [2016] OJ L173/34.

6.6.1   Listing Rules

6.6.1.1   Admission to trading

Unless certain exemptions apply, a company's listed equity shares must be admitted to trading on a regulated market for listed securities operated by a recognised investment exchange (LR 14.3.1R).

6.6.1.2   Listing Principles

Two Listing Principles apply to standard listed issuers. These are:

(1)   Listing Principle 1 (adequate systems, procedures and controls); and
(2)   Listing Principle 2 (dealing with the FCA in an open and co-operative manner).

Please see s.6.4.2 above for further information on the Listing Principles.

6.6.1.3   Shares in public hands

At least 25% of a class of the company's listed shares must be in public hands in one or more EEA states (LR 14.3.2R(1)). If it no longer complies with this requirement, it must notify the FCA as soon as possible (LR 14.3.2R(2)). The FCA may accept a percentage lower than 25% if it considers that the market will operate properly in view of the large number of shares of the same class and the extent of their distribution to the public (LR 14.2.3G). For this purpose, the FCA may take into account shares of the same class that are held (even though they are not listed) in states that are not EEA states (LR 14.2.3G).

6.6.1.4   Contact details

A company must provide the FCA with up-to-date contact details for at least one appropriate person nominated to act as the first point of contact for the FCA in relation to the company's compliance with the LRs and the DTRs (LR 14.3.8R).

6.6.1.5 Copies of documents

A company must provide copies of a number of documents to the NSM, including all circulars, notices, reports and other documents to which the LRs apply (LR 14.3.6R(1)) plus copies of all resolutions passed by the company other than those concerning ordinary business at an AGM (LR 14.3.6R(2)). The Listing Rules continue to refer to the Document Viewing Facility but, as explained in s.6.4.3.5.1 above, this requirement is now satisfied by submitting the documents to the NSM and the fact that the documents have been submitted must be notified via a RIS announcement (unless the full text of the document is set out in a RIS announcement) (LR 14.3.7R).

6.6.1.6 Notifications relating to capital

A company must notify a RIS as soon as possible of certain information relating to their capital. This includes details of any proposed change in its capital structure (save that an announcement of a new issue may be delayed while marketing or underwriting is in progress), any redemption of listed shares and the results of new issues of listed equity securities or of a public offering of existing shares or other equity securities (LR 14.3.17R).

6.6.1.7 Compliance with the Transparency Rules

A company that is not already required to comply with the transparency rules (or with corresponding requirements imposed by another EEA state) must comply with Chs 4–6 of the DTRs (LR 14.3.23R). In any case, such an issuer may have further obligations under the DTRs as described in s.6.6.2 below.

6.6.2 Disclosure Guidance and Transparency Rules

The main obligations of an issuer with a standard listing of equity shares under the DTRs are set out below, other than Chs 4 ("Periodic financial reporting") and 7 ("Corporate govern-ance") which are not dealt with in this chapter.

6.6.2.1 Disclosure Guidance and Transparency Rules 1 ("Introduction") and 2 ("Disclosure and control of inside information by issuers")

Following the EU MAR coming into effect, Chs 1 and 2 of the DTRs have been substantially amended and now provide guidance only. The substantive provisions on the disclosure and control of inside information are now primarily contained in arts 17 and 18 of the EU MAR. These apply to an issuer whose financial instruments are admitted to trading on a regulated market in the UK or for which a request for admission to such a market has been made. They therefore apply to an issuer with a standard listing of equity shares admitted, or seeking admission to, trading on a regulated market such as the Main Market of the LSE. See ss.6.2.2, 6.2.3 and 6.2.4 above for further details.

6.6.2.2 Disclosure Guidance and Transparency Rule 3 ("Transactions by persons discharging managerial responsibility and their connected persons")

As referred to above, Ch.3 of the DTRs has been substantially amended since the EU MAR came into effect and now provides guidance only. The substantive provisions on transactions by PDMRs are now primarily contained in art.19 of the EU MAR. These apply to an issuer whose financial instruments are admitted to trading on a regulated market in the UK or for which a request for admission to such a market has been made. They therefore apply to an issuer with a standard listing of equity shares admitted, or seeking admission to, trading on a regulated market such as the Main Market of the LSE. See s.6.2.5 above for further details.

6.6.2.3 *Disclosure Guidance and Transparency Rule 5 ("Vote holder and issuer notification rules")*

Chapter 5 of the DTRs applies to UK issuers trading on a regulated market or a prescribed market (such as AIM) and to non-UK issuers trading on a regulated market and for whom the UK is their home Member State. As above, these rules therefore also apply to relevant issuers with a standard listing of equity shares. See s.6.3.2 above for further information.

6.6.2.4 *Disclosure Guidance and Transparency Rule 6 ("Continuing obligations and access to information")*

The particular rules set out in DTR 6 have differing applications. Subject to certain exceptions, DTR 6.1 applies to issuers whose home Member State is the UK while DTRs 6.2 and 6.3 apply to issuers whose transferable securities are admitted to trading (on a regulated market) and whose home Member State is the UK. As mentioned previously, these rules also apply to relevant issuers with a standard listing of equity shares. See s.6.3.3 above for further details.

6.7 Cancellation of listing

The FCA may cancel a listing or an issuer may apply for a cancellation of its listing. The FCA may cancel a listing if it is satisfied that there are special circumstances that preclude normal regular dealings in its securities (LR 5.2.1R). Examples include where it appears to the FCA that the issuer no longer satisfies its continuing obligations for listing or where the relevant listing has been suspended for more than six months (LR 5.2.2G).

Normally, a company with a premium listing of equity shares which wishes to cancel its listing must obtain a 75% shareholder vote at a general meeting approving the cancellation (LR 5.2.5R(2)(a)). The circular to shareholders must state the anticipated cancellation date (which must be not less than 20 business days following shareholder approval) and the company must notify a RIS of the intended cancellation (LR 5.2.5R). However, the cancellation of listing of other types of securities does not require the approval of holders (LRs 5.2.8R and 5.2.9R), although 20 business days' notice of the intended cancellation is required.

Where a company with a controlling shareholder wishes to cancel its premium listing, the LRs require, in addition to the 75% shareholder approval requirement, the approval of a majority of votes attached to the shares of independent shareholders voting on the resolution (LR 5.2.5R(2)(b)).

The requirement to obtain shareholder approval for the cancellation of a listing of equity shares with a premium listing does not apply where (among other things):

(1) the issuer notifies a RIS that it or its group is in severe financial distress, that there is a proposal for a transaction, arrangement or other form of reconstruction necessary to ensure the survival of the issuer or its group which would be jeopardised by the continued listing and that, but for such proposal, there is no reasonable prospect that the issuer will avoid going into insolvency proceedings. The announcement must explain why the cancellation is in the best interests of those to whom the issuer or its directors have responsibilities (including shareholders and creditors) and why shareholder approval will not be sought (LR 5.2.7R);

(2) a takeover offer for an issuer becomes, or is declared, unconditional in all respects if the offeror is interested in 50% or less of the voting rights of the company and the offeror has, by virtue of its existing holding and acceptances under the offer, acquired share capital carrying 75% of the voting rights in the company, provided a prescribed statement was included in the offer document (LR 5.2.10R); and

(3) the cancellation of equity shares arises as a consequence of a takeover or restructuring of the issuer by a scheme of arrangement under Pt 26 of the Companies Act 2006;

administration or liquidation of the issuer pursuant to a court order under the Insolvency Act 1986; the appointment of an administrator or provisional liquidator; a resolution for winding-up of the issuer is passed; a company voluntary arrangement; under the Insolvency Act 1986; or the implementation of statutory winding-up or reconstruction measures in relation to an overseas issuer (LR 5.2.12R).

Different requirements apply on a takeover offer where an offeror is interested in 50% or more of the voting rights of the company before announcing its firm intention to make an offer (LR 5.2.11AR).

If a cancellation is to take place after a scheme of arrangement becomes effective and a new company is to be listed as a result of that scheme, the issuer must include, with a request to cancel the listing of securities, either a copy of the certificate from the Registrar of Companies that the scheme has become effective or documents which demonstrate adequately that the scheme will become effective on a specified date (LR 5.3.2R(3)). In practice, this requirement has been applied to a takeover via a scheme of arrangement where the target is to be delisted and new consideration shares are to be listed.

According to s.649(3)(a)(i) of the Companies Act 2006 (which provides that, unless the court orders otherwise, a reduction of capital as part of a scheme of arrangement will become effective on delivery of the court order confirming the reduction and Form SH19 ("Statement of capital") to Companies House), the issuer will be able to deliver the scheme sanction court order and reduction of capital court order to Companies House after market close on the day before the date of admission of the new company's shares, making the scheme and reduction effective before the date of admission. In such a case, the issuer's solicitors would, following such delivery, provide to the FCA a letter confirming that delivery of such court orders and Form SH19 had been made and that the scheme and reduction of capital had become effective. Depending on the time of receipt of court sanction of the scheme, a letter to the FCA confirming the court's sanction and a confirmation of expected delivery to Companies House may also be required.

Where a takeover by way of a scheme of arrangement is a cash offer and no new listing is being sought in connection with the transaction, the FCA will proceed with the delisting on the effective date of the scheme if it is provided with a copy of the court order sanctioning the scheme and approving the reduction of capital by 15.00 on the business day prior to the effective date (LR 5.3.6G). The court order may then be registered at any time on the effective date and a copy of the Registration Certification should be forwarded to the FCA during the course of that day.

When a listed company completes a reverse takeover, the FCA will generally cancel the listing of its equity shares and the company, if it wishes to retain a listing, will be required to reapply for the listing of its equity shares and satisfy relevant requirements for listing (LRs 5.6.19G and 5.6.21R). Listing Rules 5.6.23G–5.6.29G set out circumstances in which the FCA will generally be satisfied that a cancellation is not required, which are available if the target is also listed. If the issuer and the target both have the same category of listing, no cancellation is required. If they are of different listing categories and the issuer maintains its listing category, then a cancellation is not required if the enlarged issuer continues to be eligible for its existing listing category. If they are of different listing categories and the issuer changes its listing category, the issuer needs to adhere to the rules applicable to transfers between listing categories.

Issuers with listed equity shares are able to migrate between different listing segments and categories, without having to cancel a listing and reapply for a new listing. The procedures to be followed for such transfers are set out in LR 5.4A ("Transfer between listing categories: Equity shares"). See Ch.3 above for further details of this.

6.8 Suspension of listing

The FCA may suspend a listing if the smooth operation of the market is, or may be, temporarily jeopardised or if it is necessary to protect investors and may impose such conditions on the procedure for lifting the suspension as it considers appropriate (LR 5.1.1R). Examples include where it appears to the FCA that the issuer has failed to meet its continuing obligations for listing, has failed to publish financial information in accordance with the LRs, is unable to assess accurately its financial position and inform the market accordingly or there is insufficient information in the market about a proposed transaction. An issuer may request the FCA to suspend its listing (LR 5.3).

There is no automatic requirement for suspending listing when a reverse takeover is announced but the issuer, where it is a shell company (i.e. a company whose assets consist solely or predominantly of cash or short-dated securities; or whose predominant purpose or objective is to undertake an acquisition or merger, or a series of acquisitions or mergers) or, in the case of a premium listed shell company issuer, its sponsor, must contact the FCA as early as possible before announcing a reverse takeover which has been agreed or is in contemplation to discuss whether a suspension of listing is appropriate (LR 5.6.6R(1)). The FCA have stated that the Listing Rules create a rebuttable presumption that an issuer will be suspended upon announcement or leak of a reverse takeover (Technical Note on Reverse takeovers (UKLA/TN/306.3)). Where details of a reverse takeover have leaked, the FCA must be contacted as early as possible to request a suspension (LR 5.6.6R(2)). The FCA has emphasised that issuers need to ensure that they consider Listing Principle 2, which requires issuers to deal with the FCA in an open and co-operative manner, when considering the appropriate time to contact the FCA (UKLA/TN 306.3).

Examples of when the FCA will generally consider that a reverse takeover is in contemplation include if the shell company issuer has approached the target's board, where the shell company issuer has entered into an exclusivity period with a target or where the shell company issuer has been given access to begin due diligence (LR 5.6.7G). In making a decision about whether it is appropriate to consider suspension, the FCA has stated that they would expect an issuer to apply a similar rationale as they would when considering the announcement requirements under the EU MAR. The FCA have further stated that they would not, for example, expect an issuer to request a suspension where the transaction in question is too speculative to trigger an announcement under the continuing obligations regime.

Listing Rules 5.6.10G–LR 5.6.18R set out circumstances in which the FCA will generally be satisfied that a suspension is not required. These rules distinguish between targets which are admitted to a regulated market, targets admitted to an investment exchange or trading platform that is not a regulated market but for which the disclosure requirements are not materially different from those in the DTRs, and targets which are not subject to a public disclosure regime or are subject to a regime which has materially different disclosure requirements. To avoid suspension, in each case, the shell company issuer is required to publish a RIS giving certain information and confirmations the contents of which are designed to ensure that the market has sufficient information. Consequently, the information required to be included in a RIS is greatest for a target which is not subject to a public disclosure regime.

6.9   Enforcement

6.9.1   *Information gathering and publication*

Disclosure Guidance and Transparency Rule 1.3.1 used to contain provisions requiring issuers, PDMRs and connected persons to provide certain information to the FCA as soon as possible following a request. The obligation has been removed from the DTRs and a similar obligation inserted into FSMA by the 2016 Regulations. Under the new s.122A of the FSMA, the FCA may require an issuer, PDMR or person closely associated with a PDMR to provide:

(1) any information that the FCA considers appropriate to protect investors or ensure the orderly operation of the financial markets; and

(2) any other information or explanation that the FCA may reasonably require to verify whether art.17 ("Public disclosure of inside information") or art.19 ("Manager's transactions") of the EU MAR are being and have been complied with.

In addition, the new s.122G of the FSMA allows the FCA to require an issuer to publish such information as it considers appropriate to protect investors or to ensure the orderly operation of the market. If an issuer fails to comply with this requirement, the FCA can publish the information itself (this replaces the prior obligation under DTR 1.3.3R).

6.9.2 *Sanctions for breach of the EU Market Abuse Regulation and the Listing Rules*

The FCA has a variety of sanctions available to it for breaches of the EU MAR and the Listing Rules. Following the EU MAR coming into effect, these have been removed from Ch.1 ("Introduction") of the DTRs (DTR 1.5.3G) and instead are set out in Ch.5 ("Suspending, cancelling and restoring listing and reverse takeovers: all securities") of the Listing Rules and Pts VI and VIII of the FSMA.

The sanctions available to the FCA for breach of the EU MAR and the Listing Rules are:

(1) public censure of the relevant company, PDMR(s) or person closely associated with a PDMR;

(2) imposition of a fine of such amount as it considers appropriate on the relevant company, PDMR(s) or connected person;

(3) suspension of the relevant securities from trading or listing, as appropriate; and

(4) cancellation of listing of the relevant securities.

6.9.2.1 *Public censure*

Examples of cases where the FSA has publicly censured companies for breach of a listed company's continuing obligations under the pre-1 July 2005 listing regime include the Marconi, Big Food Group and SFI decisions referred to above in ss.6.2.3.3 and 6.2.3.4. In addition, in December 2005, the FSA publicly censured Eurodis Electron Plc ("Eurodis") for a breach of para.9.2(a) of the pre-1 July 2005 Listing Rules because it waited 26 days to publish an announcement of a material deterioration in its working capital position.[35] Although the FSA limited its sanction to that of public censure, the FSA went on to state, however, that it would have imposed a substantial financial penalty save for the fact that Eurodis had been in administration since 15 July 2005 and it lacked the means to pay a financial penalty. A more recent example of public censure by the FCA occurred in August 2015 when the FCA issued a public censure against The Co-operative Bank Plc ("Co-op Bank") for breaching the Listing Rules.[36]

6.9.2.2 *Fines*

The DEPP contains the FCA's policy on financial penalties for breaches of the Listing Rules and the DTRs (which it is required to prepare and issue pursuant to s.93(1) of the FSMA). DEPP 6.5.2G explains that the FCA's penalty-setting regime is based on the following principles:

(1) disgorgement: a firm or individual should not benefit from any breach;
(2) discipline: a firm or individual should be penalised for wrongdoing; and
(3) deterrence: any penalty imposed should deter the firm or individual who committed the breach, and others, from committing further or similar breaches.

---

[35] FSA, Final Notice to Eurodis Electron Plc (9 December 2005).
[36] FCA, Final Notice to The Co-operative Bank Plc (10 August 2015).

The total amount payable by a person subject to an enforcement action may be made up of two elements: (1) disgorgement of the benefit received as a result of the breach; and (2) a financial penalty reflecting the seriousness of the breach. These elements are incorporated in a five-step framework summarised in DEPP 6.5.3G.

In line with its aim to step up enforcement action against leaks of inside information and market abuse generally, the FCA has shown its willingness to impose financial penalties on both issuers and directors. The level of financial penalties imposed by it has also increased in recent years as illustrated by the cases below.

In June 2008, the FSA imposed a fine of £350,000 on Woolworths Group Plc for failing to disclose information in a timely manner as required by DTR 2.2.1R (see s.6.2.3.2 above).

In January 2009, Wolfson Microelectronics Plc ("Wolfson") was fined £140,000 for delaying disclosure of inside information in breach of DTR 2.2.1R. Wolfson lost a supply arrangement in relation to two products with a major customer, which generated approximately 18% of Wolfson's revenue. The customer, however, also informed Wolfson that it should see an increase in demand for the supply of another product. Initially, Wolfson sought advice from its investor relations advisers who concluded that no disclosure was required. A week later, Wolfson sought advice from lawyers and its corporate brokers who advised to disclose, and Wolfson disclosed the information 16 days after it had been informed of the news. The FSA emphasised that an issuer cannot "offset" negative news against positive news. It also stated that the issuer cannot refuse to disclose negative information because it believes that does not reflect the "true value" of the company. Further, it was stated that, in relation to its disclosure obligations, the company should not have relied exclusively on the advice of its investor relations advisers as it was not legal or brokerage advice. It was noted that Wolfson, as the issuer, had primary responsibility for compliance with the DTRs. Finally, it was stated that a company cannot withhold price-sensitive information due to confidentiality agreements with its clients and it was noted that Wolfson had, in any event, ultimately announced the positive news in an anonymous manner.

Also, in January 2009, Entertainment Rights Plc ("ER") was fined £245,000 for a 78-day delay in disclosing inside information, in breach of DTR 2.2.1R. ER had entered into a distribution agreement, which was subsequently varied resulting in an estimated reduction in ER's profits for 2008 of approximately US $14 million. At the time of variation, the board of ER concluded that it was too early to quantify the impact of the variation and that there would be various opportunities to mitigate the negative impact. The FSA concluded that the variation of the distribution agreement should have been disclosed to the market as soon as possible.[37] The fact that there may be opportunities to mitigate the negative impact did not justify the delay.

On 21 June 2010, the FSA published a Final Notice imposing a fine of £500,000 on Photo-Me International Plc (see s.6.2.3.6 above) and, on 26 January 2011, it issued a Final Notice imposing a fine of £455,000 on JJB Sports Plc (see s.6.2.3.2 above), both as a result of the issuers' failure to publicly disclose inside information as soon as possible in breach of DTR 2.2.1R and for breaching the Listing Principles.

On 16 August 2011, the FSA imposed a fine of £210,000 on Sir Ken Morrison, the former chairman of Wm Morrison Supermarkets Plc, for breach of DTR 5.8.3R (see s.6.3.2.8 above).

In 2013, the FSA imposed two significant fines on Lamprell Plc (see s.6.2.3.3.2 above) and Prudential Plc (see s.6.4.2.3 above) of £2.4 million and £14 million respectively, in the former case for breaches of the DTRs, Model Code and Listing Principles and, in the latter case, for a breach of the Listing Principles alongside Principle 11 of the Principles of Businesses.

---

[37] Paragraph 2.4 of FSA, Final Notice to Entertainment Rights Plc (19 January 2009).

In 2017, the FCA found that Rio Tinto breached the DTRs by failing to carry out an impairment test and to recognise an impairment loss on the value of mining assets based in the Republic of Mozambique which it acquired in August 2011 for US $3.7 billion when publishing its 2012 interim results (published 8 August 2012).[38] Had Rio Tinto complied with its obligation to carry out the test, a material impairment would have been required to have been disclosed at the time of its 2012 half-year financial reporting. Rio Tinto's financial reporting was therefore inaccurate and misleading. This continued until 17 January 2013 when Rio Tinto announced an impairment of the Mozambique assets, writing off approximately 80% of the value of the investment in the Mozambique mine. The FCA considered that Rio Tinto's delay in carrying out an impairment test given there were indicators of impairment demonstrated a serious lack of judgement. The FCA imposed a financial penalty on Rio Tinto in the amount of £27,385,400.

6.9.2.3 Suspension

Previously, examples of when the FCA could require the suspension of trading for breach of the DTRs included where an issuer failed to make a RIS announcement as required by the DTRs within the applicable time limits, which, in the opinion of the FCA, could affect the interests of investors or affect the smooth operation of the market, or where there was or may be a leak of inside information and the issuer was unwilling or unable to issue an appropriate RIS announcement within a reasonable period of time (DTR 1.4.4G). Under the new s.122I of the FSMA, the FCA may suspend trading for the purposes of exercising its functions under the EU MAR. This ultimate sanction is obviously something of a double-edged sword because penalising a company in this way may protect future investors but only at the expense of denying existing investors a market for their securities.

It should be noted that, where an issuer's securities have been suspended from listing or trading, the issuer, any PDMRs and

---

[38] FCA, Final Notice to Rio Tinto Plc (17 October 2017).

any person closely associated with a PDMR must continue to comply with the Listing Rules and the EU MAR, as appropriate (s.77(3) of the FSMA, LR 5.1.1R(2) and new s.122I(3) of the FSMA).

Chapter 7

Significant Transactions and Related Party Transactions

Chris Horton and Andrew Scott
Simmons & Simmons LLP

7.1 Introduction

This chapter describes the obligations in the Listing Rules (LRs) which apply to certain transactions carried out by listed companies. Chapter 10 of the Listing Rules deals with significant transactions, principally acquisitions and disposals, by a listed company. It applies to sales and purchases of shares, businesses and assets, and covers both agreed private deals and public takeovers. Chapter 10 describes how acquisitions and disposals are classified by reference to their size. Depending on this size classification, Ch.10 sets out requirements for notifications, circulars and shareholder approval. Chapter 11 covers transactions between parties who are in some way related and contains disclosure and shareholder approval requirements. Chapter 5 of the Listing Rules deals, among other things, with reverse takeovers. Chapter 13 deals with the contents of circulars to approve significant transactions and related party transactions.

This text is based on Chs 5, 10, 11 and 13 of the Listing Rules in effect as at 1 May 2018.

Section 7.1 provides an overview and deals with preliminary points.

Sections 7.2 and 7.3 deal with the process of classification and its consequences.

Section 7.4 deals with transactions (other than acquisitions and disposals) that are required to be classified.

Section 7.5 deals with miscellaneous issues.

Sections 7.6 and 7.7 deal with the documentation which flows from the relevant classification: notifications and shareholder circulars.

Section 7.8 sets out the procedures to be followed in the case of a Class 1 acquisition and s.7.9 provides a worked example of such an acquisition.

Section 7.10 deals with reverse takeovers.

Section 7.11 lists the requirements in relation to public takeovers which are supplementary to the provisions of the City Code on Takeovers and Mergers.

Section 7.12 sets out the provisions for related party transactions covered in Ch.11.

In this chapter, the references to "LR paragraphs" are to paragraphs of the Listing Rules. References to "Disclosure Requirements" are to arts 17, 18 and 19 of the Market Abuse Regulation.[1] References to "sections" are to the numbered sections of this text.

7.1.1 Overview

The purpose of Ch.10 is to ensure that holders of listed equity shares:

- are notified of certain transactions entered into by the listed company; and
- have the opportunity to vote on larger proposed transactions.

---

[1] Regulation 596/2014 on market abuse (market abuse regulation) and repealing Directive 2003/6 and Directives 2003/124, 2003/125 and 2004/72 [2014] OJ L173/1.

In order to achieve this purpose, Ch.10 sets out rules for the classification by size of transactions and for documentation and action consequent upon such classification. It follows that the directors of a listed company proposing to make an acquisition or disposal and its advisers need to have the potential classification in mind at an early stage.

Chapter 11 sets out safeguards that apply to:

- transactions and arrangements between a listed company and a related party; and
- transactions and arrangements between a listed company and any other person that may benefit a related party.

The safeguards in Ch.11 are intended to prevent a related party from taking advantage of its position and also prevent any perception that it might have done so.

Chapter 5 deals, amongst other things, with reverse takeovers, i.e. transactions where any percentage ratio (see below) is 100%, or which in substance result in a fundamental change in the business or a change in board or voting control of the listed company.

Where a listed company is proposing to enter into a transaction which could amount to a Class 1 transaction, a reverse takeover or a related party transaction, the listed company is required to obtain the guidance of a sponsor to assess the application of the Listing Rules and the Disclosure Requirements and the Transparency Rules.

7.1.2 *Application to listed companies and their subsidiaries*

The provisions of Chs 10 and 11 apply only to companies that have a premium listing of equity shares, referred to here as "listed companies". They do not apply to public companies generally or, in particular, to companies which have a standard listing, or to companies whose securities are traded on AIM, a market operated by London Stock Exchange Plc. The general rule is, therefore, that Chs 10 and 11 are relevant whenever the company entering into a transaction is a listed company with a premium listing or the subsidiary undertaking of such a listed company. References in this text to the "listed company" are to the relevant company in a group where the parent has a premium listing, save in respect of reverse takeovers.

The rules relating to reverse takeovers in Ch.5 apply to companies with a premium listing, a standard listing of shares or a standard listing of certificates representing equity securities.

7.1.3 Definition of "transaction"

Transactions classified under Ch.10 are principally, but not exclusively, acquisitions and disposals. Other transactions to which Ch.10 applies are the granting of certain indemnities, break fee arrangements, issues of securities by a major subsidiary undertaking and entering into or exiting joint ventures (see s.7.4 below). Transactions include not only agreements but amendments to agreements.

For the purpose of Ch.10, transactions do not include: a transaction in the ordinary course of business; an issue of securities by the listed company or a transaction to raise finance which does not involve the acquisition or disposal of any fixed asset; and intragroup transactions.

The grant to, or acquisition by, a listed company of an option will constitute a transaction as if the option had been exercised. The exception is where the exercise of the option is solely at the listed company's discretion. In that case, the transaction will be classified on exercise and only the consideration (if any) for the option will be classified at the grant or acquisition stage.

7.1.4 Ordinary course of business

Chapter 10 is intended to cover transactions that are outside the ordinary course of the listed company's business and may change a security holder's economic interest in the company's assets or liabilities (whether or not this change is recognised on the company's balance sheet). In assessing whether a transaction is in the ordinary course of business, the Financial Conduct Authority (FCA) will have regard to the size and incidence of similar transactions which the company has entered into. The FCA may determine that a transaction is not in the ordinary course of business because of its size or incidence.

7.2 Classification

7.2.1 Categories

A transaction is classified by assessing its size relative to that of the listed company proposing to make it. The comparison of size is made by using percentage ratios.

Chapter 10 lists two categories of transactions. These are, in order of ascending magnitude, Class 2 and Class 1. The class tests are also used to calculate the percentage ratios of potential reverse takeovers. Where a class test produces a result of 100% or more, the transaction will be a reverse takeover.

7.2.2 Class 2

Class 2 describes a transaction where any percentage ratio is 5% or more but each is less than 25%. Class 2 transactions are those which are of sufficient size to require a notification to a Regulatory Information Service (RIS).

7.2.3 Class 1

Class 1 describes a transaction where any percentage ratio is 25% or more. Class 1 transactions are those which are of sufficient size to require a notification, the issue of a circular to shareholders and also the prior approval of shareholders in a general meeting.

7.2.4 Reverse takeover

A reverse takeover is an acquisition by a listed company of a business, an unlisted company or assets where any percentage ratio is 100% or more, or which in substance results in either a fundamental change in the business or a change in the board or voting control of the listed company.

7.2.5 Sizing transactions

The size of a transaction is determined by comparing the size of the listed company with the size of the entity or assets acquired or disposed of. There are four tests. The first three tests, relating to gross assets, profits and a comparison of the amount of the consideration with market capitalisation, apply in all circumstances. The fourth test, relating to "gross capital", only applies to acquisitions. The value of the entity acquired or disposed of (determined by each of the tests referred to) is divided by the value (similarly determined) of the listed company.

7.2.6 Figures used for classification

The Listing Rules contain detailed provisions on the sources of figures to be used for classification purposes. Figures used for classification purposes must be, in the case of assets and profits, the figures shown in the latest published audited consolidated accounts or, where a listed company has or will have published a preliminary statement of later annual results at the time the terms of a transaction are agreed, the figures shown in that preliminary statement. If a balance sheet has been published in a subsequently published interim statement then gross assets and gross capital should be taken from that balance sheet.

The figures of the listed company must be adjusted to take account of: (1) transactions completed during the period to which the relevant published accounts, preliminary statement or interim statement relate; and (2) subsequent transactions classified and notified as Class 2 and Class 1. The figures of the target company or business must also be adjusted to take account of: (1) transactions completed during the relevant financial period (i.e. the period used as the basis for calculation of the class tests); and (2) subsequent completed transactions which would have been Class 2 or greater when classified against the target as a whole.

Figures on which the auditors are unable to report without modification must be disregarded. The FCA may modify the requirement in appropriate cases to permit figures to be taken into account.

When applying the percentage ratios to an acquisition by a company whose assets consist wholly or predominantly of cash or short-dated securities, the cash and short-dated securities must be excluded in calculating its assets and market capitalisation.

These principles will also be applied, to the extent relevant, to calculate the assets and profits of the target company or business.

7.2.7 *Anomalous results*

If a calculation under any of the class tests produces an anomalous result or if a calculation is inappropriate to the activities of the listed company, the FCA may modify the relevant rule to substitute other relevant indicators of size, including industry specific tests.

Except as provided below in relation to the profits test, where a listed company wishes to make adjustments to the figures used in calculating the class tests because it believes the test may produce anomalous results, this must be discussed with the FCA before the class tests crystallise.

If a calculation under the profits test produces an anomalous result of 25% or more and the transaction in question is not a related party transaction, a listed company may either:

(1) disregard the profits test for the purpose of classifying the transaction (provided each of the other applicable class test results falls below 5%); or

(2) make adjustments to the calculation under the profits test to reflect:

    (a) genuine one-off costs incurred by the listed company, or target company or business, in connection with its initial public offering (IPO);

    (b) genuine one-off closure costs incurred by the listed company, or target company or business, that are not part of an ongoing restructuring that will occur over more than one financial period; and

    (c) where the listed company, or target company or business, has completed an IPO, interest charges incurred under private ownership (provided that these charges were incurred under facilities that were repaid as part of the IPO capital restructuring and are substituted in the calculation of the profits test with the interest charges that would have been incurred under the new facilities for the relevant period).

If any adjustments are made to the calculation under the profits test, these should be applied equally to both the listed company and the target company or business, where applicable, to ensure a like-for-like comparison is undertaken.

A listed company is not required to consult with the FCA before disregarding or adjusting the profits test as described above but should still seek guidance from a sponsor before taking any such action.

7.3 Percentage ratio tests

7.3.1 *Gross assets*

The first of the percentage ratio tests relates to gross assets. The gross assets which are the subject of the transaction are divided by the gross assets of the listed company (i.e. the total non-current assets of the listed company plus its total current assets).

The gross assets which are the subject of the transaction are defined in different ways depending on whether a consolidated interest is being acquired or disposed of:

(1) for:
    (a) an acquisition of an interest in an undertaking which will result in the consolidation of the assets of that undertaking in the accounts of the listed company; or
    (b) a disposal of an interest in an undertaking which will result in the assets of that undertaking no longer being consolidated in the accounts of the listed company,

the gross assets the subject of the transaction means the value of 100% of that undertaking's assets, irrespective of what interest is acquired or disposed of;

(2) for an acquisition or disposal of an interest in an undertaking which does not fall within (1) above, the gross assets the subject of the transaction means:
    (a) for an acquisition, the consideration together with liabilities assumed (if any); and
    (b) for a disposal, the assets attributed to that interest in the listed company's accounts;
(3) if there is an acquisition of assets other than an interest in an undertaking, the assets the subject of the transaction means the consideration or, if greater, the book value of those assets as they will be included in the listed company's balance sheet; and

(4) if there is a disposal of assets other than an interest in an undertaking, the assets the subject of the transaction means the book value of the assets in the listed company's balance sheet.

The FCA may modify these requirements, when calculating the assets the subject of the transaction, to include further amounts if contingent assets, indemnities or similar arrangements are involved.

7.3.2 Profits

The second test is a comparison between the profits attributable to the assets to be acquired or disposed of and those of the listed company. Profits are computed after deducting all charges except taxation (profit before tax—PBT). In the case of an acquisition of an interest in an undertaking which will result in the consolidation of the assets of that undertaking in the accounts of the listed company or a disposal of an interest in an undertaking which will result in the assets of that undertaking no longer being consolidated in the accounts of the listed company, the profits will be 100% of the profits of the undertaking, irrespective of what interest is being acquired or disposed of.

The profits test does not apply to an acquisition or disposal of an interest in an undertaking that does not result in consolidation or deconsolidation of the undertaking.

The FCA in one of its Technical Notes (UKLA/TN/302.2, January 2018) has clarified the position regarding one-off costs and whether they should be excluded from PBT. The FCA has confirmed that its approach will be to consider arguments on a case-by-case basis and to take into account the specific circumstances of a listed company. The FCA has stated that adjusting the PBT figure by removing one-off costs is a modification of the Listing Rules and, as such, listed companies should always consult the FCA before relying on such an adjusted figure except where the Listing Rules expressly state that they are not required to do so.

The FCA will consider whether or not the cost in question is a genuine one-off cost and the sponsor's view on whether, in the circumstances, the item should be treated as such. The FCA will consider whether the cost appeared in previous profit and loss accounts and whether there will be a similar charge in the following year's profit and loss account. Recurring items and those which are incurred in the ordinary course of business, such as goodwill and impairment charges, are very unlikely to be considered as genuine one-off costs even if they appear in the listed company's accounts as an exceptional or extraordinary item. Likewise, items relating to a restructuring will need to be proven to be one-off rather than part of an ongoing restructuring strategy and costs incurred in a restructuring that spans more than one financial period may not be one-off.

Sponsors should address each of these issues when making a written query about the appropriate measure of profit, particularly when asking the FCA to agree that a transaction is a Class 2 transaction that would be a Class 1 transaction if actual PBT (i.e. before exclusion of one-off costs) were the profit figure used.

Listed companies and their sponsors should also take these issues into consideration when deciding whether they can rely on the concession in the Listing Rules for adjusting the profits test without consulting the FCA (see s.7.2.7 above).

The amount of loss is relevant in calculating the impact of a proposed transaction under the profits test. A listed company should include the amount of the losses of the listed company or target, i.e. disregard the negative when calculating the test.

7.3.3   Consideration

The third test is a comparison between the value of the consideration and the aggregate market value of the ordinary shares (excluding treasury shares) of the listed company. The figure used to determine market capitalisation is the aggregate market value of such shares at the close of business on the last business day before the announcement.

For these purposes:

(1) the consideration is the amount paid to the contracting party;

(2) if all or part of the consideration is in the form of securities to be traded on a market, the consideration attributable to those securities is the aggregate market value of those securities. The figures used to determine consideration consisting of securities of a class already listed is the aggregate market value of all these securities on the last business day before the announcement and for a new class of securities for which an application for listing will be made is the expected aggregate market value of all these securities;

(3) if deferred consideration is, or may be, payable or receivable by the listed company in the future, the consideration is the maximum total consideration payable or receivable under the agreement. If the total consideration is not subject to any maximum (and other class tests indicate the transaction is to be a Class 2 transaction) the transaction will normally be treated as Class 1. However, if the total consideration is not subject to any maximum (and other class tests indicate the transaction to be a transaction where all percentage ratios are less than 5%), the transaction will normally be treated as Class 2;

(4) the FCA in one of its Technical Notes (UKLA/TN/ 314.1, March 2017) has clarified that issuers still have to apply the class tests in Ch.10 when calculating the percentage ratios of a potential reverse takeover and where there is uncapped consideration in a transaction but: (a) otherwise the percentage ratios are 5% or more but less than 25%, the transaction will be treated as a class 1 transaction and not a reverse takeover; and (b) otherwise the percentage ratios are all less than 5%, the transaction will be treated as a class 2 transaction and not a class 1 transaction or a reverse takeover;

(5) the FCA may require the inclusion of further amounts in the calculation of the consideration (for instance, where the purchaser agrees to discharge any liabilities, including

the repayment of intercompany or third-party debt, whether actual or contingent, as part of the terms of the transaction); and

(6)   the FCA in one of its Technical Notes (UKLA/TN/302.2, January 2018) has stated that it regards a company's market capitalisation as significant in assessing the size and importance of a particular transaction and is generally not minded to allow enterprise value to be used as a substitute test.

7.3.4   *Gross capital*

The fourth test only applies in the case of an acquisition. The gross capital of the company or business being acquired must be compared with that of the listed company. The gross capital of the company or business being acquired means the aggregate of:

(1)   the consideration (calculated as before);
(2)   if a company is being acquired, any of its shares and debt securities which are not being acquired (and treasury shares are not to be taken into account);
(3)   all other liabilities (other than current liabilities) including, for this purpose, minority interests and deferred taxation; and
(4)   any excess of current liabilities over current assets.

The gross capital of the listed company means the aggregate of:

(1)   the market value of its shares (excluding treasury shares) and the issue amount of debt securities;
(2)   all other liabilities (other than current liabilities) including, for this purpose, minority interests and deferred taxation; and
(3)   any excess of current liabilities over current assets.

Figures used must be, for shares and debt security aggregated, the aggregate market value of all those shares (or, if not available before the announcement, their nominal value) and the issue amount of the debt security.

7.3.5 *Timing of calculation and submission of class tests to the FCA*

The percentage ratios for the class tests should be calculated at the outset of a transaction in order to determine whether the Class 2 or Class 1 requirements apply and if they do they should be carried out again before the announcement of the transaction.

Class tests do not need to be submitted to the FCA for approval. The FCA has discretion to take anomalous results into account and may be able to accept alternative tests in certain circumstances. However, except where the concession provided under the Listing Rules for anomalous profits test results in certain circumstances applies (see 7.2.7 above), a listed company and its sponsor will need to agree any substitution of alternative tests with the FCA in advance of any announcement of the transaction.

7.4 Other transactions requiring classification

7.4.1 *Indemnities and similar arrangements*

Any agreement or arrangement with a party that is not a wholly-owned subsidiary undertaking of the listed company will be treated as a Class 1 transaction in the following circumstances:

(1) the listed company agrees to discharge any liabilities for costs, expenses, commissions or losses incurred by, or on behalf of, that party, whether or not on a contingent basis;
(2) the agreement or arrangement is exceptional; and
(3) the maximum liability is either unlimited, or is equal to or exceeds, an amount equal to 25% of the average of the listed company's profits (as calculated for classification purposes) for the last three financial years (losses should be taken as "nil" profit and included in this average).

For these purposes, indemnities customarily given in connection with sale and purchase agreements, underwriting or placing agreements, indemnities given to advisers against liabilities to third parties arising out of providing advisory services and any other indemnity that is specifically permitted to be given to a director or auditor under the Companies Act 2006 are not considered by the FCA to be "exceptional".

In circumstances where the liability calculation produces an anomalous result, the FCA may disregard it and substitute other relevant indicators of the size of the indemnity or other arrangement.

The provisions referred to above are not applicable to break fee arrangements which are dealt with separately.

7.4.2 *Break fee arrangements*

The purpose of the arrangement is the key factor in determining whether an arrangement is caught.

An arrangement will be a break fee arrangement if its purpose is payment of a compensatory sum by a listed company to another party (or parties) to a proposed transaction if that proposed transaction fails or is materially impeded and there is no independent substantive commercial rationale for the arrangement (i.e. it has a "money for nothing" element).

"No shop" and "go shop" type provisions, which require payment of a sum to a party in the event the seller finds an alternative purchaser, a requirement to pay another party's material costs and non-refundable deposits will be treated as break fee arrangements. As these obligations may require shareholder approval if not capped below the relevant threshold, consideration should be given to these issues early on and individual arrangements should be considered on a case-by-case basis. Payments in the nature of damages for breach of an obligation with an independent commercial rationale such as the typical business protection covenants that apply between exchange and completion of a share or asset acquisition agreement or co-operation and information access obligations relating to obtaining merger or other clearances are not break fee arrangements.

Sums payable pursuant to break fee arrangements in respect of a transaction will be treated as a Class 1 transaction if the total value of these sums exceeds:

(1)   if the listed company is being acquired, 1% of the value of the listed company calculated by reference to the offer price; and

(2)   in any other case, 1% of the market capitalisation of the listed company.

The maximum amount payable under arrangements for a particular transaction, or for transactions relating to the same assets or business in the 12 months preceding the current arrangement, are included within the total value of the sums payable. Prior transactions can be excluded from the calculation if they were approved by shareholders.

The 1% limit is to be calculated on the basis of the fully diluted equity share capital of the listed company.

Any VAT payable is to be taken into account in determining whether the 1% limit would be exceeded (except to the extent that the VAT is recoverable by the listed company).

For a securities exchange offer, the value of the listed company is to be fixed by reference to the value of the offer at the time the transaction is announced (and is not to be taken as fluctuating as a result of subsequent movements in the price of the consideration securities after the announcement).

The City Code on Takeovers and Mergers is consistent with the Listing Rules with regard to the 1% cap applying to the aggregate of break fees agreed with all offerors.

7.4.3 *Issues by major subsidiary undertakings*

The Listing Rules cover issues of equity shares by a "major subsidiary undertaking" of the listed company. This means a subsidiary undertaking that represents 25% or more of the aggregate of the gross assets or profits (after deducting all charges except taxation) of the listed group.

If:

(1) a major subsidiary undertaking of a listed company issues equity shares for cash or in exchange for other securities or to reduce indebtedness;
(2) the issue would dilute the listed company's percentage interest in the major subsidiary undertaking; and
(3) the economic effect of the dilution is equivalent to a disposal of 25% or more of the aggregate of the gross assets or profits (after the deduction of all charges except taxation) of the group,

the issue will be treated as a Class 1 transaction with the proviso that this treatment will not apply if the major subsidiary undertaking is itself a listed company.

7.4.4 *Joint ventures*

The Ch.10 classification obligations and their consequences can apply in relation to joint ventures entered into by listed companies.

It is common, when entering into a joint venture, for the partners to include exit provisions in the terms of the joint venture agreement. These typically give each partner a combination of rights and obligations either to sell its own holding or to acquire its partner's holding should certain triggering events occur.

If the listed company does not retain sole discretion over the event which requires it either to purchase the joint venture partner's stake or to sell its own, this obligation must be classified at the time it is agreed as though it had been exercised at that time. Further, if the consideration to be paid is to be determined by reference to the future profitability of the joint venture or an independent valuation at the time of exercise, this consideration will be treated as being uncapped.

If the listed company does retain sole discretion over the triggering event, or if it is making a choice to purchase or sell following an event which has been triggered by the joint venture partner, the purchase or sale must be classified when this discretion is exercised or when the choice to purchase or sell is made.

If the consideration is uncapped, a transaction will be treated as a Class 1 transaction if the other class tests indicate that it is a Class 2 transaction. If the other class tests indicate that it is a transaction where all percentage ratios are less than 5%, it will be treated as a Class 2 transaction.

If the listed company enters into a joint venture exit arrangement which takes the form of a put or call option and the exercise of the option is solely at the discretion of the other party to the arrangement, the transaction should be classified at the time it is agreed as though the option has been exercised at that time.

The FCA has given guidance in one of its Technical Notes (UKLA/TN/302.2, January 2018) on the application of class tests to joint venture transactions. When a listed company enters into a joint venture, the FCA would expect it to classify both sides to the transaction, so that both the disposal into the joint venture and the acquisition of an interest in the joint venture are classified. The classification will depend on the facts of each case, including the value added by each partner and further funding commitments etc.

The FCA has also confirmed that, as this is effectively one transaction, it would not expect these two sets of class tests to be aggregated but the highest result from the tests will determine the overall classification of the transaction.

7.5 Miscellaneous

7.5.1 *Aggregating transactions*

Transactions completed during the 12 months before the date of the latest transaction must be aggregated with that transaction for the purposes of classification if:

- they are entered into by the company with the same person or with persons connected with one another;
- they involve the acquisition or disposal of securities or an interest in one particular company; or
- together they lead to substantial involvement in a business activity which did not previously form a significant part of the company's principal activities.

If the aggregation of transactions results in a requirement for shareholder approval, then that approval is required only for the latest transaction.

The FCA may modify these rules to require the aggregation of transactions in circumstances other than those set out above.

The FCA has clarified in one of its Technical Notes (UKLA/ TN/307.1, December 2012) that, when aggregating transactions, listed companies should add together the class test percentages of the earlier transaction (as classified at that time) with the class test percentages of the subsequent transaction. The combined percentage will indicate the aggregated classification of the transactions.

7.5.2 *Specialist companies*

Chapter 10 includes modified classification criteria for certain specialist companies. These are listed property companies, listed mineral companies and listed scientific research based companies.

7.5.3   *Disposals by companies in severe financial difficulty*

A listed company in severe financial difficulty may be permitted to dispose of a substantial part of its business within a short time frame to meet its ongoing working capital requirements or to reduce its liabilities without preparing a circular and convening a general meeting to obtain prior shareholder approval. The listed company has to demonstrate to the FCA that it is in severe financial difficulty and it could not reasonably have entered into negotiations earlier to enable shareholder approval to be sought. There are requirements for the production of documents and for the contents of an announcement to a RIS being made no later than the date the terms of the disposal are agreed.

In addition, the sponsor will be required to confirm to the FCA that, in its opinion and on the basis of the information available to it, the listed company is in severe financial difficulty and will not be in a position to meet its obligations as they fall due unless the disposal takes place according to the proposed timetable.

7.6   Notifications

7.6.1   *Timing*

Notification is required for all categories of transaction. The notification, containing the prescribed information, must be made to a RIS as soon as possible after the terms of the transaction have been agreed. The requirement for a notification is triggered once the parties have entered into a binding agreement, whether or not this is conditional.

7.6.2   *Class 2 requirements*

Notification of a Class 2 transaction must include:

(1)   details of the transaction, including the name of the other party to the transaction;

(2) a description of the business carried on by, or using, the net assets the subject of the transaction;
(3) the consideration, and how it is being satisfied (including the terms of any arrangements for deferred consideration);
(4) the value of the gross assets the subject of the transaction;
(5) the profits attributable to the assets the subject of the transaction;
(6) the effect of the transaction on the listed company including any benefits which are expected to accrue to the company as a result of the transaction;
(7) details of any service contracts of proposed directors of the listed company;
(8) for a disposal, the application of the sale proceeds;
(9) for a disposal, if securities are to form part of the consideration received, a statement as to whether such securities are to be sold or retained; and
(10) details of key individuals important to the business or company the subject of the transaction.

7.6.3   Class 1 requirements

Notifications for Class 1 transactions have to include the same information as Class 2 notifications.

7.6.4   Supplementary notification

A listed company must notify a RIS as soon as possible if, at any time after a notification referred to in s.7.6.2 or 7.6.3 above has been made, the listed company becomes aware that:

(!) there has been a significant change affecting any matter contained in that earlier notification; or
(2) a significant new matter has arisen which would have been required to be mentioned in that earlier notification if it had arisen at the time of the preparation of that notification.

The supplementary notification must give details of the change or new matter and also contain a statement that, except as disclosed, there has been no significant change affecting any matter contained in the earlier notification and no other significant new matter has arisen which would have been required to be mentioned in that earlier notification if it had arisen at the time of the preparation of that notification.

For these purposes, "significant" means significant for the purpose of making an informed assessment of the assets and liabilities, financial position, profits and losses and prospects of the listed company, and the rights attaching to any securities forming part of the consideration. It includes a change in the terms of the transaction that affects the percentage ratios and requires the transaction to be reclassified into a higher category.

7.6.5   Change in terms

If there is a material change to the terms of a Class 1 transaction or reverse takeover after obtaining shareholder approval but before the completion of the Class 1 transaction or reverse takeover, the listed company must comply again separately with the notification and shareholder approval requirements set out in Ch.10. The FCA would (amongst other things) generally consider an increase of 10% or more in the consideration to be a material change for these purposes.

7.7   Circulars

7.7.1   Introduction

A circular to shareholders is required for Class 1 and reverse takeover transactions. Chapter 13 of the Listing Rules sets out requirements for the content and approval procedure for circulars, including Class 1 circulars. The contents of Class 1 circulars are prescribed in Ch.13 and in Annex 1 to Ch.13. The table in Annex 1 to Ch.13 identifies (by reference to certain paragraphs of Annexes 1 and 3 to the Prospectus Directive Regulation)[2] the additional information required to be

---

[2]   Regulation 809/2004 implementing Directive 2003/71 as regards information

included in a Class 1 circular relating to the listed company and the undertaking the subject of the transaction, including working capital and significant change statements.

If a listed company produces a circular containing proposals to be put to shareholders in a general meeting relating to a reconstruction or a refinancing (not defined in the Listing Rules), the circular must include a working capital statement. FCA guidance in one of its Technical Notes (UKLA/TN/301.1, December 2012) is that typically the following indicators suggest a proposal may be a refinancing or reconstruction:

- the listed company will invariably be in a rescue situation, e.g. it has a pressing need for funds for working capital purposes; and
- often shareholders are being asked to vote on giving away significant rights in the company and/or its assets. This may be in the form of a significant dilution or a debt for equity swap.

7.7.2   Chapter 13 requirements

A listed company must ensure that circulars issued to holders of its listed equity shares comply with the requirements of Ch.13.

Every circular sent by a listed company to holders of its listed securities must provide a clear and adequate explanation of its subject matter, giving due prominence to its essential character-istics, benefits and risks. Where, as in the case of Class 1 circulars, voting is required, the circular must contain all information necessary to allow the security holders to make a properly informed decision. The circular must also contain a recommendation from the board of directors as to the action security holders should take, indicating whether or not the proposal described in the circular is, in the board's opinion, in the best interests of security holders as a whole.

---

contained in prospectuses as well as the format, incorporation by reference and publication of such prospectuses and dissemination of advertisements [2004] OJ L149/3.

Circulars may incorporate, by reference, up-to-date information contained in a prospectus or listing particulars or any other published document filed with the FCA.

Class 1 circulars require the approval of the FCA and the appointment of a sponsor under Ch.8 of the Listing Rules.

7.7.3 *Specific requirements for Class 1 circulars*

A Class 1 circular must comply with the general requirements relating to circulars referred to in s.7.7.2 above and must include the following information:

(1) the information given in the notification (see s.7.6.3 above);
(2) the information required by Annex 1R to Ch.13 (see s.7.7.1 above);
(3) if applicable, certain financial information required by LR 13.5 (see s.7.7.4 below);
(4) a declaration by the listed company and its directors in the following form (with appropriate modifications):

> "The [company] and the directors of [the company], whose names appear on page [ ], accept responsibility for the information contained in this document. To the best of the knowledge and belief of the [company] and the directors (who have taken all reasonable care to ensure that such is the case) the information contained in this document is in accordance with the facts and does not omit anything likely to affect the import of such information" (LR 13.4.1(4)R);

(5) a statement of the effect of the acquisition or disposal on the earnings and assets and liabilities of the group; and
(6) if a statement or report attributed to a person as an expert is included in a circular (other than one incorporated by reference from a prospectus or listing particulars), a statement that it is included, in the form and context in which it is included, with the consent of that person.

7.7.4   Financial information in Class 1 circulars

Listing Rule 13.5 deals with the financial information to be contained in Class 1 circulars. Such information is required where the listed company seeks to acquire an interest in a target which will result in a consolidation of the target's assets and liabilities with those of the listed company or seeks to dispose of an interest in a target which will result in the assets and liabilities no longer being consolidated. Financial information may also be required under LR 13.5.1(3) where a target has itself acquired a further target.

All financial information disclosed in a Class 1 circular must be in a form which is consistent with the accounting policies adopted in the listed company's own latest annual consolidated accounts and the listed company must identify the source of all such financial information.

Listing Rule 13.5 contains detailed information on the requirements for financial information tables, accountants' opinions, profit forecasts and profit estimates, synergy benefits and the subsequent publication of unaudited financial information.

Where a company includes details of expected synergies or other quantified estimated financial benefits in the Class 1 circular, it has to include:

(1)   the basis for the belief that those synergies or other quantified estimated financial benefits will arise;

(2)   an analysis and explanation of the constituent elements of the synergies or other quantified estimated financial benefits (including any costs) sufficient to enable the relative importance of those elements to be understood, including an indication of when they will be realised and whether they are expected to be recurring;

(3)   a base figure for any comparison drawn;

(4)   a statement that the synergies or other quantified estimated financial benefits are contingent on the Class 1 transaction and could not be achieved independently; and

(5) a statement that the estimated synergies or other quantified estimated financial benefits reflect both the beneficial
elements and relevant costs.

7.7.5 *Formal approval of circulars*

A listed company must appoint a sponsor on each occasion
that it is required to produce a Class 1 circular. The duties of
the sponsor include providing assurance to the FCA when
required that the responsibilities of the listed company under
the Listing Rules have been met and guiding the listed
company in understanding and meeting its responsibilities
thereunder and under the Disclosure Requirements and
Transparency Rules.

The following documents (to the extent applicable) must be
lodged with the FCA in final form before it will approve the
circular:

(1) a Sponsor's Declaration for the Production of a Circular
completed by the sponsor;
(2) a letter setting out any items of information required by
Ch.13 that are not applicable for the particular Class 1
circular (in practice, this is addressed by indicating
non-applicable items when submitting the relevant circular contents checklists to the FCA); and
(3) any other document that the FCA has sought in advance
from the listed company or its sponsor.

Drafts of the Class 1 circular, the Sponsor's Declaration and the
derogations letter (if any) must be submitted at least 10 clear
business days before the date on which it is intended to publish
the circular.

If a circular submitted for approval is amended, copies of
amended drafts must be resubmitted, marked to show
changes.

The FCA will approve the circular if it is satisfied that the
requirements of Ch.13 have been met.

7.8   Procedure for a Class 1 acquisition

Typically, the procedure followed in a Class 1 acquisition of a private company by a premium listed company (such as the example in s.7.9 below) would be as follows.

First, the target is selected by the listed company and the financial advisers to the acquiring company appraise the potential target from published information and any other available sources. Class tests should be carried out at an early stage to determine whether the transaction falls into Class 1 or Class 2 (or not).

If, on at least one of the four classification tests, the ratio produced is 25% or more, the acquisition will be a Class 1 acquisition and require notification to a RIS, a circular and shareholder approval. The acquiring company must appoint a sponsor.

Secondly, there will be discussions between the boards of the two companies leading to agreement in principle on the terms of the acquisition. Once terms have been agreed in principle, the acquiring company will usually instruct its accountants to investigate and report on the target. At the same time, the solicitors for the acquiring company will be instructed to prepare a sale and purchase agreement and, once the first draft is available, negotiation of the terms of that agreement will begin.

The purchaser may want to fund the consideration for the acquisition by an issue of equity share capital. However, the sellers may want the bulk of the consideration to be received by them in cash. If the financial advisers to the listed acquiring company believe that there is a market for new shares of the purchaser then such financing may be possible by way of a placing (which may be subject to clawback in an open offer—see below). This will call for the production, by solicitors acting for the financial advisers, of an agreement covering the placing of those shares.

If the number of shares to be issued will increase the issued equity share capital of the acquiring company by 20% or more, or if the shares to be listed are to be offered to the public before admission, and if none of the exemptions apply, then a prospectus will be required.

The Class 1 circular to the shareholders of the acquiring company will have to be accompanied by, or incorporate, the prospectus, if required. It will also contain a notice of a general meeting at which resolutions to approve the acquisition and, if necessary, authorise the directors to allot the shares and to disapply pre-emption rights (if applicable) will be proposed.

A number of documents will be produced in parallel: the sale and purchase agreement; the placing agreement; the notification; the Class 1 circular; and, if required, the prospectus.

A further consequence of the purchaser's issued share capital being increased by 10% or more is that compliance with the guidelines issued by the Investment Association will require the new shares to be offered to existing shareholders pro rata to their holdings. This will typically be done by a placing with clawback by way of an open offer to existing shareholders. The shares to be issued will be placed under the terms of the placing agreement (typically, to institutional shareholders who may or may not be existing shareholders of the company), but such placing will be conditional upon shareholder approval of the acquisition and admission of the new shares to listing and will be subject to the right of existing shareholders to subscribe for their pro rata portion of those shares in preference to the placees.

The timetable runs along the following lines. Work on all the documents proceeds in parallel up to a proposed impact date when the sale and purchase is announced and the shares are conditionally placed. On the evening before that date, the placing agreement—the agreement under which the cash to finance the consideration is to be raised—will be executed in escrow. At the same meeting, the sale and purchase agreement, which is conditional upon shareholder approval, is also signed and held in escrow. First thing the next morning, both the sale and purchase agreement and the placing agreement are released from escrow and become binding, subject to their conditions. The agreed notification of the acquisition is released on a RIS. The financial adviser to the acquiring company places the shares, conditional upon shareholder approval and admission of the new shares to listing, by reference to a substantially final proof or "P-proof" of the Class 1 circular and prospectus.

The FCA provides written confirmation of its approval of the prospectus and the circular, and the prospectus is then published and the circular is despatched to shareholders.

The resolution to approve the transaction and to authorise allotment of the shares will normally be an ordinary resolution. A special resolution will be needed if pre-emption rights are being disapplied. The offer to existing shareholders to take up new shares must be made available to them for at least 10 business days. So, on the appropriate day, the general meeting will be held and the company's registrars will separately notify the purchaser's financial advisers of the number of shares taken up by existing shareholders from which the financial advisers will determine the number of shares which will be placed with placees.

7.9 Example of a Class 1 acquisition

7.9.1 *The transaction*

Acquisico Plc, a company whose shares are admitted to the premium segment of the Official List of the FCA, is considering the acquisition of the entire issued share capital of Target Ltd, a private company owned by five shareholders. The directors of Acquisico agree with the shareholders of Target that Acquisico will acquire Target for £15 million.

The Target shareholders wish to receive cash. Acquisico wishes to finance the acquisition of Target by the issue of new ordinary shares. Acquisico's share price is currently 105 pence. At a price of 100 pence per share (allowing for a discount on the placing of Acquisico's shares), the acquisition of Target will require the issue of 15 million ordinary shares of Acquisico.

7.9.2   Financial information on Acquisico

The latest report and accounts for Acquisico show that in the year ended 31 December 2017, Acquisico made profits before tax and extraordinary items of £10 million on turnover of £170 million and had gross assets of £95 million.

Acquisico has released a half-yearly financial report recording unaudited profits before tax of £7.5 million in the six months ended 30 June 2018 and containing an unaudited balance sheet showing gross assets of £100 million.

Acquisico has unlisted debt securities of £15 million. The latest report and accounts for Acquisico show that the total liabilities of Acquisico (other than current liabilities), including minority interests and deferred taxation as at 31 December 2017, were £20 million (in addition to the debt securities of £15 million). At that date, the current assets of Acquisico exceeded its current liabilities.

The gross capital of Acquisico is £84.88 million—Acquisico's issued shares (excluding treasury shares) with a market value of £49.88 million, plus its debts securities of £15 million nominal value, plus its additional liabilities of £20 million.

7.9.3   Financial information on Target

The latest report and accounts for Target show that in the year ended 31 December 2017, Target made profits before tax and extraordinary items of £3 million on turnover of £25 million and had gross assets of £10 million.

Target has no debt securities. The latest report and accounts for Target show that the total liabilities of Target (other than current liabilities) including minority interests and deferred taxation as at 31 December 2017 were £5 million. At that date, the current assets of Target exceeded its current liabilities.

The gross capital of Target is £20 million—the consideration of £15 million plus Target's liabilities of £5 million.

7.9.4 The class tests

Gross assets—Target's gross assets of £10 million divided by Acquisico's gross assets (derived from the balance sheet in the half yearly report) of £100 million—10%.

Profits—Target's profits of £3 million divided by Acquisico's profits of £10 million (taken from the latest full year accounts)—30%.

Consideration to market capitalisation—consideration of £15 million divided by the aggregate market value of Acquisico's issued shares (excluding treasury shares) of £49.88 million—30%.

Gross capital—Target's gross capital of £20 million divided by Acquisico's gross capital of £84.88 million—24%.

7.9.5 Classification

Two of the class tests produce a result in excess of 25%. As a result, the acquisition will be a Class 1 transaction. Note that because each of the other class test results exceeds 5%, Acquisico may not disregard the profits test result of 30% even if it is anomalous (see s.7.2.7 above).

7.9.6 Consequences

The transaction will require notification to a RIS, a Class 1 circular to shareholders and the approval of shareholders in a general meeting.

Because the transaction will involve an increase in Acquisico's issued ordinary share capital of more than 20% (specifically

32%) and those shares will be admitted to trading on a regulated market, the transaction will require the publication of a prospectus. A prospectus will also be required, unless an exemption applies, if there is to be a public offer of the new Acquisico ordinary shares.

Because the new shares will be issued for cash, under LR 9.3.11R, they must be offered pro rata to existing Acquisico shareholders unless the Acquisico shareholders have authorised a disapplication of statutory pre-emption rights in accordance with the Companies Act 2006. In addition, because the placing of the new shares will increase Acquisico's issued ordinary share capital by more than 10%, guidance issued by the Investment Association requires the new shares to be offered pro rata to existing Acquisico shareholders.

Shareholder approval would also be required if issuing the shares at more than a 10% discount to the prevailing market price under LR 9.5.10R.

7.9.7 Documentation

(1) Sale and purchase agreement—between the shareholders in Target and Acquisico—is conditional on the placing agreement becoming unconditional in all respects, save for any condition requiring completion of the sale and purchase agreement;

(2) placing agreement—between the sponsor/underwriter and Acquisico—under which the sponsor/underwriter agrees with Acquisico to act as sponsor and to procure placees to subscribe for Acquisico's shares on the terms that the proceeds are applied in satisfaction of the consideration due to be paid to the vendor shareholders in Target. This agreement will be conditional, amongst other matters, on:

    (a) shareholder approval of the transaction and the share issue;

    (b) completion of the sale and purchase agreement;

    (c) admission of the new shares;

(3) the placing will be made subject to the conditions of the placing agreement and subject to a right of first refusal on the new shares for the existing shareholders of Acquisico under an open offer;

(3) notification of the transaction with the information referred to in s.7.6.3 above; and

(4) circular to shareholders of Acquisico comprising:

    (a) a letter from the chairman of Acquisico describing the transaction;

    (b) an open offer to Acquisico shareholders of new Acquisico shares;

    (c) financial information on Acquisico and Target;

    (d) a prospectus;

    (e) notice of general meeting to propose an ordinary resolution to approve the transaction and, if required, authorise the directors to allot shares.

7.9.8 Timetable

Key points

Tuesday (Day 1) (evening)	Sign sale and purchase agreement and placing agreement and hold in escrow.
Wednesday (Day 2)	Release sale and purchase agreement and placing agreement from escrow. Notify transaction. Conditionally place new shares to the placees. Approval and publication of the prospectus. Despatch Class 1 circular and prospectus.
Wednesday (Day 16)	Open offer to existing shareholders closes (10 business days).
Friday (Day 18)	Hold the general meeting (likely to be 14 clear days' notice or 14 working days if applying the UK Corporate Governance Code).
Monday (Day 21)	Underwriter pays funds from the placing and registrar pays funds from the open offer to Acquisico. Complete sale and purchase agreement. Admission of new Acquisico shares effective.

7.10 Reverse takeovers

7.10.1 Introduction

A reverse takeover is an acquisition by a listed company of a business, company or assets, where any percentage ratio is 100% or more, or which in substance results in a fundamental change in the business or in a change in board or voting control of the listed company.

When calculating the percentage ratios for a reverse takeover, a listed company must apply the class tests in Ch.10 and apply the aggregation provisions in LR 10.2.10R. This is to ensure that transactions cannot be artificially broken up to avoid reverse takeover requirements.

The FCA considers that the following factors are indicators of a fundamental change:

* the extent to which the transaction will change the strategic direction or nature of its business;
* whether its business will be part of a different industry sector following completion; or
* whether its business will deal with fundamentally different suppliers and end users.

A reverse takeover by a listed company of another listed company will not constitute a reverse takeover provided that the other company has the same category of listing as the company (thus preventing a listed company from using a reverse takeover to move from one listing category to another without having to satisfy the eligibility conditions for the new category). However, a listed company with a premium listing must, in relation to a reverse takeover, comply with the Class 1 requirements for that transaction.

7.10.2 Reverse takeover requirements

Listing Rule 5.6 deals with reverse takeovers. This rule applies to a listed company with a premium listing, a standard listing of shares or a standard listing of certificates representing equity securities.

A listed company with a premium listing must, in relation to a reverse takeover, comply with the Class 1 requirements for that transaction—appointment of a sponsor, notification, circular and shareholder approval.

7.10.3 Suspension

Previously, all listed companies were subject to the rebuttable presumption that there was insufficient information available to the market in the event of a reverse takeover and that a suspension of listing was therefore appropriate. However, in its Policy Statement (PS 17/22) published in October 2017, the FCA explained that it considers in most cases that the information disclosed as part of a listed company's obligations under the Disclosure Requirements allows the market to operate smoothly without the need for a presumption of suspension. As a result, with effect from 1 January 2018, the FCA amended the Listing Rules to remove the presumption of suspension in the case of reverse takeovers for all listed companies except "shell companies" (defined in LR 5.6 as companies whose assets consist solely of cash or short-dated securities or whose predominant purpose or objective is to undertake one or more acquisitions or mergers).

The shell company (or, if it has a premium listing, its sponsor) must contact the FCA as early as possible: (1) before announcing a reverse takeover which has been agreed or is in contemplation, to discuss whether a suspension of listing is appropriate; or (2) once details of the reverse takeover have leaked, to request a suspension. The FCA expects early engagement on reverse takeovers.

Examples of where the FCA will consider that a reverse takeover is in contemplation include situations where:

- the shell company has approached the target's board;
- the shell company has entered into an exclusivity period with a target; or
- the shell company has been given access to begin due diligence work (whether or not on a limited basis).

Generally, on the announcement of a reverse takeover by a shell company, or if it is leaked, it will be appropriate to suspend the shares of the listed company as there will be insufficient publicly available information about the proposed transaction and the shell company will be unable to assess accurately its financial position and inform the market accordingly. However, the FCA may agree that suspension is not required if it is satisfied that there is sufficient publicly available information about the proposed transaction.

The FCA has issued guidance in one of its Technical Notes (UKLA/TN/420.2, January 2018) that in making a decision about whether it is appropriate to consider suspension, it would expect a company to apply a similar rationale as it would when considering announcement requirements under the Market Abuse Regulation. The FCA would not expect a listed company to request a suspension when the transaction in question is too speculative to trigger an announcement under the continuing obligations regime.

The FCA will generally be satisfied that there is sufficient publicly available information about the proposed transaction if:

(1) the target has shares or certificates representing equity securities admitted to a regulated market; and
(2) the shell company makes an announcement by means of a RIS stating that the target has complied with the disclosure requirements applicable on that regulated market and providing details of where information disclosed pursuant to those requirements can be obtained.

The FCA will generally be satisfied that there is sufficient publicly available information about the proposed transaction if the target has securities admitted to an investment exchange or trading platform that is not a regulated market and the shell company:

(1) confirms, in a form acceptable to the FCA, that the disclosure requirements in relation to financial information and inside information of the investment exchange or trading platform on which the target's securities are admitted are not materially different from the disclosure requirements under the Disclosure Requirements; and
(2) makes an announcement by means of a RIS to the effect that:
   (a) the target has complied with the disclosure requirements applicable on the investment exchange or trading platform to which its securities are admitted and provides details of where information disclosed pursuant to those requirements can be obtained;
   (b) there are no material differences between those disclosure requirements and the disclosure requirements under the Disclosure Guidance and Transparency Rules.

Where a shell company has a premium listing, the written confirmation must be given by the shell company's sponsor.

Where the target in a reverse takeover is not subject to a public disclosure regime, or if the target has securities admitted on an investment exchange or trading platform that is not a regulated market but the shell company is not able to give the confirmation and make the announcement contemplated above, the FCA will generally be satisfied that there is sufficient publicly available information about the proposed transaction such that a suspension is not required where the shell company makes an announcement by means of a RIS containing:

(1) financial information on the target covering the last three years. Generally, the FCA would consider the following information to be sufficient:

    (a) profit and loss information to at least operating profit level;

    (b) balance sheet information, highlighting at least net assets and liabilities;

    (c) relevant cash flow information;

    (d) a description of the key differences between the shell company's accounting policies and the policies used to present the financial information on the target;

(2) a description of the target which includes key non-financial operating or performance measures appropriate to the target's business operations and the information as required under Prospectus Rule (PR) Appendix 3 Annex 1 Item 12 ("Trend information") for the target;

(3) a declaration that the directors of the shell company consider that the announcement contains sufficient information about the business to be acquired to provide a properly informed basis for assessing its financial position; and

(4) a statement confirming that the shell company has made the necessary arrangements with the target vendors to enable it to keep the market informed without delay of any developments concerning the target that would be required to be released were the target part of the shell company.

Where a shell company has a premium listing, a sponsor must provide written confirmation to the FCA that, in its opinion, it is reasonable for the shell company to provide the declarations described above in (3) and (4).

Where the FCA has agreed that a suspension is not necessary, as a result of such an announcement, the shell company must comply with the obligation under art.17(1) of the Market Abuse Regulation on the basis that the target already forms part of the enlarged group.

7.10.4 *Cancellation*

When a listed company completes a reverse takeover, the FCA will generally cancel the listing of its equity securities and the company will be required to reapply for listing and satisfy the relevant requirements for listing.

Where a listed company acquires the shares or certificates representing equity securities of a target with a different listing category from its own and the listed company wishes to maintain its existing listing category, the FCA will generally be satisfied that a cancellation is not required on completion of a reverse takeover if:

(1) the listed company will continue to be eligible for its existing listing category following completion of the transaction;
(2) the listed company provides an eligibility letter setting out how the listed company as enlarged by the acquisition satisfies each listing rule requirement that is relevant to it being eligible for its existing listing category; and
(3) the listed company makes an announcement or publishes a circular explaining:
    (a) the background and reasons for the acquisition;
    (b) any changes to the acquiring listed company's business that have been made or are proposed to be made in connection with the acquisition;
    (c) the effect of the transaction on the acquiring listed company's obligations under the Listing Rules;
    (d) (where appropriate) how the acquiring listed company will continue to meet the eligibility requirements referred to in LR 5.6.21;
    (e) any other matter that the FCA may reasonably require.

An eligibility letter prepared for these purposes must be provided to the FCA not less than 20 business days prior to the announcement of the transaction. Where a listed company has a premium listing, the eligibility letter must be provided by a sponsor.

The FCA will generally be satisfied that a cancellation is not required on completion of a reverse takeover if the target is listed with a different listing category from that of the listed company, the listed company wishes to transfer its listing to a different listing category in conjunction with the acquisition and the listed company as enlarged by the relevant acquisition complies with the relevant requirements of LR 5.4A to transfer to a different listing category.

7.11 Takeovers

7.11.1 Class 1 takeover offers

The Listing Rules can have application to takeover offers; that is, acquisitions by a listed company of a public company. The term "takeover offer" is not defined by the Listing Rules. These requirements come into play where the takeover offer constitutes a Class 1 transaction for the acquiring listed company.

7.11.2 Contents of circulars

The contents requirements for a Class 1 circular relating to a takeover offer are contained in LRs 13.4.3 and 13.5.27:

(1) if a Class 1 circular relates to a takeover offer which is recommended by the offeree's board and the listed company has had access to due diligence information on the offeree at the time the Class 1 circular is published, the listed company must prepare and publish the working capital statement on the basis that the acquisition has taken place;

(2) if a Class 1 circular relates to a takeover offer which has not been recommended by the offeree's board or the listed company has not had access to due diligence information on the offeree at the time the Class 1 circular is published, then the listed company must comply with (3)–(6) below;

(3) the listed company must prepare and publish the working capital statement on the listed company on the basis that the acquisition has not taken place;

(4) other information on the offeree required by LR 13 Annex 1R should be disclosed in the Class 1 circular on the basis of information published or made available by the offeree and of which the listed company is aware and is free to disclose;

(5) if the takeover offer has been recommended but the listed company does not have access to due diligence information on the offeree, the listed company must disclose in the Class 1 circular why access has not been given to that information; and

(6) unless a dispensation is granted, where the target is either admitted to trading on a regulated market or is a company whose securities are either listed on an investment exchange that is not a regulated market or admitted to a multilateral trading facility, where appropriate standards as regards the production, publication and auditing of financial information are in place and none of the financial information included in the target's financial information table is subject to a modified report (i.e. an accountant's or auditor's report in which the opinion is modified or which contains an emphasis-of-matter paragraph), the listed company must include in the Class 1 circular either: (a) a reconciliation of financial information on the target for all periods covered by the financial information table on the basis of the listed company's accounting policies, accompanied by an accountant's opinion that sets out whether the reconciliation of financial information in the financial information table has been properly compiled on the basis stated and whether the adjustments are appropriate for the purpose of presenting the financial information (as adjusted) on a basis consistent in all material respects with the listed company's accounting policies; or (b) a statement by the directors that no material adjustment needs to be made to the target's financial information to achieve consistency with the listed company's accounting policies. The FCA will make its assessment of whether the accounting and other standards applicable to an investment exchange or multilateral trading facility as a result of securities being admitted to trading are appropriate, having regard to at least the following matters in relation

to the legal and regulatory framework applying to the target by virtue of its admission to that market:

(a) the quality of auditing standards compared with International Standards on Auditing;

(b) requirements for independence of auditors;

(c) the nature and extent of regulation of audit firms;

(d) the quality of accounting standards compared with International Financial Reporting Standards;

(e) the requirements for the timeliness of publication of financial information;

(f) the presence and effectiveness of monitoring of the timely production and publication of the accounts;

(g) the existence and level of external independent scrutiny of the quality of accounts and the disclosures therein.

Where a listed company proposes to rely on (6) above, its sponsor must submit to the FCA an assessment of the appropriateness of the standards applicable to an investment exchange or multilateral trading facility against the factors set out above and any other matters that it considers should be noted. The assessment must be submitted before or at the time the listed company submits the draft Class 1 circular.

7.12 Transactions with related parties

7.12.1 *Introduction*

Chapter 11 sets out the rules relating to transactions and arrangements between a listed company and related parties, such as current or recent directors or substantial shareholders (or associates of either). It also covers transactions and arrangements between a listed company and any other person that may benefit a related party. The purpose of Ch.11 is to provide safeguards intended to prevent a related party from taking advantage of its position and also to prevent any perception that it may have done so. Chapter 11 only applies to companies with a premium listing.

Where any transaction is proposed between a listed company (or any of its subsidiary undertakings) and a related party, an announcement, a circular and the prior approval of the shareholders in a general meeting will generally be required and the related party will not be permitted to vote. Any circular sent to shareholders must provide a clear and adequate explanation of its subject matter, giving due prominence to its essential characteristics, benefits and risks.

The circular must include a statement by the board of the listed company that the transaction is fair and reasonable so far as the security holders of the company are concerned and that the directors have been so advised by a sponsor.

A company proposing to enter into a transaction that is or could be a related party transaction is required under LR 8.2.3R to obtain the guidance of a sponsor to assess the potential application of the Listing Rules, the Disclosure Requirements and the Transparency Rules.

7.12.2 Definition of "related parties"

A "related party" means:

(1) a person who is (or was within the 12 months before the date of the transaction or arrangement) a "substantial shareholder" (as defined below);

(2) a person who is (or was within the 12 months before the date of the transaction or arrangement) a director or shadow director of the listed company or of any other company which is (and, if he has ceased to be such, was while he was a director or shadow director of such company) its subsidiary undertaking or parent undertaking or a fellow subsidiary undertaking of its parent undertaking;

(3) a person exercising significant influence; or

(4) an associate of a related party referred to in (1), (2) and (3) above.

The term "associate" is defined as follows:

(1) in relation to a director, substantial shareholder, or person exercising significant influence, who is an individual:

    (a) that individual's spouse, civil partner or child (together "the individual's family");

    (b) the trustees (acting as such) of any trust of which the individual or any of the individual's family is a beneficiary or a discretionary object (other than a trust which is either an occupational pension scheme or an employees' share scheme which does not, in either case, have the effect of conferring benefits on persons all or most of whom are related parties);

    (c) any company in whose equity securities the individual or any member or members (taken together) of the individual's family or the individual and any such member or members (taken together) are directly or indirectly interested (or have a conditional or contingent entitlement to become interested) so that they are (or would on the fulfilment of the condition or the occurrence of the contingency be) able:

        (i) to exercise or control the exercise of 30% or more of the votes able to be cast at general meetings on all, or substantially all, matters; or

        (ii) to appoint or remove directors holding a majority of voting rights at board meetings on all, or substantially all, matters; and

    (d) any partnership whether a limited partnership or limited liability partnership in which the individual or any member or members (taken together) of the individual's family are directly or indirectly interested (or have a conditional or contingent entitlement to become interested) so that they hold or control or would on the fulfilment of the condition or the occurrence of the contingency be able to hold or control:

        (i) a voting interesting greater than 30% in the partnership; or

        (ii) at least 30% of the partnership.

For the purpose of (c) above, if more than one director of the listed company, its parent undertaking or any of its subsidiary undertakings is interested in the equity securities of another company, then the interests of those directors and their associates will be aggregated when determining whether that company is an associate of the director; and

(2) in relation to a substantial shareholder, or person exercising significant influence, which is a company:

   (a) any other company which is its subsidiary undertaking or parent undertaking or fellow subsidiary undertaking of the parent undertaking;

   (b) any company whose directors are accustomed to act in accordance with the substantial shareholder's or person exercising significant influence's directions or instructions; and

   (c) any company in the capital of which the substantial shareholder or person exercising significant influence and any other company under (a) or (b) taken together is (or would on the fulfilment of a condition or the occurrence of a contingency be) able to exercise power of the type described in (1)(c)(i)–(ii) of this definition.

The term "substantial shareholder" is defined as follows.

Any person who is entitled to exercise, or to control the exercise of, 10% or more of the votes able to be cast on all or substantially all matters at general meetings of the company (or of any company which is its subsidiary undertaking or parent undertaking or of a fellow subsidiary undertaking of its parent undertaking). However, the following can be disregarded for the purposes of the definition of "substantial shareholder":

(1) any voting rights which such a person exercises (or controls the exercise of) independently in its capacity as bare trustee, investment manager, collective investment undertaking or a long-term insurer in respect of its linked long-term business if no associate of that person interferes by giving direct or indirect instructions, or in any other way, in the exercise of such voting rights (except to the

extent any such person confers or collaborates with such an associate which also acts in its capacity as investment manager, collective investment undertaking or long-term insurer); or

(2) any voting rights which a person may hold (or control the exercise of) solely in relation to the direct performance, by way of business, of:

    (a)   underwriting the issue or sale of securities; or

    (b)   placing securities, where the person provides a firm commitment to acquire any securities which it does not place; or

    (c)   acquiring securities from existing shareholders or the listed company pursuant to an agreement to procure third-party purchases of securities; and

    (d)   where the conditions in (i)–(iv) below are satisfied:

        (i)   the activities set out in (2)(a)–(c) are performed in the ordinary course of business;

        (ii)   the securities to which the voting rights attach are held for a consecutive period of five trading days or less, beginning with the first trading day on which the securities are held;

        (iii) the voting rights are not exercised within the period for which securities are held; and

        (iv) no attempt is made directly or indirectly by the firm to intervene in (or attempt to intervene in) or exert (or attempt to exert) influence on the management of the listed company within the period the securities are held.

The exemption in (1) above allows holdings held by investment managers to be disaggregated if they are held in separately managed funds.

7.12.3 Related party transactions

A "related party transaction" means:

(1) a transaction (other than a transaction in the ordinary course of business) between a listed company (or any of its subsidiary undertakings) and a related party;

(2) an arrangement (other than an arrangement in the ordinary course of business) pursuant to which a listed company (or any of its subsidiary undertakings) and a related party each invests in, or provides finance to, another undertaking or asset; or

(3) any other similar transaction or arrangement (other than a transaction in the ordinary course of business) between a listed company (or any of its subsidiary undertakings) and any other person, the purpose and effect of which is to benefit a related party.

Note that this is different from, and wider than, the definition of "transaction" in Ch.10.

In assessing whether a transaction is in the ordinary course of business under Ch.11, the FCA will have regard to the size and incidence of the transaction and also whether the terms and conditions of the transaction are unusual.

7.12.4 *Transactions to which related party transaction rules do not apply*

The provisions of Ch.11 do not apply to the following kinds of transactions:

• a transaction or arrangement where each of the applicable percentage ratios for the class tests referred to in s.7.3 above is equal to or less than 0.25%; or

• certain transactions agreed before the person became a related party.

If the transaction or arrangement is of the kind referred to in s.7.12.4.1–7 below, the provisions of Ch.11 will not apply provided that the transaction or arrangement does not have any unusual features.

7.12.4.1   Issue of new securities and sale of treasury shares

A transaction that consists of:

(1) the take up by a related party of new securities or treasury shares under its entitlement in a pre-emptive offering; and
(2) an issue of new securities made under the exercise of conversion or subscription rights attaching to a listed class of securities.

7.12.4.2   Employees' share schemes and long-term incentive schemes

The:

(1) receipt of any asset (including cash or securities of the listed company or any of its subsidiary undertakings) by a director of the listed company, its parent undertaking or any of its subsidiary undertakings;
(2) grant of an option or other right to a director of the listed company, its parent undertaking, or any of its subsidiary undertakings to acquire (whether or not for consideration) any asset (including cash or new or existing securities of the listed company or any of its subsidiary undertakings); or
(3) provision of a gift or loan to the trustees of an employee benefit trust to finance the provision of assets as referred to in (1) or (2),

in accordance with the terms of an employees' share scheme or a long-term incentive scheme.

7.12.4.3   Credit

A grant of credit (including the lending of money or the guaranteeing of a loan):

(1) to the related party on normal commercial terms;

(2) to a director for an amount and on terms no more favourable than those offered to employees of the group generally; or

(3) by the related party on normal commercial terms and on an unsecured basis.

7.12.4.4 *Directors' indemnities and loans*

(1) A transaction that consists of:
  (a) granting an indemnity to a director of the listed company (or any of its subsidiary undertakings) if the terms of the indemnity are in accordance with those specifically permitted to be given to a director under the Companies Act 2006;
  (b) maintaining a contract of insurance if the insurance is in accordance with that specifically permitted to be maintained for a director under the Companies Act 2006 (whether for a director of the listed company or for a director of any of its subsidiary undertakings); or
  (c) a loan or assistance to a director by a listed company or any of its subsidiary undertakings if the terms are in accordance with those specifically permitted under s.204 or s.205 of the Companies Act 2006; and

(2) applies to a listed company that is not subject to the Companies Act 2006 if the terms of the indemnity or contract of insurance are in accordance with those that would be specifically permitted under that Act (if it applied).

7.12.4.5 *Underwriting*

(1) The underwriting by a related party of all or part of an issue of securities by the listed company (or any of its subsidiary undertakings) if the consideration to be paid by the listed company (or any of its subsidiary undertakings) for the underwriting:
  (a) is no more than the usual commercial underwriting consideration;
  (b) is the same as that to be paid to the other underwriters (if any); and

(2) does not apply to the extent that a related party is underwriting securities which it is entitled to take up under an issue of securities.

7.12.4.6 *Joint investment arrangements*

(1) An arrangement where a listed company, or any of its subsidiary undertakings, and a related party each invests in, or provides finance to, another undertaking or asset if the following conditions are satisfied:

    (a) the amount invested, or provided, by the related party is not more than 25% of the amount invested, or provided, by the listed company or its subsidiary undertaking (as the case may be) and the listed company has advised the FCA in writing that this condition has been met;

    (b) a sponsor has provided a written opinion to the FCA stating that the terms and circumstances of the investment or provision of finance by the listed company or its subsidiary undertakings (as the case may be) are no less favourable than those applying to the investment or provision of finance by the related party; and

(2) the advice in (1)(a) and the opinion in (1)(b) above must be provided before the investment is made or the finance is provided.

7.12.4.7 *Insignificant subsidiary undertaking*

(1) A transaction or arrangement where each of the conditions in (2)–(6) below (as far as applicable) is satisfied;

(2) the party to the transaction or arrangement is only a related party because:

    (a) it is (or was within the 12 months before the date of the transaction or arrangement) a substantial shareholder or its associate; or

    (b) it is a person who is (or was within the 12 months before the date of the transaction or arrangement) a director or shadow director or his associate, of a subsidiary undertaking or subsidiary undertakings of the listed company that has, or if there is more than one subsidiary undertaking that have in aggregate, contributed less than 10% of the profits of, and represented less than 10% of the assets of, the listed company for the relevant period;

(3) the subsidiary undertaking or each of the subsidiary undertakings (as the case may be) have been in the listed company's group for one full financial year or more;

(4) in (2), "relevant period" means:

    (a) if the subsidiary undertaking or each of the subsidiary undertakings (as the case may be) has been consolidated in the listed company's group for one full financial year or more but less than three full financial years, each of the full financial years before the date of the transaction or arrangement for which accounts have been published;

    (b) if the subsidiary undertaking or any of the subsidiary undertakings (as the case may be) has been consolidated in the listed company's group for three full financial years or more, each of the three full financial years before the date of the transaction or arrangement for which accounts have been published;

(5) if the subsidiary undertaking or any of the subsidiary undertakings (as the case may be) are themselves party to the transaction or arrangement or if securities in the subsidiary undertaking or any of the subsidiary undertakings or their assets are the subject of the transaction or arrangement, then the ratio of consideration to market capitalisation of the listed company is less than 10%; and

(6) in this rule, the figures to be used to calculate profits, assets and consideration to market capitalisation are the same as those used to classify profits, assets and consideration to market capitalisation in LR 10 Annex 1 (as modified or added to by LR 10.7, where applicable).

7.12.5   Related party transaction requirements

If a listed company enters into a related party transaction, the listed company must:

(1)   make a notification containing the details required for a Class 2 transaction and also the name of the related party and details of the nature and extent of the related party's interest in the transaction or arrangement;

(2)   send to its shareholders a circular prepared in accordance with the relevant provisions of LRs 13.3 and 13.6. The effect is that, where the related party transaction is also Class 1, the listed company must comply with the requirements applicable to a Class 1 circular and that all related party circulars must contain written confirmation from a sponsor that the terms of the transaction or arrangement are fair and reasonable as far as the share-holders of the listed company are concerned (an "inde-pendent fairness opinion");

(3)   obtain the approval of its shareholders for the transaction or arrangement either before it is entered into or, if the transaction or arrangement is expressed to be conditional on that approval, before it is completed; and

(4)   ensure that the related party does not vote on the relevant resolution and takes all reasonable steps to ensure that its associates do not vote thereon.

7.12.6   Supplementary notification

A listed company has to comply with the same rules on supplementary notifications as for a Class 1 transaction, see s.7.6.4 above.

7.12.7   Change in terms

If there is a material change to the terms of a related party transaction after obtaining shareholder approval but before its completion, the listed company must comply again separately with the notification and shareholder approval requirements set out in Ch.11. The FCA would (amongst other things) generally consider an increase of 10% or more in the consideration to be a material change for these purposes.

7.12.8 Smaller related party transactions

The requirements set out in s.7.12.5 above will not be applied to a related party transaction if each of the percentage ratios for the class tests referred to in s.7.3 above is less than 5% but one or more of the percentage ratios exceeds 0.25%. In this case, the listed company must:

(1) before entering into the transaction or arrangements, get a (private) fairness opinion in writing from a sponsor; and
(2) announce the transaction or arrangement via a RIS announcement as soon as possible after it has been entered into. The announcement has to include the related party's identity, the value of the consideration, a brief description of the transaction or arrangement, the fact that it is a smaller related party transaction and any other relevant circumstances.

7.12.9 Aggregation

If a listed company enters into transactions or arrangements with the same related party (and any of its associates) in any 12-month period and the transactions or arrangements have not been approved by shareholders (including transactions or arrangements falling under s.7.12.8 above and small transactions by reference to the criteria set out in LR 11 Annex 1R), the transactions or arrangements must be aggregated.

If any percentage ratio is 5% or more for the aggregated transactions or arrangements, then the listed company must comply with the obligations referred to in s.7.12.5 above in respect of the latest transaction or arrangement. Details of each of the transactions or arrangements being aggregated must be included in the circular.

If transactions or arrangements that are small transactions by reference to the criteria set out in LR 11 Annex 1R are aggregated and each of the percentage ratios is less than 5% but one or more of the percentage ratios exceeds 0.25%, then the listed company has to obtain a (private) fairness opinion in writing from a sponsor in respect of the latest small transaction; and must make the announcement referred to in s.7.12.8 above in respect of the aggregated small transactions.

7.12.10 *Transactions or arrangements with controlling shareholders*

The Listing Rules have specific requirements for companies with a premium listing which have a "controlling shareholder". A controlling shareholder is defined as any person who exercises or controls on their own, or together with any person with whom they are acting in concert, 30% or more of the votes able to be cast on all or substantially all matters at general meetings of the company. Certain voting rights are disregarded for these purposes.

One of these requirements is for a controlling shareholder to have an "independence agreement" in place with the listed company.

This agreement has to be in writing and legally binding and is intended to ensure as a minimum that:

(1) transactions and relationships with the controlling shareholder (and/or any of its associates) will be conducted at arm's length and on normal commercial terms;
(2) neither the controlling shareholder nor any of its associates will take any action that would have the effect of preventing the listed company from complying with its obligations under the Listing Rules; and
(3) neither the controlling shareholder nor any of its associates will propose or procure the proposal of a shareholder resolution which is intended or appears to be intended to circumvent the proper application of the Listing Rules.

If a listed company has more than one controlling shareholder, the listed company does not have to enter into a separate agreement with each one provided that it reasonably considers, in light of its understanding of the relationship between those controlling shareholders, that one of them can procure that the others comply with the terms of the agreement and, in the agreement, that the controlling shareholder agrees to procure their compliance and the non-signing controlling shareholders are named.

If certain circumstances occur, then all transactions with the controlling shareholder (and its associates) (including ordinary course transactions) will be related party transactions and none of the exemptions in LR 11 will apply so that all transactions will require independent shareholder approval (the independent shareholders being all holders of shares except the controlling shareholders(s)), thus, in effect, providing minority shareholders with a veto in respect of all transactions between the company and its controlling shareholder.

The circumstances are:

(1) the listed company does not have the required independence agreement in place with any controlling shareholder including the relevant independence provisions;
(2) the listed company has not complied with the independence provisions in an independence agreement;
(3) the listed company becomes aware that a controlling shareholder or any of its associates is not complying with an independence provision in an independence agreement;
(4) the listed company becomes aware that a procurement obligation in an independence agreement has not been complied with by a controlling shareholder; or
(5) an independent director declines to support the directors' statement of compliance (which is a statement by the board in the company's annual report and accounts confirming compliance with the rules on "independence agreements", if relevant).

Where the non-compliance is by the controlling shareholder (or any of its associates), these rules only apply when the company becomes aware of the breach but the listed company's systems and controls need to be adequate to ensure that these breaches are identified. An unreasonable delay before becoming aware would be inconsistent with Listing Principle 1.

The sanction that all transactions/arrangements require independent shareholder approval will continue to apply until the listed company publishes an annual financial report which has a clean statement of compliance, with no dissent from an independent director.

The FCA has the ability to modify the sanctions but the FCA would expect to enter into detailed discussions with the company about the relative severity of any breaches before agreeing to do so.

7.12.11   Section 190 of the Companies Act 2006

When examining a proposed transaction to determine if it is a related party transaction, it is important also to consider s.190 of the Companies Act 2006. That section covers substantial property transactions involving directors. It has the effect of prohibiting certain arrangements whereby a director of the company or its holding company or a connected person acquires assets from the company, or where the company acquires assets from such a person. If the price payable for such asset is not less than £5,000 but (subject to that) exceeds £100,000, or 10% of the company's asset value, the arrangement must first be approved by a resolution of the shareholders in a general meeting and, in certain cases, its holding company or be conditional on such approval.

Unlike related party transactions, s.190 does not require the approval of the holding company in a general meeting of a purchase by the director of a subsidiary unless the subsidiary director is also a director of the holding company. Further, for s.190 purposes, the definition of a connected person of a director covers companies in which the director has at least a 20% interest in the share capital (see s.252 of the Companies

Act 2006) whereas, for the purposes of related party transactions, a corporate associate of a director is one in which the director has a 30% interest.

Where shareholder approval is required under s.190 but not required under Ch.11, the circular convening the shareholders' meeting must comply with the relevant provisions of Ch.13 but would not need the FCA's prior approval.

Chapter 8

Overseas Companies, Investment Entities, Debt and Specialist Securities and Mineral Companies and the High Growth Segment

Simon FT Cox
Solicitor, Norton Rose Fulbright LLP

8.1 Introduction

This chapter addresses four principal categories of securities which are identified within the Listing Rules of the UK Listing Authority (UKLA) (which is part of the Financial Conduct Authority (FCA) which replaced the Financial Services Authority (FSA) as the competent authority for listing) as being subject to separate rules. These are securities issued by overseas companies, securities issued by investment entities, certain specialist securities (such as eurobonds and depositary receipts) and securities of mineral companies. Rather than examining in detail all the Listing Rules relating to these categories, this chapter concentrates on the rules which differ from those which apply generally to the listing of ordinary shares of a company incorporated in the UK.

A range of changes to the Prospectus Directive (PD)[1] regime have been proposed, although, at the time of production of this

---

[1] Directive 2003/71 on the prospectus to be published when securities are offered to the public or admitted to trading and amending Directive 2001/34 [2003] OJ L345/64.

chapter, the final text has not been adopted. A number of the provisions referred to in this chapter will be affected. References have been made to some of the most relevant proposed changes but it is beyond the scope of this edition to address all the consequent changes in detail. The extent to which the EU-based provisions will remain relevant for companies listing in London following Brexit is unknown.

The following table sets out the principal listing categories for the Main Market of the London Stock Exchange (LSE), most of which are addressed in this chapter. In addition, the Professional Securities Market (PSM) and the Specialists Fund Segment (SFS) are available for certain types of securities, as addressed later in this chapter. A section on the High Growth Segment (HGS) of the Main Market can be found at the end of this chapter.

Securities Category	Examples of types of Companies/Securities	Listing Rule Chapter
Equity Shares	Commercial Companies	LR 6
Equity Shares	Closed-ended Investment Funds	LR 15
Equity Shares	Open-ended Investment Companies	LR 16
Shares		LR 14
Global Depositary Receipts		LR 18
Debt Securities	Bonds	LR 17
Other Debt-like Securities	Convertible/ Exchangeable Securities; Asset-backed Securities; and Preference Shares.	LR 17
Securitised Derivatives		LR 19
Miscelaneous Securities	Options; and Warrants	LR 20

8.2 Overseas companies

8.2.1 Background

The following table shows the number of companies whose securities are listed on the Official List and traded on the LSE in London as at 31 May 2018, showing which market they are traded on—being the Main Market, the PSM, the SFS or the HGS. In addition, a total of 941 companies (of which 145 are non-UK companies) have securities traded on the AIM market.

	UK Companies	Overseas Companies
Main Market	944	221
PSM	65	34
SFS	30	7
HGS	-	1

These statistics do not distinguish between UK companies with a domestic business and those whose business is completely or substantially outside the UK. They do show, however, that the listing of overseas companies (being those incorporated outside the UK) is an important part of the business of the LSE and has raised a wide-ranging discussion of eligibility criteria, particularly in relation to corporate governance issues.

Many of the basic rules and requirements relating to the application procedure and continuing obligations for overseas companies are those found elsewhere in the Listing Rules for listed securities generally. However, there are some variations in the case of foreign companies, although, since April 2010, the treatment of UK and overseas companies has been more closely aligned. The FCA has made various amendments and deletions to the *FCA Handbook* (Listing Rules and the Disclosure Guidance and Transparency Rules (DTRs) sourcebook (which was previously known as "The Disclosure Rules and Transparency Rules Sourcebook") through various statutory instruments implementing the Market Abuse Regulation

(MAR) which took effect on 3 July 2016.[2] There have been a number of changes, including in relation to areas such as disclosure of inside information to the market, maintenance of insider lists and disclosure of/restrictions on dealing by directors and persons discharging managerial responsibilities (PDMRs) (now largely covered by MAR arts 17, 18 and 19), which have an impact on UK and overseas companies. Parts of the DTRs, particularly in DTRs 2 and 3, have now been replaced by provisions of the MAR with the DTR text directing readers to relevant MAR provisions. The implications of the MAR implementation are covered in Ch.6 above and the detail is beyond the scope of this chapter.

The rules applicable to overseas companies depend in part on whether they are incorporated in or outside the European Economic Area (EEA) and in part on the nature of their listing in the UK (i.e. whether it is premium or standard).

Apart from the application of the PD, the principal rationale for distinguishing the treatment of overseas companies is the existence of other regulations relating to the issuer by reason of its country of incorporation and/or any other listing maintained for its securities. Where a non-UK applicant whose securities are listed on a foreign exchange seeks a listing, it must be in compliance with the requirements of that exchange.

8.2.2 The implications of the Prospectus Directive for overseas companies

As stated elsewhere in this guide, the implementation of the PD has resulted in two regimes for the production and publication of a PD compliant prospectus—where the securities are offered to the public in an EEA state and/or where they are admitted to trading (not just listing) on a regulated market. This has a number of implications for overseas companies, and also for other issuers, such as those of debt and other securities, as addressed later in this chapter.

---

[2] Regulation 596/2014 on market abuse (market abuse regulation) and repealing Directive 2003/6 and Directives 2003/124, 2003/125/ and 2004/72 [2014] OJ L173/1.

Any issuer making a public offer of securities or applying to have securities admitted to trading on a regulated market in the EEA must have a home Member State ("Home State"), even if the issuer itself is not based in the EEA. Each EEA state must nominate a competent authority for the approval of prospectuses. The FCA is the competent authority in the UK.

8.2.2.1 *Home State must approve the prospectus*

The competent authority in the issuer's Home State is responsible for vetting the prospectus and for ensuring that the obligations for issuers and others under the PD are met. This means that the general principle is that it is to the competent authority of their Home State to which issuers must submit prospectuses for approval in the first instance, no matter where the public offer is to be made or where the securities to be issued are to be admitted to trading.

8.2.2.2 *Transfer of approval of prospectus from the Home State*

In some circumstances, an issuer may apply to have the function of approving a prospectus transferred to the competent authority of another EEA state. If the Home State is the UK, the person making the request must do so in writing to the FCA at least 10 working days before the date the transfer is sought (Prospectus Rule (PR) 3.1.12R). The request must:

- set out the reasons for the proposed transfer;
- state the name of the competent authority to whom the transfer is sought; and
- include a copy of the draft prospectus.

The FCA will consider transferring the function of approving a prospectus to the competent authority of another EEA state if requested to do so by the issuer, offeror or person seeking admission or by another competent authority, or in other cases if the FCA considers it would be more appropriate for another competent authority to perform that function (PR 3.1.13G). The FCA has stated that it will only transfer the approval of the prospectus to the competent authority of another EEA state if, in all the circumstances, it considers such transfer to be in the best interests of investors. The competent authority of the other EEA state must also agree to the transfer.

8.2.2.3 Determining an issuer's Home State

An issuer will always have the same Home State except where it is issuing "Relevant Bonds" (see s.8.2.2.3.1 below). Therefore, where issuers have a choice of Home State and are considering making an election, they should be aware that their choice is binding for all future issues of securities other than Relevant Bonds, subject to the limited ability to seek to have the approval function transferred as described above. If the issuer is an EEA issuer of securities, then, save as set out below, its Home State will always be the EEA state in which it has its registered office.

8.2.2.3.1 Issuer of Relevant Bonds (EEA or non-EEA)

Whether the issuer is an issuer of securities incorporated in the EEA or outside the EEA, if it is proposing to issue:

* non-equity securities whose denomination per unit (assumed to mean par or nominal value) is less than €1,000 (or the equivalent in another currency); and
* convertible non-equity securities giving the right on conversion or exercise to acquire transferable securities or to receive a cash amount, provided that the issuer of the non-equity securities is not the issuer of the underlying securities or a member of its group,

(together, the "Relevant Bonds"), it (or the offeror) will be able to choose its Home State from the following:

* the EEA state in which it has its registered office (if applicable);
* the EEA state in which the securities were, or are to be, admitted to trading on a regulated market; or
* the EEA state in which the securities are offered to the public.

8.2.2.3.2   Non-EEA issuer of securities other than Relevant Bonds

If the issuer is an issuer of securities (other than Relevant Bonds) incorporated outside the EEA, its Home State will be (art.2(1)(m)(iii) of the PD):

- the EEA state where the securities are intended to be offered to the public for the first time after the date of entry into force of the Prospectus Directive; or
- the EEA state where the first application for admission to trading on a regulated market is made,

at the choice of the issuer, the offeror or the person asking for admission, as the case may be. Issuers incorporated in a third country may override this election if the Home State was not determined by their choice or, alternatively, if its securities are no longer admitted to trading on a regulated market in its Home State but are admitted to trading in one or more other Member States. The issuer can then choose from amongst those Member States where its securities are admitted to trading on a regulated market and the Member State where the issuer has its registered office (if applicable).

Since 26 November 2015, all issuers have been required to disclose their Home State to:

- the competent authority of the Member State where it has its registered office, where applicable;
- the competent authority of the Home State; and
- the competent authorities of all host Member States.

It is considered that, in determining whether an offer has been made to the public prior to 1 July 2005, the interpretation of whether there was a public offer should apply the local law of the jurisdiction where the potential offer was made as in force at that time. For the purposes of offers post-1 July 2005, the term "offer of securities to the public" is defined in art.2(1)(d) of the PD as:

"a communication to persons in any form and by any means, presenting sufficient information on the terms of the offer and the securities to be offered, so as to enable an investor to decide to purchase or subscribe to these securities".

It may be the case that an offer which is exempt from the requirement to publish a prospectus under art.3(2) of the PD would not be treated as a public offer for the purposes of identification of the Home State because such an offer would be limited in scope and comprise:

- an offer addressed only to qualified investors;
- an offer addressed to fewer than 150 persons per EEA state other than qualified investors (this is not necessarily the construction of this provision offered by all relevant authorities);
- an offer addressed to investors who pay a minimum of €100,000 per investor for each separate offer; and/or
- an offer where the denomination per unit amounts to at least €100,000.

Furthermore, the requirement to publish a prospectus under the PD would not apply to an offer of securities with a total consideration in EEA states of less than €5 million (which limit shall be calculated over a period of 12 months). Under the proposed changes to the PD regime, the mandatory level for a prospectus will be increased to €8 million but Member States may require a prospectus for issues of between €1 million and €8 million or establish other disclosure requirements below €8 million.

8.2.2.3.3   Non-EEA issuers that are already listed

If the issuer is a non-EEA issuer which already has securities listed on a regulated market, the PD provides that such issuer must choose its Home State in accordance with art.2(1)(m)(iii) (as summarised at s.8.2.2.3.2 above).

If such an issuer does not make an appropriate notification and intends to list or offer to the public any securities (other than Relevant Bonds), the EEA state in which it makes (or has made) such an offer or applies for listing may be considered its choice of Home State. Notifications should be made as soon as possible for issuers in this category to remove doubt about the Home State. This is particularly important in the case of issuers with multiple listings.

8.2.2.3.4   Non-EEA issuers already listed (in the UK)

Issuers seeking confirmation of their Home State should decide (or seek separate advice) on what they believe is a valid Home State election and then consider applying to the FCA by:

- submitting a letter to the FCA electing the UK as their Home State;
- offering their securities to the public for the first time in the UK; or
- making their first application for their securities to be admitted to trading on a regulated market in the UK.

In summary:

- a UK issuer issuing equity securities will have the UK as its Home State, wherever it is seeking listing and wherever it proposes to make a public offer;
- a non-EEA issuer seeking to have equity shares admitted to the Official List and which has not already established a Home State can choose as its Home State the UK or any other EEA state where it wishes to offer its shares to the public (although, as the choice of Home State is, in most cases, binding for all time, care will need to be taken if "forum shopping" is proposed);
- for a UK-listed issuer seeking to issue convertible/ exchangeable bonds out of an EEA special purpose vehicle (SPV) (which would presumably be part of the same group as the UK-listed issuer), which convert into the shares of the UK-listed issuer, the Home State will be where the SPV has its registered office (and not the UK).

The same will apply for the issue of non-convertible bonds, save that, if the bonds have a denomination of more than €1,000, then the Home State may be chosen from the state in which the issuer has its registered office, the state in which the application for listing is made or, if there is an offer to the public, the state in which the offer is made;

- for a UK-listed issuer seeking to issue convertible/ exchangeable bonds out of a non-EEA SPV (presumably part of the same group as the UK issuer) which convert into the shares of the UK-listed issuer, the Home State will be where the application for listing of the bonds will be made (or the offer to the public of bonds is made) and not necessarily the UK. The same will apply for the issue of non-convertible bonds and, for different reasons, bonds which have a denomination of more than €1,000;

- an issuer seeking admission of its shares to a non-EEA regulated market (such as AIM) without making an offer to the public (or by making an offer to the public which is exempt from the requirement to publish a prospectus) will not need to publish a prospectus (though the relevant market may require a document in connection with the admission to trading of the relevant securities); and

- if a non-UK company listed on, say, the Johannesburg Stock Exchange makes a takeover offer for a UK officially listed company and makes that offer into different jurisdictions in the EEA (because of the wide shareholder base of the UK target), it may be able to choose which of these EEA states will be its Home State. The fact that the target is a UK company is irrelevant. Even if the South African company is also applying for a standard listing in the UK, there would still appear to be no obligation to choose the UK as its Home State. However, as stated above, this should be checked with the FCA on a case-by-case basis to determine whether these circumstances arise.

8.2.2.3.5 Offering securities to the public or seeking admission to trading on a regulated market outside the Home State

If an overseas company wishes to offer securities to the public in the UK and the UK is not its Home State, it must produce to the FCA a certificate of approval of the prospectus issued by the competent authority in the Home State and a copy of the prospectus as approved. The prospectus it has produced is then valid for an offer to the public in the UK and the FCA may not undertake any approval or administrative procedures relating to the prospectus other than (if applicable) to require a translation of the summary of the prospectus. Technical requirements for the submission of an application for approval of a prospectus (such as the format of the prospectus required for submission) have been set out in Regulation 2016/301 (Omnibus II Regulation).[3]

If an issuer is seeking admission to trading on the regulated market of the LSE, the position is broadly similar to that in relation to a public offering of securities, except that the FCA may set its own eligibility criteria for admission to its markets. For example, the Listing Rules will apply to any issuer seeking admission to the Official List.

8.2.2.3.6 Prospectus

The application of the PD to an overseas company with a standard listing will be substantially dependent on the above rules and the application of the Prospectus Rules to determine which Annexes to Regulation 809/2004 (PD Regulation)[4] will apply as the basis for the contents of the prospectus. Once in

---

[3] Regulation 2016/301 supplementing Directive 2003/71 with regard to regulatory technical standards for approval and publication of the prospectus and dissemination of advertisements and amending Regulation 809/2004 [2016] OJ L58/13.

[4] Regulation 809/2004 implementing Directive 2003/71 as regards information contained in prospectuses as well as the format, incorporation by reference and publication of such prospectuses and dissemination of advertisements [2004] OJ L149/3.

force, the proposed New Prospectus Regulation[5] will replace the PD, the PD Regulation and amending Directive 2010/73.[6]

8.2.3 *The Listing Rules' structure*

Not all the EEA or other exchanges draw a distinction between companies with a premium (formerly in the UK "primary") listing (being, where there is a distinction, the listing where the issuer is subject to the full set of rules—subject to appropriate modifications applicable by reason of their overseas status) and those with a standard (formerly in the UK "secondary") listing (being where the extent of the regulation is reduced to minimum EU directive standards). This distinction has, however, been maintained in the UK.

Chapter 14 of the Listing Rules, which provides the directive minimum (standard) listing regime, was formerly only available to eligible overseas companies. Since October 2009, however, the Ch.14 regime has also been available for eligible UK companies. The fact that it does not qualify issuers for the Financial Times Stock Exchange (FTSE) UK series indices may have discouraged some UK companies and may be the reason why in practice the regime has principally been used by overseas companies. Companies of certain specific types (for example, mineral companies) may have to comply with additional provisions of the Listing Rules and others (such as certain investment companies, as described below) may not be eligible for a standard listing.

---

5   Regulation 2017/1129 on the prospectus to be published when securities are offered to the public or admitted to trading on a regulated market, and repealing Directive 2003/71 [2017] OJ L168/12.
6   Directive 2010/73 amending Directives 2003/71 on the prospectus to be published when securities are offered to the public or admitted to trading and 2004/109 on the harmonisation of transparency requirements in relation to information about issuers whose securities are admitted to trading on a regulated market [2010] OJ L327/1.

8.2.4 Premium listing applicants

Chapters 6 (which is covered in Ch.2 of this guide above), 7, 8, 9, 10, 11, 12 and 13 of the Listing Rules apply to issuers applying for a premium listing. "Premium listings" are defined (in summary) as listings of equity shares (formerly, Ch.6 was available to the wider category of equity securities, which included securities convertible into equity shares) where the issuer is required to comply with Ch.6 (or in the case of closed-ended investment funds or open-ended investment companies, Ch.15 or Ch.16 respectively) in addition to other Listing Rules which apply to securities with a premium listing. A commercial company seeking a premium listing of its equity shares will, for example, have to show published or filed historical financial information that covers at least three years (LR 6.2.1(1)R), that it carries on an independent business as its main activity and that it has sufficient working capital available for the next year from the date of publication of the prospectus or listing particulars (LR 6.7.1R). The FCA's recent Consultation Paper (CP) 17/4 in February 2017 proposes to make clarifications (in a new LR 6.2.4R) regarding the requirement for premium listing, including explicitly stating that the additional financial information (which may be required where there have been acquisitions during the three-year track-record period) needs to be audited. If these changes are implemented, the requirement for financial information and track record will become more important to obtaining premium listing and the FCA intends to delete the current guidance in LRs 6.1.13G–6.1.15G which provides the "cases where the FCA may modify accounts and track record requirements" because maintaining such a reference is misleading as the FCA does not normally waive these requirements. Many of the provisions described in relation to standard listings below will apply to issuers with a premium listing, including, for example, the rule that a company's listed securities (other than those to which Ch.4 (the PSM) applies) must be admitted to trading at all times on a regulated market for listed securities operated by a recognised investment exchange (LR 2.2.3R). Non-UK regulated markets are able to seek such recognition in order for equity securities admitted to trading on their market to be eligible for a UK listing.

Some types of security, such as global depositary receipts (GDRs) and debt instruments, are not eligible for premium listing, in some cases as a result of the change in the eligibility requirement from equity securities to equity shares. GDRs are generally not relevant for UK issuers and are covered later in this chapter.

Most of the Ch.6 rules apply to issuers irrespective of their place of incorporation, although there are some provisions applicable, or of particular relevance, to overseas companies.

These include:

(1) admission: LR 6.15.1R provides that, where a company is incorporated in a non-EEA state and its shares are not listed in the country of incorporation or where the majority of its shares are held, the FCA must be satisfied that the absence of such a listing is not due to the need to protect investors;

(2) accounts: the issuer's accounts must have been independently audited in accordance with the auditing standards applicable in an EEA state or an equivalent standard (LR 6.1.3R(1)(d));

(3) the restraints on application of the procedures under s.793 of the Companies Act 2006 (notice by company requiring information about interests in its shares) do not apply to non-UK issuers as the relevant provisions would not in any event be applicable to them (LRs 9.3.9R and 9.3.10G);

(4) previously, the Listing Rule which required a listed company making a further issue of equity securities for cash to make that issue subject to pre-emption rights did not apply to overseas companies with a primary listing. Now, in order to provide uniformity and clarity to the premium listing segment, overseas companies with a premium listing are required, when issuing shares for cash, to offer pre-emption rights to their shareholders unless there has been prior shareholder consent for the

company to issue shares other than in accordance with this rule (LRs 9.3.11R and 9.3.12R). Such consent must be within the terms of an authority equivalent to that required by s.570 or s.571 of the Companies Act 2006 or in accordance with the law of its country of incorporation provided that the country has implemented art.29 of Directive 77/91 or art.33 of Directive 2012/30 (LR 9.3.12R(4)).[7] If the law of the country of incorporation for the overseas company does not confer on shareholders equivalent rights to the pre-emption rights that protect shareholders of UK companies, an overseas company applying for a premium listing will need to ensure that its constitution provides for such pre-emption rights and be satisfied that conferring pre-emption rights will not be incompatible with the law of its country of incorporation (LR 6.9.2R);

(5) LR 9.4.1R, which requires certain employee share schemes and long-term incentive plans to be approved by share-holders, applies to listed companies incorporated in the UK and any of its major subsidiary undertakings, even if that major subsidiary undertaking was incorporated, or operates, outside of the UK; and

(6) overseas companies with premium listings have to "com-ply or explain" against the UK Corporate Governance Code (LR 9.8.7R); this is in contrast to the lesser "compare and contrast" test which some were advocating for overseas companies.

As a result of the implementation of the Transparency Directive (TD) in the UK (effective from 20 January 2007),[8] a number of

---

[7] Directive 77/91 on coordination of safeguards which, for the protection of the interests of members and others, are required by Member States of companies within the meaning of the second paragraph of Article 58 of the Treaty, in respect of the formation of public limited liability companies and the maintenance and alteration of their capital, with a view to making such safeguards equivalent [1977] OJ L26/1; Directive 2012/30 on coordination of safeguards which, for the protection of the interests of members and others, are required by Member States of companies within the meaning of the second paragraph of Article 54 of the Treaty on the Functioning of the European Union, in respect of the formation of public limited liability companies and the maintenance and alteration of their capital, with a view to making such safeguards equivalent [2012] OJ L315/74.

[8] Directive 2004/109 on the harmonisation of transparency requirements in

the provisions in Ch.9, which were applicable to all overseas companies with what were then primary listings, were removed and/or replaced by provisions in the Disclosure Guidance and Transparency Rules which as described above have now in part been modified by the MAR. Of particular interest to overseas companies may be the rules on Periodic Financial Reporting (DTR 4) and Vote Holder and Issuer Notification Rules (DTR 5).

As with the PD, the TD applies to all companies (whether incorporated within or outside the EEA) whose securities are admitted to trading on a regulated market in the EEA. The DTRs are applicable to UK issuers with shares traded on a regulated market and non-EEA issuers whose shares are traded on a regulated market and for whom the UK is their Home State (there are exemptions from certain of the requirements under the DTRs for non-EEA issuers whose domestic regime is deemed equivalent by the FCA, in which case, such issuers will remain subject to certain requirements regarding filing of information with the FCA, language provisions and the dissemination of information provisions (DTR 6)). As non-UK EEA issuers will be subject to these equivalent provisions, the following DTR requirements will therefore only be applicable to UK issuers and relevant non-EEA issuers (provided such issuers are not deemed to comply with "equivalent require-ments"):

(1)   there are detailed obligations on issuers to disclose, on an ongoing basis, details of the changes to their share capital. Upon receipt of a disclosure notification from a share-holder pursuant to DTR 5, a company must publish all of the information contained in the shareholder notification to the market. A UK issuer is required to notify as soon as possible and, in any event, no later than the end of the trading day following receipt of notification of major shareholdings to it, or obtained by it, pursuant to provisions of the Companies Act 2006 (DTR 5.8.12R(1)). A non-EEA issuer will be treated as meeting equivalent

---

relation to information about issuers whose securities are admitted to trading on a regulated market and amending Directive 2001/34 [2004] OJ L390/38.

requirements to those set out for non-UK issuers in DTR 5.8.12R(2) (issuer to make public notifications of major shareholdings by close of the third day following receipt), provided that the period of time within which the notification of the major shareholding is to be given to the issuer and is to be made public by the issuer is in total equal to, or shorter than, seven trading days (DTR 5.11.1R). An overseas company will also be exempted from the requirements of DTRs 5.5.1R (notifications relating to acquisition or disposal of own shares), 5.6.1R (notification of changes in total voting rights) and 5.8.12R(2) if the law of the non-EEA state in question lays down equivalent requirements or the issuer complies with requirements of the law of the non-EEA State that the FCA considers equivalent (DTR 5.11.4R). A list of those non-EEA states with equivalent requirements is maintained by the FCA (DTR 5.11.5G). The normal disclosure obligations under LR 9.6 in relation to board change and directors' details continue to apply to an overseas company with a premium listing; and

(2) among the various obligations in relation to periodic financial reporting, an issuer must produce:

(a) half-yearly financial reports: DTR 4.2 sets out more prescriptive contents requirements for the half-yearly report, which must include, in addition to a condensed set of financial statements, appropriate statements of assurance (or responsibility statements) from persons responsible in the company. There are no additional requirements for the half-yearly report in the Listing Rules;

(b) annual financial reports: the core requirements for the annual financial report are set out in DTR 4.1 but listed companies will still need to comply with those additional requirements in Ch.9 of the Listing Rules. The application of DTR 7.2 (relating to corporate governance statements) extends to all companies with shares or GDRs listed, including overseas companies (LR 9.8.7A). As a result, all such companies must make statements about their corporate governance and describe their internal control and risk management. The precise application of these rules and the relationship with LR 9.8 will depend on the rules to which the overseas company is otherwise subject;

(c) reports on payments to governments: equity issuers who are active in the extractive or logging of primary forest industries must prepare a report annually on payments made to governments for each financial year and these reports must be made public at the latest six months after the end of each financial year and the issuers must ensure that the report on payments to governments remains publicly available for at least 10 years (DTRs 4.3A.4–4.3A.6).

8.2.4.1 *Premium listing for sovereign-controlled commercial companies*

Following an earlier consultation process, on 1 July 2018, the FCA introduced new rules (principally LR 21 and related amendments) related to the creation of a new premium listing category for "sovereign-controlled commercial companies" (SCCs), which are companies 30% or more of the voting rights of which are controlled by a sovereign shareholder (i.e. the sovereign or other head of State in their public capacity, the Government of that State, a department of that State or an agency or special purpose vehicle of that State). SCCs which satisfy this requirement, and the other eligibility criteria, will be able to benefit from a premium listing with some relaxation of the controlling shareholder and related party rules and with the ability to obtain a premium listing for their depositary receipts (DRs), as summarised in greater detail below.

Other premium listing requirements will apply to SCCs, including that the issuer must adopt the UK Corporate Governance Code, the issuer must give shareholders pre-emption rights on further issuances for cash and "weighted voting shares" are not to be eligible for listing.

Independent shareholder approval will be required for a transfer from an existing premium listing into the new category, for transfers from the new category to a standard listing and for delisting.

8.2.4.1.1 Related party rules

The requirements set out in Ch.11 of the Listing Rules for companies to seek prior independent shareholder approval and obtain a fair and reasonable opinion from the company's sponsor in connection with certain related party transactions will not apply in respect of transactions with the sovereign controlling shareholder or one of its associates. Disclosure of such transactions will still, however, be required in order to ensure transparency. The requirements for approval for relevant significant transactions will apply.

8.2.4.1.2 Controlling shareholder rules

The requirement for the company to have a controlling shareholder agreement (or "relationship agreement") in place will not apply in respect of the sovereign controlling shareholder. However, the rules requiring the appointment or reappointment of independent directors to be approved by independent shareholders as well as by shareholders as a whole will apply to SCCs with a premium listing in the same way as for any other premium listed company with a controlling shareholder.

8.2.4.1.3 Ability to list depositary receipts

In contrast to normal companies seeking a premium listing, SCCs will be able to list depositary receipts with which international investors may be more comfortable. However, there are specific eligibility conditions. These include that the SCC must be able to demonstrate (and have in place arrangements that ensure) that the rights attached to the equity shares underlying the DRs are capable of being exercised by the DR holders as if they were holders of those underlying shares and that the underlying shares are able to be voted on those matters on which the premium listing rules require shareholder approval to be obtained. The arrangements will also have to provide for an independent vote where required.

The FCA will continue to have the right to allow a listing where the standard minimum free float level of 25% is not satisfied, provided there is sufficient liquidity in the shares to be listed; however, since the free float is determined on the basis of the particular security being listed, where DRs are to be listed, the percentage free float of the issuer's total underlying equity represented by the DRs could be very low, although the DRs themselves meet the 25% level. Whether a premium listing of DRs by an issuer which is able to satisfy the nationality or enhanced free float requirements will enable inclusion in the FTSE UK Index Series remains to be determined and will depend materially on the approach of the index operators.

8.2.5 Standard listings

Chapter 14 of the Listing Rules applies to standard listings of equity shares, which are defined as listings that are not premium listings. Chapter 14 was amended on 6 October 2009 to apply to all companies, rather than just overseas companies, so that UK companies can apply for a standard listing. This section of this chapter focuses principally on the application of the relevant provisions to overseas companies.

Compliance only with the provisions of Ch.14 of the Listing Rules is less onerous than compliance with the enhanced obligations applicable to companies with a premium listing in London.

8.2.5.1 Continuing obligations for companies with a standard listing in London

Many of the provisions of the Listing Rules (such as rules relating to continuing obligations in Ch.9—which have been amended to give effect to the MAR)—significant transactions in Ch.10 and related party transactions in Ch.11) are expressed to apply to issuers with a premium listing of equity securities. As such they do not apply to issuers who do not have securities so listed. The relevant DTRs and the continuing obligations in LR 14.3 do, however, apply to relevant companies with a standard listing in London.

An overseas company with a standard listing is subject to a similar disclosure regime to that applying to companies established in the UK, with certain modifications principally resulting from the different regulatory regimes in different countries. A non-UK EEA issuer must comply with the corresponding rules laid down in their Home State implementing the TD. Other companies incorporated in a non-EEA state and for whom the UK is the Home State must comply with the major shareholder notifications and other share capital disclosures contained in DTR 5. The company must, on receipt of a shareholder notification of its holding in the company, as soon as possible and in any event by not later than the end of the third trading day following receipt of the notification, make public all of the information contained in the notification. The disclosure thresholds at which a person must notify a non-UK issuer of changes in his voting rights differ slightly from those for a UK issuer (DTR 5.1.2R).

All the DTRs, relevant MAR provisions and related guidance apply in most respects to relevant overseas listed issuers. Thus, the provisions in relation to such issues as market rumours, which together with other issues in relation to disclosure are addressed in Ch.6 of this guide, should be taken into account. The overriding disclosure principle is to enable holders of a company's listed securities and the public to appraise the position of the issuer, to avoid a false market and to disseminate information on major new developments which could lead to substantial price movements. In addition, changes in the financial condition of the company, in its trading performance and in the directors' expectation of its performance must be disclosed, if knowledge of that change is likely to lead to a substantial share price movement. These provisions are now addressed in Ch.3 of the MAR ("Disclosure Requirements"). These provisions include reference to circumstances where the disclosure of inside information which would otherwise be disclosable can be delayed as well as the related procedures. The European Securities and Markets Authority (ESMA) has published guidelines to provide guidance by giving examples to assist issuers in their decision to delay public disclosure of inside information under art.17(4) of the MAR and further detail and guidance on delayed disclosure are set out in DTR 2.5.

The MAR provides the regime for selective disclosure of inside information ahead of announcement and the DTRs provide additional guidance on this issue (DTRs 2.5.7G–2.5.9G). An issuer may, depending on the circumstances, be justified in disclosing inside information to certain categories of recipient in addition to those employees of the issuer who require the information to perform their functions, including potentially advisers, counterparties, employee representatives and regulators. These provisions, as are other provisions such as the maintenance of insider lists, may all be relevant to overseas companies listed in London and subject to these regimes.

The Market Abuse Regulation Instrument 2016 deleted DTR 2.4 (Equivalent Information) which included DTR 2.4.1R which required a company which has multiple listings to ensure that equivalent information to that given to other exchanges is made available to a RIS for release to the market at the same time. DTR 1.3.6G (Notification when a RIS is not open for business), which was previously DTR 1.3.6R, provides that, if an announcement has to be made when a RIS is closed, the information may be distributed as soon possible to not less than two UK national newspapers, two newswire services operating in the UK. In addition, the information must also be announced to a RIS for release as soon as it is open. Disclosure Guidance and Transparency Rule 1.3.6G, which was previously DTR 1.3.6R, as a result of the Market Abuse Regulation Instrument 2016 has now been converted to guidance.

As mentioned above, the application of DTR 7.2 (relating to corporate governance statements) has been extended to all companies with equity shares or GDRs listed, including overseas companies with a standard listing. Listing Rule 14.3.24 provides that a listed company that is not already required to comply with DTR 7.2, or with corresponding requirements imposed by another EEA Member State, must comply with DTR 7.2 as if it were an issuer to which that section applies.

The requirement that application for listing be made in respect of any further issues of securities already listed repeats the time limit in the Admissions Directive.[9] Listing Rule 14.3.4R requires that application be made as soon as possible and, in any event, within one year of the allotment.

An overseas company for which the UK is a Home State, for the purposes of the TD, must appoint a registrar in the UK if it has 200 or more UK resident investors or if 10% or more of its shares are held by UK resident investors (LR 14.3.15). Stamp duty issues should be considered in such cases.

It is both a basic condition of listing and one of the continuing obligations that the accounts of the company be prepared and independently audited in accordance with standards appropriate for companies of international standing and repute. There are detailed provisions in DTR 4 in relation to annual accounts, which cover such issues as the need for independent audit, consolidation and publication within four months of the end of the relevant financial period.

There are requirements as to the auditor's report. These have the result that, for example, a report conforming to US, rather than to UK, auditing practice is acceptable. The FCA should be consulted if the company is not incorporated in the EEA and is not required to draw up its accounts so as to give a true and fair view. There are also detailed rules for the timing, publication and contents of half-yearly reports. These are also set out in DTR 4, which has been amended.

---

[9] Directive 2001/34 on the admission of securities to official stock exchange listing and on information to be published on those securities [2001] OJ L184/1.

Listing Rule 14.3.1R states that a company's listed equity securities (other than those to which Ch.4 (the PSM) applies) must be admitted to trading at all times on a regulated market for listed securities operated by a recognised investment exchange. As stated above, non-UK regulated markets are able to seek such recognition in order for equity securities admitted to trading on their market to be eligible for a UK listing.

The issuer must have sufficient shares of any listed class in public hands at all times in the relevant jurisdictions and must notify the FCA as soon as possible if these holdings fall below the level set out in LR 14.2.2R.

There are a range of other continuing obligations applicable to these issuers. These include requirements as to:

- forwarding of circulars and other documentation to the FCA for publication through the document viewing facility (LR 14.3.6 and related notification to a RIS (LR 14.3.7);
- the provision to the FCA of contact details of appropriate persons nominated to act as a first point of contact with the FCA in relation to compliance with the Listing Rules and DTRs (LR 14.3.8);
- temporary and renounceable documents of title (LR 14.3.9);
- equality of treatment for all holders of equity securities who are in the same position (DTR 6.1.3R);
- making available in the Home State all information and facilities necessary to enable holders of shares to exercise their rights and preservation of data integrity (DTR 6.1.4R); and
- RIS notification obligations in relation to a range of debt and equity capital issues, with a potential deferral (subject to compliance with DTR 2) of certain information to allow completion of underwriting in the context of an under-written issue (LRs 14.3.17–14.3.18R).

8.2.6 *International Order Book and Order book for Retail Bonds*

Dealings in international securities can be effected on the LSE through the International Order Book (IOB). The IOB is administered by the LSE. The IOB enables trading of depositary receipts. During the month of March 2018, average turnover on the IOB formed around 5% of the total order book on the LSE.[10]

The IOB enables trading in these securities. This is not the same as a listing. If a security is not listed in London, to be eligible for the IOB it must be listed on at least one exchange that is a member or corresponding member of the World Federation of Exchanges. The IOB is an order driven system, whereby orders are submitted by a member firm, usually on behalf of a client, and are executed electronically.

The LSE launched its electronic Order book for Retail Bonds (ORB) on 1 February 2010. The ORB is not a separate market but is a trading platform designed for gilts and retail-sized bonds listed on the LSE's EU-regulated Main Market and was modelled after the established Italian electronic bond market (Borsa Italiana's MOT market). New bond issues have proven to be popular options for private investors looking for alternatives to cash deposits and shares in blue chip companies. Bonds can be an attractive form of finance for companies seeking to diversify away from loans which may also avoid many covenants typically associated with loans.

As at 31 March 2018, there are 72 gilts and 92 corporate bonds available on the ORB, mostly from well-known issuers.[11] There are criteria which must be satisfied before securities are admitted to the ORB in order to ensure that they are suitable for the retail market. These requirements are:

---

[10] See LSE, IOB Factsheet (March 2018) available at: *http://www.londonstockexchange. com/statistics/trading/international-order-book/international-order-book-archive-2018/ iob-factsheet-march-2018.pdf* [Accessed 6 June 2018].

[11] See LSE, Retail Bonds Factsheet (March 2018) available at: *http://www. londonstockexchange.com/statistics/historic/retail-bonds/orb-monthly-archive-2018/ retail-bonds-trading-statistics-march-2018.pdf* [Accessed 11 July 2018].

- the bond must be listed in a EU regulated market;
- the bond must have a committed market maker willing to supply electronic two-way prices throughout the trading day;
- the bond must be tradable in units of no larger than £10,000 and in practice many have much smaller tradable units;
- the disclosure requirements specified in the Prospectus Rules must be satisfied (e.g. for corporate issuers Annexes IV and V); and
- the bond must be set up for settlement in the CREST settlement system.

Once admitted, all securities are continually priced throughout the trading day by market makers. The full order book functionality allows brokers to set their own price to buy or sell by entering a priced limit order directly on the ORB. The ORB allows for electronic on-book execution and straight-through processing to the CREST settlement system, therefore creating efficiencies by instructing settlement in CREST on behalf of the counterparties. Routing of trade information to Euroclear and/or Clearstream is possible as well via CREST Depositary Interests (CDIs).

8.2.7 *Turquoise*

Turquoise is the European multilateral trading facility (MTF) majority owned by the London Stock Exchange Group (LSEG) in partnership with the user community. With a single connection, members can trade shares, depository receipts, exchange-traded funds (ETFs) and European rights issues of 19 European countries with an Open Access model that allows members to choose among three interoperable central counter-parties (CCPs) to clear these trades. Members include banks, brokers, specialist trading firms and retail intermediaries.

The Turquoise trading platform is hosted in LSEG data centres and features interfaces common to other LSEG markets, including the LSE and Borsa Italiana, ensuring that customers accessing other LSEG markets can enjoy access to Turquoise with little incremental cost or effort.

Turquoise features two electronic orders book services, Turquoise Integrated Lit combines simple limit and iceberg orders with large-in-scale hidden orders. Turquoise® Midpoint Dark, renamed Turquoise Plato™ prioritises orders by size and allows users to configure minimum execution size; it features two distinct mechanisms, each executing at the midpoint of the primary market best bid and offer: continuous matching and Turquoise Plato Uncross™, an innovation that provides randomised uncrossings during the trading day, which are ideal for larger and less time sensitive passive orders. Turquoise Plato Block Discovery™ matches undisclosed Block Indications that execute in Turquoise Plato Uncross™.

Turquoise Plato Dark Lit Sweep™ is an order that interacts firstly with the Turquoise Plato™ order book at the primary midpoint price and then continues to interact with any balance resting in Turquoise Integrated Lit.

The ability to trade after a company lists on primary stock exchanges is a key ingredient to successful capital raisings. These Turquoise innovations offer market participants additional execution mechanisms for trading securities listed on primary stock exchanges, including LSEG markets such as the LSE and Borsa Italiana.

8.2.8 *International Securities Market*

The LSE launched a new MTF, the International Securities Market (ISM), in early May 2017. With this new MTF, the LSE aims to compete directly with popular exchange-regulated markets such as the Irish Stock Exchange's (ISE's) Global Exchange Market (GEM) and the Luxembourg Stock Exchange's Euro MTF (Euro MTF) for debt securities sold to "professional investors". Products that will trade on the ISM include "plain vanilla" bonds as well as a range of specialist debt products such as structured products, convertible debt, derivative securities, high yield bonds and asset-backed securities.[12] Equities and GDRs will not be eligible for trading on the ISM.

On 8 May 2017, the final ISM Rulebook came into effect.

The headline benefits of ISM are as follows:

- issuers will benefit from the well-recognised and highly reputable LSE brand and global reach, which attracts a deep and varied pool of investors;
- products that will trade on the ISM include plain vanilla bonds (including sovereign bonds) as well as a range of specialist debt products such as structured products, convertible debt, high yield bonds, asset-backed and derivative securities;
- securities admitted to trading on the ISM will be subject to the ISM Rulebook, which has been designed to be flexible and pragmatic, and actively encourages dialogue with ISM officials as part of the admission process. As an exchange-regulated MTF, the ISM will offer greater flexibility for issuers as compared to regulated markets such as the LSE's Main Market;
- the ISM has a Primary Markets Regulation team comprising senior and experienced personnel from the UKLA and leading law firms;
- the ISM will deliver a customer-centric approach and an efficient admission process. For example, turnaround times on the review of admission documentation will mirror those of the GEM and Euro MTF (three business day review for initial submission and two business days for subsequent review);
- no annotation of offering documents is required;
- securities that are issued or guaranteed by Member States of the Organisation for Economic Co-operation and Development (OECD) and their regional or local authorities and issued by public international bodies or non-profit

---

[12] For the purposes of this chapter, "securities" means "debt securities" unless otherwise indicated.

organisations will be exempt from the requirement to provide a full offering document;

- simplified disclosure will be available for sovereign debt issuers in the reg.S (of the US Securities Act 1933) markets and to issuers with securities already admitted on certain specified categories of exchange/market;
- the ISM Rulebook aims to eliminate the need for derogations and instead hardwires in matters that frequently require derogation requests from the rules of the GEM and Euro MTF. For example, the inclusion of financial statements for upstream guarantors and the incorporation by reference of financial statements;
- the ISM will not charge issuers annual fees; and
- no listing agent will be required. Issuers and their counsel will have direct access to the ISM.

Securities trading on the ISM were previously outside the scope of the "Quoted Eurobond Exemption" as, although the LSE was a "recognised stock exchange", it was unable to provide an "official listing" to securities that trade on the ISM for the purposes of the Income Tax Act 2007. Accordingly, issuers of securities trading on the ISM with UK source income were obliged to pay interest subject to UK withholding tax. On 15 March 2018, the Finance Act 2018 came into force and amended s.987 of the Income Tax Act 2007 to extend coverage of the "Quoted Eurobond Exemption" to, among other things, securities admitted on a MTF operated by an EEA-regulated recognised stock exchange. This amendment has effect in relation to payments made on or after 1 April 2018. It follows that interest payments for securities trading on the ISM (an MTF) from issuers with UK source income will be exempt from UK withholding tax from and including 1 April 2018.

8.2.8.1   *Principal aims of the International Securities Market*

The ISM represents a departure from the current UK listing and trading market landscape for debt securities, which lack a market equivalent in operational terms to the GEM or Euro MTF. As an exchange-regulated EU MTF, the day-to-day regulation (including scrutiny of disclosure and admission decisions) will be undertaken by the LSE rather than the UKLA.

Most debt securities listed in the UK are listed on the regulated market and admitted to the Official List in the "standard listing—debt and debt-like securities" subcategory. Because they are admitted to trading on the regulated market, the PD, TD and MAR apply. The UKLA (a division of the FCA) applies a high (and often time-consuming) PD and TD compliant standard of disclosure review to issuers' listing and admission documentation. This is also the case for securities listed on LSE's PSM which, as a MTF, should have been competitive to the GEM and Euro MTF. However, issuers listing on the PSM (requiring UKLA approval) are obliged to provide PD-compliant disclosure and TD-level transparency, removing some of the practical disclosure and timing advantages to listing on a MTF. This is the principal reason why the PSM failed to gain traction with many issuers who have otherwise listed wholesale debt securities on the GEM or Euro MTF.

According to the FCA's Discussion Paper (DP) 17/12 in February 2017, a significant proportion of market participants reported that they considered the UK market offering to be incomplete, with companies (UK and otherwise) that could not meet certain main market disclosure requirements (and/or whose deal timetables could not accommodate lengthy and multiple review processes) effectively forced to list their wholesale debt securities in another jurisdiction, often on the GEM or Euro MTF.

There has been a decline in the use of the UK as a trading venue for corporate debt since 2009 and almost all UK-listed debt trades on the regulated market. By contrast, 28% of debt securities in Ireland and Luxembourg are now listed on MTFs, while less than 1% of UK issuances are on a MTF.

As a MTF, the ISM falls outside the scope of the PD and TD. Securities admitted to the ISM will be subject instead to the ISM Rulebook, which should avoid some of the technical regulatory disclosure challenges that caused some issuers to move their listings away from EU regulated markets. For example, vanilla bond issuers should be able to supplement their programmes and incorporate by reference future financial disclosure. The LSE has also promised that ISM issuers can look forward to a marked focus on customer service, including tighter turnaround times, commercial understanding and a tailored approach.

The ISM also has the advantage of the LSE's global reach and international standing. According to the LSE, London is home to over 2,300 companies from more than 70 countries around the world.[13] 70% of all bond secondary trading activity is conducted out of London and, as such, issuers on the ISM will have access to one of the deepest pools of global capital. In addition, the ISM offers the reputational benefits and name recognition from listing on London's distinguished global exchange.

8.2.8.2   *Market Abuse Regulation requirements apply*

As with listing on any other PD-compliant regulated market or MTF in the EEA, the usual prohibitions against insider trading, market manipulation and market abuse continue to apply under the MAR to issuers whose debt securities are admitted to trading on the ISM. Issuers must maintain insider trading lists, post and maintain all inside information required to be disclosed publicly on their websites for a period of at least five years, and take all reasonable steps to ensure that any person on the insider list acknowledges in writing the legal and regulatory duties entailed and is aware of the sanctions applicable to insider dealing and unlawful disclosure of inside information.

Persons discharging managerial responsibilities and "persons closely associated" with them must notify promptly the issuer

---

[13] LSE, "International Securities Market: London Stock Exchange's Enhanced Offering for Fixed Income Securities" available at: *http://www.londonstockexchange. com/companies-and-advisors/international/securities/market.htm* [Accessed 11 July 2018].

and the FCA of transactions relating to ISM-listed securities of the issuer. Persons discharging managerial responsibilities are also unable to deal with the issuer's listed securities (on their own account or for a third party, directly or indirectly) during a closed period of 30 calendar days before the announcement of an interim financial report or a year-end report, which issuers are obliged to make public according to the ISM Rulebook.

8.3 Investment entities

8.3.1 *Regulatory background*

The types of investment vehicle which can be established under English law include open-ended investment companies (OEICs), closed-ended investment companies including investment companies as so defined within s.833 of the Companies Act 2006 (including those qualifying as venture capital trusts under Ch.3 Pt 6 of the Income Tax Act 2007 (as amended) and investment trusts under Ch.4 Pt 24 of the Corporation Tax Act 2010 (as amended)), limited partnerships, limited liability partnerships, authorised unit trusts and unauthorised unit trusts. An OEIC must have a depositary which holds the OEIC's property on trust for the OEIC. Both the authorised corporate director and the depositary are regulated by the FCA.

Closed-ended investment funds and OEICs are governed by Chs 15 and 16 respectively. Unlike Ch.15, which provides a body of super-equivalent rules appropriate for the governance of closed-ended investment funds, Ch.16 provides a lighter touch regime for OEICs, which are already subject to the FCA or other EEA authority authorisation. Chapter 14 has been limited in scope and is not available to investment entities— they can only seek a premium listing. An investment entity is only able to obtain a standard listing for a further class of its equity shares if it already has, and for as long as it maintains, a premium listing of a class of its equity shares.

Investment entities seeking to list depositary receipts representing their shares can only do so if the underlying shares themselves are listed in London or are the subject of an application for listing at the same time.

8.3.2   Closed-ended investment funds

The following are the key provisions of Ch.15 of the Listing Rules which apply to closed-ended investment funds:

(1)   a listed closed-ended fund must at all times invest and manage its assets in a way which is consistent with its object of spreading investment risk (LRs 15.2.2 and 15.4.2(1)R);

(2)   publication of an investment policy: under the rules, a closed-ended investment fund must at all times have a published investment policy (LRs 15.2.7 and 15.4.1AR) and invest and manage its assets in compliance with it (LR 15.4.2(2)R). The term "investment policy" does not have a formal definition and the Listing Rules are not prescriptive in terms of the specific content of the "investment policy". In particular, the Listing Rules do not prescribe any specific maximum investment exposures. This is intended to provide boards with some flexibility as to how they would approach formulating the investment policy, which is in line with the FCA's principles-based approach. The investment policy should give adequate information about risks to which a potential investor may be exposed. According to the guidance previously issued by the UKLA, an investment policy should:

> "not be expressed in difficult-to-understand legalese or technical jargon that only asset management professionals understand . . . the language should be firm so that it binds the company to its chosen course of action" (*List!* Issue No.17 (UKLA Publications, November 2007), para.3);

(3)   specifically, the investment policy must provide information to potential investors and existing shareholders about

the fund's policies in relation to asset allocation, risk diversification and gearing, and must also include maximum permitted exposures (LR 15.2.7R). The published investment policy must include quantitative information concerning maximum exposures and be sufficiently precise and clear to enable an investor to: (a) assess the investment opportunity; (b) identify how the objective of risk spreading is to be achieved; and (c) assess the significance of any proposed change of investment policy (LR 15.2.8G). The rationale of this "quantification" requirement is to enable a closed-ended investment fund to demonstrate that it invests and manages its assets in a way which is consistent with its object of spreading the investment risk, as required under LR 15.2.2R. Further, there is a requirement to submit any proposed "material change" to a published investment policy to the FCA for approval and, having obtained such approval from the FCA, to obtain prior shareholder approval unless LR 15.4.8AR applies (LR 15.4.8R). It is not a requirement to seek the FCA's approval if the change is proposed to enable the winding-up of the closed-ended investment fund and the winding-up: (a) is in accordance with the constitution of the closed-ended investment fund; and (b) will be submitted for approval by the shareholders of the closed-ended investment fund at the same time as the proposed material change to the investment policy (LR 15.4.8AR);

(4) controlling positions: there is no restriction on closed-ended investment funds taking controlling positions in investee companies, provided the fund can demonstrate that it has the objective of managing its assets with a view to spreading investment risk (and therefore should avoid cross-financing between the businesses forming part of its investment portfolio and the operation and common treasury functions as between the fund and investee companies (LR 15.2.4AG). Additionally, a closed-ended investment fund and its subsidiary undertakings must not conduct any "trading activity" which is "significant" in the context of its group as a whole, but this will not

prevent businesses forming part of the investment portfolio of the fund from carrying out trading activities
themselves (LR 15.2.3AR);

(5) experience of the investment manager: there is no listing
requirement that the manager of a closed-ended investment company, as an applicant for listing, must have
"sufficient and appropriate experience";

(6) board independence: board independence is an important
element of any premium-listed investment entity in
ensuring that the rights and interests of shareholders are
protected. The board of directors or equivalent body of a
fund must be able to act independently of the investment
manager appointed to manage the investments of the fund
and, if a fund has an investment policy of principally
investing its funds in another company or fund that
invests in a portfolio of investments (a master fund), the
board of the feeder fund must also be able to act
independently of the master fund (LR 15.2.11R). The
chairman of the fund must be independent of the manager,
however, there is no restriction on representatives of the
manager being on the board, with the effect that an
independent chairman together with a simple majority of
independent directors will suffice to meet the board
independence criteria. There are detailed rules contained
in LR 15.2.12AR about who is not independent, to provide
extra clarity on this important tenet of the listing regime as
it affects investment entities. Annual re-election of non-
independent directors will also help to maintain board
independence (LR 15.2.13AR);

(7) feeder funds: the rules permit feeder funds to list without
the board being able to exercise control over the master
fund, i.e. another company or fund into which the listed
closed-ended investment entity principally invests. The
board of directors of the listed feeder fund must, however,
be satisfied that the investment policy of the master fund
is consistent with the listed feeder fund's investment
policy and provides for spreading of investment risk, and
the master fund does, in fact, invest in accordance with
that investment policy and spreads risk when investing
and managing its investments (LR 15.2.6R). If the listed

feeder fund becomes aware that the master fund (or intermediary) is not managing or investing its investments in accordance with the above rule, it must immediately consider withdrawal of its funds from the master fund (or intermediary) or take other action to ensure that it is not in breach of the Listing Rules (LR 15.4.6AG);

(8) periodic disclosure of holdings: a quarterly portfolio disclosure is not required, save for disclosure of cross-holdings in other listed closed-ended investment funds (LR 15.6.8R). The FSA concluded previously that for some issuers a regular portfolio disclosure represents a disincentive to list in the UK and the resultant disclosure regime is based on:

(a) the requirements for the disclosure of inside information set out in DTR 2 (as substantially replaced by equivalent provisions of the MAR);

(b) the reporting cycle of annual, half-yearly and interim management reports established by the TD and given effect by DTR 4;

(c) notifications by listed funds of major shareholdings in other companies, as required by DTR 5;

(d) the quarterly disclosure of cross-holdings in other listed closed-ended investment funds that the FSA proposed in CP 07/12 and implemented in LR 15.6.8R;

In addition, a closed-ended listed fund must ratify any change in its taxation status to a regulatory information service as soon as possible (LR 15.6.1R);

(9) transactions with related parties: an investment manager (and any member of its group) is deemed a related party of the listed fund for the purposes of Ch.11 of the Listing Rules ("Related Party Transactions") (LR 15.5.4R). There is an exemption from the related party rules to facilitate co-investment by listed investment entities and transactions with other clients of the investment manager or the investment manager's group. This co-investment would either involve an investment in, or the provision of finance to, a particular company or asset. Such co-investment arrangement will be exempted, provided that the investment is made either at the same time and on substantially

the same economic and financial terms, or referred to in the published investment policy, or made in accordance with a pre-existing agreement between the fund and its investment manager (LR 15.5.5R(1)). For the purposes of the foregoing, a pre-existing agreement is an agreement entered into at the time the investment manager was appointed (LR 15.5.5R(2));

(10) significant transactions: a closed-ended investment fund must comply with the Listing Rules relating to significant transactions in Ch.10 and the rules relating to reverse takeovers in LR 5.6 unless the transaction is executed in accordance with the scope of its published investment policy (LR 15.2.2R);

(11) working capital: investment entities are subject to the same requirements to have sufficient working capital and there is a requirement for a working capital statement as applies to other listed companies (LRs 6.1.16R–6.1.18G). This is unlikely to cause problems for most investment companies, although it could be more complicated for leveraged funds investing in illiquid assets;

(12) further issues: except where authorised by it shareholder, the listed fund may not issue further shares of an existing class (including treasury shares) for cash at a discount to net asset value unless they are first offered on a pre-emptive and pro-rata basis to the existing holders of that class (LR 15.4.11R); and

(13) pre-emption rights: if the law of the country in which a fund is incorporated does not confer on shareholders pre-emption rights on the issue of new shares in that fund (which in the case of many offshore jurisdictions will be the case), the fund must: (a) ensure its constitution provides for rights which are at least equivalent to the rights provided for in LR 9.3.11R (as qualified by LR 9.3.12R); and (b) be satisfied that conferring such rights would not be incompatible with the law of the country of its incorporation. It may be possible to disapply the pre-emption rights entrenched in a fund's constitution by shareholder resolution.

8.3.3 The Alternative Investment Fund Managers Directive

The Alternative Investment Fund Managers Directive (2011/ 61) (AIFMD)[14] was published in the *Official Journal of the European Union* on 1 July 2011 and came into force on 21 July 2011. EU Member States, such as the UK, were required to implement it by 22 July 2013 and the UK has done so primarily through the Alternative Investment Fund Managers Regulations 2013 (SI 2013/1773) and the *Investment Fund Sourcebook*, which has been added to the *FCA Handbook*. The European Commission published an implementing regulation (Regulation 231/2013) (the Regulation) on 22 March 2013,[15] which became directly applicable in EU Member States from 22 July 2013. The AIFMD regulates the managers of a wide range of funds that are not authorised under the Undertakings for Collective Investment in Transferable Securities (UCITS) Directive[16]—including hedge funds, private equity, property, listed funds, funds of funds and commodity funds (each an alternative investment fund—AIF). It governs the activities of alternative investment fund managers (AIFMs) whose regular business is managing AIFs. While it does not directly regulate AIFs, certain requirements for an AIFM may influence an AIF's operation. EU AIFMs are caught by the scope of the AIFMD, as are non-EU AIFMs that manage EU AIFs or market AIFs to EU investors.

Under the AIFMD, an AIF shall have only one AIFM (art.5(1)) which must either be an external AIFM or the AIF itself (a "self-managed" AIF). In addition, if the external AIFM or self-managed AIF is within the EU, it must become authorised in its Home State (which is the Member State in which it has its registered office).

---

[14] Directive 2011/61 on Alternative Investment Fund Managers and amending Directives 2003/41 and 2009/65 and Regulations 1060/2009 and 1095/2010 [2011] OJ L174/1.

[15] Regulation 231/2013 supplementing Directive 2011/61 with regard to exemptions, general operating conditions, depositaries, leverage, transparency and supervision [2013] OJ L83/1.

[16] Directive 2014/91 amending Directive 2009/65 on the coordination of laws, regulations and administrative provisions relating to undertakings for collective investment in transferable securities (UCITS) as regards depositary functions, remuneration policies and sanctions [2014] OJ L257/186.

In the context of closed-ended investment funds most, if not all, listed closed-ended investment funds will be AIFs given the broad definition of an AIF under the AIFMD. Therefore, the operation of those funds will be affected by the requirements imposed on AIFMs by the AIFMD to the extent those funds are managed or marketed in the EU. Where the AIFM is authorised in the EU, the fund's management, depositary and custody arrangements in particular will need to be reviewed to ensure that they are compliant with the AIFMD, the Regulation and any other implementing requirements in the AIFM's Home State.

The Listing Rules were amended as a result of the AIFMD. A new eligibility requirement was introduced requiring the board of directors of the closed-ended investment fund to be in a position to effectively monitor and manage the performance of its key service providers, including any investment manager (LR 15.2.19R). This requirement has been mirrored in a continuing obligation (LR 15.4.7AR). These rules were introduced to ensure that the board of directors (or equivalent body) of a listed closed-ended investment fund maintains ultimate responsibility for the control and management of the fund, rather than the investment manager.

A description of the full range of implications for investment funds of implementation of the AIFMD is beyond the scope of this chapter. The provisions of the AIFMD (described above) may also affect any OEICs that are not authorised as UCITS funds.

8.3.4   Open-ended investment companies

Under Ch.16 of the Listing Rules, and specifically LR 16.2, an OEIC must satisfy the following conditions for listing:

(1)   the requirements for listing set out in Ch.2 of the Listing Rules; and
(2)   an OEIC must not have warrants or options to subscribe for equity shares which exceed 20% of the issued equity

share capital (excluding treasury shares) of the OEIC as at the time of issue of the warrants or options (LR 6.1.22R).

The only OEICs that can apply for a premium listing of equity securities are:

(1) an OEIC that has been granted an authorisation order by the FCA; and
(2) an overseas collective investment scheme that is a recognised scheme.

No other OEIC is permitted to list its equity securities (LR 16.1.1R).

Listing of OEICs is effected by means of listing particulars and the content is determined by reference to LR 4.2.5G (see s.8.3.5.1 below).

There are some additional continuing obligations provisions contained in LR 16.4 which an OEIC must observe to remain listed. Among these is a requirement to notify the RIS of instances when the OEIC becomes aware of the interests of any single person or entity exceeding 10% of the issued shares of any class (LR 16.4.3R).

The provisions of Chs 10 ("Significant transactions") and 12 ("Dealing in own securities and treasury shares") do not apply to OEICs (LR 16.4.4R). The requirements for a percentage of shares to be in public hands are disapplied for OEICs (LR 16.4.1R).

8.3.5 The application of the Prospectus Directive to investment entities

The PD exempts units in an open-ended collective investment scheme from its scope. Article 1(2) ("Purpose and scope") of the PD states that "this Directive shall not apply to: (a) units issued by collective investment undertakings other than the closed-end type". The definition of "collective investment undertakings other than the closed-end type" is set out in art.2(1)(o) of the PD, which states that

> "a 'collective investment undertaking other than the closed-end type' means unit trusts and investment companies: (i) the object of which is the collective investment of capital provided by the public, and which operate on the principle of risk-spreading; (ii) the units of which are, at the holder's request, repurchased or redeemed, directly or indirectly, out of the assets of these undertakings".

However, listing particulars will still need to be published where an issuer applies for admission of such securities to the Official List (LR 4.1.1R(1)).

The guidance in LR 4.2.5G is that the FCA expects issuers to follow the most appropriate schedules and building blocks in the PD Regulation to determine the minimum information to be included in listing particulars. Thus, in effect, issuers of such units would have to comply with Annexes I and III of the PD Regulation in any event.

Where the collective investment undertaking is of the closed-ended type, the PD will apply and issuers will have to comply (inter alia) with the minimum disclosure requirements of Annex XV of the PD Regulation.

8.3.5.1 *Annex XV of the Prospectus Directive Regulation*

Annex XV to the PD Regulation details the minimum disclosure requirements that closed-ended investment companies must comply with when issuing their registration documents, in addition to other mandatory requirements for the prospectus. Most of the provisions of Annex I to the PD Regulation apply and the prospectus must, inter alia, contain (to the extent applicable) the following:

- a detailed description of the investment objective and policy which the collective investment undertaking will pursue and a description of how that investment objective and policy may be varied, including any circumstances in which such variation requires the approval of investors, together with a description of any techniques and instruments that may be used in the management of the collective investment undertaking; borrowing and/or leverage limits and, if there are no such limits of the collective investment undertaking, it should include a statement to that effect;

- the issuer's regulatory status together with the name of any regulator in its country of incorporation;
- the profile of a typical investor for whom the collective investment undertaking is designed;
- a statement of the investment restrictions which apply to the collective investment undertaking, if any, and an indication of how the holders of securities will be informed of the actions that the investment manager will take in the event of a breach;
- where more than 20% of the gross assets of any collective investment undertaking (subject to certain exemptions) may be: (1) invested in, either directly or indirectly, or lent to any single underlying issuer (including the underlying issuer's subsidiaries or affiliates); (2) invested in one or more collective investment undertakings which may invest in excess of 20% of its or their gross assets in other collective investment undertakings (open-ended and/or closed-ended type); or (3) exposed to the creditworthiness or solvency of any one counterparty (including its subsidiaries or affiliates) (if collateral is advanced to cover that portion of the exposure to any one counterparty in excess of 20% of the gross assets of the collective investment undertaking, details of such collateral arrangements must be provided), a range of information has to be disclosed about each underlying issuer/collective investment undertaking/counterparty. This requirement shall not apply where the 20% is exceeded due to appreciation or depreciation in value, changes in exchange rates, by reason of the receipt of rights, bonuses, benefits in the nature of capital or by reason of any other action affecting every holder of that investment, provided the investment

manager has regard to the threshold when considering changes in the investment portfolio;

- where a collective investment undertaking may invest in excess of 20% of its gross assets in other collective investment undertakings (open-ended and/or closed-ended), a description of if and how risk is spread in relation to those investments. In addition, the provisions summarised above shall apply, in aggregate, to its underlying investments as if those investments had been made directly;

- where a collective investment undertaking may invest in excess of 40% of its gross assets in another collective investment undertaking either of the following must be disclosed: (1) information relating to each underlying collective investment undertaking as if it were an issuer under minimum disclosure requirements for the registration document schedule for securities issued by collective investment undertakings of the closed-ended type; or (2) if securities issued by an underlying collective investment undertaking have already been admitted to trading on a regulated or equivalent market or the obligations are guaranteed by an entity admitted to trading on a regulated or equivalent market, the name, address, country of incorporation, nature of business and name of the market in which its securities are admitted;

- where a collective investment undertaking invests directly in physical commodities a disclosure of that fact and the percentage that will be so invested;

- where a collective investment undertaking is a property collective investment undertaking, disclosure of that fact, the percentage of the portfolio that is to be invested in property, as well as a description of the property, and any material costs relating to the acquisition and holding of such property. In addition, a valuation report relating to the properties must be included;

- derivatives financial instruments/money market instruments/currencies: where a collective investment undertaking invests in derivatives, financial instruments, money market instruments or currencies other than for the purposes of efficient portfolio management (i.e. solely for the purpose of reducing, transferring or eliminating investment risk in the underlying investments of a collective investment undertaking, including any technique or instrument used to provide protection against exchange and credit risks), a statement whether those investments are used for hedging or for investment purposes and a description of if and how risk is spread in relation to those investments;

- in relation to the applicant's service providers:
  — the actual or estimated maximum amount of all material fees payable directly or indirectly by the issuer for any services under arrangements entered into on, or prior to, the date of the registration document and a description of how these fees are calculated, together with a description of any fee payable directly or indirectly by the collective investment undertaking which cannot be quantified in this way and which is, or may be, material. If any service provider to the issuer is in receipt of any benefits from third parties (other than the issuer) by virtue of providing any services to the issuer, and those benefits may not accrue to the issuer, a statement of that fact, the name of that third party if available and a description of the nature of the benefits;
  — the name of the service provider which is responsible for the determination and calculation of the net asset value of the collective investment undertaking;
  — a description of any material potential conflicts of interest which any of the service providers to the issuer may have as between their duty to the issuer and duties owed by them to third parties and their other interests, together with a description of any arrangements which are in place to address such potential conflicts;
- in respect of any investment manager, a variety of corporate information must be disclosed together with a description of its regulatory status and experience. In the case of a property scheme, disclosure under this head extends to the valuation entity and any other entity responsible for the administration of the property. The

name and a brief description of any entity providing investment advice in relation to the assets of the collective investment undertaking must be included;

- a full description of how the assets of the collective investment undertaking will be held, and by whom, and any fiduciary or similar relationship between the collective investment undertaking and any third party in relation to custody. Where a custodian, trustee, or other fiduciary is appointed, information about them, the obligations of such party under the custody or similar agreement, their delegates and the regulatory status of such party and delegates should be provided. There are additional disclosure obligations where any other entity holds any assets of the issuer;
- a description of how often, and the valuation principles and the method by which, the net asset value of the collective investment undertaking will be determined, distinguishing between categories of investments and a statement of how such net asset value will be communicated to investors;
- details of all circumstances in which valuations may be suspended and a statement of how such suspension will be communicated or made available to investors;
- in the case of an umbrella collective investment undertaking, a statement of any cross-liability that may occur between classes or investments in other collective investment undertakings and any action taken to limit such liability;
- financial information: where, since the date of incorporation or establishment, a collective investment undertaking has not commenced operations and no financial statements have been made up as at the date of the registration document, a statement to that effect. Where a collective investment undertaking has commenced operations, the provisions of Item 20 of Annex I on the Minimum Disclosure Requirements (in the Listing Rules) for the share registration document apply; and
- a comprehensive and meaningful analysis of the collective investment undertaking's portfolio (if unaudited, clearly marked as such). An indication of the most recent net asset

value per security must be included in the securities note schedule (and, if unaudited, clearly marked as such).

8.4   Venture capital trusts

The Listing Rules define a venture capital trust (VCT) as a company which is, or which is seeking to become, approved as a VCT in accordance with Ch.3 Pt 6 of the Income Tax Act 2007 (as amended). Under the rules, VCTs are subject to the same set of rules, including conditions for listing and continuing obligations, as other listed closed-ended funds under Ch.15.

The FSA specifically stated in CP 06/21 that it is of paramount importance that the chairman of a listed investment entity is, and is perceived to be, independent and free of any potential conflict of interest. Accordingly, VCTs are required to have the same level of independence between boards and investment managers as are other forms of investment entities (LRs 15.2.11R and LR 15.4.7R).

Individual investors can claim income tax relief in respect of subscriptions for new eligible shares in a VCT, provided that the VCT shares are held for at least five years. The subscription must raise money for the VCT. Eligible shares are new ordinary shares in the VCT which, for a period of five years from the date of issue, have no present or future preferential rights to dividends, assets in a winding-up or redemption. The amount of the relief is the lower of 30% of the amount subscribed (up to a maximum subscription of £200,000 per tax year) and the amount which reduces the individual's income tax liability to zero. Subject to certain conditions, individual investors are exempt from income tax on respect of dividends in respect of shares held by those investors within the "permitted maxi-mum" (currently £200,000). In addition, gains and losses accruing to individuals who dispose of VCT shares (being either new or existing shares) are neither chargeable gains nor allowable losses so long as the company was a VCT both when the individual acquired the shares and when he disposed of them. Although VCTs are now governed by Ch.15, depending on the circumstances, other specific chapters may be applicable. Examples may include an overseas company seeking to qualify as a VCT, in which case the requirements of both Chs 14 and 15 could be relevant.

8.5   Property investment companies

As is the case with closed-ended investment funds, in 2007, the FSA also changed the rules relating to property investment companies quite substantially. The rules governing concentration limits and gearing and placing limits on short leaseholds and unoccupied property were removed.

As there is a unitary listing regime for closed-ended investment funds, there is no longer a differentiation between various types of vehicles, formats or strategies. It is now the responsibility of the closed-ended fund itself to ensure that it operates within the spirit of the rules by having and pursuing an investment policy which has, at its core, the objective of investing to spread investment risk. The result is that the same rules apply now to property investment companies as they do generally to closed-ended investment funds.

There are, however, some additional valuation requirements in relation to property investment companies contained in LR 15.6.3R. A closed-ended investment fund with 20% of the assets invested in property at the end of its financial year must include a summary of the valuation of its property portfolio in the annual financial report. The valuation must comply with either the Appraisal and Valuation Standards issued by the Royal Institution of Chartered Surveyors or, if the valuation does not comply in all applicable respects with the Appraisal and Valuation Standards (6th edn), it must include a statement which sets out a full explanation for such non-compliance. The valuation must also be made by an external valuer as defined in the Appraisal and Valuation Standards (6th edn) (LR 15.6.4R). The "summary" referred to above must contain (LR 15.6.5R):

- the total value of properties (as defined in the Listing Rules) held at the year-end;
- the total cost of the properties acquired;
- the net book value of properties disposed of during the year; and
- an indication of the geographical location and type of properties held at the year-end.

The FSA, among other things, also removed the requirement that property-focused investment entities must subject significant purchases or sales of property to shareholder approval. This exemption applies provided such transactions fall within the scope of the fund's published investment policy. This indicates that the FSA took the view that shareholders of property-focused investment entities should rely on the entity's published investment policy as the key control mechanism. The benefit of this includes the FCA no longer having to approve circulars prepared by property investment companies which has clear administrative and economic advantages.

8.6   Real Estate Investment Trusts

Real Estate Investment Trusts (REITs) are investment vehicles designed to enable tax efficient investment in a professionally managed real estate portfolio. In the UK, the REIT regime was introduced on 1 January 2007 when nine property groups became the UK's first real estate investment trusts. Under ss.534 and 535 of the Corporation Tax Act 2010 (as amended) (2010 Act), the effect of converting into a REIT is that, provided various conditions are adequately satisfied, the REIT will qualify for exemption from UK corporation tax on the profits and capital gains resulting from its qualifying property rental business. Distributions of such profits and capital gains are treated as UK property income in the hands of shareholders and 20% withholding tax is (subject to certain exceptions) imposed on such distributions. Prior to 17 July 2012, companies which converted into a REIT were subject to a joining tax charge of 2% on the gross market value of the property assets within the qualifying property rental business. However, the Finance Act 2012 abolished this entry charge for companies joining the REIT regime on or after 17 July 2012.

The UK REIT regime is governed by Pt 12 of the 2010 Act and the following regulations:

- the Real Estate Investment Trusts (Breach of Conditions) Regulations 2006 (SI 2006/2864);
- the Real Estate Investment Trusts (Financial Statements of Group Real Estate Investment Trusts) Regulations 2006 (SI 2006/2865);
- the Real Estate Investment Trusts (Assessment and Recovery of Tax) Regulations 2006 (SI 2006/2867);
- the Real Estate Investment Trusts (Joint Ventures) Regulations 2006 (SI 2006/2866);
- the Real Estate Investment Trusts (Breach of Conditions) (Amendment) Regulations 2007 (SI 2007/3540);
- the Real Estate Investment Trusts (Joint Venture Groups) Regulations 2007 (SI 2007/3425);
- the Real Estate Investment Trusts (Prescribed Arrangements) Regulations 2009 (SI 2009/3315); and
- the Real Estate Investment Trust (Amendments to the Corporation Tax Act 2010 and Consequential Amendments) Regulations 2014 (SI 2014/518).

8.6.1 Qualifying conditions

In order to qualify as a REIT, a company must satisfy all of the qualifying conditions set out below. A group of companies qualifies for REIT status if the group's principal company satisfies the "company conditions" and the group satisfies the "business conditions" set out below.

Company conditions:

(1) the company must be tax resident in the UK and nowhere else;
(2) the company must not be an OEIC;
(3) the company must not be a close company or, if it is a close company, it must be only by virtue of having as a

participator an "Institutional Investor" (such as a limited partnership which is a collective investment scheme);

(4) it must only have one class of ordinary share capital in issue and the only other shares it may issue are non-voting restricted preference shares and non-voting convertible preference shares;

(5) it must not be a party to a loan where the interest payable depends on the results of the company, entitles the lender to an excessive amount of interest or entitles the lender to an excessive repayment; and

(6) its shares must be included in the official UK list or be officially listed in a qualifying country outside the UK or be traded on a recognised stock exchange.

Business conditions:

(1) the company must have a property rental business that satisfies conditions of a "tax exempt business" throughout the relevant accounting period, including the following:
   (a) the business must comprise at least three rental properties;
   (b) no one property can represent more than 40% of the total value of the rental properties of the business;
   (c) no property in the business must be owner-occupied;
   (d) at least 90% of the profits arising from the property rental business (along with 100% of distribution received from other REITS) must be distributed by way of dividend;

(2) the profits from the property rental business must comprise at least 75% of the company's total profits; and

(3) at the beginning of each accounting period, the value of the assets in the property rental business must comprise at least 75% of the company's total assets. If this condition is not met, it does not mean that the REIT status is lost provided that this condition is met at the beginning of the next accounting period.

There are no regulatory borrowing restrictions on a company wishing to qualify as a REIT. However, a tax charge will be incurred if the REIT's income profits from its property rental business do not cover its related finance costs by at least 1.25 times.

It should also be noted that a REIT will be subject to a tax charge if it makes a distribution to a body corporate which is beneficially entitled to 10% or more of the REIT's shares or dividends or who controls 10% or more of the voting rights. The amount of the charge reflects the tax withheld on the distribution which the holder of excessive rights could reclaim under a double taxation treaty. This is generally equivalent to basic rate tax (currently 20%) on:

- the profits of the REIT's qualifying tax-exempt business distributed to such shareholders in respect of their ordinary shares; and
- any REIT profits distributed to such shareholders in respect of their preference shares.

8.6.2 Converting into a Real Estate Investment Trust

In order to convert into a REIT, the following steps must be taken:

(1) a company must serve a notice on Her Majesty's Revenue and Customs prior to the accounting period for which it wishes to convert (s.524 of the Corporation Tax Act 2010); and

(2) there is a need to amend the REIT's Articles of Association. This is because REITs must take "reasonable steps" to avoid paying distributions to shareholders that are beneficially entitled to 10% or more of the shares or dividends of the REIT or control 10% or more of the voting rights in the REIT. If this is not done, the REIT may be exposed to a tax penalty (s.551 Corporation Tax Act 2010).

8.6.3 Real Estate Investment Trusts and the Listing Rules

If a REIT has a policy of spreading investment risk, it may be listed under Ch.15 of the Listing Rules whereas, if the REIT does not spread investment risk then it may still be listed under Ch.6 of the Listing Rules. If the REIT is conducting significant trading activities then it is likely to be listed under Ch.6. If, on the other hand, the REIT has an investment policy, the objective of which is the spreading of investment risk, Ch.15 may be suitable and the same rules will apply to the REIT as they apply to closed-ended investment entities. It follows that an existing issuer who is listed under Ch.15 will not be required to have its obligations changed if it were to convert into a REIT, unless it changes its nature of business rather substantially. Conversely, if a Ch.6 issuer obtains a REIT status, it would normally remain so listed under Ch.6.

8.7 Specialist Fund Segment

The Specialist Fund Segment (SFS), formally known as the Specialist Fund Market, which was launched on 1 November 2007, is the LSE's regulated market for highly specialised, UK or non-UK investment entities that wish to target institutional, professional and highly knowledgeable investors only. It is not intended for investment products targeted at non-professional and non-institutional investors including private equity funds, some feeder funds and hedge funds. The SFS was developed in response to the growth of more complex investment vehicles and the well-publicised listing of certain high profile private equity funds on Amsterdam's NYSE Euronext. It is an EU regulated market as defined in the markets in MiFID[17] (and for the purposes of the UCITS Directive) and a structure which is compliant with the EU's Financial Services Action Plan.

Securities admitted to trading on the SFS should be transferable securities admitted to a regulated market for the purposes

---

[17] Directive 2004/39 on markets in financial instruments amending Council Directives 85/611 and 93/6 and Directive 2000/12 and repealing Directive 93/22 [2004] OJ L145/1.

of the UCITS Directive. However, as securities do not need to be approved for public notification on the Official List as a prerequisite for admission, the SFS is an unlisted market with a more flexible regulatory regime. Admission to trading on the SFS is a two-stage process requiring: (1) the approval of a prospectus by the applicant's EEA competent authority; and (2) following approval of the prospectus, application to the LSE for admission to trading on the SFS. As at 25 June 2018, 51 securities were traded on the SFS.

8.8   Debt and specialist securities

This section addresses the listing of debt and specialist securities and the related PSM. Specialist securities (such as eurobonds) are, for the purposes of the Listing Rules, broadly defined as securities which, because of their nature, are normally bought and traded by a limited number of investors who are particularly knowledgeable in investment matters.

This chapter concentrates on debt securities and GDRs. These securities are not eligible for premium listing and in most cases there will be a choice between a standard listing and: (1) trading on the Main Market (under LR 17 or LR 18); or (2) trading on the PSM. For those securities traded on the Main Market, there is a distinction between the "wholesale" and "retail" regimes as described below. The New Prospectus Regulation (defined further below)[18] will aim to extend the scope of the wholesale disclosure regime to include issues of debt securities that are admitted to an EU regulated market where access is limited to qualified investors.

For debt securities, the denomination is important for the purposes of determining which EEA state(s) qualifies as the issuer's Home State (see s.8.2.2.3 above). In relation to the listing of debt securities and GDRs, the prospectus regime to be

---

[18] Regulation 2017/1129 on the prospectus to be published when securities are offered to the public or admitted to trading on a regulated market, and repealing Directive 2003/71 [2017] OJ L168/12.

followed will depend upon whether the securities are categorised as "retail" or "wholesale" investments. Retail offers require more detail in respect of the information to be provided in the prospectus. Wholesale offers will require less detail to be disclosed in the prospectus and have greater flexibility in some other respects. Whether an offer is retail or wholesale is not determined by reference to the target audience for an issue, as was the case when the distinction was drawn between a retail offer being one to the general public and a wholesale offer being one to professional investors. The difference is now defined by reference to the denomination of the security.

Issuers of debt securities and depositary receipts that are denominated below €100,000 (or the equivalent amount in another currency) will, subject to what is addressed below, be required to follow the requirements of the retail regime. The wholesale regime is available only to issuers of such securities that are denominated at or above €100,000 (or the equivalent amount in another currency). The €100,000 limit was increased from €50,000 on 1 July 2012. Issuers of debt securities that are convertible or exchangeable into equity securities, which as a class are already admitted to trading on a regulated market, also have to follow the retail or wholesale requirements, depending on the denomination of the securities. However, issuers of debt securities that are convertible or exchangeable into shares, the class of which are not yet admitted to trading on a regulated market, will have additional disclosure requirements aligned with those of equity issuers and might be subject to stamp duty.

Compliance with the retail regime includes the need to have a PD-compliant prospectus as applicable for admission of those securities to listing and the requirement for an issuer following a retail regime to prepare its financial information according to International Financial Reporting Standards (IFRS) or an equivalent standard. If the financial information is not equivalent, it must be presented in the form of restated financial statements. Preparing a restatement of financial information according to IFRS is not a requirement under the wholesale regime. However, issuers would be required to provide a description of the key differences between the accounting standards used and the IFRS. The wholesale regime also involves different PD requirements, including the absence of a need for a summary.

8.8.1 *The Professional Securities Market*

The wholesale regime provides a less onerous prospectus regime than that applicable to retail debt, but it is not available to all issuers and, for issuers such as those who may want to list convertible bonds or securities denominated below €100,000, the retail or equity regime could be costly to comply with. This is particularly so for those issuers from outside the EEA, whose accounting standards may not be deemed equivalent to the IFRS (not least as a result of there being considerable uncertainty as to what is considered to be equivalent). The cost of restating or providing additional disclosures under a retail regime could be prohibitive.

To address concerns set out in the paragraph above and, with a view to retaining London's competitive position, the LSE and in July 2005 the FCA established an additional platform—the PSM—which provides a third option for debt, convertibles or depositary receipt issuers listing in London (in addition to the choice between the retail and wholesale markets), which will enable them to follow a wholesale regime irrespective of the denomination of the security.

The PSM (which is equivalent in regulatory status to the Euro MTF market in Luxembourg) is a market operated and regulated by the LSE. Securities admitted to such a market are therefore admitted to the Official List of the UKLA and to trading on a market operated by the LSE but that market is not a "regulated market" for the purposes of the PD, which means that issuers would not fall within the scope of the FCA Prospectus Rules (other than the public offer limb) or the DTRs, unless they are otherwise subject to these provisions. Listing Rule 4 sets out the requirements for listing particulars for (inter alia) specialist securities to be traded on the PSM. Once listed, the issuer must comply with the obligations under the Listing Rules.

Admission to the PSM can apply to any type of eligible debt security or depositary receipt, including those carrying a right to convert or acquire equity, of any denomination and follow, in effect, a wholesale regime. Admission to the PSM is not available for equity securities. If an issuer wants its equity securities to be publicly traded in the UK, other than through admission to the Official List and trading on the LSE's regulated market (premium or standard Segment), available options may include the AIM market or the HGS, both of which are operated by the LSE. The HGS is a new segment of LSE's Main Market and was launched in March 2013 and further information on which is set out below. It is a transitional segment designed to attract high growth, mid-sized UK and European companies looking to obtain an official listing over time.

In respect of securities traded on the PSM, companies wanting to raise capital without being restricted in the type or value of securities they issue may do so without the potentially greater cost of following a retail or equity regime. Issuers of debt, convertibles and depositary receipts will not be required to report historical financial information in accordance with the IFRS or an EEA approved equivalent standard either in listing documents or as a continuing obligation requirement, as these issuers can continue to use their domestic accounting stand-ards. The PSM therefore provides an alternative for issuers who do not prepare or do not wish to prepare their financial information in accordance with the IFRS or equivalent account-ing standards (US Generally Accepted Accounting Principles (GAAP), Canadian GAAP and Japanese GAAP) or who wish to offer lower denomination securities.

The PSM is operated, and is approved, as a MTF as defined under the MiFID. Approval of PSM listing particulars does not provide a passport to other European markets.

The LSE has stated that they believe that a consistent approach is the right way forward for issuers and that the starting point for its PSM should be the PD requirements but with the flexibility built in to address the specific issues it has identified.[19] This alignment with the PD regime which is now the standard for the EEA will provide more comfort for investors who want the assurance of a robust regulatory approach.

For a number of reasons, many issuers continue to seek admission to trading on the regulated market for securities which would be eligible for the PSM.

The provisions of Ch.17 of the Listing Rules apply (among other securities) to both retail and wholesale debt securities. An issuer of such securities must comply with Chs 2 ("Requirements for listing") and 3 ("Listing applications") of the Listing Rules.

8.8.2   Listing debt securities

8.8.2.1   Admission and marketing

There are a number of different ways in which specialist debt issues are affected. The most common procedure is for the lead manager of the issue to invite a number of financial institutions to be co-managers. These managers will then organise the issue, for a fee, and will normally undertake to subscribe for the whole of the issue, with or without other parties.

The result is that all the bonds or notes are likely to be issued in the first instance to members of those groups and/or their clients and only subsequently will there be a wider dissemination of the notes or debentures into the market, with subsequent dealings being cleared normally through Euroclear and/or Clearstream, and/or the Depository Trust Company for any US tranche. One consequence of such a marketing

---

[19] LSE, "The Professional Securities Market" available at: *http://www. londonstockexchange.com/companies-and-advisors/psm/professional-securities-market.pdf* [Accessed 11 July 2018].

technique is that the investors, who will be making a decision to subscribe for these securities by participating in the primary offer rather than by acquiring them in the secondary market, are likely to be experienced operators in this market.

An issuer of specialist debt securities must (in addition to compliance with the relevant provisions if they are an overseas company) comply with the normal requirements in Ch.2 (subject to certain modifications). There are a number of variations in the prospectus content requirements which may, in effect, impact on eligibility to seek admission. These are summarised below.

As in the case of an ordinary equity issue, issuers (other than states and their regional or local authorities) of these securities must prepare prospectuses and have them approved by the FCA (unless the securities are listed on the PSM, in which case listing particulars will need to be produced and approved). Applicants for debt securities need not appoint a sponsor under Ch.8 of the Listing Rules in respect of the application for admission.

8.8.2.2   *Prospectus/listing particulars requirements*

The PD sets a high standard of disclosure for debt issuers. It is partially relaxed for wholesale debt, which is more narrowly defined than specialist securities (see above). Information required to be disclosed in a prospectus drawn up in accordance with the PD wholesale regime is in effect the same as that for listing particulars for a PSM issuer.

A prospectus must include risk factors, the reason for the offer and use of proceeds, information about the administrative, management and supervisory bodies of the issuer, the issuer's corporate practices, information about potential conflicts of interest as well as both interim and final financial information. Under the Prospectus Rules, historical financial information will have to be prepared in accordance with the IFRS or national accounting standards where these are deemed to be equivalent to the IFRS. Under the New Prospectus Regulation, an issuer will need to assess the materiality of the risk factors based on the probability of their occurrence and expected magnitude of negative impact. The risk factors will need to be categorised depending on their nature, with the most material risk factors being mentioned first in each category.

As stated above, an issuer of the relevant securities can qualify for the less onerous disclosure regime by: (1) selecting a denomination per unit of at least €100,000; or (2) applying for trading (irrespective of denomination) on the PSM. Chapter 4 of the Listing Rules sets out the listing particulars requirements for the PSM and certain other securities. The chapter applies to an issuer that has applied for the admission of certain of the types of securities listed in Sch.11A to the FSMA and other specialist securities for which a prospectus is not required under the PD. Chapter 4 requires inclusion of certain minimum information from the Prospectus Rules which is broadly commensurate with that required for debt and derivative securities with a denomination per unit of at least €100,000. If the issue is guaranteed, information on the guarantor as set out in the guarantee building block, Annex VI of the PD Regulation, is required.

The general standard of disclosure for an issuer of non-equity securities is in many respects the same as that for an issuer of equity securities in that the prospectus is required to contain all information which, according to the particular nature of the issuer and securities in question, is necessary to enable investors to make an informed assessment of the assets and liabilities, financial position, profits and losses, and prospects of the issuer and of any guarantor, and of the rights attaching to such securities. It should also include a summary for retail debt.

However, the specific information set out in the schedules and building blocks of the PD Regulation which is required to be set out in a prospectus for non-equity securities is not as extensive or detailed as that which is required for equity securities.

There are a number of relaxations from the Prospectus Rules for issuers of wholesale debt (and other issues subject to LR 4) as opposed to retail debt. These include:

- a prospectus relating to the admission to trading of wholesale debt does not have to include a summary;
- where admission to trading is being sought, the prospectus can be drawn up in either a language accepted by the competent authorities of the Home State and host state of the person seeking admission or in a language customary in the sphere of international finance (in all other cases where the UK is the Home State, the prospectus must be drawn up in at least English depending on where the offer is to be made or admission to trading is to be sought); and
- less information is required to be disclosed in the prospectus for an offer or issue of wholesale debt than for retail debt.

In the case of a convertible debt issue where it is stated that the equity is to be listed in London upon conversion, provided that the equity is of the same class as the equity already listed, it will not normally be necessary to obtain a formal clearance for the future listing at the time of issue of the convertible debt. The FCA has stated that the exemption in PR 1.2.3R(7) from the need to publish a prospectus for admission of securities of a class already listed which arises on the exercise of conversion rights will apply unless the issuer appears to be abusing the exemption, such as introducing an artificial convertible to avoid the publication of a prospectus (*List!* Issue No.16 (July 2007) and restated in UKLA/TN/602.1). ESMA has suggested that were such abuse to take place, then the competent authorities are free to take enforcement actions, where appropriate, or cancel the transactions (ESMA, *Questions and Answers: Prospectuses*, ESMA/2015/1874 (December 2015)). Under the New Prospectus Regulation and with effect from 20 July 2017, this exemption is available only where the resulting shares represent, over a period of 12 months, less than 20% of the number of shares of the same class already admitted to trading on the same regulated market. The New Prospectus Regulation shall not apply to the admission to trading on a regulated market of the shares irrespective of their proportion in relation to the number of shares of the same class already admitted to trading on the same regulated market where:

- a prospectus was drawn up in accordance with either the New Prospectus Regulation or the PD upon the offer to the public or admission to trading of the securities giving access to the shares;
- the securities giving access to the shares were issued before 20 July 2017;
- the shares qualify as Common Equity Tier 1 instruments and result from the conversion of Additional Tier 1 instruments issued by a financial institution due to occurrence of a trigger event as set out in Regulation 575/2013[20]; or
- the shares qualify as eligible own funds or eligible basic own funds as set out in Directive 2009/138[21] and result from the conversion of other securities, triggered for the purposes of fulfilling certain solvency or minimum capital requirements as contained in that directive.

Where the issuer itself is a state, or a regional or local authority, the amount of information which is required to be given in the equivalent offering document is materially reduced.

Under Ch.4 of the Listing Rules, information may be included in listing particulars by reference, and equivalent information may be included, as if the PD applied to the listing particulars.

On 30 November 2015, the European Commission proposed a revision of the PD which harmonises the rules for publishing prospectuses associated with equity finance.[22] For companies, the current rules constitute a lot of legal paperwork and require complex legal terminology that investors find difficult to

---

[20] Regulation 575/2013 on prudential requirements for credit institutions and investment firms and amending Regulation 648/2012 [2013] OJ L176/1.

[21] Directive 2009/138 on the taking-up and pursuit of the business of Insurance and Reinsurance (Solvency II) [2009] OJ L335/1.

[22] Proposal for a Regulation on the prospectus to be published when securities are offered to the public or admitted to trading COM(2015) 583 final.

interpret. The Commission's proposal addresses these weaknesses whilst ensuring an appropriate level of disclosure in clear and accessible language. By turning the current directive into a regulation, a more streamlined and coherent approach will be ensured across the EU. The revision will consider the overall structure of the European markets and look to reduce national fragmentation by supporting innovative and growing sectors of the economy. On 20 July 2017, the New Prospectus Regulation entered into force and will repeal and replace the existing PD regime with full effect from 21 July 2019.

8.8.2.3 *Chapter 17: Continuing obligations*

The specific continuing obligations provisions which are set out in Ch.17 of the Listing Rules do not apply to issues by a state, a regional or local authority except that such an issuer must comply with LR 17.3.2R (admission to trading). An issue by a state, regional or local authority must, however, comply with certain Disclosure Guidance and Transparency Rules in DTRs 5 and 6, even if that issuer is not already required to comply with the DTRs.

Chapters 10 ("Significant transactions") and 11 ("Related party transactions") and other provisions expressed to apply to companies that have a premium listing of equity securities will not apply to issuers whose only listed securities are those covered by Ch.17, even if the securities are convertible.

The continuing obligations which do apply include:

- the requirement that an issuer's listed securities must be admitted to trading at all times on a recognised investment exchange's market for listed securities and that the issuer must notify the FCA in writing and without delay of requests to any recognised investment exchange for (inter alia) admission, cancellation or suspension of trading or if it has been informed by the relevant exchange that the trading of its securities will be cancelled or suspended this is otherwise to occur (LR 17.3.2R);

- equal treatment of all holders of debt securities ranking pari passu in respect of all rights attaching to such securities (DTR 6.1.3R);
- the publication of annual reports and accounts as soon as possible after they have been approved and within four months after the end of the financial period to which they relate (subject to certain exceptions) (DTR 4); and
- the requirements in relation to circulars to be sent to holders in relation to amendments to trust deeds and early redemptions (LRs 17.3.10R and 17.3.12R).

Under DTR 6.1.10, the issuer must disclose to the public without delay any changes in the rights of holders, including changes in the terms and conditions which could indirectly affect those rights, resulting in particular from a change in loan terms or interest rates.

8.8.2.4 *Costs*

In normal circumstances, the cost of listing a specialist security may be less than that of obtaining a listing for an equity issue for the equivalent amount.

8.8.2.5 *Debt issuance programmes*

The information memorandum for a debt issuance programme is referred to as the "base prospectus" and the pricing supplements are called "final terms". A base prospectus contains all the relevant information concerning the issuer (or multiple issuers) or the securities to be admitted to trading or offered to the public. The information in a base prospectus must be supplemented in the normal way if required. If the final terms of the offer are not included in either the base prospectus or a supplementary prospectus, the final terms must be provided to investors and filed with the FCA. ESMA issued a Consultation Paper on 15 March 2013,[23] setting out

---

[23] ESMA, Consultation Paper on "Draft regulatory standards on specific situations that require the publication of a supplement to the prospectus", ESMA/2013/316 (2016).

proposals for specific situations that require the publication of a supplement to the prospectus, which are now reflected in Regulation 382/2014.[24]

A base prospectus must be approved by the competent authority of the issuer's Home State in the normal way. The relevant competent authorities in the host Member States act in co-operation with the competent authority in the issuer's Home State (and, provided that certain conditions are met) to "passport" the base prospectus into the host Member States to enable the base prospectus to be used for the public offer or admission to trading of securities on a regulated market in such host Member State.

Base prospectuses, like the other types of prospectus, are valid for 12 months after publication subject to being updated by a supplementary prospectus if necessary. Issuers in a programme using a base prospectus would therefore have to produce a new one (or update the existing one) and have it approved by the relevant competent authority every 12 months for so long as they continue to use the programme.

Following the issue by ESMA of a technical advice paper on possible delegated acts concerning the PD, to the European Commission, important changes to the format and content of documentation for the issue of debt securities were introduced on 1 July 2012 by Regulation 486/2012.[25] Some of the key changes are set out in the next section.

8.8.2.6 Contents of a base prospectus

A base prospectus must be composed of the following parts:

- contents;
- summary;

---

[24] Regulation 382/2014 supplementing Directive 2003/71 with regard to regulatory technical standards for publication of supplements to the prospectus [2014] OJ L111/36.

[25] Regulation 486/2012 amending Regulation 809/2004 as regards the format and the content of the prospectus, the base prospectus, the summary and the final terms and as regards the disclosure requirements [2012] OJ L150/1.

- risk factors linked to the issuer and type of securities to be covered by the issue(s) that will be made under it;
- the information set out in the relevant schedules and building blocks for the type of debt being issued;
- the final terms (if not contained in a separate document); and
- Category A information, as further set out in Annex XX to the PD Regulation.

The schedules and building blocks are set out as Annexes to the PD Regulation. Prospectus Regulation 2.3 and Annex XIII to the PD Regulation determine which schedules and building blocks of the PD Regulation are applicable to any particular issue. For example, for an issue of retail debt securities, the minimum disclosure requirements for the registration document are set out at Annex IV to the PD Regulation and, for the securities note, are set out at Annex V to the PD Regulation. For an issue of wholesale debt securities, the minimum disclosure requirements for the registration document are set out in Annex IX to the PD Regulation and, for the securities note, are set out at Annex XIII to the PD Regulation. If the bonds are to be guaranteed, the information set out at Annex VI to the PD Regulation would also have to be included. This effectively requires the same information as is provided in relation to the non-equity securities issuers to be provided in relation to the guarantor. There is also a building block for underlying shares (Annex XIV to the PD Regulation) but this is only required to be used where the shares have not been admitted to trading on a regulated market at the time of approval of the prospectus. Note that the New Prospectus Regulation will replace the above rules when it is fully in force.

Where a base prospectus relates to different securities, it should contain a single summary for all the securities but the information about each of the securities should be clearly segregated. Where the summary in the base prospectus needs to be updated, this can be done by either integrating the new information into the existing summary or producing a supplement to the summary. If the information is integrated, investors must easily be able to identify the changes in particular by way of footnotes. The final terms can be presented as a separate document or incorporated into the base prospectus. If they are presented as a separate document, they may replicate some of the information in the base prospectus provided that the new terms are easily identifiable as such. The final terms must also include a statement that the full information on the issuer and the offer is only available on the basis of the combination of the base prospectus and final terms and where the base prospectus is available.

Regulation 486/2012 stated the following key changes are to be implemented:

- final terms: the final terms should be prepared in an easily analysable and comprehensible form and should only contain Categories B and C information. Details of what this information includes are further set out in an Annex XX to the PD Regulation. A summary of the individual issue should be annexed to the final terms. As the summary forms part of the final terms, it will be subject to the same requirements of the PD Regulation. The final terms should contain a clear and prominent statement, indicating, inter alia, that in order to get the full information, both the base prospectus and the final terms must be read in conjunction and that the summary is annexed to the final terms;
- final terms may include additional information limited to the information in Annex XXI and the signature of the legal representative of the issuer or the person responsible for the prospectus according to the relevant national law or the signature of both; and
- final terms must not amend or replace any information in the base prospectus. The final terms should also not reproduce information in relation to the securities note which is included in the base prospectus.

8.9 Specialist certificates representing other securities

Specialist certificates representing other securities (DRs) are covered by Ch.18 of the Listing Rules. For such securities, the issuer of the shares is the issuer for the purpose of the Listing Rules and the application will be dealt with on this basis.

On 1 July 2018, as summarised in s.8.2.4 above, the FCA has introduced a new regime for the premium listing of SCCs which includes that, subject to the other eligibility criteria being satisfied, a premium listing can be obtained for their DRs. Only a standard listing can be obtained for the DRs of other companies. There are various other modifications to the rules applicable to DR listings where the underlying securities are issued by DRs.

Issuers of DRs may request admission to the Official List of a greater number of DRs than they initially intend to have admitted to trading which, in principle, could allow further DRs to be admitted to trading for a period without the need for a new prospectus or listing application. This may be particularly relevant if shares can be put into the DR programme by their holders. There has been uncertainty and discussion about when an additional prospectus would be required in the context of the issue of additional GDRs.

In an ESMA's *Questions and Answers: Prospectuses* in June 2012 (ESMA/2012/381) and republished in April 2016 (ESMA/2016/576), ESMA stated that it recognised that, in a typical GDR facility, the number of GDRs in issue fluctuates due to investors having the possibility to exchange shares for GDRs (and vice versa) at any time which is outside the issuer's control. This should therefore be accommodated by a pragmatic approach to the application of the PD. ESMA believes:

> "that it is acceptable for a person applying for admission of GDRs to trading to produce a prospectus covering the admission of 'up to' a specified number of GDRs. The number of GDRs can be no more than the equivalence of

100% of the issued capital of the issuer at the date of the GDR prospectus" (ESMA, *Questions and Answers: Prospectuses* (2016), Answer to Question 77).

ESMA further clarifies that no new prospectus is required as long as the GDRs in issue do not exceed the amount originally covered by the prospectus. More importantly, ESMA states that this would allow new shareholders, holding newly issued shares, issued after the date the GDR facility was established, to exchange their shares for GDRs. This is subject to the number of GDRs in issue not exceeding the amount of the "up to" facility. The application of the rules and the ESMA guidance would need to be analysed by reference to the specific facts of any issue.

The regimes are similar to those summarised above in relation to debt securities. If the denomination of a unit is at least €100,000, the wholesale regime will apply (Annex IX to the PD Regulation). Depositary receipts are eligible for trading on the PSM, which as described above is an alternative route to what is, in effect, the wholesale regime.

The principal conditions for the listing of these securities in those two circumstances, in addition to any special conditions imposed by the FCA, are similar to those for wholesale debt securities save where applicable to the different nature of the securities. They include (LRs 18.2.3R–18.2.14R):

- that the issuer must be duly incorporated according to the relevant laws of its place of incorporation or establishment and operating in conformity with its constitution;
- the securities which the certificates represent must conform with the law of the issuer's place of incorporation, be duly authorised according to the requirements of the issuer's constitution and be fully paid up and freely transferable;
- if the represented securities are equity shares of an overseas issuer, at least 25% of the certificates for which admission is sought must normally be in public hands in one or more EEA states or where they are otherwise listed;

- if the represented securities are equity shares of a UK company or of an investment entity, such shares must be listed or be subject to a listing application;
- the certificates representing the securities must satisfy the requirements of LRs 2.2.2–2.2.11R; and
- the depositary must maintain adequate arrangements to safeguard certificate holders' rights to the securities and to all rights relating to the securities and all monies and benefits it may receive in respect of them, subject only to payment of the remuneration and proper expenses of the issuer of the certificates (LR 18.2.14). Listing Rule 18.2.14 came into force on 1 May 2013 and amended the previous requirement by the Listing Rules that the depositary must hold the represented securities (and related rights) on trust for the DR holders and must be a suitably authorised and regulated financial institution acceptable to the FCA. Following a consultation in October 2012 (CP 12/27) by the FSA, it was found that this is not a requirement under the PD and therefore imposes a higher standard than is demanded by the market. The consultation proposed that LR 18.2.14 should be amended to the above. Part of the proposal was that these arrangements would need to be described in the prospectus.

A further amendment to LR 18, implemented on 1 May 2013 following the proposal issued by the FSA, was the deletion of LR 18.2.13R. Under LR 18.2.13R, a depositary that issues GDRs had been required to be a suitably authorised and regulated financial institution acceptable to the FCA. It was noted that, since in practice GDR issuers do not tend to use UK depositaries, it was difficult to enforce this rule. In addition, this requirement is not a requirement under the PD and the FCA felt that it would be sufficient to rely on disclosure to deliver an appropriate level of investor protection.

The listing application must comply with the relevant sections of Ch.3 of the Listing Rules and, in addition, a copy of the executed final form deposit agreement must be kept for six years following admission and provided to the FCA on request.

8.9.1 Continuing obligations

The continuing obligations provisions are in many respects similar to those applicable to specialist debt securities (compliance with LR 17.3 is required) but with a number of variations including some consequent upon the different nature of the securities. Among the additional provisions in LR 18.4 are:

- if the represented securities are equity shares of a UK issuer, it must comply with Ch.9 ("Continuing Obligations");
- if the represented securities are equity shares of an overseas issuer, it must comply with some of the continuing obligations set out in LR 14.3 and with certain articles of Regulation 596/2014[26]; and
- prior to any change of the depositary of the represented securities, the new depositary must satisfy the FCA that it meets the requirements of LRs 18.2.11R–18.2.14R (as set out in LR 18.4.4R) and any such change must be notified to a RIS by 07.30 on the following business day and the announcement must contain the required information (LR 18.4.5R).

8.10 Mineral companies

8.10.1 Application for admission and eligibility

For the purposes of the Listing Rules, a mineral company is a company or group whose principal activity is, or is planned to be, the extraction of mineral resources (which may or may not include exploration for mineral resources). Mineral resources include metallic and non-metallic ores, mineral concentrates, industrial minerals, construction aggregates, mineral oils, natural gases, hydrocarbons and solid fuels including coal, and extraction includes mining, quarrying or similar activities and the reworking of mine tailings or waste dumps.

---

[26] Regulation 596/2014 on market abuse (market abuse regulation) and repealing Directive 2003/6 and Directives 2003/124, 2003/125 and 2004/72 [2014] OJ L173/1.

When a mineral company seeks a premium listing, the normal eligibility rules apply but with certain modifications summarised below.

A mineral company seeking admission of its equity shares does not need three years' historical financial information prepared to IFRS or equivalent (as required by LR 6.2.1R(1)) if it has been operating for a shorter period of time, although it must have published or filed historical financial information since the inception of its business (LR 6.10.1R(1)). Further, where a mineral company has operated for less than three years, there are derogations available from LR 6.2.1R(2), which requires the historical financial information to represent at least 75% of a company's business for the relevant period and LRs 6.2.1R(3)–(4), 6.2.4 and 6.2.6, as to the content of the historical financial information and status of the auditors. The result of these derogations (contained in LR 6.10.1R(2)) is that LRs 6.2.1R(2)–(4), 6.2.4 and 6.2.6 apply to such a mineral company only with regard to the period for which the company has published or filed historical information. In addition, the requirements in LR 6.3.1R as to the revenue earning track record of an issuer do not apply to a mineral company applying for the admission of its equity shares (LR 6.10.2).

Under LR 6.6.1R, it is a requirement that a new applicant can demonstrate that it exercises operational control over the business it carries on as its main activity. Where a new applicant's business consists principally of holdings of shares in entities that it does not control, it would normally not satisfy the control requirement. This is, however, relaxed for mineral companies provided that, if the mineral company does not hold controlling interests in a majority (by value) of the properties, fields, mines or other assets in which it has invested, it can demonstrate that it has a reasonable spread of direct interests in mineral resources and has rights to participate actively in their extraction, whether by voting or through other rights which give it influence in decisions over the timing and method of extraction of those resources (LR 6.10.3R).

8.10.2 Class tests

Listing Rule 10.7.5R provides that, in addition to the class tests in LR 10 Annex 1, listed mineral companies undertaking a transaction involving significant mineral resources (or rights thereto) must apply an additional test, the reserves test. The reserves test, set out in LR 10.7.5R(2), is calculated by dividing the volume or amount of the proven and probable reserves to be acquired or disposed of pursuant to the transaction by the volume or amount of the aggregate proven and probable reserves of the mineral company making the acquisition or disposal. If the mineral resources are not directly comparable, the FCA may modify LR 10.7.5R(2) to permit valuations to be used instead of amounts or volumes (LR 10.7.6G). When calculating the size of a transaction under LRs 10 Annex 1 and 10.7.5R, account must be taken of any associated transactions or loans effected, or intended to be effected, and any contingent liabilities or commitments (LR 10.7.7R).

In addition, if a Class 1 transaction relates to an acquisition or disposal of mineral resources or rights to mineral resources, the circular must contain a mineral expert's report and a related glossary (LR 13.4.6R). A "mineral expert's report" is a competent person's report (CPR) prepared in accordance with the recommendations for the consistent implementation of the PD Regulation published by ESMA (ESMA/2011/81) (ESMA Recommendations).[27] A revised version of the ESMA Recommendations was issued in March 2013[28] and the requirements for a CPR are contained in para.133 and the Appendices (see s.8.10.3 below).

However, the FCA may modify the information requirements in LR 13.4.6R if it considers that the information set out would not provide significant additional information. In those circumstances, the FCA would generally require only the information

---

[27] ESMA, *ESMA update of the CESR recommendations: The consistent implementation of Regulation 809/2004 implementing the Prospectus Directive*, ESMA/2011/81 (23 March 2011).

[28] ESMA, *ESMA update of the CESR recommendations: The consistent implementation of Regulation 809/2004 implementing the Prospectus Directive*, ESMA/2013/319 (20 March 2013).

set out in LR 13.4.7G provided it is presented in accordance with reporting standards acceptable to the FCA. The requirements of LR 13.4.7G essentially mirror the information required to be included in a mineral company's prospectus under para.132 of the ESMA Recommendations (see s.8.10.3 below).

8.10.3 Prospectuses

The normal contents requirements for a prospectus are the same for a mineral company as for other new issuers, with one major exception. Additional disclosure obligations are placed on mineral companies (as defined in the ESMA Recommendations rather than the Listing Rules) by paras 131–133 of the ESMA Recommendations. Note that the definition of a "mineral company" under the Listing Rules is not the same as the definition used in the ESMA Recommendations and, whilst in most cases a mining or oil and gas company will fall within both definitions, in some cases care will be needed.

The ESMA Recommendations aim to achieve appropriate levels of transparency and assurance over the reserves and resources figures reported to the market. The ESMA Recommendations define "mineral companies" as "companies with material mineral projects" and the term "mineral projects" is defined as exploration, development, planning or production activities (including royalty interests) in respect of minerals including: metallic ore; industrial minerals; gemstones; hydrocarbons; and solid fuels (para.131).

Materiality is assessed from the point of view of the investor and projects will be considered "material" where evaluation of the resources and/or reserves and/or exploration results the project seeks to exploit is necessary to enable investors to make an informed assessment of the prospects of the issuer. Evaluation of mineral projects is presumed to be necessary: (1) where the projects seek to extract minerals for their resale value as commodities; or (2) where the minerals are extracted to supply (without resale to third parties) an input into an industrial production process and in both cases there exists uncertainty as to either the existence of economically recoverable resources in the quantities required or the technical feasibility of their recovery. In their feedback statement in March 2013,[29] ESMA confirmed that the information required in relation to paras 131–133 of the ESMA Recommendations is solely required for material mineral projects as defined in para.131(c) and that a mineral project may be considered material for a small company but non-material if it belongs to a large diversified group. The materiality of mineral projects therefore should be assessed having regard to all the company's mineral projects relative to the issuer and its group taken as a whole. It should be noted that the ESMA Recommendations are related principally to disclosure and not eligibility, and whether a company will be eligible for listing needs to be assessed by reference to the Listing Rules.

Paragraph 132 of the ESMA Recommendations requires that a prospectus produced by any mineral company should contain:

* details of mineral resources and, where applicable, reserves (presented separately) and exploration results or prospects presented in accordance with one or more of the ESMA endorsed standards (contained in Appendix 1—see below for details);
* anticipated mine life and exploration potential or similar duration of commercial activity in extracting reserves;
* an indication of the duration and main terms of any licences or concessions and the legal, economic and environmental conditions for exploring and developing those licences or concessions;
* indications of the current and anticipated progress of mineral exploration and/or extraction and processing including a discussion of the accessibility of the deposit; and
* an explanation of any exceptional factors that have influences on the matter in the above.

---

[29] ESMA, "Feedback Statement: Consultation Paper on proposed amendments to the ESMA update of the CESR recommendations for the consistent implementation of the Prospectuses Regulation regarding mineral companies", ESMA/2013/318 (2013).

If the transaction described in the prospectus includes the acquisition of a mineral company or of reserves and/or resources and the acquisition constitutes a significant gross change, then the issuer should, in addition to information on its existing assets, include the information above on the assets being acquired. When presented in the prospectus, the new assets should be clearly segmented from the existing assets.

As well as the information required by para.132, pursuant to para.133 of the ESMA Recommendations, a CPR reporting on the issuer's mineral resources, and where applicable reserves and exploration results, will be required for all prospectuses issued by a mineral company (as defined in para.131 rather than the Listing Rules) for a public offer or admission to trading of equity securities, and depositary receipts issued over shares with a denomination per unit of less than €100,000. There is, however, an exemption from this requirement and, to qualify for it, an issuer must: (1) have its equity securities admitted to either a regulated market, an "appropriate multi-lateral trading facility" or an "equivalent third country market" (each as defined in para.131); and (2) have reported on its reserves/resources and exploration results annually in accordance with one of the ESMA endorsed standards (contained in Appendix I) for at least three years. If the issuer has not reported on three financial years since admission, this exemption condition will be deemed fulfilled if it has reported as required since its admission (provided, in the case of issuers admitted to multi-lateral trading facilities, it produced a CPR on admission). A CPR is not required for mineral company issuers of only non-equity securities (other than depositary receipts). The CPR must contain information on the company's mineral projects, having regard to the information set out in Appendix II or III to the ESMA Recommendations (as applicable) being: legal overview; geological overview, statement of resources and/or reserves; valuation of reserves (where applicable); environmental, social and facilities; historic production/expenditures; infrastructure; maps and diagrams; and any special factors. The Appendices also clarify that site visits by the competent person are not obligatory.

The CPR must be dated no more than six months prior to the date of the prospectus (provided that, if it is not dated on or around the date of the prospectus, the issuer affirms that there are no material changes since the date of the CPR the omission of which would make the CPR misleading) and must be prepared by a suitably qualified and experienced independent expert. This means the individual must either possess the required competencies as prescribed by the relevant reporting standard or, if there are no such prescribed requirements, then must be professionally qualified and a member in good standing of an appropriate recognised professional association and have at least five years' relevant experience. For the individual to be independent they must be independent of the company, its directors and advisers and they must have no economic or beneficial interest in the company or any of the mineral assets and their fee must not be linked to the admission or valuation of the mineral company.

Appendix 1 to the ESMA Recommendations sets out a list of permitted reporting standards that can be used. The permitted standards for mining companies are: the JORC Code; SAM-REC; CIM Guidelines; the *Guide prepared by the US Society for Mining, Metallurgy and Exploration*, as amended; PERC; Certification Code as published by the *Instituto de Ingenieros de Minas de Chile*, as amended; or NAEN Code. The permitted standards for oil and gas companies are: the Petroleum Resources Management System; *COGE Handbook*; or the Norwegian Petroleum Directorate classification system for resources and reserves. There are also specified standards for valuation of reserves/resources: VALMIN; SAMVAL; and CIMVAL. ESMA has stated that, for the purposes of meeting certain exemptions to produce a competent person's report under the ESMA Recommendations, predecessors of these standards are acceptable. Currently, the Chinese National Standards are excluded.

8.10.4 New UK reporting requirements for extractive companies

8.10.4.1 EU Accounting Directive

Chapter 10 of the EU Accounting Directive (2013/34)[30] requires certain entities active in the extractive and logging of primary forest industries to report on the payments they make to governments worldwide on a country and project basis. The intention is to give citizens of resource-rich countries the information they need to hold governments to account. These EU requirements have been implemented in the UK through the Reports on Payments to Governments Regulations 2014 (SI 2014/3209) , as amended in December 2015 by the Reports on Payments to Governments (Amendment) Regulations 2015 (SI 2015/1928) (the Regulations).

The Regulations apply to UK registered "large undertakings" or "public interest entities" which are involved in mining or quarrying for products such as oil, minerals and gas or the logging of primary forests. "Public interest entities" include, in broad terms, undertakings whose transferable securities are admitted to a regulated market (the Official List in the UK), certain credit institutions and certain insurance institutions.

Under the Regulations, a company needs to prepare a report each financial year specifying: the government (and country) to which each payment has been made; the total amount of payments made to each government; the total amount per type of payment made to each government (e.g. taxes, royalty payments, dividends, licence fees, rental fees etc); and, where payments have been attributed to a specific project, the total amount per type of payment made for each such project and the total amount of payments for each such project will need to be stated. The report must be delivered as an XML document via the extractives service provided by Companies House to

---

[30] Directive 2013/34 on the annual financial statements, consolidated financial statements and related reports of certain types of undertakings, amending Directive 2006/43 and repealing Directives 78/660 and 83/349 [2013] OJ L182/19.

the Registrar of Companies at Companies House within 11 months of the financial year-end.

Payments, activities and projects cannot be artificially split or aggregated to avoid the application of the Regulations and payments in kind must also be reported. So, if a royalty liability was satisfied by the delivery of 1,000 barrels of oil, the report needs to provide both the monetary value of the oil and the volume delivered.

There are a number of exemptions, for example, payments below a threshold of £86,000 need not be reported if the payment relates to a single obligation and is not part of a series of related payments. So a single payment of £75,000 for a licence in a year would not have to be reported but a series of four quarterly payments of £25,000 for a single licence would need to be reported in aggregate. In addition, subsidiaries are exempt from preparing a report if the payments to governments are included in the consolidated report drawn up by a parent undertaking either in accordance with the Regulations or in accordance with provisions implementing Ch.10 of the EU Accounting Directive in any other EU Member State.

The aim of the Regulations is to seek compliance, so if Companies House becomes aware of a missing report or an incomplete report, companies have 28 days to comply or are asked to confirm why they have not produced a report. Failure to comply with a notice to produce a report is an offence for both the company and the directors, with the punishment on conviction being a fine. It is also an offence knowingly or recklessly to submit a statement in a report that is misleading, false or deceptive.

In April 2016, the International Association of Oil and Gas Producers published industry guidance in relation to the Regulations to assist entities subject to the reporting requirements and to promote consistency in the reporting of payment information.

8.10.4.2 EU Transparency Directive

As well as the requirements in the EU Accounting Directive, the EU TD (as amended)[31] introduced similar country-by-country reporting requirements for listed companies in the extractive or logging of primary forest industries. Disclosure Guidance and Transparency Rule 4.3A requires such companies to prepare a report each year on their payments to governments. That report should follow the format in the Regulations described above but payments must be reported at the consolidated level. In addition, DTR 4.3A.5 requires that that report is published within six months of the financial year-end (rather than the 11 months permitted by the Regulations).

Disclosure Guidance and Transparency Rule 4.3A.10 requires that the report must be uploaded to the FCA's National Storage Mechanism in XML format. This means that companies that have to make a report under both the Regulations and the DTRs can prepare a report which meets the requirements of both in one format, with the report required by the Regulations being filed with Companies House and the report required by the DTRs filed with the FCA. It is worth noting that the filing requirement under DTR 4.3A.10 will result in duplicate filing of reports required by the DTRs since the DTR 6.3 requirements relating to the disclosure, dissemination and filing of regulated information (which includes reports on payments to governments) mean human readable versions of reports on payments to the Government must also be disclosed, disseminated and filed.

---

[31] The EU TD was amended by Directive 2013/50 amending Directive 2004/109 on the harmonisation of transparency requirements in relation to information about issuers whose securities are admitted to trading on a regulated market, Directive 2003/71 on the prospectus to be published when securities are offered to the public or admitted to trading and Directive 2007/14 laying down detailed rules for the implementation of certain provisions of Directive 2004/109 [2013] OJ L294/13 in November 2013.

8.10.4.3 Extractive Industries Transparency Initiative

In October 2014, the Government announced that the UK had been admitted as a candidate country for the Extractive Industries Transparency Initiative (EITI). Governments that voluntarily sign up to the EITI choose to implement the EITI's Standard. In summary, this means that extractive companies operating in the UK and paying taxes in the UK need to report on their payments to the Government which in turn reports on the payments it receives. These reports are made to an Independent Administrator who reconciles the information it receives from companies and from the tax authorities on behalf of the Government. The UK's first EITI report, in respect of payments made in 2014, was published in April 2016.[32]

8.11 High Growth Segment

In September 2012, the Department for Business Innovation and Skills and the LSE announced proposals to introduce a new segment to the Main Market for high growth companies, designed as a transitional admission route to the Official List. Following a consultation period, the *Rulebook for the High Growth Segment* (HGS) (the Rulebook) was published by the LSE on 27 March 2013 and republished in Sch.5 to the Admission and Disclosure Standards, effective from 4 April 2016. The segment is intended to:

> "cater specifically for high growth, UK and European businesses that require access to further capital and access to the Main Market to continue their growth".

The Rulebook requires that an applicant for the HGS was be incorporated in an EEA state. However, there is some flexibility in the application of this rule and the only company whose securities are currently traded on the HGS is incorporated in Israel.

---

[32] UK EITI, *UK EITI Report for 2014* (April 2016) available at: *https://assets.publishing. service.gov.uk/government/uploads/system/uploads/attachment_data/file/537177/bis-16-194-uk-eiti-report-2014.pdf* [Accessed 11 July 2018].

8.11.1 Admission

The HGS has EU Regulated Market status but sits outside the UK's Listing Regime so that the Listing Rules do not apply to companies listed on the HGS. HGS companies are subject to LSE's Rulebook and existing Admission and Disclosure Standards. In addition, as a Regulated Market under the EU Financial Services Action Plan (FSAP), the relevant directives (including the PD, TD and the Market Abuse Directive) apply. The key sections of the Rulebook are summarised below:

- issuers with securities admitted to or applying for admission to the HGS must comply with parts of the FCA Disclosure Guidance and Transparency Rules, the Prospectus Rules, the Admission and Disclosure Standards issued by the LSE as well as national law and regulation of its country of incorporation;
- the LSE will determine admission to the HGS on the basis of information and submissions relating to eligibility given by the issuer and its "Key Adviser" (as defined in the Rulebook) and on the basis that the prospectus has been approved by the FCA or other EEA state competent authority;
- eligibility for admission: to be eligible for admission, the issuer, together with its subsidiary undertakings, must be a trading business[33]; the issuer must:
  (1) control the majority of its assets;
  (2) be able to demonstrate growth in audited consolidated revenue, prepared in a form consistent with that which will be adopted in the issuer's next published financial statements, of at least 20% on a Compound Annual Growth Rate (CAGR)[34] basis over the prior three financial years;
  (3) have at least 10% of the number of securities to be admitted in public hands. The securities in public hands must have a value of at least £30 million and the majority of the £30 million must be raised at

---

[33] The guidance to the Rulebook provides that "an Issuer should not, for example, be a mineral resource company at exploration stage, or an investment entity".
[34] Further information on the CAGR is set out in the Rulebook.

admission by the issue of new securities or sale of existing securities from the same class as that to be admitted;

(4) have a sufficient number of registered holders of the securities to be admitted to provide an orderly market in the securities following admission. The securities to be admitted must form part of the issuer's equity share capital, must conform with the laws and regulations of the issuer's place of incorporation and be duly authorised according to the requirements of the issuer's constitution as well as having any other necessary consents. The issuer must be duly incorporated or otherwise validly established in an EEA State and must operate in conformity with its constitution, and be a public limited company or similar EEA corporate structure;

• the issuer must publish prior to admission a prospectus in relation to the securities to be admitted that has been approved by the FCA or the competent authority of another EEA state. The prospectus should, amongst other requirements, contain a non-binding statement, in the section in the prospectus that deals with information about the issuer, setting out that the issuer intends to apply for admission to the Official List in the future and how it intends to satisfy the eligibility criteria for admission to the Official List; and

• an issuer must have appointed a Key Adviser in relation to the admission.

8.11.2 *Continuing obligations*

An issuer with securities admitted to the HGS will be subject to continuing obligations, the key sections of which are summarised below:

• *continuing eligibility requirements*: whilst the issuer has securities admitted to the HGS, most of the criteria (except those at rr.2.3, 2.5 and 2.5 of the Rulebook) for admission will apply on a continuing basis (s.B1 of the Rulebook). In addition, an issuer must: (1) deal with the LSE in an open and co-operative way and deal with all enquiries raised by the LSE promptly; (2) promptly notify the LSE if it becomes aware that it is likely to fail or has failed to comply with its obligations under the Rulebook or the Admission and Disclosure Standards; and (3) provide to the LSE any information or explanation the LSE might reasonably require for the purpose of verifying whether the issuer is or has been complying with the Rulebook;

- *advice of Key Advisers*: an issuer must obtain the guidance of a Key Adviser to assist it with the application of the rules set out in the Rulebook and the Admission and Disclosure Standards where it (or any of its subsidiary undertakings) is proposing to enter into or undertake any significant transaction or a significant event occurs, including a transaction which, due to its size or nature, could amount to a notifiable transaction, related party transaction or reverse takeover; cancellation of its admission; a further issue of securities or a purchase of own securities of the same class to that which is admitted; or severe financial difficulty, including in relation to any associated restructuring, reconstruction or disposal. More detailed rules in relation to notifiable transactions, related party transactions and reverse takeovers are set out in the Rulebook;

- *requirement for notifications to a RIS*: an issuer must notify a RIS without delay in several circumstances, including the resignation, dismissal or appointment of any director giving the date of such occurrence and, in the case of an appointment, including the usual biographical information about such director as might be found in a prospectus, including details of any holding of securities in the issuer; any change in its accounting reference date, registered office address or legal name; any decision to make any payment in respect of the securities; the admission or cancellation of any of the issuer's securities; any proposed or actual change in the issuer's capital structure and the results of any new issue of securities; and details of all resolutions passed at a general meeting of the issuer other than resolutions concerning ordinary business passed at an annual general meeting;

- *continuing website disclosures*: an issuer must, from admission, maintain a website on which there should be easily available and free of charge, inter alia, a description of the group's business; the name of the issuer's directors and brief biographical details of each; a description of the responsibilities of the members of the board of directors and details of any committees of the board of directors and their responsibilities; the issuer's country of incorporation and main country of operation; its current constitutional documents; details of any other exchanges or trading platforms on which the issuer has applied or agreed to have any of its securities admitted or traded; the number of securities in issue (noting any held as treasury shares); details of any restrictions on the transfer of its securities; its most recent annual financial report and any subsequent half-yearly, quarterly or similar reports; information in relation to corporate governance required to be included in an issuer's financial report in accordance with relevant sections of the Rulebook; all notifications to a RIS the issuer has made in the past 12 months; taking into account any restrictions in relation to applicable securities laws, its most recent prospectus together with any circulars or documents sent to shareholders within the past 12 months; and details of its key professional advisers;
- *corporate governance*: an issuer must ensure that certain information is included in its annual financial report on an ongoing basis. This includes details of the corporate governance code to which the issuer is subject and/or details of the corporate governance code or practices which the issuer may have voluntarily decided to apply, and where such code and practices are publicly available, as well as a statement as to how the issuer has applied the main principles set out in such codes and practices in a manner that would enable shareholders to evaluate how the principles have been applied; and a statement specifying which provisions of the code or practice the issuer has complied with throughout the accounting period; where it has not complied with a provision explaining the reasons

for non-compliance; for provisions of a continuing nature, the period during which it did not comply with some or all of those provisions;

- *cancellation of admission*: other than in specific examples as set out in the Rulebook, an issuer that wishes to cancel its admission of securities must obtain, at a general meeting, the consent of not less than 75% of the shareholders. To convene the meeting, a notice conforming to the issuer's constitution or applicable law should be sent to the shareholders setting out the reasons for the cancellation, the anticipated date of cancellation (which must not be less than 20 business days following the passing of the resolution as required above) and all relevant information to enable the shareholders to make an informed decision.[35] The issuer must notify a RIS at the same time the notice convening the meeting is sent to shareholders and notify a RIS of the outcome of the meeting. It is stated that the provisions in the Rulebook supersede, where relevant, the requirements of the Admission and Disclosure Standards in relation to cancellation of admission; and
- *disciplining of issuers*: where the exchange considers that an issuer is in breach of its responsibilities and obligations under the Rulebook, the LSE may take disciplinary action against such issuer and the compliance procedures set out in the Admission and Disclosure Standards shall apply to breaches of these rules as well as to breaches of the Admission and Disclosure Standards.

8.11.3 *Key Advisers*

The issuer must engage a Key Adviser for admission and other certain events occurring after admission.

An issuer must ensure that, prior to engaging a person to act as Key Adviser, that person is on the list of Key Advisers, available from the LSE. The issuer must ensure that the LSE is

---

[35] Guidance notes to this Rule provide that LR 13.3.1R should be used as guidance in relation to the contents of the circular. For the avoidance of doubt, the LSE does not approve the contents of the circular to be sent to shareholders.

informed promptly of the name and contact details of the Key Adviser appointed in accordance with the Rulebook.

An issuer must notify the LSE in writing at the earliest possible opportunity of the resignation or dismissal of any Key Adviser that it had appointed. In case of a dismissal, the reason for the dismissal must be included in the notification. The notification must be copied to the Key Adviser.

An issuer must co-operate with its Key Adviser in relation to its performance of the Key Adviser role by providing the Key Adviser with all information reasonably requested by the Key Adviser for the purpose of performing the Key Adviser role.

Index

All indexing is to heading number

481